YOU CAN'T DO THAT

Beatles

Bootlegs &
Novelty Records

YOU CAN'T DO THAT

Beatles

Bootlegs & Novelty Records

CHARLES REINHART

Includes John Lennon tribute records

Contemporary Books, Inc.
Chicago

The inclusion of photographs of bootleg and counterfeit recordings and/or the associated jackets of such recordings in this volume should not be construed or interpreted as an endorsement of the practice of record piracy by either the author or the publisher.

The reproduction of proprietary cover art used on bootleg and other pirated record jackets pictured herein which may have first appeared as part of or in accompaniment with original recordings released by EMI Records Limited or its affiliates worldwide has been cleared with EMI Records Ltd., London. All applicable rights of property and/or copyright are hereby reaffirmed.

The reproduction of proprietary cover art appearing on novelty record jackets and sleeves pictured herein has been cleared with the following organizations: photograph of **Do The Beetle** (Crown Records CST 399) reproduced courtesy of Cadet Records, Los Angeles; photograph of **The Beatles Greatest Hits** (Canadian American Records SCALP 1017) reproduced courtesy of Dawn Productions Ltd., Mt. Gretna, Pennsylvania; photograph of **Francois Glorieux Plays The Beatles** (Vanguard VSD 79417) reproduced courtesy of Victor Records, Shinko Music, Tokyo, Japan, and Vanguard Recording Society, Inc., New York City. Used by permission. All Rights Reserved.

All other proprietary cover art reproduced on pirated record jackets has otherwise been unidentifiable in terms of ownership due to uncredited misuse. Reasonable attempts have been made to secure permissions to include reproductions of the other recording jackets pictured in the novelty section of this book. Efforts to identify and locate owners or other principals involved have been unsuccessful, however, due to a variety of factors. It is not the intention of the author or publisher to usurp legitimate rights of ownership or copyright in artwork depicted herein, but for which ownership could simply not be determined. Any reasonable requests for proprietary attribution and/or compensation for use will be honored for any materials in which ownership can be proven.

DEDICATION

To my wife Erna.

Without her unceasing love,
support and understanding,
I could not have completed this work.

Contents

Contents continued ▶

◄Contents continued

Illustrations

BOOTLEGS & COUNTERFEITS

NOVELTIES

Foreword

Neither Harry Castleman nor I would ever have done this book. To be blunt, we have long felt that, with few exceptions, most bootlegs are worthless. Nonetheless, one of the most frequent questions we've received from readers of **All Together Now** and **The Beatles Again** has always been: "Where is there more information on bootleg records?" The answer is now in hand.

Probably the best aspect of Charles Reinhart's exhaustive compilation is that it clearly demonstrates the fact that most bootleg records do *not* contain secretly suppressed studio-quality gems. All too often, in fact, the same poorly recorded material is repackaged again and again and again. (Consult the *Let It Be* and *Get Back* entries in the song title index as illustration.) Yet, maddeningly, there are a few worthwhile nuggets out there, and this book provides the sorely-needed guidance required for any search through the vinyl jungle.

In a way, **You Can't Do That** serves as a consumer's reference tool similar to **All Together Now** and **The Beatles Again**, but focuses instead on an area that those books did not cover (quite intentionally, I might add). To ardent collectors looking for information on particular bootleg packages, this will be a welcome organizer. For rock historians, Charlie Reinhart's extensive documentation provides not only important background on the discs themselves, but also on the events and personalities which were deemed important enough to record and sell. Even the nameless bootleggers will no doubt learn something about their own "mini-industry" by paging through the text.

For fans uninterested in any of the bootleg releases, however, **You Can't Do That** also provides information on some legitimately released collectibles including novelty records, "break-ins," and cash-ins. There is even a list of twenty-five clues "proving" that the members of Klaatu probably were maybe really The Beatles except that they weren't. A guest piece by publisher Tom Schultheiss ends it all with a detailed discussion of the legal morass surrounding bootleg, counterfeit, and pirate discs. This is required reading for those planning to issue their own illegal wares.

And there will be more bootlegs. **You Can't Do That** shows that people most certainly *can* and *will* persist, despite stern warnings and occasional legal action. Ironically, though, the detailed information in this book may also prove to be the best possible deterrent against bootleg purchases. Stripped of their air of mystery, most bootlegs pale in comparison to such legitimate favorites as **Abbey Road, Band On The Run**, and **Imagine**.

As one who has listened to more than his share of awful "collector's records," I'm glad Charlie Reinhart did this long overdue book. (Now Harry and I won't ever be tempted.) A friendly parting shot: Your job has only begun, Charlie! Wait until the lists of corrections, objections, additions, and discrepancies begin to arrive, as they did with our books. Not to mention the inevitable calls for even more esoteric follow-ups such as guides to video tapes and video discs!

Stay tuned for further developments . . .

—**Wally Podrazik**

Preface

The research for what was to become this book grew out of my own needs as a collector. Many times, I have ordered two or three differently titled bootlegs only to receive them and find that they all contained the same material, or bought a bootleg because of a newly listed song only to find it was a widely available song that some bootlegger had decided to retitle. There are gaps in my research; nobody knows that better than I do. Hopefully, some of you reading and using this book will be able to fill in those missing bits of information. Pubilius Syrus said centuries ago, "It is a very hard undertaking to seek to please everybody." Hard, yes, but I feel there is something here for everyone interested in the Beatles and their recordings. The indexes alone should prove an invaluable aid to the collector and researcher.

Charles Reinhart

Introduction

BOOTLEGGING THE BEATLES

Beatle bootlegging is big business. Just like everything else surrounding the Beatles, bootlegging has flourished. There are more Beatle bootlegs (group and solo) than there are for any other artist. Several factors may have led to the great number of Beatle bootlegs in existence. First, while still together as a group, the Beatles released no live albums. They did many concerts over the years and tapes of several of these were made. Some of these tapes, the Hollywood Bowl concert for example, were recorded by record company personnel for possible release, while others were recorded by persons in the audience. Secondly, the Beatles made many radio, TV and film appearances, especially from late 1962 through 1964. As with concerts, many of these appearances were taped. Another factor is that the Beatles spent vast amounts of time in recording studios over the years, and many songs or bits of songs were recorded. Most of these were never polished to the point where they could have been commercially released, and many were, in fact, never meant for release at all. With so much unreleased material available, it seems inevitable that a large bootlegging industry would grow up around the Beatles.

At this point it might be wise to make a distinction between the various types of non-original Beatle records that are available. These fall into three main categories: bootlegs, pirates, and counterfeits. Bootlegs are often referred to as "underground" records. As mentioned before, these consist mainly of live concerts, studio outtakes, films, and radio and TV appearances -- in other words, material that is not available in any legitimately released form. Pirated records consist of material that has been commercially released by a record company, but with no attempt made to make the pirate look like the original. While the original may have a printed label, a full-color jacket, and possibly an attractive sleeve, the pirate will most often have a plain label and a plain jacket with an insert. The sound quality of the pirated songs will most likely not be as good as the originals. Counterfeits are attempts at exact copies of previously released material, and are designed to be passed off as originals. Many dealers will not tell you that you're buying a counterfeit, but when you buy a $100 album for $10 you can be almost certain that is is one.

Pirates and counterfeits cost artists and record companies vast amounts of money. According to a report in *Zodiac* (November 6, 1979), the market for counterfeit LP's in the U.S. alone stands at $400 million a year. Worldwide that figure may reach $1 billion a year. Bootlegging also causes a financial loss, but many feel it's not a serious loss because much of the material is usually not of commercial quality and would not have been released anyway. Most bootleg runs are small; sometimes as few as 100 are pressed, but the normal range seems to be 1000–2000 copies. Because of this, the amount lost is minimal, but a copyright has been infringed, there is still a loss, and bootlegging, like pirating and counterfeiting, is illegal.

There is now a law to protect artists and record companies, although, hard as it may be to believe, sound recordings did not receive any copyright protection under U.S. Federal law until February 15, 1972. On that date the copyright law, known as Act S. 646, became law. A loophole does exist in this law: it does not apply to any bootlegs or counterfeits made before its passage. Therefore, any bootlegs or counterfeits first manufactured before February 15, 1972, do not break the federal law, although they are still illegal under various state laws. Also, the copyright act refers only to performances on records, and concerts cannot be copyrighted as such. Bootleggers have tried different ways to avoid prosecution. Some have printed on their labels that they are paying royalties to the artist, and while some may actually do this, the majority probably do not. Many bootlegs are apparently made in other countries; France, Germany and many of the Southeast Asian countries appear to be the most popular places for bootlegging. Some may actually be made in these countries but, again, many are just marked that they were made there when they actually were manufactured in the U.S. Some bootleggers even dream up imaginary countries which they then list as the country of origin. Melvin Records is one label that has done this. The F.B.I. in the U.S. and various law enforcement agencies around the world continue to crack down on counterfeiters, pirates and bootleggers, but the list of new bootlegs is still increasing.

Occasionally, a bootleg will cause some reaction from a record company; for example, when Capitol Records announced that it would be releasing an album of live material from the Beatles' Hollywood Bowl concert and some radio stations began playing cuts from that concert which were already available on bootlegs, Capitol had to move up its planned release date. **WINGS FROM THE**

WINGS, a three-record set of all the songs performed by Paul and Wings on their 1976 U.S. tour, was released months before the commercial version became available. In this case, the legitimate release was in direct competition with the bootleg. The commercial release of albums like **THE BEATLES AT THE HOLLYWOOD BOWL**, **WINGS OVER AMERICA** and **THE BEATLES LIVE AT THE STAR CLUB** have in turn cut into bootleg sales of these concerts.

YOUR FRIENDLY NEIGHBORHOOD BOOTLEGGER

The big four bootleg labels, as far as Beatles material is concerned, are The Amazing Kornyphone Record Label (TAKRL), Contraband Music (CBM), Trade Mark Of Quality (TMOQ) and Wizardo. Let's take a short look at each of these labels:

TAKRL –   This label was supposedly run by a fictitious character named Dr. Terremce H. "Telly" Fone. Kornyphone went out of business in July, 1976 when Fone "died." Others now have the Kornyphone plates and continue to issue records. New releases have deluxe black-and-white covers. The Kornyphone logo is a man with a pig's head (see Figure 1). Several releases, purportedly put out by Kornyphone, were in fact issued by another company using the Kornyphone name and logo. These same people were probably also responsible for the TKRWM releases.

CBM –   Contraband records are hard to keep track of because the bootleggers didn't always number their early issues. Sometimes it is possible to pick up a number in the run-off wax of the record. CBM is also responsible for at least three other labels: Shalom, King Kong and Instant Analysis. The King Kong releases in particular are usually of poor quality (see Figure 2 for their logo).

TMOQ –   This may actually be two different companies both using the same name. There are two logos. One is an entire pig (Figure 3A), while the other is just a pig's head (Figure 3B). Many of the early TMOQ releases were pressed on colored vinyl. Some TMOQ discs are again being pressed on colored vinyl by the K&S label. TMOQ's subsidiary labels include Highway Hi Fi (HHCER), and Pig's Eye. Their 1975 issues were

FIGURE 1
The Amazing Kornyphone Record Label

FIGURE 2
Contraband Music

FIGURES 3A & 3B
Trade Mark Of Quality

FIGURE 4
Wizardo

stamped Silver Galaxy Records.

WIZARDO -- The Wizardo logo is shown in Figure 4. Many of the Wizardo numbers appeared on two or more albums with different titles, although usually the albums contained the same material. This again can lead to confusion when trying to purchase bootlegs.

Some of the other labels that have released Beatle bootlegs are:

AMAZON
ETCETRA -- Usually reissued material already available from other labels. The quality, in general, is not as good as that of the original bootleg. The jackets on many Amazon releases are a single sheet of thin cardboard folded to make a pocket for the record.

BERKELEY -- This is listed as a British label. For the most part they reissue other bootleg labels' material. The sound quality is inferior to that of the original bootleg. Most of their releases have laminated covers, with the pictures printed directly onto the jacket.

BEAT--L --   All four of these labels have been used by a Beatle
HIT   fan club. Usually only 10--20 copies of each record
RAM   have been pressed. Most of these are not true vinyl,
RING   but rather an aluminum disc with a thin layer of vinyl around it. The grooves are cut into the vinyl. There are some rarities here that have not as yet been released by any other sources. They are hard to find, but worth the look.

DECCAGONE --These records were released by one of the Beatle fan clubs. After buying the original tapes, the club began releasing two cuts at a time as 45s. Each was pressed on colored vinyl and came with a full-color picture sleeve. Unfortunately, as quick as a record was released, another person copied it and undersold the original.

K&S -- This label specializes in re-issuing other bootlegs on colored vinyl. All are done in extremely limited editions, usually only 100--150 are pressed.

MELVIN -- Although Melvin is one of the newer bootleg labels, it has quickly made a name for itself. Much of the material it issues has not been issued before; also, its jackets and sleeves are very well structured and thought out.

TOBE--MILO -- This label started out by releasing six EPs in hard sleeves. Several of these EPs contained previously released material, but the packaging was always new and very nice. The jackets were all laminated, some were in color. Several of the records were also pressed on colored vinyl. Most were limited to 500 or 1,000 copies, with the jackets being numbered.

ZAP -- Ze Anonym Plattenspieler. Many of the albums released by ZAP contain concert material. Some have cuts from several concerts, and because of this they make good samplers for those who want to hear the Beatles live from several sources.

A word about the quality of Beatle bootlegs is also in order here. The quality for one show will vary tremendously from one bootleg to another. A song from, say, an "Ed Sullivan Show" may sound almost perfect on one LP but be nearly inaudible on another. You are always taking a chance on quality unless you get to hear the record before you purchase it. Re-releasing causes a lot of the loss of sound quality. Bootleg copies are usually made from other bootleg records, not from the original tapes, so it's possible to go through two, three, or many more generations of copies with the resultant progressive sound quality deterioration.

The trend over the last few years has been to issue 7--inch records, 45s and EPs. Many of these are issued with sleeves and on colored vinyl. Albums, too, are more and more being issued with laminated covers, many in color. Since 1979, picture discs have also been a big item. There have been 45s, EPs and LPs issued as picture discs. The quality (of the pictures) has been consistently high, and the pressing runs low. This has made many of the bootleg picture discs instant collector's items, selling for highly inflated prices.

WHAT YOU *CAN DO* WITH *YOU CAN'T DO THAT*

The bootleg discography which makes up most of this volume is divided into six separate sections: The Beatles (as a group), George Harrison bootlegs, John Lennon bootlegs, Lennon/McCartney bootlegs, Paul McCartney/Wings bootlegs, and Ringo Starr bootlegs. There is also a separate section on Beatle counterfeits (group and solo). Within the bootleg and counterfeit sections, all entries are arranged in alphabetical order, letter--by--letter, according to the title of the record, ignoring the article "the" when it begins a title (articles "a" and "and" do figure in the alphabetical order, however.) Each entry has been assigned a number (001--891). This number is used in the various indexes to facilitate finding the desired entry. In the case of an untitled 45 or EP, the songs have been listed alphabetically, and an entry appears only under the first song. For example, *HEY JUDE/REVOLUTION* is listed under "H" only, and is not relisted in the "R" section. Picture sleeves released without a record are handled the same way. In the case of albums, the various cuts have been listed according to side, beginning on the left side of the page (side one), and moving to the right side of the page (side two), and so on. If it was not known which songs were on side one or two, the listings were split evenly between two assumed sides. For the most part, label names are spelled out. Some common abbreviations are used and these have already been discussed earlier in this section.

The bootleg and counterfeit sections have been indexed in several ways to help both the collector and the researcher quickly and easily find the facts needed. The three principal indexes are devoted to personal names, song titles (and some album title variations not provided for in the discography itself), and record labels/numbers.

The **Personal Name Index** lists more than 350 people mentioned throughout the various bootleg and counterfeit sections, with more than 1,000 references to the entries which mention their names. This index lists all those persons mentioned either in a bootleg itself or in the credits for a particular bootleg. References to John, Paul, George and Ringo are listed here, but references to the Beatles as a group are not. In a few cases, especially with the individual Beatles themselves, only the first (or last) name will appear in the bootleg listed. A variety of forms of entry for names of people and groups has been used in the index to accommodate the varied approaches – fan, collector, researcher – users will bring to this book.

The **Label Index** lists 178 labels on which bootlegs have been issued, as well as nearly 900 label numbers and their corresponding entry numbers within the discography. Labels are listed alphabetically and, under each label, are listed, numerically, all the records appearing on that label. Often the label of a record was known, but the number is not; entries of this type are placed at the end of the list for that label. In other cases, the label was unknown, but the number was known. These are all listed together, numerically, under "U" for unknown label. In still other cases, neither the label nor number was known, and these, of course, are not listed in this index at all.

The largest, and hopefully most useful, index is the **Song & Album Title Index**. This lists not only all the songs appearing on all the bootlegs -- over 1,000 song titles -- but also breaks each song down by origin: concert, radio appearance, TV appearance, soundtrack, etc. For example, under *A Hard Day's Night*, you will find listings for the Hollywood Bowl concert, Shea Stadium concert, "Top Of The Pops" radio show, soundtrack for the film, and many others. In this way, it can quickly be determined what versions of the song are available and on what bootlegs they can be found. Taking all this into consideration, there are nearly 2,200 song entries in this index. Additionally, a few song and album sub-titles or other title elements which might be presumed by some to be the title (or might otherwise have simply been incorrectly remembered as a song or album title) have been included in this index to facilitate the location of desired entries. If nothing appears after a song title, it may be assumed that it is done by the Beatles as a group. If done solo, the following notations appear after the title: (G) = George, (J) = John, (P) = Paul/Wings, (R) = Ringo.

In addition to these three principal indexes, there are fourteen smaller indexes to the bootleg and counterfeit sections grouped together as the **Topical Index**. These indexes cover such subjects as CHRISTMAS RECORDS, CONCERTS, INTERVIEWS, PICTURE DISCS, SOUNDTRACKS, and so on. Access to 56 concerts, 18 radio appearances, and 40 TV appearances recorded on bootlegs is provided by this index section.

Misspellings of words in album and song titles in the discography section reflect the spelling carried on the bootleg; references to songs are listed under the correct spelling of the song title in indexes, however. Otherwise, throughout the bootleg and counterfeit sections and indexes, jacket information has been followed unless it was definitely known to be incorrect.*

HAVE YOU HEARD THE WORD: The question of whether John Lennon had any part in the recording of *Have You Heard The Word* has been raging for quite some time. The problem may now have been solved. In their book *All Together Now* (Pierian Press), Harry Castleman and Wally Podrazik dealt with this question. When they asked Beatles' road manager Mal Evans if John was involved in the session, the answer was 'no'. But, if it wasn't John, who was it? Well, Harry and Wally have uncovered the answer and have graciously granted me permission to discuss it here. They've discovered that *Have You Heard The Word* was recorded by Steve Kipner and Maurice Gibb. A check into the history of Kipner and Gibb suggests that this might indeed be possible.

In the 60s, Kipner formed the group Tin Tin in his native Australia. Besides Kipner, the group (at various times) included Fred Goodman, Steve Groves and John Vallins. Tin Tin left Australia in early 1970 and moved to London. In London, they caught the attention of Maurice Gibb, who volunteered to pro-

NOVELTIES: BEATLEMANIA ON RECORD

The Beatles generated more novelty records than any other artist in history. Even the rush of novelties that followed the death of Elvis Presley did not push his total over that of the Beatles. Most of the Beatle novelties appeared in the early days of Beatlemania in 1964 and 1965, but the really amazing thing is that novelty records are continuing to appear even though the group has not been together for ten years.

Beatle novelties can easily be divided into several categories: (1) There were those records by artists who copied the group's name, using the Beatles name directly or characterizing themselves as the American Beatles, Female Beatles, and so forth. Various other insects were also used as names by some groups, clearly in parody of the Beatles. Even the Beatles' hometown, Liverpool, was used in the names of some novelty groups. (2) Then there were those artists who tried to capitalize on Beatlemania by recording Beatle songs. Early songs like *I Want To Hold Your Hand* and *She Loves You* were much recorded. Some artists even used Beatle song titles to make up the lyrics to their own songs. (3) The largest number of novelties came from those who recorded songs *about* the Beatles. Lately, many of these novelties have pleaded for the group to get back together again. Sometimes these novelties are about only one member of the Beatles -- Ringo came out on top here with 40 songs dedicated to him. (4) Several comedy records were done about the Beatles. Some artists, like Fisher and Marks, did straight comedy albums, while others used the Beatles in break-in comedy records. (5) At least two former Beatles tried to make it on their own utilizing their "Beatles connection." Pete Best and Jimmy Nicol both failed without their former partners. (6) Family and friends of the Beatles account for several novelties. John's father, Freddie, tried his hand at singing. Harry Nilsson and David Peel, Beatle friends, have also done novelty material. (7) Several artists answered Beatle songs. Here we have songs like

---

duce some songs for them. This puts Kipner and Gibb together in a recording studio in 1970. Most persons agree that *Have You Heard The Word* was recorded in 1970, probably in June.

Tin Tin went on to have their first hit, *Toast And Marmalade For Tea*, in early 1971 (Atco 6794 in the U.S.). It was produced for them by none other than Maurice Gibb. A follow-up, *Is That The Way* (Atco 6821), was co-produced by Maurice and Billy Lawrie. Lawrie will be remembered by Beatle fans for having co-written *Rock And Roller* with Ringo Starr; Billy also recorded the song and it was released in England in 1973 (RCA 2439).

Tin Tin broke up shortly after their last hit. Kipner formed a new group, Friends, with Darryl Cotton and Michael Lloyd. Their 1973 album, **FRIENDS** (MGM SE-4901), is apparently the last record involving Kipner to be released in the U.S.

Yes You Can Hold My Hand. (8) December, 1964, saw many Christmas novelties including *I Want A Beatle For Christmas* and *Santa, Bring Me Ringo.* (9) Many novelties were dances. Included here are songs like *The Beatle Walk* and *Beatle Bop.* (10) Several novelties are listed here because of their sleeves. Records like **LYNDON JOHNSON'S LONELY HEARTS CLUB BAND**, a take-off on the **SGT. PEPPER** cover, fall into this last category.

Several types of records were not listed in this discography. First, normal interview records of the Beatles have not been listed. This includes not only the Ed Rudy-type interviews, but also albums like Louise Harrison Caldwell's **ALL ABOUT THE BEATLES.** Secondly, Beatle songs performed in a normal way by other artists are not listed, so that records of Beatle material by the Hollyridge Strings, Boston Pops and many more have been left out of the discography. On the other hand, a song like *I Want To Hold Your Hand* done Italian-style by Lou Monte, or the **BEATLE COUNTRY** album by the Charles River Boys, with all songs done country style, are listed as novelties. This is a novelty discography and not an attempt to list all Beatle songs "covered" by other artists.

Within three novelty sections, more than 390 novelty records are listed in alphabetical order by artists. Many entries also have complete artist information, including the names of the individual members for group entries. As with bootlegs and counterfeits, there are also several indexes for quick and easy access to titles, labels, people and many other topics. Many indexes following the novelty sections have further introductory remarks which should be read before using that index.

ACKNOWLEDGEMENTS

Many thanks to Wally Podrazik and Harry Castleman who, without realizing it, inspired this book. In their two fine books, **All Together Now** and **The Beatles Again** (both published by Pierian Press), they chose not to deal with bootlegs in any great detail. In reading those books, I realized that a similar book on bootlegs would also be of value to the collector and historian, and immediately began work on this volume. Also, a special thanks to Wally for taking time from his busy schedule to read my manuscript and make several suggestions for improving it. Wally also provided the Foreword for this edition.

Words alone cannot express my gratitude to Tom Schultheiss of Pierian Press for his seemingly unending patience with this novice author. In the beginning, Tom's letters of encouragement always seemed to arrive at just the right time to lift my spirits and keep me working. Later, he suffered through many pages of questions, corrections and additions, all of which helped to make the book much better. His *Everything You Always Wanted To Know About Bootlegs, But Were Too Busy Collecting Them To Ask* is an exhaustive look at bootlegging which could stand well on its own. I am glad that it could be part of this book.

I would also like to extend my appreciation to my wife, Erna, for her continuing faith in me. And to my sons, Jeff and Greg, who had to do without their father at times so that deadlines could be met. They're all Beatle fans and probably know more about bootlegs than they ever thought they would.

Finally, I would like to thank the following individuals for their kindness and courtesy in allowing us to use their materials to illustrate this work: Mr. Martin Haxby of EMI Records Limited; Mr. Howard Alperin of Cadet Records; Mr. Joey Welz of Dawn Productions; Mr. Katsumi Kita of Shinko Music Publishing and Mr. Maynard Solomon of Vanguard Recording Society.   **C. R.**

The Beatles

001   ABBEY ROAD REVISITED   Wizardo 353   (LP)

1. *You Really Got A Hold On Me*
2. *Have You Heard The Word*
3. *Don't Let Me Down*
4. *Those Were The Days*
5. *Mean Mr. Mustard*
6. *All Together On The Wireless Machine*
7. *Step Inside Love*
8. *Bye Bye Bye*
9. *Cottonfields*
10. *Twist And Shout*
11. *Dizzy Miss Lizzy*
12. *From Me To You*
13. *Twist And Shout*
14. *This Boy*
15. *I Saw Her Standing There*
16. *She Loves You*
17. *I Want To Hold Your Hand*
18. *Please Please Me*
19. *All My Loving*

Cuts 1,10: Recorded October 30, 1963, for the Swedish TV show "Drop In." The show was aired November 3, 1963.
Cut 2: Recorded in June of 1970. Reportedly this is John and at least some of the Bee Gees. This version is somewhat longer than the version found on some other albums. (For discussion, see footnote on pages xxiv-xxv.)
Cuts 3–4: Recorded in the fall of 1968, live at a press conference.
Cuts 5–6, 8: Depending on the source, these three songs were either recorded in the spring of 1969 or the spring of 1970.
Cut 7: Demo cut by Paul in February, 1968. The song was later given to Cilla Black.
Cut 9: Recorded January, 1968 by John as part of an interview with Kenny Everett.
Cut 11: Original record.
Cuts 12–13, 15–18: From the Beatles' second appearance on the "Ed Sullivan Show." Broadcast live from the Deauville Hotel in Miami Beach on February 16, 1964. There were 3,400 fans in attendance.
Cuts 14, 19: From the Beatles' first appearance on the "Ed Sullivan Show." Recorded in New York City on February 7, 1964. Shown on February 9, 1964.
SEE ALSO: **ABBEY ROAD REVISITED** (CBM 3907); **CAVERN DAYS -- SUPER STUDIO SERIES 5; RENAISSANCE MINSTRELS I** (side two); **THOSE WERE THE DAYS.**

002   ABBEY ROAD REVISITED   CBM 3907   (LP)

1. *You Really Got A Hold On Me*
2. *Have You Heard The Word*
3. *Don't Let Me Down*
4. *Those Were The Days*
5. *Mean Mr. Mustard*
6. *All Together On The Wireless Machine*
7. *Step Inside Love*
8. *Bye Bye Bye*
11. *From Me To You*
12. *Twist And Shout*
13. *This Boy*
14. *I Saw Her Standing There*
15. *She Loves You*
16. *I Want To Hold Your Hand*
17. *Please Please Me*
18 *All My Loving*

9. *Cottonfields*
10. *Twist And Shout*
NOTES: Same as **ABBEY ROAD REVISITED** (Wizardo 353) except *Dizzy Miss Lizzy* is not included at the end of side one.
SEE ALSO: **CAVERN DAYS -- SUPER STUDIO SERIES 5; RENAISSANCE MINSTRELS I; THOSE WERE THE DAYS.**

003   **ABC MANCHESTER 1964**   Wizardo 361   (LP)

1. *Introduction*
2. *From Me To You*
3. *She Loves You*
4. *Twist And Shout*
5. *Interview*
6. *Paperback Writer*
7. *Rain*
8. *I Want To Hold Your Hand*
9. *This Boy*
10. *All My Loving*
11. *Money*
12. *Twist And Shout*

Cuts 1--2: Unknown, possibly from the "Ed Sullivan Show" of February 16, 1964.
Cuts 3--4: Recorded in Manchester, England at the Ardwick Apollo on November 20, 1963. The show was filmed by Pathe British News and the resulting eight–minute film was released on December 22, 1963. These two songs are a part of that film.
Cut 5: Interview from June, 1965.
Cuts 6--7: From the BBC–TV show "Top Of The Pops" June 16, 1966. The film was later shown on "Thank Your Lucky Stars" (June 25, 1966) and on the "Ed Sullivan Show" in August, 1966.
Cuts 8--12: From the TV show "Sunday Night At The London Palladium" which aired October 13, 1963. This was the Beatles first major TV appearance.
SEE ALSO: **BEATLES LIVE AT A.B.C. MANCHESTER; LIVE AT A.B.C. MANCHESTER.**

004   **A/B SINGLE ACETATE**   Wizardo 315   (LP)

1. *Save The Last Dance For Me*
2. *Don't Let Me Down*
3. *I Dig A Pony*
4. *I've Got A Feeling*
5. *Get Back*
6. *One After 909*
7. *For You Blue*
8. *Teddy Boy*
9. *Two Of Us*
10. *Dig It*
11. *Let It Be*
12. *The Long And Winding Road*
13. *Get Back*

Cuts 1--13: Recorded January of 1969 at the Twickenham Studio on London during the **LET IT BE** sessions. Essentially, this is the **LET IT BE** album before Phil Spector got his hands on it.
SEE ALSO: **THE BEATLES LET IT BE; LET IT BE: BEFORE PHIL SPECTOR; ORIGINAL "GET BACK" ACETATE; STEREO ACETATE FOR LET IT BE (BEFORE PHIL SPECTOR).**

005   **ACROSS THE UNIVERSE**   Tobe--Milo 5Q3   (EP)
NOTES: This is a seven–inch 33 1/3 rpm, one–sided recording. It was made to look like a test pressing. This version of the song was recorded in early February, 1968 and was included on the British album **NO ONE'S GONNA CHANGE OUR WORLD** (EMI Star Line SRS 5013). The proceeds from this album went to the World Wildlife Fund. All four Beatles appear on this version, along with George Martin on organ and Lizzie Bravo and Gayleen Pease on backing vocals.

006   *A DAY IN THE LIFE/GET BACK*   Beat–L 003   (45)
NOTES: Seven–inch 45 rpm bootleg single. The two songs are both original recordings. There are also comments on these Beatle recordings by Alan

A Hard Day's Night/Long Tall Sally (45)   **Beat 12-142 (Entry 009)**

Parsons. Comments are from the 1979 DJ album **AUDIO GUIDE TO THE ALAN PARSONS PROJECT** (Arista SP 68).

007   **A HARD DAY'S NIGHT**   Wizardo 303   (2 LPs)

1. *A Hard Day's Night*
2. *I Should Have Known Better*
3. *I Wanna Be Your Man*
4. *Don't Bother Me*

5. *All My Loving*
6. *If I Fell*
7. *Can't Buy Me Love*

8. *And I Love Her*
9. *I'm Happy Just To Dance With You*
10. *Instrumental*

11. *A Hard Day's Night*
12. *Can't Buy Me Love*
13. *Tell My Why*
14. *If I Fell*
15. *I Should Have Known Better*
16. *She Loves You*
17. *A Hard Day's Night*
18. *Skinnie Minnie*

Cuts 1–17: Recorded at EMI Abbey Road Studios from March 2 until April 27, 1964. All songs and the dialogue between them are from the soundtrack of the film "A Hard Day's Night."

Cut 18: Original. Recorded by Tony Sheridan and the Beat Brothers. No Beatle involvement with this record.

SEE ALSO: **A HARD DAY'S NIGHT + SKINNIE MINNIE; CINELOGUE 3 – A HARD DAY'S NIGHT; COMPLETE SOUNDTRACK TO A HARD DAY'S NIGHT; HARD DAY'S NIGHT SOUNDTRACK.**

008   **A HARD DAY'S NIGHT + SKINNIE MINNIE**   Unknown   (2 LPs)
NOTES: This double album is the same as **A HARD DAY'S NIGHT** (Wizardo 303), except for the different title.

SEE ALSO: **CINELOGUE 3 – A HARD DAY'S NIGHT; COMPLETE SOUND--TRACK TO A HARD DAY'S NIGHT; HARD DAY'S NIGHT SOUND--TRACK.**

009   *A HARD DAY'S NIGHT/LONG TALL SALLY*   BEAT 12–142   (45)
NOTES: This 45 was pressed on red vinyl and came with a picture sleeve. Front of sleeve shows black–and–white photo of the Beatles. Back is printed in red and shows song titles and recording information. *A Hard Day's Night* is marked as having been recorded on April 2, 1964 and *Long Tall Sally* as April 1, 1964. Both are alternate takes. "Small" Stan is given credit for having cut these two songs.

010   **ALIVE AT LAST IN ATLANTA**   Walrus TVC 1001   (LP)

1. *Twist And Shout*
2. *You Can't Do That*
3. *All My Loving*
4. *She Loves Me*
5. *Things We Said Today*
6. *Roll Over Beethoven*

7. *Can't Buy Me Love*
8. *If I Fell*
9. *I Want To Hold Your Hand*
10. *Boys*
11. *A Hard Day's Night*
12. *Long Tall Sally*

NOTES: The "Whiskey Flat" cuts are probably the hardest to track down. Various sources will list them as being from three different concerts – Hollywood Bowl (8–23--64), Atlantic City Convention Center (8–30–64), and Philadelphia Convention Hall (9–2–64). There seems to be no clear cut idea as to which of these concerts the cuts were taken from. Since all the following albums have the same cuts, we can be fairly sure they all come from the same show. But, which one? The best guess appears to be the Hollywood Bowl. Just to keep things straight, these cuts will be listed in the index as being from the "Whiskey Flat" concert with no date or place listed.

SEE ALSO: BEATLES ALIVE IN ATLANTA AT LAST; BEATLES IN
ATLANTA WHISKEY FLAT; IN ATLANTA WHISKEY FLAT; LIVE
AT HOLLYWOOD BOWL; LIVE AT THE ATLANTA WHISKEY FLAT;
LIVE CONCERT ATLANTA; LIVE CONCERT ATLANTA, GEORGIA;
LIVE CONCERT AT WHISKEY FLATS; LIVE IN ATLANTA WHISKEY
FLAT; LIVE IN HOLLYWOOD.

011   ALL YOU NEED IS CASH   Rut 546   (LP)

1. *Get Up and Go*
2. *Medley*
3. *Goose Step Momma*
4. *Number One*
5. *Made For Each Other (Between Us)*
6. *With A Girl Like You*
7. *Hold My Hand*
8. *I Must Be In Love*
9. *Living In Hope*
10. *Ouch*
11. *Looking Good* (Live)
12. *Good Times Roll*
13. *Love Life*
14. *Nevertheless*
15. *Piggy In The Middle*
16. *Cheese And Onions*
17. *Let's Be Natural*
18. *You Need Feet*
19. *Get Up And Go*
20. *Doubleback Alley*

NOTES: Not the Beatles, but the Rutles. From the TV special of March 22,
1978. This is the complete dialogue and music track. The show starred the
Rutles, George Harrison, Mick Jagger and Paul Simon. The Rutles are (were?)
Eric Idle as Dirk McQuickly, Neil Innes as Ron Nasty, Rikki Fataar as Stig
O'Hara and John Halsey as Barry Wom.

012   ALPHA OMEGA VOL. 1   Audio Tape ATRBH 3583   (4 LPs)

1. *Act Naturally*
2. *All I've Got To Do*
3. *All My Loving*
4. *And I Love Her*
5. *Baby's In Black*
6. *Yesterday*
7. *Ballad Of John And Yoko*
8. *Bangla Desh*
9. *Can't Buy Me Love*
10. *Come Together*
11. *Day Tripper*
12. *Do You Want To Know A Secret*
13. *Eight Days A Week*
14. *Eleanor Rigby*
15. *Uncle Albert*

16. *I Should Have Known Better*
17. *It Won't Be Long*
18. *I Want To Hold Your Hand*
19. *Lady Madonna*
20. *Ticket To Ride*
21. *Lucy In The Sky With Diamonds*
22. *Michelle*
23. *Mr. Moonlight*
24. *I Feel Fine*
25. *If I Fell*
26. *I'll Be Back*
27. *Hey Jude*
28. *I'm A Loser*
29. *I'm Happy Just To Dance With
   You*
30. *I Saw Her Standing There*

31. *Nowhere Man*
32. *Ob--La--Di Ob--La--Da*
33. *Paperback Writer*
34. *Penny Lane*
35. *Help*
36. *Roll Over Beethoven*
37. *Sgt. Pepper's Lonely Hearts Club
   Band*
38. *Get Back*
39. *Hello Goodbye*
40. *Revolution No. 1*
41. *Here Comes The Sun*
42. *I'll Follow The Sun*
43. *Imagine*
44. *Honey Don't*

45. *We Can Work It Out*
46. *With A Little Help From My Friends*
47. *Yellow Submarine*
48. *Baby You're A Rich Man*
49. *You Can't Do That*
53. *She Loves You*
54. *Something*
55. *Strawberry Fields Forever*
56. *Tell Me Why*
57. *The Long And Winding Road*

50. *You've Got To Hide Your Love*
    Away
51. *Maybe I'm Amazed*
52. *A Hard Day's Night*
58. *Let It Be*
59. *Everybody's Trying To Be My*
    Baby

Cuts 1–59: Original recordings.
SEE ALSO: **BEATLES VOL. 1; GREATEST HITS: COLLECTOR'S EDITION; VOLUME ONE.**

013   **ALPHA OMEGA VOL. 2**   Audio Tape ATRB 4   (4 LPs)

1. *No Reply*
2. *Rock And Roll Music*
3. *Too Many People*
4. *Heart Of The Country*
5. *Back Of My Car*
6. *Magical Mystery Tour*
7. *Fool On The Hill*
8. *Lovely Rita*
9. *When I'm Sixty--Four*
10. *A Day In The Life*
11. *Getting Better*
12. *You've Got To Hide Your Love*
    Away
13. *Another Girl*
14. *Good Day Sunshine*

15. *Taxman*
16. *She Said She Said*
17. *All Together Now*
18. *Pepper Land* (George Martin)
19. *Crippled Inside*
20. *Oh Yoko*
21. *I'm Looking Through You*
22. *I've Just Seen A Face*
23. *Norwegian Wood*
24. *You Won't See Me*
25. *Lovely Linda*
26. *Drive My Car*
27. *Dr. Robert*
28. *What Goes On*
29. *My Sweet Lord*

30. *All Things Must Pass*
31. *Apple Scruffs*
32. *Baby It's You*
33. *A Taste Of Honey*
34. *You Never Give Me Your Money*
35. *She Came In Through The*
    Bathroom Window
36. *Maxwell's Silver Hammer*
37. *Golden Slumbers*
38. *Mean Mr. Mustard*
39. *Love Me Do*
40. *Twist And Shout*
41. *Please Please Me*
42. *P.S. I Love You*
43. *Dizzy Miss Lizzy*
44. *Rocky Raccoon*
45. *Helter Skelter*

46. *Kansas City*
47. *Tell Me What You See*
48. *I Don't Want To Spoil The Party*
49. *Back In The USSR*
50. *Birthday*
51. *Goodnight*
52. *Why Don't We Do It In The Road*
53. *Across The Universe*
54. *Maggie Mae*
55. *Two Of Us*
56. *I've Got A Feeling*
57. *I Dig A Pony*
58. *All You Need Is Love*
59. *I Am The Walrus*
60. *Being For The Benefit Of Mr.*
    Kite

Cuts 1–60: Original recordings.
SEE ALSO: **BEATLES VOL. 2; VOLUME TWO.**

014   **ALPHA OMEGA VOL. 3**   Audio Tape 1–4   (2 LPs)
       NOTES: Exact cuts included are unknown, but all are presumed to be original.
       SEE ALSO: **VOLUME THREE.**

015   **AMERICAN TOUR WITH ED RUDY 1964**   Unknown   (LP)
       NOTES: This is a copy of the original Ed Rudy interview album.
       SEE ALSO: **ED RUDY I -- TALK ALBUM; ED RUDY VOL. I; 1964 TALK ALBUM.**

6

016   **AMERICAN TOUR WITH ED RUDY 1965**   Unknown   (LP)
NOTES: This is a copy of the original 1965 Ed Rudy interview album with the Beatles.
SEE ALSO: **ED RUDY VOL. II; 1965 TALK ALBUM.**

017   **AND THE BEATLES WERE BORN**   Napoleon 11044   (LP)

1. *Boys*
2. *A Hard Day's Night*
3. *Long Tall Sally*
4. *Twist And Shout*
5. *You Can't Do That*
6. *All My Loving*
7. *Twist And Shout*
8. *Diddy Wah Diddy* (Buffalo Springfield)
9. *Moonchild* (Capt. Beefheart)
10. *Blue Bird* (Buffalo Springfield)
11. *Frying Pan* (Capt. Beefheart)
12. *A Quick One And He's Away* (Who)

Cuts 1–7: Recorded live at the Hollywood Bowl August 23, 1964.
Cuts 8–12: Not the Beatles. Recorded by the artists listed.
NOTES: This album has a deluxe cover. It is sometimes listed as a legitimate Italian release.
SEE ALSO: **BEATLES WERE BORN; ONCE UPON A TIME . . .**

018   *ANNA/OH DARLING*   ESR   (45)
NOTES: Seven–inch 45 rpm. The originals were pressed on red vinyl. A later edition was on black vinyl.

019   **APPLE SLICES**   Beat–L 005   (LP)

1. *Six O'Clock*
2. *Dark Horse*
3. *Spiritual Regeneration*
4. *Happy Birthday Mike Love*
5. *Within And Without You*
6. *Savoy Truffle*
7. *Hey Bulldog*
8. *The Fool On The Hill*
9. *I Am The Walrus*
10. *Peace Of Mind*
11. *Mean Mr. Mustard*
12. *All Things Must Pass*
13. *Oriental Nightfish*
14. *Get Back*
15. *I Should Have Known Better*
16. *From Us To You*
17. *Kansas City*
18. *Long Tall Sally*
19. *If I Fell*
20. *Boys*

Cut 1: This is the original, long version of the song from the **RINGO** album.
Cut 2: A Harrison outtake.
Cuts 3–4: Recorded March 15, 1968 in Riskikesh, India. *Spiritual Regeneration* is sometimes listed as *Indian Rope Trick.*
Cut 5: Outtake.
Cuts 6–7: 1968 outtakes? (Or just originals with one of the sound tracks dropped?)
Cuts 8–9: 1967 outtakes? (Or just originals with one of the sound tracks dropped?)
Cut 10: Recorded in June 1967, found in the Apple trash can in 1970.
Cut 11: Outtake with extra verse.
Cut 12: 1969 Beatles' version.
Cut 13: 1973 demo by Paul and Linda.
Cut 14: From the **LET IT BE** sessions of early 1969.
Cut 15: From the soundtrack of the film "A Hard Day's Night."
Cut 16: From the BBC radio show "From Us To You" which aired December 26, 1963.
Cuts 17–20: Alternate takes.
NOTES: This was originally released as a collector's tape, but was later pressed in very limited quantity for a fan club.

020   **APPLETRAX ONE '69**   CBM B218   (2 LPs)
NOTES: The cuts are unknown, but presumably the same as those on **SWEET APPLE TRAX VOL. ONE** (CBM 4182), which are listed below.

1. *Old Hillbilly Way*
2. *House Of The Rising Sun*
3. *Commonwealth Song*
4. *Get Off White Power*

5. *Winston Richard And John*
6. *Yakety Yack*
7. *For You Blue*
8. *Let It Be*

9. *Get Back*
10. *Don't Let Me Down*
11. *On Our Way Home*
12. *Ba Ba Black Sheep*
13. *Encore*

14. *Suzy Parker*
15. *Oh Yeah (I've Got A Feeling)*
16. *No Pakistanis*

Cuts 1–16: Recorded live in early 1969 at Twickenham Studios, London, during
the **LET IT BE** sessions.
SEE ALSO: **SWEET APPLE TRAX** (sides one and two); **SWEET APPLE TRAX
VOL. ONE; SWEET APPLE TRAX 1.**

021   APPLETRAX TWO '69   CBM B219   (2 LPs)
NOTES: The cuts are unknown, but presumably the same as those on **SWEET
APPLE TRAX VOL. TWO** (CBM 4181), which are listed below.

1. *Let It Be*
2. *Be Bop A Lou*
3. *Silver Spoon*
4. *Tuesday Speaking*
5. *Hi Heel Sneakers*

6. *I'll Be Mine*
7. *One After 909*
8. *Norwegian Wood*
9. *Bathroom Window*

10. *A Long And Winding Road*
11. *Shakin' In The 60's*
12. *Everybody's Rockin'*
13. *Across The Universe*
14. *On Our Way Home*

15. *Momma You've Been On My
    Mind*
16. *Da De Da*

Cuts 1–16: Recorded in early 1969 at the Twickenham Studios in London during
the **LET IT BE** sessions.
SEE ALSO: **SWEET APPLE TRAX** (sides three and four); **SWEET APPLE
TRAX VOL. TWO.**

022   AROUND THE BEATLES   Wizardo 349   (LP)

1. Medley:
   Love Me Do
   Please Please Me
   From Me To You
   She Loves You
   I Want To Hold Your Hand
2. *Can't Buy Me Love*
3. *Long Tall Sally*
4. *She Loves You*
5. *Act Naturally*

6. *Can't Buy Me Love*
7. *Baby's In Black*
8. *Help*
9. *I'm Down*
10. *I Feel Fine*
11. *Dizzy Miss Lizzy*
12. *Ticket To Ride*

Cuts 1–3: Recorded April 27–28, 1964 for the Rediffusion TV show "Around
The Beatles." The show aired May 6, 1964.
Cut 4: From the February 16, 1964 Ed Sullivan Show. Broadcast live from the
Deauville Hotel in Miami Beach.
Cuts 5–12: Recorded live during the Shea Stadium concert on August 15, 1965.
SEE ALSO: **AROUND THE BEATLES; SECRET.**

023   AROUND THE BEATLES   Wizardo 349   (LP)

1. *Twist And Shout*
2. *Roll Over Beethoven*

8. *1966 Tour Interviews With Ken
    Douglas*

3. *I Wanna Be Your Man*
4. *Long Tall Sally*
5. Medley:
   Love Me Do
   Please Please Me
   From Me To You
   She Loves You
   I Want To Hold Your Hand
6. *Can't Buy Me Love*
7. *Shout*

Cuts 1–7: Recorded April 27–28, 1964 for the Rediffusion TV show "Around The Beatles." The show aired May 6, 1964.

Cut 8: Parts of the Ken Douglas interviews, recorded during the Beatles' U.S. tour.

NOTES: This album was originally issued on color vinyl.

SEE ALSO: **AROUND THE BEATLES.**

024 **AS IT HAPPENED: THE BEATLES AND MURRAY THE K** Fairway 526 (EP)
NOTES: This is the original Murray The K interview EP complete with the songs *She Loves You* and *Shout*.
SEE ALSO: **MURRAY THE K AND THE BEATLES: AS IT HAPPENED.**

025 **AS SWEET AS YOU ARE** CBM 3316; Dittolino Discs No. 0001; KO–408 (LP)

1. *I Got A Woman*
2. *Glad All Over*
3. *I Just Don't Understand*
4. *Slow Down*
5. *Please Don't Ever Change*
6. *A Shot Of Rhythm And Blues*
7. *I'm Sure To Fall*
8. *Nothing's Shakin' But The Leaves On The Trees*
9. *Lonesome Tears In My Eyes*
10. *Everyone Wants Someone*
11. *I'm Gonna Sit Right Down And Cry Over You*
12. *Crying, Waiting, Hoping*
13. *To Know Her Is To Love Her*
14. *Bound By Love*

Cuts 1–14: Recorded from a BBC radio broadcast in November, 1962.
SEE ALSO: **DON'T PASS ME BY; 14 UNRELEASED SONGS; JUDY; YELLOW MATTER CUSTARD** (Shalom 3316C/3316D); **YELLOW MATTER CUSTARD** (TMO 71032).

026 **A STUDIO RECORDING** Catso Records (LP)

1. *Let It Be*
2. *Get Back No. 1*
3. *Don't Let Me Down*
4. *I've Got A Feeling*
5. *Anything You Want*
6. *Teddy, Don't Worry Your Mommy Is Here*
7. *We're On Our Way Home*
8. *I Love You Girl*
9. *Across The Universe*

Cuts 1–9: Recorded during the **LET IT BE** sessions early in 1969 at London's Twickenham Studios.

027 *A TRIP TO MIAMI/A TRIP TO MIAMI PT. 2* Lee Alan Presents (45)
NOTES: Recorded in February of 1964 at the Deauville Hotel in Miami Beach. Lee Allen, a Detroit DJ, did the interview. The original record had an insert telling the whole story of the interview. The boots do not have this sheet.

028 **AT THE CAVERN CLUB** Unknown (LP)
NOTES: Cuts are unknown, but it is possibly the same as **CAVERN CLUB** (CBM 3906).

029   AT THE HOLLYWOOD BOWL   TMOQ S–208   (LP)

1. *Twist And Shout*
2. *You Can't Do That*
3. *All My Loving*
4. *She Loves You*
5. *Things We Said Today*
6. *Roll Over Beethoven*
7. *Can't Buy Me Love*
8. *If I Fell*
9. *I Wanna Be Your Man*
10. *Boys*
11. *A Hard Day's Night*
12. *Long Tall Sally*

Cuts 1–12: Recorded live at the Hollywood Bowl on August 23, 1964. The recording was made by George Martin for possible release, so the quality is good.

030   AT THE RAREST   Joker--Saar SM 3591   (LP)

1. *Boys*
2. *Do You Want To Know A Secret*
3. *All My Loving*
4. *Please Please Me*
5. *Misery*
6. *Twist And Shout*
7. *You Can't Do That*
8. *Carol*
9. *I Just Want To Make Love To You*
10. *Cry To Me*
11. *Walking The Dog*
12. *You Can Make It If You Try*
13. *Route 66*

Cuts 1–7: These were supposed to have been recorded live during the Beatles tour of Italy in June of 1965. They are, however, studio tracks.

Cuts 8–13: These cuts are by the Rolling Stones, not the Beatles.

NOTES: Cuts 1, 3, 6 and 7 are live cuts of unknown origin. Cuts 2, 4 and 5 are studio cuts.

SEE ALSO: **BEATLES AND ROLLING STONES; BEATLES/STONES LIVE.**

031   A WAY WITH WORDS   Wizardo 505   (3 LPs)

1. Medley:
   Tutti Frutti (Little Richard)
   Back In The Jungle (Eternals)
   She Bop (unknown)
   Roll Over Beethoven (Chuck Berry)
   Fever (Little Willie John)
   The Great Pretender (Platters)
   Duke of Earl (Gene Chandler)
   Let's Go To The Hop (Danny & The Juniors)
   Chantilly Lace (The Big Bopper)
   As I Walk Along (Del Shannon)
   Blue Moon (Marcels)
   The Wanderer (Dion)
   Wake Up Little Suzy (Everly Bros.)
   Bye Bye Love (Everly Bros.)
   That Loving Feeling (Righteous Bros.)
   Love Me Tender (Elvis)
   Don't Be Cruel (Elvis)
   Hound Dog (Elvis)
   Jailhouse Rock (Elvis)
   Are You Lonesome Tonight (Elvis)
   Dizzy Miss Lizzy
   Ticket To Ride
   Help
   Act Naturally

2. *Eleanor Rigby*
3. *Scottish Lock*
4. *Paperback Writer*
5. *Sgt. Pepper*
6. *With A Little Help From My Friends*
7. *Good Morning*
8. *When I'm Sixty–Four*
9. *Within You Without You*

10. *Magical Mystery Tour*
11. *Fool On The Hill*
16. *Get Back*
17. *Happiness Is A Warm Gun*

10

Back In 1964 At The Hollywood Bowl (LP)   **Berkeley 2027 (Entry 032)**

12. *Rhymes And Lessons*	18. *My Sweet Lord*
13. *Flying*	19. *Nowhere Man*
14. *Here Comes The Sun*	20. *Revolution*
15. *Lucy In The Sky*	21. *Forgotten Lyrics: Give Peace A Chance*
	22. *Gimme A Dime*
	23. *All You Need Is Love*
	24. *Strawberry Fields*
25. *Yesterday*	29. *Interviews: John; Paul (with a version of "Teddy Boy"); George; Ringo.*
26. *Ain't No Cherry*	
27. *Hey Jude*	
28. *Let It Be*	

Cut 1: All songs in this medley are by the artist listed with the last four being Beatles' cuts from Shea Stadium, August 15, 1965.
Cuts 2–28: Original recordings.
Cut 3: This is really *Norwegian Wood.*
Cut 12: This is really *Glass Onion.*
Cut 22: This is really George Harrison's *Give Me Love.*
Cut 26: This is really *The Ballad Of John And Yoko.*

032   BACK IN 1964 AT THE HOLLYWOOD BOWL   Lemon CSR 143; Berkeley 2027
         (LP)

1. *Twist And Shout*	7. *Can't Buy Me Love*
2. *You Can't Do That*	8. *If I Fell*
3. *All My Loving*	9. *I Want To Hold Your Hand*
4. *She Loves You*	10. *Boys*
5. *Things We Said Today*	11. *A Hard Day's Night*
6. *Roll Over Beethoven*	12. *Long Tall Sally*

Cuts 1–12: Recorded live at the Hollywood Bowl concert in Los Angeles, August 23, 1964. The concert was recorded by George Martin and the boots were made from this tape.
NOTES: The Berkeley LP has a special laminated black--and--white cover.
SEE ALSO: **BACK IN 1964 AT THE HOLLYWOOD BOWL** (CBM 4178);
BEATLES 1964; HOLLYWOOD BOWL '64; LIVE AT HOLLYWOOD BOWL; LIVE AT THE HOLLYWOOD BOWL; LIVE AT SHEA; THE ONLY LIVE RECORDING (Kustom); **THE ONLY LIVE RECORDING** (unknown); **THE SHEA STADIUM CONCERT 1964; THE SHEA STADIUM "MORE OR LESS" STEREO; SHEA: THE GOOD OLD DAYS** (Kustom); **SHEA: THE GOOD OLD DAYS** (Pine Tree).

033   BACK IN 1964 AT THE HOLLYWOOD BOWL   CBM 4178; Instant Analysis 1032
         (LP)

1. *Twist And Shout*	5. *She Loves You*
2. *You Can't Do That*	6. *Things We Said Today*
3. *All My Loving*	7. *Roll Over Beethoven*
4. *Can't Buy Me Love*	8. *If I Fell*
	9. *I Want To Hold Your Hand*
	10. *Boys*
	11. *A Hard Day's Night*
	12. *Long Tall Sally*

Cuts 1–12: Same as **BACK IN 1964 AT THE HOLLYWOOD BOWL** (Lemon CSR 143).
SEE ALSO: **BEATLES 1964; HOLLYWOOD BOWL '64; LIVE AT HOLLY-WOOD BOWL; LIVE AT THE HOLLYWOOD BOWL; LIVE AT SHEA; THE ONLY LIVE RECORDING** (Kustom); **THE ONLY LIVE RECORDING**

(unknown); **THE SHEA STADIUM CONCERT 1964; THE SHEA STADIUM "MORE OR LESS" STEREO; SHEA: THE GOOD OLD DAYS** (Kustom); **SHEA: THE GOOD OLD DAYS** (Pine Tree).

034   BACK IN THE SADDLE -- 8TH AMENDMENT   ZAP 7872   (LP)

1. *Murray The K Fan Club Messages '65*
2. *I Saw Her Standing There*
3. *You Can't Do That*
4. *Johnny B. Goode*
5. *Slow Down*
6. *Ain't Nothin' Shakin' But The Leaves On The Trees*
7. *I'm Gonna Sit Right Down And Cry Over You*
8. *Honey Don't*
9. *Rock And Roll Music*
10. *Dizzy Miss Lizzy*

Cut 1: Murray The K interviews with all four Beatles. Includes the songs *She Loves You* and *Shout*.
Cuts 2–3: Recorded live at the Melbourne, Australia concert June 16, 1964.
Cut 4: Recorded May 25, 1963 from the BBC radio show "Saturday Club."
Cuts 5--7: Recorded from a BBC radio show in November of 1962.
Cut 8: Recorded from a BBC radio show in 1963. John is singing lead.
Cut 9: Recorded live in 1966.
Cut 10: Unknown.
NOTES: A live version of *Money* appears between no. 9 and no. 10, but is not listed on the cover.

035   BACK UPON US ALL   ZAP 7864   (LP)

1. *Day Tripper*
2. *Two Of Us*
3. *Maggie Mae*
4. *Twist And Shout*
5. *You Can't Do That*
6. *All My Loving*
7. *Dig It*
8. *When You Get To Suzy Parker's Everybody Gets Well Done*
9. *Let It Be*
10. *Dizzy Miss Lizzy*
11. *Sie Liebt Dich*
12. *Honey Don't*
13. *I'm Sure To Fall*
14. *I Need You*
15. *For You Blue*

Cut 1: Recorded live at Budokan Hall in Tokyo on July 2, 1966.
Cuts 2–3, 7--9, 15: Recorded during the **LET IT BE** sessions early 1969 at Twickenham Studios in London.
Cuts 4--6: Recorded live at the Hollywood Bowl on August 23, 1964.
Cut 10: Live, unknown.
Cut 11: Original recording.
Cut 12: From a BBC radio show in 1963. John is singing lead.
Cut 13: From a BBC radio show broadcast in November of 1962.
Cut 14: From the soundtrack of "Help." Some dialogue is also included.
SEE ALSO: **BACK UPON US ALL** (Kornyphone 1969); **MORE FROM THE FAB FOUR** (side two); **POWER BROKERS** (side two); **UPON US ALL -- 4TH AMENDMENT.**

036   BACK UPON US ALL   Kornyphone 1969   (LP)

1. *Day Tripper*
2. *Two Of Us*
3. *Maggie Mae*
4. *Twist And Shout*
5. *You Can't Do That*
6. *All My Loving*
7. *Suzy Parker*
8. *Suzy Parker*
9. *Let It Be*
10. *Dizzy Miss Lizzy*
11. *Sie Liebt Dich*
12. *Honey Don't*
13. *I'm Sure To Fall*

7. *Dig It*   14. *I Need You*
15. *For You Blue*

Cuts 1–15: All cuts are the same as on **BACK UPON US ALL** (ZAP 7864), except no. 8 which is simply listed as *Suzy Parker* here.

SEE ALSO: **MORE FROM THE FAB FOUR** (side two); **POWER BROKERS** (side two); **UPON US ALL -- 4TH AMENDMENT.**

037   **BACTRAX**   King Kong 3922   (2 LPs)

1. *You Really Got A Hold On Me*
2. *Have You Heard The Word*
3. *You Really Got A Hold On Me*
4. *What's Yer New Mary Jane*
5. *Teddy Boy*
6. *Dig It*
7. *L.S. Bumblebee*
8. *Maxwell's Silver Hammer*
9. *Besame Mucho*
10. *Crying, Waiting, Hoping*
11. *Shakem Rattle And Roll*

12. *Let It Be*
13. *Dialogue*
14. *Rain*
15. *Paperback Writer*
16. *Get Back*
17. *The Candle Burns*
18. *Hey Jude*
19. *I Should Have Known Better*
20. *If I Fell*
21. *And I Love Her*
22. *Tell My Why*

Cut 1: Recorded October 30, 1963, for the Swedish TV show "Drop In." The show was aired November 3, 1963.

Cut 2: Recorded in June of 1970. Reportedly this is John and at least some of the Bee Gees. (For discussion, see footnote on pages xxiv-xxv.)

Cut 3: Live, unknown.

Cut 4: Recorded by John, August 14, 1968.

Cuts 5-6, 8-9, 11-12, 16, 18: All recorded during the **LET IT BE** sessions early in 1969 at London's Twickenham Studios.

Cut 7: This cut was released in the U.K. on January 27, 1967 (Decca 12551) and was generally thought to be by the Beatles. In fact, it is by Dudley Moore and Peter Cook. The song appears on many Beatles' bootlegs even though none of the Beatles has anything to do with it.

Cut 10: From a BBC radio broadcast of November, 1962.

Cuts 13-15: Recorded for the BBC--TV show "Top Of The Pops," this clip was shown on that show on June 16, 1966. It was later shown on "Thank Your Lucky Stars" and in August, 1966, it was shown on the "Ed Sullivan Show."

Cut 17: An Apple outtake supposedly found in the Apple trash can in 1970. The recording date appears to be 1967. Also known as *Peace Of Mind.*

Cuts 19-22: From the soundtrack of "A Hard Day's Night."

SEE ALSO: **BYE BYE BYE**; **SUPERTRACKS VOL. I**; **SUPERTRACKS I** (CBM 3922); **SUPERTRACKS 1** (CBM); **SUPERTRACKS II** (HHCER 102).

038   **BAKE A FAKE -- THE GREAT IMPOSTERS**   Riverbreeze Discs   (LP)

NOTES: This is not the Beatles, but a sound--alike group.

039   **BATTLE**   Battle No. 24; N 2027; TMOQ RP 24   (LP)

1. *Looking Tired*
2. *How Many Times*
3. *In The Bottom*
4. *Brian's Blues*
5. *High Heeled Sneakers*
6. *I Feel Fine*
7. *I'm Down*
8. *Act Naturally*
9. *Ticket To Ride*
10. *Yesterday*
11. *Help*

Cuts 1--5: Rolling Stones 1964 Chicago studio sessions.

Cuts 6-11: Taped before a live audience on August 14, 1965, for the "Ed Sullivan Show." The show was broadcast September 12, 1965.

The Beatles (LP)   TMOQ 73030 (Entry 043)

NOTES: Cover shows a different order for side two. Cuts listed as 6, 7, 8, 10, 9, 11.
SEE ALSO: **FROM THE BEGINNING.**

040   **B.C. 64**   Wizardo 340   (2 LPs)

1. *Interviews*
2. *Press Conference*
3. *Press Conference Pt. II*
4. *Radio Coverage*

5. *Radio Coverage Pt. II*
6. *Twist And Shout*
7. *You Can't Do That*
8. *All My Loving*

9. *Things We Said Today*
10. *Roll Over Beethoven*
11. *Can't Buy Me Love*
12. *If I Fell*

13. *Boys*
14. *A Hard Day's Night*
15. *Long Tall Sally*

Cuts 1--15: Recorded live August 22, 1964 at the Empire Stadium in Vancouver, British Columbia.
SEE ALSO: **BRITISH COLUMBIA '64; VANCOUVER 1964** (TMQ); **VAN-- COUVER 1964** (K&S).

041   **BEAT LEGGED LIVE**   Unknown   (LP)
NOTES: Cuts are unknown.

042   **BEATLEMANIA; 1963--69 TWENTY NEVER PUBLISHED SONGS**
Zakatecas ST 57 633XU   (LP)

1. *Christmas Time*
2. *Good Rockin' Tonight*
3. *Hi Ho Silver*
4. *Shakin' In The 60's*
5. *High Heeled Sneakers*
6. *I Me Mine*
7. *House Of The Rising Sun*
8. *Some Other Guy*
9. *Suzy Parker*
10. *Get Back*
11. *Tennessee*

12. *Crying, Waiting, Hoping*
13. *Bound By Love*
14. *Nothing Shakin' But The Leaves On The Trees*
15. *Everyone Wants Someone*
16. *I'm Gonna Sit Right Down And Cry*
17. *A Shot Of Rhythm And Blues*
18. *I'm Sure To Fall*
19. *To Know Her Is To Love Her*
20. *This Is The Wishin'*

Cut 1: A short section of the 1967 Christmas record.
Cuts 2–11: Recorded during the **LET IT BE** sessions early in 1969 at the Twickenham studio in London.
Cuts 12–19: Recorded from a BBC radio broadcast of November, 1962.
Cut 20: From a Christmas disc.
NOTES: European bootleg with a deluxe color cover.

043   **BEATLES**   TMOQ 73030   (LP)

1. *Till There Was You*
2. *I Want To Hold Your Hand*
3. *This Boy*
4. *All My Loving*
5. *Yesterday*
6. *Nowhere Man*
7. *She's A Woman*
8. *Everybody's Trying To Be My Baby*

9. *Rock And Roll Music*
10. *I Feel Fine*
11. *Ticket To Ride*
12. *Johnny B. Goode*
13. *Memphis*
14. *Some Other Guy*
15. *You Really Got A Hold On Me*
16. *Shout*

NOTES: This is the same as **THE BEATLES** (CBM X3), except *Everybody's Trying To Be My Baby* has been substituted for *Can't Buy Me Love*. This cut is also from the Paris concert. The label doesn't list *Happy Birthday*, either, but it does appear on the album.

Beatles (45)   **92444 C/D (Entry 044)**

044   *BEATLES*   92444C/D   (45)
> NOTES: Seven--inch picture disc. The picture used here is a xeroxed copy of John, George and Ringo as they appeared on the cover of the **ROCK AND ROLL** album. The record is not a Beatle record, but instead is a tribute to Elvis Presley done by Paul Lichter. There were supposedly 60 different picture records made of the Beatles.
> SEE ALSO: **GEORGE HARRISON; DENNY LAINE; JOHN LENNON; JOHN LENNON/ELVIS PRESLEY; PAUL McCARTNEY; RINGO STARR; WINGS.** The same recording was used for all these picture discs.

045   **THE BEATLES**   CBM X3   (LP)

1. *Till There Was You*
2. *I Want To Hold Your Hand*
3. *This Boy*
4. *All My Loving*
5. *Yesterday*
6. *Nowhere Man*
7. *She's A Woman*
8. *Can't Buy Me Love*
9. *Rock And Roll Music*
10. *I Feel Fine*
11. *Ticket To Ride*
12. *Johnny B. Goode*
13. *Memphis, Tenn.*
14. *Happy Birthday*
15. *Some Other Guy*
16. *You Really Got A Hold On Me*
17. *Shout*

Cuts 1--6: Unknown.
Cuts 7--11: Recorded live at the Paris Palais Des Sports during the June 20, 1965 concert.
Cuts 12--14, 16: Recorded from the BBC radio show "Saturday Club" on May 25, 1963.
Cut 15: Recorded live at the Cavern Club by Granada TV on October 13, 1962. Shown on the "People And Places" show on November 7, 1962.
Cut 17: Recorded from the BBC show, "The Alan Freeman Show," in August, 1964.
SEE ALSO: **THE BEATLES** (TMQ).

046   **THE BEATLES**   Gamma Alpha Records on CBM 3609   (2 LPs)

1. *Michelle*
2. *Yellow Submarine*
3. *A Hard Day's Night*
4. *Tell Me Why*
5. *I Should Have Known Better*
6. *If I Fell*
7. *And I Love Her*
8. *Can't Buy Me Love*
9. *I Want To Hold Your Hand*
10. *I Saw Her Standing There*
11. *It Won't Be Long*
12. *All I've Got To Do*
13. *Here Comes The Sun*
14. *She Loves You*
15. *I'm Happy Just To Dance With You*
16. *All My Loving*

17. *Hey Jude*
18. *Ballad Of John And Yoko*
19. *Paperback Writer*
20. *Lady Madonna*
21. *Revolution*
22. *Eight Days A Week*
23. *Let It Be*
24. *Dig It*
25. *Long And Winding Road*
26. *Get Back*
27. *Strawberry Fields Forever*
28. *Penny Lane*

Cuts 1--28: All original recordings.

047   **THE BEATLES**   Unknown   (4 LPs)

1. *Twist And Shout*
2. *It Don't Come Easy*
3. *Mr. Kite*
4. *It's Getting Better*
9. *Can't Buy Me Love*
10. *Come Together*
11. *Day Tripper*
12. *Do You Want To Know A Secret*

18

The Beatles And The Rolling Stones (LP)   Joker-Saar SM 3591 (Entry 050)

5. *Good Night*
6. *Because*
7. *Why Don't We Do It In The Road*
8. *What You're Doing*

13. *Eight Days A Week*
14. *Eleanor Rigby*
15. *Uncle Albert*

16. *I Should Have Known Better*
17. *It Won't Be Long*
18. *I Want To Hold Your Hand*
19. *Lady Madonna*
20. *Ticket To Ride*
21. *Lucy In The Sky*
22. *Michelle*
23. *Mr. Moonlight*

24. *I Feel Fine*
25. *If I Fell*
26. *I'll Be Back*
27. *Hey Jude*
28. *I'm A Loser*
29. *I'm Happy Just To Dance*
30. *I Saw Her Standing There*

31. *Crippled Inside*
32. *Lovely Linda*
33. *And I Love Her*
34. *Every Little Thing*
35. *Ringo's Theme* (George Martin)
36. *Long Tall Sally*
37. *Please Mr. Postman*

38. *If I Needed Someone*
39. *Don't Let Me Down*
40. *Rain*
41. *Old Brown Shoe*
42. *I've Got A Feeling*
43. *Kansas City*
44. *Tell Me What You See*

45. *Maxwell's Silver Hammer*
46. *Oh Darling*
47. *Octopusses Garden*
48. *You Never Give Me Your Money*
49. *She Came In Through The
    Bathroom Window*
50. *Golden Slumbers*
51. *Across The Universe*
52. *Maggie Mae*

53. *She Loves You*
54. *Something*
55. *Strawberry Fields Forever*
56. *Tell Me Why*
57. *Long And Winding Road*
58. *Let It Be*
59. *Everybody's Trying To Be My
    Baby*

Cuts 1–59: Original recordings.
NOTES: This album is similar, but not the same as the **ALPHA & OMEGA** series.
The songs on the album do not match the songs listed as being included.

048 **BEATLES ALIVE** Unknown (LP)

1. *Twist And Shout*
2. *Roll Over Beethoven*
3. *I Wanna Be Your Man*
4. Medley:
   Love Me Do
   Please Please Me
   From Me To You
5. *Can't Buy Me Love*
6. *Shout*

7. *Beatles Interview from 1966*

Cuts 1--3: Recorded live during the 1964 tour.
Cuts 4–6: Recorded April 27–28, 1964, for Rediffusion TV. It was shown on
the show "Around The Beatles" on May 6, 1964.
Cut 7: Portions of the Ken Douglas interviews.

049 **BEATLES ALIVE IN ATLANTA AT LAST** Walrus Records TVC 1001 (LP)
NOTES: See comments under **ALIVE AT LAST IN ATLANTA**.

050 **BEATLES AND ROLLING STONES** Joker--Saar SM 3591 (LP)
NOTES: This is the same as **AT THE RAREST**.
SEE ALSO: **BEATLES/STONES LIVE**.

The Beatles Broadcasts (LP)   **Circuit LK 4450 (Entry 053)**

051   BEATLES APART   Crash Records 1016   (LP)

1. *Too Many People*
2. *Yer Blues*
3. *Smile Away*
4. *Give Me Some Truth*
5. *Maybe I'm Amazed*
6. *Imagine*

7. *Isn't It A Pity*
8. *Some People Never Know*
9. *My Sweet Lord*

Cuts 1–9: Original recordings.
NOTES: *Imagine* is not listed on the album cover. Cuts 1, 3, 5, 8 are by Paul; cuts 2, 4, 6 by John; and 7 and 9 by George. Has a deluxe color cover.

052   BEATLES AT SHEA STADIUM   Idle Mind 1180   (LP)
NOTES: Cuts are unknown. May possibly be from the Shea concert of August 15, 1965.

053   BEATLES BROADCASTS   Circuit LK4450   (LP)
NOTES: Issued in mid–1980, too late for full information to be included here. All material on the album is from BBC broadcasts and several never released takes. Comes with a full color deluxe cover.

054   THE BEATLES BY ROYAL COMMAND   Vewy Queen Wecords 1108   (EP)

1. *From Me To You*
2. *She Loves You*

3. *Till There Was You*
4. *Twist And Shout*

Cuts 1–4: Recorded at the Prince of Wales Theatre during the Royal Command Variety Show, November 4, 1963.
NOTES: Issued with a picture sleeve. One side shows the Beatles meeting the Queen and the other side shows them on stage. Issued with a small center hole. Originals were pressed on color vinyl and in several colors, including: blue and white marbled and orange and black marbled.

055   THE BEATLES BY ROYAL COMMAND   Deccagone 1108   (EP)

1. *From Me To You*
2. *She Loves You*

3. *Till There Was You*
4. *Twist And Shout*

Cuts 1–4: Recorded at the Prince of Wales Theatre during the Royal Command Variety Show, November 4, 1963.
NOTES: This is a re–issue of the Vewy Queen Wecords disc. It was also issued with a picture sleeve and a small center hole. It came pressed on clear vinyl.

056   THE BEATLES BY ROYAL COMMAND   Deccagone 1108   (EP)

1. *From Me To You*
2. *She Loves You*

3. *Till There Was You*
4. *Twist And Shout*

Cuts 1–4: Recorded at the Prince of Wales Theatre during the Royal Command Variety Show, November 4, 1963.
NOTES: This is a boot of a boot. It is a copy of the original Deccagone EP. Unlike the original, it has a large center hole. The picture sleeve is also different. On the originals, the word "BEATLES" appears in a grey area at the top along with the words "BY ROYAL COMMAND." "BEATLES" is in red and the rest is in blue. On these copies, "BEATLES" is in black, with the song titles appearing under it in blue. The picture is not as clear as the original. These copies were pressed in several colors of vinyl, including: yellow, violet, blue, gold, orange, and red.

The Beatles By Royal Command (EP)   Deccagone 1108 (Entry 055)

057   **THE BEATLES COLLECTOR'S ITEMS**   Capitol SPRO–9462   (LP)

1. *Love Me Do*
2. *From Me To You*
3. *Thank You Girl*
4. *All My Loving*
5. *This Boy*
6. *Sie Liebt Dich*
7. *I Feel Fine*
8. *She's A Woman*
9. *Help*
10. *I'm Down*

11. *Penny Lane*
12. *Baby You're A Rich Man*
13. *I Am The Walrus*
14. *The Inner Light*
15. *Across The Universe*
16. *You Know My Name (Look Up My Number)*
17. *Sgt. Pepper Inner Groove*

Cut 1: Alternate take recorded September 11, 1962.
Cuts 2–3, 6–7, 9, 13–14, 16: Original recordings.
Cut 4: With high hat introduction.
Cut 5, 8, 10, 12: Stereo versions, not previously released on U.S. albums.
Cut 11: DJ version with trumpet ending.
Cut 15: Recorded early 1968, this version appeared on the album **NO ONE'S GONNA CHANGE OUR WORLD** (EMI Star Line SRS 5013) which was released only in the U.K. The proceeds from the album went to the World Wildlife Fund.
NOTES: Full color laminated front cover showing Beatle memorabilia, including a "butcher" cover, Beatle game, Sgt. Pepper picture disc and many, many more. The back cover is in black and white and shows the cover of all Capitol Beatle albums. The jacket pictured for **YESTERDAY AND TODAY** is an alternate picture of the Beatles and the trunk, and not the cover that was finally used for that album. The album was made to look like a regular Capitol release and even had the purple label that Capitol was using at that time.

058   **BEATLES DEC. 1963**   ODD–Four–A/ODD–Five–B   (LP)

1. *From Me To You*
2. *I Saw Her Standing There*
3. *All My Loving*
4. *Roll Over Beethoven*
5. *Boys*
6. *Till There Was You*
7. *She Loves*

8. *This Boy*
9. *I Want To Hold Your Hand*
10. *Money*
11. *Twist And Shout*
12. *Rock And Roll Music*
13. *Everybody's Trying To Be My Baby*
14. *I'll Follow The Sun*
15. *Kansas City*

Cuts 1–11: From the Beatles Christmas show at the Liverpool Empire on December 22, 1963.
Cuts 12–13, 15: Unknown.
Cut 14: Unknown, but probably original.

059   *BEATLES FRIENDS*   Beat–L 007   (45)

1. *Billy Preston*   2. *Robert Palmer*
NOTES: Billy Preston talks about his first meeting with George Harrison and the Beatles while he was on tour with Little Richard. Robert Palmer talks about playing at Eric Clapton's wedding with Eric, Paul, George and Ringo.

060   **THE BEATLES GET TOGETHER**   Tobe–Milo 4Q1–2   (EP)

1. *Kenny Everett Interviews The Beatles Featuring "Cottonfields"*
2. *When Everybody Comes To Town*
3. *I'd Have You Anytime*

4. *Loving Sacred Loving*
5. *Shapes Of Orange*
6. *Too Many Cooks*

The Beatles Collector's Items (LP)   Capitol SPRO-9462 (Entry 057)

The Beatles Get Together (EP)   Tobe-Milo 4Q1-2 (Entry 060)

Cut 1: Recorded by the Beatles and Kenny Everett in January of 1968.

Cuts 2–3: George Harrison and Bob Dylan outtakes from May, 1970.

Cuts 4–5: EP jacket states that the Beatles are involved with these cuts, but they were not.

Cut 6: This cut features Mick Jagger on vocals, Ringo on drums and John Lennon handling production. Recorded by Apple, but never released because of contract problems.

NOTES: This is a 33 1/3 rpm seven–inch, small hole EP. Released with a hard picture cover. The original 500 copies were issued on yellow vinyl. Another 500 were later released on black vinyl.

061   BEATLES HAPPY BIRTHDAY   CBM 5030   (LP)

1. *Johnny B. Goode*
2. *Shout*
3. *Pop Goes The Beatles*
4. *You Really Got A Hold On Me*
5. *Memphis, Tenn.*
6. *Happy Birthday*
7. *This Boy*
8. *Twist And Shout*
9. *I Want To Hold Your Hand*
10. *Interviews*
11. *Roll Over Beethoven*
12. *Tell Me Why*
13. *If I Fell*
14. *I Should Have Known Better*

Cuts 1, 4–6: Recorded from the BBC radio "Saturday Club" show, May 25, 1963.

Cuts 2, 10–11: From the BBC radio "Top Of The Pops" show, August, 1964. Interview by Brian Matthews.

Cut 3: Theme song for the "Pop Goes The Beatles" radio show. This 30–minute show ran for 15 weeks, from June to September of 1963.

Cuts 7–9: Recorded August 19, 1963 for Granada TV show, "Scene At 6:30."

Cuts 12–14: From the soundtrack of "A Hard Day's Night." Recorded March 2–April 27, 1964.

SEE ALSO: **HAPPY BIRTHDAY; RARE BEATLES; RARE SESSIONS.**

062   BEATLES IN ATLANTA WHISKEY FLAT   TMOQ 71007   (LP)
NOTES: See cuts and comments under **ALIVE AT LAST IN ATLANTA.**

063   BEATLES IN ITALY   Parlophone 31506   (LP)

1. *Long Tall Sally*
2. *She's A Woman*
3. *Matchbox*
4. *From Me To You*
5. *I Want To Hold Your Hand*
6. *Ticket To Ride*
7. *This Boy*
8. *Slow Down*
9. *I Call Your Name*
10. *Thank You Girl*
11. *Yes It Is*
12. *I Feel Fine*

NOTES: This was supposed to be a legitimate Italian release of a live concert from the Beatles 1965 tour. Instead, all cuts are original recordings. Comes with a color laminated cover.

064   BEATLES IN ITALY   Parlophone 31506   (LP)
NOTES: This is a picture disc and contains the same songs as **BEATLES IN ITALY** album. The picture is also the same as used on the other album and shows the Beatles all holding wine glasses. The other side of the picture disc shows the back of the album cover and the song list.

065   BEATLES IN ITALY   Unknown
NOTES: Cuts are unknown, but possibly the same as **LIVE IN ITALY** (CBM 4178).

The Beatles In Italy (LP)   **Parlophone 31506 (Entry 063)**

066 THE BEATLES IN ITALY   Unknown   (EP)

NOTES: This EP was issued in mid--1980 with a black--and--white picture sleeve. It includes three songs and a live interview from the Beatles 1965 tour of Italy.

067 THE BEATLES IN PERSON SAM HOUSTON COLISEUM   Milo XMilo 10Q3/4 (LP)

1. *Intro. I, II, III*
2. *Twist And Shout*
3. *She's A Woman*
4. *I Feel Fine*
5. *Dizzy Miss Lizzy*
6. *Ticket To Ryde*
7. *Everybody's Trying To Be My Baby*
8. *Can't Buy Me Love*
9. *Baby's In Black*
10. *A Hard Day's Night*
11. *Help*
12. *I'm Down*

Cuts 1--12: Recorded live during the evening show (8 p.m.) August 19, 1966.

NOTES: Contains the full 12:33 introduction with bits from Brenda Holloway and Sounds, Inc. The LP has a black--and--white laminated cover. *Ticket To Ryde* is deliberately misspelled to coincide with the company name of the people who issued the album.

SEE ALSO: **BEATLES LIVE IN HOUSTON.**

068 BEATLES INTRODUCE NEW SONGS   Capitol PRO 2720/2721   (EP)

1. *John Lennon Introduces "It's For You" – Cilla Black. John Lennon Signs Off.*
2. *Paul McCartney Introduces "I Don't To See You Again" -- Peter & Gordon. Paul Signs Off.*
3. *It's For You* (Cilla Black)
4. *I Don't Want To See You Again* (Peter & Gordon)

NOTES: Released September of 1964 for Capitol to promote the two new records with songs written by John and Paul, but performed by other artists.

SEE ALSO: **BEATLES INTRODUCE NEW SONGS; THE BEATLES INTRO-DUCE NEW SONGS.**

069 THE BEATLES INTRODUCE NEW SONGS   Capitol PRO 2720   (EP)

1. *John Lennon Introduces "It's For You" – Cilla Black. John Signs Off.*
2. *Paul McCartney Introduces "I Don't Want To See You Again" – Peter & Gordon. Paul Signs Off.*
3. *Shout*

Cuts 1--2: From a Capitol promo disc issued September, 1964 to promote two new records with songs written by John and Paul, but performed by other artists.

Cut 3: Recorded before a live audience on April 27--28, 1964, for the Rediffusion TV show "Around The Beatles." The show aired May 5, 1964. Portions were shown in the U.S. on ABC–TV on November 15, 1964.

SEE ALSO: **BEATLES INTRODUCE NEW SONGS; BEATLES INTRODUCE NEW SONGS.**

070 *BEATLES INTRODUCE NEW SONGS*   Beat–L 001   (45)

1. *John Lennon Introduces "It's For You" – Cilla Black. John Signs Off.*
2. *Paul McCartney Introduces "I Don't Want To See You*

Again" – Peter & Gordon.
Paul Signs Off.
NOTES: This was originally released in September of 1964 as an EP by Capitol Records. It also appears in other bootleg forms.
SEE ALSO: **BEATLES INTRODUCE NEW SONGS; THE BEATLES INTRODUCE NEW SONGS.**

071 **THE BEATLES "JOHN, PAUL, GEORGE AND JIMMY" COPENHAGEN '64**
Wizardo 501 (LP)

1. *I Wanna Be Your Man*
2. *All My Loving*
3. *She Loves You*
4. *Till There Was You*
5. *Roll Over Beethoven*
6. *Can't Buy Me Love*
7. *This Boy*
8. *Twist And Shout*
9. *She Loves You*
10. *All My Loving*
11. *Twist And Shout*
12. *Roll Over Beethoven*
13. *Long Tall Sally*
14. *Can't Buy Me Love*

Cuts 2–8: Recorded live in Copenhagen, June 4, 1964, with Jimmy Nicol replacing Ringo on drums.
Cuts 1, 9–14: Unknown. Sometimes listed from BBC in 1964 with Ringo.
SEE ALSO: **COPENHAGEN 1964; JOHN, PAUL, GEORGE AND JIMMY.**

072 **THE BEATLES LET IT BE** Wizardo 315
NOTES: Same as **A/B SINGLE ACETATE.**
SEE ALSO: **LET IT BE: BEFORE PHIL SPECTOR; ORIGINAL "GET BACK" ACETATE; ORIGINAL STEREO ACETATE FOR LET IT BE (BEFORE PHIL SPECTOR).**

073 **BEATLES LIVE** BE 1001 (LP)

1. *Twist And Shout*
2. *I Feel Fine*
3. *Dizzy Miss Lizzy*
4. *Ticket To Ride*
5. *Can't Buy Me Love*
6. *Baby's In Black*
7. *A Hard Day's Night*
8. *Help*
9. *I Feel Fine*
10. *I'm Down*
11. *Act Naturally*
12. *Ticket To Ride*
13. *Yesterday*
14. *Help*

Cuts 1–8: Recorded live at Shea Stadium, August 16, 1965.
Cuts 9–14: Recorded before a live audience for the "Ed Sullivan Show" on August 14, 1965. Show was aired September 12, 1965.
SEE ALSO: **DAWN OF OUR INNOCENCE; EARLY BEATLES LIVE; LIVE.**

074 **BEATLES LIVE AT SHEA STADIUM** Benbecula Records 242813 (LP)

1. *Twist And Shout*
2. *You Can't Do That*
3. *All My Loving*
4. *She Loves You*
5. *Things We Said Today*
6. *Roll Over Beethoven*
7. *Can't Buy Me Love*
8. *Boys*
9. *A Hard Day's Night*
10. *Long Tall Sally*
11. *Please Don't Bring Your Banjo Back*
12. *Everywhere It's Christmas*
13. *What's The New Mary Jane*

Cuts 1–10: Recorded live at the Hollywood Bowl concert August 23, 1964.
Cuts 11–12: From the Beatles 1966 Christmas record for the fan club.
Cut 13: Recorded August 14, 1968 by John. This was to have been released on Apple, but never was.
NOTES: This European bootleg came with a deluxe red cover.
SEE ALSO: **LIVE AT SHEA STADIUM** (Benbecula 242813).

075   **BEATLES LIVE AT THE A.B.C. MANCHESTER**   Wizardo 360   (LP)

1. *Twist And Shout*	6. *I Want To Hold Your Hand*
2. *She Loves You*	7. *This Boy*
3. *Interviews*	8. *All My Loving*
4. *Paperback Writer*	9. *Money*
5. *Rain*	10. *Twist And Shout*

Cuts 1–2: Recorded in Manchester, England, at the Ardwick Apollo on November 20, 1963. The show was filmed by Pathe British News and the resulting 8–minute film was released on December 22, 1963.

Cut 3: Interview from June, 1965.

Cuts 4–5: Recorded live for the BBC–TV show "Top Of The Pops." It was first shown June 16, 1966. It was later shown on "Thank Your Lucky Stars," June 25, 1966, and in August it was shown on the "Ed Sullivan Show."

Cuts 6–10: From the TV show, "Sunday Night At The London Palladium," which aired October 13, 1963.

SEE ALSO: **A.B.C. MANCHESTER 1964; LIVE AT A.B.C. MANCHESTER.**

076   **BEATLES LIVE IN HOUSTON**   X Milo 5Q 1/2   (EP)

1. *Introduction*	3. *Ticket To Ryde*
2. *Dizzy Miss Lizzy*	4. *Phony New York Telephone Ad*
	(Not listed on cover)

NOTES: This is a seven–inch, small–hole EP and originals came with a black–and–white, laminated, hard cover. The original press run was 500. It was later sold without the cover. *Ticket To Ryde* was spelled this way on purpose to correspond to the spelling used by the company that released this EP. Recorded live at the concert in Houston, August 19, 1965.

SEE ALSO: **LIVE AT SAM HOUSTON COLISEUM.**

077   **BEATLES LIVE IN HOUSTON**   Milo XMilo 10Q3/4   (LP)
NOTES: Same as **THE BEATLES IN PERSON SAM HOUSTON COLISEUM.**

078   **THE BEATLES LIVE IN WASHINGTON, D.C.**   CBM 3795 C1/3571 B   (LP)

1. *Roll Over Beethoven*	10. *Kansas City*
2. *From Me To You*	11. *I'm A Loser*
3. *I Saw Her Standing There*	12. *Boys*
4. *This Boy*	13. *Hey Jude*
5. *All My Loving*	14. *Revolution*
6. *I Wanna Be Your Man*	
7. *Please Please Me*	
8. *Till There Was You*	
9. *I Want To Hold Your Hand*	

Cuts 1–9: Recorded live at the Washington Colosseum on February 11, 1964.

Cuts 10–12: Recorded at the Granville Theatre in England on October 9, 1964. Shown on the TV show "Shindig" on January 20, 1965 in the U.S.A.

Cut 13: Recorded for the David Frost British TV show on September 4, 1968. The show aired September 8, 1968.

Cut 14: Shown on the British TV show "Top Of The Pops" on September 19, 1968.

SEE ALSO: **THE BEATLES LIVE IN WASHINGTON, D.C.; DISTRICT OF COLUMBIA; LIVE IN EUROPE/U.S. TELECASTS (side two); LIVE IN EUROPE/U.S. TV CASTS (side two).**

079   **BEATLES 1964**   Unknown   (LP)
NOTES: Same as **BACK IN 1964 AT THE HOLLYWOOD BOWL** (Lemon CSR 143).
SEE ALSO: **BACK IN 1964 AT THE HOLLYWOOD BOWL** (CBM 4178);

The Beatles On Stage In Japan
   — The 1966 Tour (LP)   TAKRL 1900 (Entry 080)

HOLLYWOOD BOWL '64; LIVE AT HOLLYWOOD BOWL; LIVE AT THE HOLLYWOOD BOWL; L.A.; LIVE AT SHEA; THE ONLY LIVE RECORDING (Kustom); THE ONLY LIVE RECORDING (Unknown); THE SHEA STADIUM CONCERT 1964; THE SHEA STADIUM "MORE OR LESS" STEREO; SHEA: THE GOOD OLD DAYS (Kustom); SHEA: THE GOOD OLD DAYS (Pine Tree).

080   BEATLES ON STAGE IN JAPAN THE 1966 TOUR   TAKRL 1900; Pigs Eye No. 1
       (LP)

1. *Rock And Roll Music*
2. *She's A Woman*
3. *If I Needed Someone*
4. *Day Tripper*
5. *Baby's In Black*
6. *I Feel Fine*
7. *Yesterday*
8. *I Wanna Be Your Man*
9. *Nowhere Man*
10. *Paperback Writer*
11. *I'm Down*

Cuts 1–11: Recorded live at Budokan Hall in Tokyo on July 2, 1966.
SEE ALSO: **FIVE NIGHTS IN A JUDO ARENA; ON STAGE IN JAPAN 1966; TOKYO 1966.**

081   BEATLES RAREST NO. 1   TAKRL 1985   (LP)

1. *Let It Be (By The Numbers)*
2. *Shakin' In The 60's*
3. *Good Rockin' Tonight*
4. *Across The Universe*
5. *Two Of Us*
6. *Momma, You're Been On My Mind*
7. *Tennessee*
8. *House Of The Rising Sun*
9. *Back To Commonwealth*
10. *White Power Promenade*
11. *Hi Ho Silver*
12. *For You Blue*
13. *Let It Be*

Cuts 1–13: Recorded in early 1969 at Twickenham Studio in London during the **LET IT BE** sessions.
SEE ALSO: **VERY BEST OF THE BEATLES RAREST NO. 1**

082   BEATLES RAREST NO. 2   TAKRL 1986   (LP)

1. *Twist And Shout*
2. *She Loves You*
3. *Things We Said Today*
4. *Roll Over Beethoven*
5. *Love Me Do*
6. *Please Please Me*
7. *Can't Buy Me Love*
8. *If I Fell*
9. *I Want To Hold Your Hand*
10. *Boys*
11. *A Hard Day's Night*
12. *Long Tall Sally*
13. *Till There Was You*
14. *I Saw Her Standing There*

Cuts 1–14: All recorded live at various concerts, including Washington, D.C., Hollywood Bowl and Shea Stadium (February 11, 1964; August 23, 1964; and August 15, 1965 respectively).
SEE ALSO: **VERY BEST OF THE BEATLES RAREST NO. 2**

083   BEATLES RAREST NO. 3   TAKRL 1987   (LP)

1. *Rock And Roll Music*
2. *She's A Woman*
3. *If I Needed Someone*
4. *Day Tripper*
5. *Baby's In Black*
6. *I Feel Fine*
7. *Yesterday*
8. *I Wanna Be Your Man*
9. *Ain't She Sweet*
10. *P.S. I Love You*
11. *There's A Place*
12. *From Me To You*
13. *Nowhere Man*
14. *Paperback Writer*
15. *I'm Down*

Cuts 1–8, 13–15: Recorded live at Budokan Hall in Tokyo, July 2, 1966.
Cut 9: Original recording.

Cuts 10–12: EMI outtakes from 1963.
SEE ALSO: **VERY BEST OF THE BEATLES RAREST NO. 3**

084   **BEATLES RAREST NO. 4   TAKRL 1988   (LP)**

1. *Nowhere Man*
2. *No Pakistanis*
3. *What A Shame Mary Jane Had A Pain At The Party*
4. *All My Loving*
5. *The Walk*
6. *Teddy Boy*
7. *Maxwell's Silver Hammer*
8. *Besame Mucho*
9. *You Really Got A Hold On Me*
10. *Do You Want To Know A Secret*
11. Medley:
    Love Me Do
    Please Please Me
    From Me To You
    She Loves You
    I Want To Hold Your Hand
12. *White Power*
13. *You Can't Do That*
14. *A Hard Day's Night*

Cut 1: Recorded live in Japan at Budokan Hall on July 2, 1966.
Cuts 2–3, 5–9, 12: Recorded at Twickenham Studios in early 1969 during the **LET IT BE** sessions.
Cut 4: Recorded at Teddington Studios February 23, 1964. Shown on the TV show "Big Night Out" on February 29, 1964.
Cut 10: Unknown.
Cut 11: Recorded April 27–28, 1964, for the Rediffusion TV show "Around The Beatles." The show was shown May 6, 1964.
Cut 13: Unknown.
Cut 14: Recorded live at Shea Stadium August 15, 1965.
SEE ALSO: **VERY BEST OF THE BEATLES RAREST NO. 4**

085   **BEATLES RAREST NO. 5   TAKRL 1989   (LP)**

1. *Day Tripper*
2. *Two Of Us*
3. *Maggie Mae*
4. *Twist And Shout*
5. *You Can't Do That*
6. *All My Loving*
7. *Dig It*
8. *Suzy Parker*
9. *Till There Was You*
10. *I Want To Hold Your Hand*
11. *This Boy*
12. *All My Loving*
13. *Yesterday*
14. *Nowhere Man*
15. *I Feel Fine*
16. *Can't Buy Me Love*

Cuts 1, 13–15: Recorded live in Japan at the Budokan Hall, July 2, 1966.
Cuts 2–3, 7–8: Recorded during the **LET IT BE** sessions at Twickenham Studios in London early in 1969.
Cuts 4–6: Recorded live at the Hollywood Bowl concert August 23, 1964.
Cuts 9–12, 16: Unknown.
SEE ALSO: **VERY BEST OF THE BEATLES RAREST NO. 5.**

086   **BEATLES RAREST NO. 6   TAKRL 1995   (LP)**

1. *Instrumental No. 42*
2. *Save The Last Dance For Me*
3. *Don't Let Me Down*
4. *I Dig A Pony*
5. *I've Got A Feeling*
6. *Get Back*
7. *One After 909*
8. *For You Blue*
9. *Teddy Boy*
10. *Two Of Us*
11. *Maggie Mae*
12. *Dig It*
13. *Let It Be*
14. *Long And Winding Road*

Cuts 1–14: Recorded at London's Twickenham Studios early in 1969 as part of the **LET IT BE** sessions. This was the original George Martin disc that was to have been the **LET IT BE** album.
SEE ALSO: **NEXT TO LAST RECORDING SESSION -- 5TH AMENDMENT; VERY BEST OF THE BEATLES RAREST VOL. 6**

087　BEATLES RAREST NO. 7　TAKRL 1998　(LP)

1. *Paperback Writer*
2. *A Hard Day's Night*
3. *From Me To You*
4. *From Us To You*
5. *Have You Heard The Word*
6. *Get Back*
7. *I Want To Hold Your Hand*
8. *Long Tall Sally*
9. *Words Of Love*
10. *Hi Ho Silver*
11. *Johnny B. Goode*
12. *Act Naturally*
13. *I'm Down*
14. *Love Me Do*
15. *I Dig A Pony*
16. *Hippy Hippy Shake*
17. *She Loves You*

Cuts 1, 13: Recorded live in Tokyo at the Budokan Hall, July 2, 1966.
Cuts 2, 12: Recorded live at Shea Stadium August 15, 1965.
Cut 3: Unknown.
Cut 4: From the BBC radio show "From Us To You" broadcast December 26, 1963.
Cut 5: Recorded June 1970. This is supposed to be John and at least a few of the Bee Gees. (For discussion, see footnote on pages xxiv-xxv.)
Cuts 6, 10, 15: From the **LET IT BE** sessions at London's Twickenham Studios early in 1969.
Cuts 7–8: Recorded live at the Hollywood Bowl concert August 23, 1964.
Cuts 9, 14, 17: Listed as 1964 demos, these are probably originals.
Cut 11: From the BBC radio show "Saturday Club," May 25, 1963.
Cut 16: From the BBC radio, March, 1963.
SEE ALSO: **THE VERY BEST OF THE BEATLES RAREST VOL. SEVEN**

088　*BEATLES SHOW*　Beat--L 006　(45)
　　1. *Interview/Yesterday*
NOTES: From the weekly Top--30 show of July 21, 1979, with host Mark Elliott. This is a one--sided disc.

089　BEATLES '66　Smilin' Ears 7704　(LP)

1. *Rock And Roll Music*
2. *She's A Woman*
3. *If I Needed Someone*
4. *Day Tripper*
5. *Baby's In Black*
6. *I Feel Fine*
7. *Yesterday*
8. *I Wanna Be Your Man*
9. *Paperback Writer*
10. *I'm Down*
11. *Interview*

Cuts 1--11: Recorded live at the Tokyo, Budokan Concert on July 2, 1966.
NOTES: Deluxe black--and--white laminated cover. Back cover has pictures from the "Revolver" period. Title is somewhat confusing. Spine says **BEATLES '66**, but the record label says just **BEATLES.**
SEE ALSO: **BEATLES 66 TOKYO LIVE CONCERT.**

090　BEATLES '66　Tobe--Milo 4Q 7-10　(2 EPs)

1. *Rock And Roll Music*
2. *She's A Woman*
3. *If I Needed Someone*
4. *Day Tripper*
5. *Baby's In Black*
6. *I Feel Fine*

7. *Yesterday*
8. *I Wanna Be Your Man*
9. *Nowhere Man*
10. *Paperback Writer*
11. *I'm Down*
12. *Interview*

Cuts 1–12: Recorded live at Budokan Hall in Tokyo on July 2, 1966.
NOTES: Came with a hard cover which folded out. The records are seven--inch, 33 1/3 rpm, small hole. Came with a post card. Only 1,000 copies were pressed, all numbered.
SEE ALSO: **FIVE NIGHTS IN A JUDO ARENA.**

091   **BEATLES 66 TOKYO LIVE CONCERT**   Smilin' Ears SE 7704   (LP)

1. *Rock And Roll Music*
2. *She's A Woman*
3. *If I Needed Someone*
4. *Day Tripper*
5. *Baby's In Black*
6. *I Feel Fine*
7. *Yesterday*
8. *I Wanna Be Your Man*
9. *Paperback Writer*
10. *I'm Down*
11. *Interview*

Cuts 1–11: Recorded live at Budokan Hall, Tokyo, July 2, 1966.
NOTES: Deluxe black--and--white cover.
SEE ALSO: **BEATLES '66** (Smilin' Ears 7704).

092   **BEATLES/STONES**   Smilin' Ears 2--7700   (2 LPs)
SEE ALSO: **SING THIS ALL TOGETHER** for full deatils on this album.

093   **BEATLES STONES LIVE**   Joker--Saar 3591
NOTES: Same as **AT THE RAREST.**
SEE ALSO: **BEATLES AND ROLLING STONES.**

094   **BEATLES STORY PT. 1: THE BIRTH OF THE LIVERPOOL SOUND**
BS 1000   (LP)

1. *Jezabel* (Frankie Laine)
2. *Cry* (Johnny Ray)
3. *Rock Around The Clock* (Bill Haley)
4. *Heartbreak Hotel* (Elvis Presley)
5. *All Shook Up* (Elvis Presley)
6. *Rock Island Line* (Lonnie Donegan)
7. *Whole Lotta Shakin' Goin On*
    (Jerry Lee Lewis)
8. *Peggy Sue* (Buddy Holly)
9. *No Particular Place To Go* (Chuck Berry)
10. *Bye Bye Love* (Everly Brothers)
11. *Please Please Me*
12. *All My Loving*
13. *Help*
14. *Norwegian Wood*
15. *Yellow Submarine*
16. *Sgt. Pepper*
17. *Ob--La--Di Ob--La--Da*
18. *Come Together*
19. *Let It Be*
20. *Maggie Mae*
21. *Lucille* (Live)
22. *I Forgot To Remember*
23. *Money*
24. *Twist And Shout* (Live)
25. *Roll Over Beethoven* (Live)
26. *Long Tall Sally* (Live)
27. *Dizzy Miss Lizzy*
28. *Cry For A Shadow*
29. *My Bonnie*
30. *Ain't She Sweet*

NOTES: This is part 1 of Brian Matthews' 13-part "Beatles Story" which was made special for radio broadcast. Most songs are only played in part. This disc also includes many interviews with people like John Lennon, Paul McCartney, George Harrison, Bill Harry, Larry Parnes, Allan Williams, Bob Wooler, Tony Barrow, Peter Eckhorn, Gerry Marsdan and Tony Sheridan.

095   **BEATLES STORY PT. 2: GETTING IT ONTO WAX**   BS 1001   (LP)

1. *From Us To You*
2. *My Bonnie*
3. *Slow Down*
4. *Rock And Roll Music*
5. *I Saw Her Standing There*
6. *Bad Boy*
7. *Please Mr. Postman*
8. *Some Other Guy*
9. *I Wanna Be Your Man*
10. *P.S. I Love You*
11. *Love Me Do*
12. *I Am The Greatest* (Ringo)

NOTES: This is part 2 of Brian Matthew's 13--part "Beatles Story." Also
included on this disc are interviews with many Beatle people, including:
Bob Wooler, Brian Epstein, Allistar Taylor, Clive Epstein, Paul, George
Harrison (of the *Liverpool Echo*), Queenie Epstein, Ringo, Dick James
and Norman Smith.

096   BEATLES STORY PT. 3: CHART SUCCESS   BS 1002   (LP)

1. *Love Me Do*
2. *We Can Work It Out*
3. *You Really Got A Hold On Me*
4. *Please Please Me*

NOTES: This is part 3 of Brian Matthew's 13--part "Beatles Story." This record
also includes interviews with many people including: Ringo, John, Paul,
George, David Jacobs, Tony Barrow, Rory Storm's mother, the manager of
the Star Club and Arthur Howe.

097   BEATLES STORY PT. 4: PACKAGE TOURS   BS 1003   (LP)

1. *Please Please Me*
2. *Thank You Girl*
3. *From Me To You*
4. *Chains*
5. *Boys*
6. *Do You Want To Know A Secret*
7. *There's A Place*
8. *Twist And Shout*
9. *Photograph* (Ringo)
10. *Ram On* (Paul)

NOTES: This is part 4 of Brian Matthew's 13–part "Beatles Story." Also included
are interviews with Helen Shapiro, Dick James, Tony Bramwell, Tony Barrow,
George Martin, Paul and Bob Wooler.

098   BEATLES STORY PT. 5: THE START OF BEATLEMANIA   BS 1004   (LP)

1. *She Loves You*
2. *All Together Now*
3. *She Loves You*
4. *I'll Get You*
5. *It Won't Be Long*
6. *Back In The USSR*
7. *I Want To Hold Your Hand*
8. *All My Loving*
9. *Don't Bother Me*
10. *She Loves You*
11. *I Want To Hold Your Hand*
12. *Till There Was You*
13. *Can't Buy Me Love*
14. *And I Love Her*
15. *I'll Cry Instead*
16. *A Hard Day's Night*

NOTES: This is part 5 of Brian Matthew's 13--part "Beatles Story." Also
included are many interviews with persons including: Hunter Davies, Freda
Kelly, Tony Barrow, George, John, Paul, George Martin, Brian Sommerville,
Ringo, Peter Woods and George Harrison (of the *Liverpool Echo*).

099   BEATLES STORY PT. 6: REWARDS OF SUCCESS   BS 1005   (LP)

1. *I Feel Fine*
2. *Eight Days A Week*
3. *I'll Follow The Sun*
4. *Kansas City*
5. *Everybody's Trying To Be My Baby*
6. *She's A Woman*
7. *I'm A Loser*
8. *1964 Christmas Record*
   (Parts only)
9. *Baby's In Black*
10. *Yesterday*
11. *Ticket To Ride*

NOTES: This is part 6 of Brian Matthew's 13--part "Beatles Story." Also
included are interviews with people like: Klaus Sperling, John, George,
Paul, Ringo, Les Coleman, Tony Barrow, Allistar Taylor and Jimmy Seville.

100   BEATLES STORY PT. 7: WHEN THE TOURING HAD TO STOP   BS 1006   (LP)

1. *Help*
2. *Act Naturally*
3. *Help*
4. *You've Got To Hide Your Love*
9. *Day Tripper*
10. *Her Majesty*
11. *Norwegian Wood*
12. *Girl*

                         Away   13. *Nowhere Man*
        5. *Ticket To Ride*   14. *Michelle*
        6. *All My Loving*   15. *Paperback Writer*
        7. *Can't Buy Me Love*   16. *Eleanor Rigby*
        8. *Run For Your Life*
        NOTES: This is part 7 of Brian Matthew's 13–part "Beatles Story." Also
            contains interviews with John, Paul, George, Alf Bicknell, Tony Barrow,
            George Martin and Rick Lewis.

101   BEATLES STORY PT. 8: THE MAKING OF SGT. PEPPER   BS 1007   (LP)

        1. *Strawberry Fields Forever*   6. *A Day In The Life*
        2. *Sgt. Pepper*   7. *Sexie Sadie*
        3. *Lucy In The Sky With Diamonds*   8. *Here, There and Everywhere*
        4. *Good Morning, Good Morning*   9. *Hello Goodbye*
        5. *When I'm 64*
        NOTES: This is part 8 of Brian Matthew's 13–part "Beatles Story." Also
            included are interviews with George Martin, John, Al Aronowitz, Paul,
            Maharishi Mahesh Yogi, Hunter Davies, George, George Harrison (of
            Liverpool Echo), Joanne Neufield and Allistar Taylor.

102   BEATLES STORY PT. 9: MAGICAL MYSTERY TOUR AND APPLE
        BS 1008   (LP)

        1. *You And Me Babe* (Ringo)   9. *Hey Jude*
        2. *Magical Mystery Tour*   10. *Yellow Submarine*
        3. *Fool On The Hill*   11. *Revolution No. 1*
        4. *I Am The Walrus*   12. *Glass Onion*
        5. *Wonderwall Music*   13. *While My Guitar Gently Weeps*
        6. *Cottonfields*   14. *Revolution No. 9*
        7. *Don't Pass Me By*   15. *Maybe I'm Amazed* (Paul)
        8. *Lady Madonna*   16. *Hello Goodbye*
        NOTES: This is part 9 of Brian Matthew's 13–part "Beatles Story." Also
            interviewed on this disc are Paul, Kenny Everett, John, Jane Asher, Derek
            Taylor, George Martin, Tony Bramwell, George and Ritchie Yorke.

103   BEATLES STORY PT. 10: LET IT BE AND APPLE PROBLEMS   BS 1009   (LP)

        1. *Come Together*   10. *Hare Krishna Mantra*
        2. *Piggies*   11. *Blue Suede Shoes* (Live)
        3. *Let It Be*   12. *Dizzy Miss Lizzy* (Live)
        4. *Polythene Pam*   13. *Come Together*
        5. *Get Back*   14. *Here Comes The Sun*
        6. *Music From: Life With The Lions* 15. *Carry That Weight*
        7. *Music From: Electronic Sounds* 16. *You Never Give Me Your Money*
        8. *Ballad Of John And Yoko*   17. *Cold Turkey*
        9. *Give Peace A Chance*   18. *Something*
        NOTES: This is part 10 of Brian Matthew's 13–part "Beatles Story." Also
            included are interviews with John, Paul, Allistar Taylor, George, Derek
            Taylor, Allen Klein, Yoko, Ringo and Ritchie Yorke.

104   BEATLES STORY PT. 11: INDIVIDUAL BEATLES   BS 1010   (LP)

        1. *All Things Must Pass*   8. *Beaucoups Of Blues*
        2. *Instant Karma*   9. *What Is Life*
        3. *Let It Be*   10. *Isn't It A Pity*
        4. *Maybe I'm Amazed*   11. *Well, Well, Well*
        5. *That Would Be Something*   12. *Love*
        6. *Two Of Us*   13. *If I Fell* (Live)

The Beatles Studio Outtakes (EP)   Tobe-Milo 4Q 11/12 (Entry 107)

7. *The Long And Winding Road*   14. *It Don't Come Easy* (Bangla Desh)
NOTES: This is part 11 of Brian Matthew's 13–part "Beatles Story." Also
included are interviews with John, George, Paul and Tony Bramwell.

105   BEATLES STORY PT. 12: THE JOHN, PAUL, GEORGE AND RINGO SHOW
BS 1011   (LP)

1. *Uncle Albert*   4. *How Do You Sleep*
2. *Back Seat Of My Car*   5. *Imagine*
3. *Too Many People*   6. *Mumbo*
NOTES: This is part 12 of Brian Matthew's 13--part "Beatles Story." Also
includes interviews with Peter Asher, Paul and John.

106   BEATLES STORY PT. 13: THE END   BS 1012   (LP)

1. *Two Of Us*   4. *Back Off Boogaloo*
2. *I Dig A Pony*   5. *Mary Had A Little Lamb*
3. *Bangla Desh* (Live)   6. *Little Woman Love*
NOTES: This is part 13 of Brian Matthew's 13--part "Beatles Story." Also
included are interviews with Paul, Linda and Ringo.

107   THE BEATLES STUDIO OUTTAKES   Tobe–Milo 4Q 11/12   (EP)

1. *Hey Jude*   4. *Day Tripper*
2. *I Am The Walrus*   5. *Fool On The Hill*
3. *Oh My Love*   6. *Voulez Vous Coucher Avec Moi*
                          7. *Mommy's Little Girl*
Cut 1: Short version from the **LET IT BE** sessions.
Cut 2: Demo.
Cut 3: Beatles' version of song later done solo by John.
Cut 4: John with Jimi Hendrix.
Cut 5: 1968 demo with Paul on the piano.
Cut 6: John Lennon doing a very short bit of LaBelle's hit.
Cut 7: 1972 McCartney outtake.
NOTES: Seven--inch 33 1/3 rpm, small hole EP. Came with a hard picture cover.
Only 1,000 copies pressed.

108   BEATLES TALK   Beat--L 002   (LP)
NOTES: This is the complete Beatle interview by disc jockey Red Robinson.
The commercial LP released of these interviews was only 19 minutes long.
This one is nearly 40 minutes in length.

109   BEATLES TAPES   PBR 7005/6   (2 LPs)

1. *John Lennon With Yoko Ono*   2. *Paul McCartney*
   A. *Interview Pt. 1 June 1969*   A. *Interview Pt. 1 March 1970*
   B. *Give Peace A Chance*   B. *Because*
   C. *Interview Pt. 2 June 1969*   C. *Interview Pt. 2 March 1970*
   D. *Imagine*   D. *Yesterday*
   E. *Interview Pt. 3 June 1969*   E. *Interview Pt. 3 March 1970*
   F. *Come Together*   F. *Hey Jude*
   G. *Interview October 1969*

3. *George Harrison*   4. *Ringo Starr*
   A. *Interview Pt. 1 March 1969*   A. *Interview December 1968*
   B. *Here Comes The Sun*   B. *Interview July 1970*
   C. *Interview Pt. 2 March 1969*   C. *Interview Pt. 1 December*
   D. *Something*   *1973*
                                          D. *Octopus's Garden*

40

         E.   *Interview Pt. 2 December*
              1973
         F.   *Yellow Submarine*

NOTES: This is the same as the **BEATLES TAPES, INTERVIEWS BY DAVID WIGG** which was released in the U.K. on the Polydor label. This double set came with a fully laminated, brown–tone jacket and was pressed on blue vinyl. The Beatle songs included are instrumentals and are not by the Beatles themselves. This LP may be a legitimate release, but it had only a very limited distribution in the U.S.

110   BEATLES: THEIR GREATEST UNRELEASED   Melvin MM001   (LP)

1. *Lucille*
2. *Cry Over You*
3. *I Don't Understand*
4. *Love Of The Loved*
5. *Crying, Waiting, Hoping*
6. *Hippy Hippy Shake*
7. *Soldier Of Love*
8. *Please Don't Ever Change*
9. *Honeymoon Song*
10. *What's Yer New Mary Jane*
11. *Step Inside Love*
12. Medley:
    Besame Mucho
    Cottonfields
    When You Walk
    Whole Lotta Shakin' Goin' On
    Suzy Parker
13. *Bye Bye Bye*
14. *All Together On The Wireless Machine*
15. *Have You Heard The Word*

Cut 1: Live unknown.
Cuts 2–3, 5, 8–9: Recorded from a BBC radio broadcast in November of 1962.
Cut 4: From the Decca sessions, January 1, 1962.
Cut 6: From a BBC radio broadcast, 1963.
Cut 7: Studio outtake from 1963.
Cut 10: Recorded by John on August 14, 1968. This was to have been an Apple single, but it was scrapped.
Cut 11: Demo done by Paul in the spring of 1968. This song was later given to Cilla Black.
Cut 12: *Cottonfields* is by John and is from an interview done by Kenny Everett in January, 1967. All others in this medley are from the **LET IT BE** sessions, early in 1969 at Twickenham Studio in London.
Cuts 13–14: Studio outtakes from the spring of 1970.
Cut 15: Recorded June of 1970. This is supposedly John and at least some of the Bee Gees. (For discussion, see footnote on pages xxiv-xxv.)

111   BEATLES TOUR – THE GREAT TAKE OVER   Wizardo 502   (LP)

1. *Press Conference In Tokyo*
2. *Welcome To The Beatles*
3. *Rock And Roll Music*
4. *She's A Woman*
5. *If I Needed Someone*
6. *Day Tripper*
7. *Baby's In Black*
8. *I Feel Fine*
9. *Yesterday*
10. *I Wanna Be Your Man*
11. *Paperback Writer*
12. *I'm Down*

Cuts 1–2: Recorded in Tokyo before the concert at the Budokan Hall.
Cuts 3–12: Recorded during the Budokan concert July 2, 1966.
SEE ALSO: **THE GREAT TAKEOVER.**

112   BEATLES TRIBUTE ALBUM
NOTES: This is not the Beatles, but a group of novelty records about the Beatles.
SEE ALSO: Entry 1343 in the novelty section of this book for full details.

113 **THE BEATLES UNDOCTORED**   Unknown   (LP)

1. *Two Of Us*
2. *Jazz Piano Song*
3. *Suzy Parker*
4. *For You Blue*
5. *Besame Mucho*
6. *Long And Winding Road Cha Cha Cha*
7. *Shake, Rattle And Roll*
8. *Kansas City*
9. *Lawdy Miss Clawdy*
10. *Dig It*
11. *People Say*
12. *Together*
13. *Shout*

Cuts 1--10, 12: From the **LET IT BE** sessions recorded early 1969 at London's Twickenham Studio.

Cut 11: Not the Beatles. Some say this is Pete Best or the Nurk Twins. The original 45 of this lists the artist as John and Paul.

Cut 13: From the "Around The Beatles" TV show which was first shown in England on May 6, 1964. Recorded for Rediffusion TV, April 27--28, 1964.

114   **BEATLES VS CHUCK BERRY**   Original Rock 1000   (LP)

1. *Rock And Roll Music*
2. *Rock And Roll Music*
3. *Roll Over Beethoven*
4. *Roll Over Beethoven*
5. *Carol*
6. *Carol*
7. *Memphis*
8. *Memphis*
9. *Little Queenie*
10. *Little Queenie*
11. *I'm Talking About You*
12. *I'm Talking About You*

Cuts 1, 3: Beatles, original recordings.

Cuts 2, 4, 6, 8, 10, 12: All original recordings by Chuck Berry.

Cut 5: Beatles from radio Luxembourg, January 18, 1963.

Cut 7: Beatles from the Decca audition sessions, January 1, 1962.

Cut 9: Beatles, recorded at the Star Club in Hamburg, Germany, December, 1962.

Cut 11: Unknown; probably Star Club, Hamburg, Germany, December, 1962.

115   **BEATLES VS DON HO**   Melvin MM08   (LP)

1. *Too Much Monkey Business*
2. *My Girl Is Red Hot*
3. *A Hard Day's Night Promo Spot*
4. *Sitar Play & Discussion With George*
5. *Interview With John And Paul*
6. *I'll Be On My Way*
7. *Help Promo Spot*
8. *All You Need Is Love*
9. *Beatles Christmas Message*
10. *Think For Yourself*
11. *A Quick One And He's Away*
12. *Beyond The Valley Of A Day In The Life*
13. *Give Peace A Chance*
14. *Twist And Shout*
15. *Carol*
16. *Lend Me Your Comb*
17. *Everybody's Trying To Be My Baby*
18. *Soldier Of Love*
19. *Mellotron Music*
20. *Maxwell's Silver Hammer*
21. *Honey Don't*
22. *Guitar Blues*
23. *I'm Down*
24. *Tiny Bubbles*

Cut 1: Recorded from the BBC radio in 1962.

Cut 2: Recorded live at the Star Club in Hamburg, Germany in December, 1962.

Cuts 3, 7: Radio commercials for Beatles' movies.

Cut 4: George on the David Frost Show.

Cut 5: The interview was done in Los Angeles in 1965.

Cut 6: From the BBC in 1962.

Cut 8: From the "Our World" TV show. Recorded June 25, 1967.

Cut 9: Listed as BBC TV film from 1963.

Cut 10: Short version from the film "Yellow Submarine."

Cut 11: Unknown, possibly the Who.

Cut 12: Not the Beatles, but a group known as the Residents.

Cut 13: A 1969 rehearsal version.

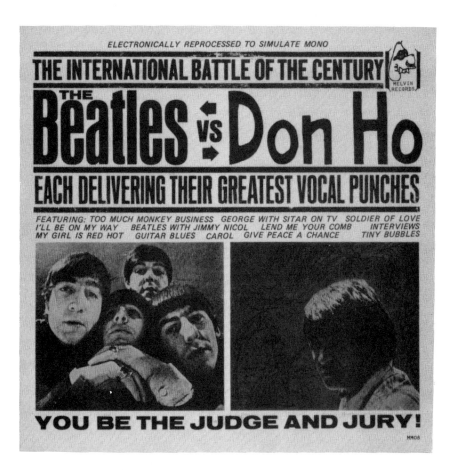

The Beatles Vs. Don Ho (LP)   Melvin MM08 (Entry 115)

Cut 14: Recorded live in Copenhagen on June 4, 1964, with Jimmy Nicol on drums.

Cuts 15--16: Recorded from radio Luxembourg, January 18, 1963.

Cut 17: BBC radio, 1964 with an interview.

Cut 18: A 1963 demo recording.

Cut 19: From the 1967 film "Magical Mystery Tour."

Cut 20: Outtake.

Cut 21: Recorded in 1963 from the BBC radio with John on lead vocals.

Cut 22: Recorded 1964 in New York.

Cut 23: Recorded live at the Hollywood Bowl (?).

Cut 24: Not the Beatles, but Don Ho.

NOTES: At the opening of side one of this album is a phony phone call giveaway by a William Campbell. He's trying to give a woman a copy of this album, but she doesn't want it.

116	**BEATLES VS COWBOY COPAS**
117	**BEATLES VS ERNEST TUBB**
118	**BEATLES VS UNCLE REMUS**
119	**BEATLES VS CHI CHI RODRIGUEZ**
120	**BEATLES VS ORSON BEAN**
121	**BEATLES VS BIG MAYBELLE**
122	**BEATLES VS PHAST PHRANK**
123	**BEATLES VS CHOCOLATE MILK**
124	**BEATLES VS HEARTBREAK OF PSORIASIS**
125	**BEATLES VS HOGFAT JACKSON**
126	**BEATLES VS MARCEL MARCEAU**
127	**BEATLES VS THE ATLANTA BRAVES**
128	**BEATLES VS SONNY BONO'S REFRIGERATOR**

NOTES: None of the above were ever released. These are listed on the back cover of the **BEATLES VS DON HO** album as being also available in this series.

129 **BEATLES VS BUDDY HOLLY AND THE ISLEY BROTHERS**   Original Rock 1001   (LP)

1. *Reminiscing*
2. *Reminiscing*
3. *Words Of Love*
4. *Words Of Love*
5. *Crying, Waiting, Hoping*
6. *Crying, Waiting, Hoping*
7. *Twist And Shout*
8. *Twist And Shout*
9. *Shout*
10. *Shout*

Cut 1: Beatles at the Star Club in Hamburg, Germany, 1962.

Cuts 2, 4, 6: Originals by Buddy Holly.

Cuts 3, 7: Beatles, original recordings.

Cut 5: Beatles, recorded from a BBC radio broadcast of November, 1962.

Cuts 8, 10: Originals by the Isley Brothers.

Cut 9: Beatles, recorded for the Rediffusion TV show "Around The Beatles" between April 27 and 28, 1964. The show aired May 6, 1964.

130 **BEATLES VS LITTLE RICHARD AND LARRY WILLIAMS**   Original Rock 1002 (LP)

1. *Long Tall Sally*
2. *Long Tall Sally*
3. *Good Golly Miss Molly*
4. *Good Golly Miss Molly*
5. *Lucille*
6. *Lucille*
7. *Bad Boy*
8. *Bad Boy*
9. *Slow Down*
10. *Slow Down*
11. *Dizzy Miss Lizzy*
12. *Dizzy Miss Lizzy*

Cuts 1, 7, 9, 11: Beatles, original recordings.

Cuts 2, 4, 6: Little Richard, original recordings.
Cut 3: Beatles, from the **LET IT BE** sessions recorded early in 1969.
Cut 5: Beatles, from a 1963 broadcast over BBC radio.
Cuts 8, 10, 12: Larry Williams, original recordings.

131 BEATLES VS CARL PERKINS Original Rock 1003 (LP)

1. *Everybody's Trying To Be My Baby*
2. *Everybody's Trying To Be My Baby*
3. *Lend Me Your Comb*
4. *Lend Me Your Comb*
5. *Matchbox*
6. *Matchbox*
7. *Blue Suede Shoes*
8. *Blue Suede Shoes*
9. *Honey Don't*
10. *Honey Don't*
11. *Glad All Over*
12. *Glad All Over*
13. *Sure To Fall*
14. *Sure To Fall*

Cuts 1, 5, 9: Beatles original recordings.
Cuts 2, 4, 6, 8, 10, 12, 14: Carl Perkins, original recordings.
Cut 3: Beatles, from a broadcast over radio Luxembourg, January 18, 1963.
Cut 7: John, live in Toronto.
Cut 11: Beatles, recorded from a BBC radio broadcast in November, 1962.
Cut 13: Beatles, from the Decca auditions, January 1, 1962.

132 BEATLES VS THE GIRLS Original Rock 1004 (LP)

1. *Boys*
2. *Boys*
3. *Baby It's You*
4. *Baby It's You*
5. *Chains*
6. *Chains*
7. *Please Mr. Postman*
8. *Please Mr. Postman*
9. *Devil In Her Heart*
10. *Devil In His Heart*
11. *Till There Was You*
12. *Till There Was You*

Cuts 1, 3, 5, 7, 9, 11: Beatles, original recordings.
Cuts 2, 4: Shirelles, original recordings.
Cut 6: Cookies, original recording.
Cut 8: Marvelettes, original recording.
Cut 10: Donays, original recording.
Cut 12: Anita Bryant, original recording.

133 BEATLES VS THE WORLD VOL. I Original Rock 1005 (LP)

1. *Hippy Hippy Shake*
2. *Hippy Hippy Shake*
3. *I Remember You*
4. *I Remember You*
5. *Kansas City*
6. *Kansas City*
7. *Money*
8. *Money*
9. *Sheila*
10. *Sheila*
11. *Searchin'*
12. *Searchin'*

Cut 1: Beatles, from a BBC radio broadcast in 1962.
Cut 2: Swingin' Blue Jeans, original recording.
Cuts 3, 9: Beatles, live at the Star Club in Hamburg, Germany, in December, 1962.
Cut 4: Frank Ifield, original recording.
Cuts 5, 7: Beatles, original recordings.
Cut 6: Wilbert Harrison, original recording.
Cut 8: Barrett Strong, original recording.
Cut 10: Tommy Roe, original recording.
Cut 11: Beatles, recorded during the Decca audition session, January 1, 1962.
Cut 12: Coasters, original recording.

134 BEATLES VS THE WORLD VOL. II Original Rock 1006 (LP)

1. *Take Good Care Of My Baby*
2. *Take Good Care Of My Baby*
7. *Lonesome Tears In My Eyes*
8. *Lonesome Tears In My Eyes*

3. *Act Naturally*	9. *Save The Last Dance For Me*
4. *Act Naturally*	10. *Save The Last Dance For Me*
5. *Anna*	11. *Shake, Rattle And Roll*
6. *Anna*	12. *Shake, Rattle And Roll*

Cut 1: Beatles, Decca audition sessions, January 1, 1962.
Cut 2: Bobby Vee, original recording.
Cuts 3, 5: Beatles, original recordings.
Cut 4: Buck Owens, original recording.
Cut 6: Arthur Alexander, original recording.
Cut 7: Beatles, from a BBC radio broadcast of November, 1962.
Cut 8: Johnny Burnette Trio, original recording.
Cuts 9, 11: Beatles, recorded during the **LET IT BE** sessions early in 1969.
Cut 10: Drifters, original recording.
Cut 12: Joe Turner, original recording.

135   **BEATLES VS THE WORLD VOL. III**   Original Rock 1007   (LP)

1. *Hallelujah I Love Her So*	7. *To Know Him Is To Love Him*
2. *Hallelujah I Love Her So*	8. *To Know Him Is To Love Him*
3. *The Saints*	9. *You Win Again*
4. *The Saints*	10. *You Win Again*
5. *You Really Got A Hold On Me*	11. *Good Rockin' Tonight*
6. *You Really Got A Hold On Me*	12. *Good Rockin' Tonight*

Cut 1: Beatles, recorded live at the Star Club in Hamburg, Germany in December, 1962.
Cut 2: Ray Charles, original recording.
Cuts 3, 5: Beatles, original recordings.
Cut 4: Bill Haley & Comets, original recording.
Cut 6: Miracles, original recording.
Cut 7: Beatles, recorded during the Decca audition session, January 1, 1962.
Cut 8: Teddy Bears, original recording.
Cuts 9, 11: Beatles, recorded during the **LET IT BE** sessions early in 1969.
Cut 10: Hank Williams, original recording.
Cut 12: Elvis Presley, original recording.

136   **BEATLES VOL. I**   TV 8467   (LP)
NOTES: Same as **ALPHA OMEGA VOL. I.**
SEE ALSO: **GREATEST HITS: COLLECTOR'S EDITION; VOLUME ONE.**

137   **BEATLES VOL. 2**   TV 8468   (LP)
NOTES: Same as **ALPHA OMEGA VOL. 2.**
SEE ALSO: **VOLUME TWO.**

138   **BEATLE VIEWS**   BV 1966   (LP)

1. *John – Religion And Movies*	5. *Paul – Impressions*
2. *Paul – Songwriting*	6. *Jim Stagg In Liverpool*
3. *Ringo -- Home Life*	7. *Cleveland And Memphis,*
4. *George – Hamburg Beginnings*	*Touring Plans*
	8. *Beatles -- Hobbies And Future*
	Plans

NOTES: Recorded during the 1966 U.S. tour, except for Jim Stagg's bit in
    Liverpool. The narrator is Ken Douglas. At the beginning of side two there
    is a short version of *I Feel Fine* from the concert in Cleveland, Ohio on
    August 14, 1966.
SEE ALSO: **VIEWS.**

Besame Mucho/To Know Him
Is To Love Him (45)

Deccagone 1106 (Entry 140)

139   BEATLES WERE BORN   Napoleon 11044   (LP)
       NOTES: Same as AND THE BEATLES WERE BORN.
       SEE ALSO: ONCE UPON A TIME . . .

140   *BESAME MUCHO/TO KNOW HIM IS TO LOVE HIM*   Deccagone 1106   (45)
       NOTES: Originally released by one of the Beatle fan clubs.
            The 45 came with a full–color picture sleeve and was pressed on green vinyl.
            It was later booted by another outfit. Songs are from the Decca audition,
            January 1, 1962.

141   *BESAME MUCHO/TO KNOW HIM IS TO LOVE HIM*   Deccagone 1106   (45)
       NOTES: This is a boot of the original Deccagone boot put out by one of the
            Beatle fan clubs. Originals had a light cream while these had a bright orange
            label. Original picture sleeve had a white area at the top with "THE
            BEATLES" printed in light blue, "TO KNOW HIM IS TO LOVE HIM" in
            brown and "BESAME MUCHO" in red. On this issue the area at the top of
            the sleeve is orange and both song titles are in light blue. The records were
            pressed on several different colors of vinyl, including blue, gold, red, violet
            and yellow.

142   BEST OF 1967   Unknown   (LP)
       NOTES: This LP is considered by many to be the first bootleg (actually it's a
            pirate) to be distributed on a large scale. It was even mentioned in *Rolling
            Stone* magazine on November 23, 1967. The album included songs by the
            Beatles, Doors, Monkees and others.

143   BEST OF THE BEATLES & JETHRO TULL   CBM   (LP)

       1. *Nothing Is Easy*   7. *Christmas Message 1967*
       2. *Dig It*   8. *Christmas Message 1968*
       3. *Christmas Message 1963*   9. *Christmas Message 1969*
       4. *Christmas Message 1964*
       5. *Christmas Message 1965*
       6. *Christmas Message 1966*
       Cut 1: Jethro Tull, not the Beatles.
       Cut 2: From the LET IT BE sessions, recorded early in 1969 at London's
            Twickenham Studios.
       Cuts 3--9: Beatles Christmas recordings for their fan club members. All original.
       SEE ALSO: COMPLETE CHRISTMAS COLLECTION; DON'T PASS ME BY.

144   BEST OF TOBE MILO PRODUCTIONS   Tobe Milo 10Q 1/2   (LP)

       1. *Guinness Book Of World Records*   7. *Hey Jude*
       2. *My Carnival*   8. *And The Roof Almost Came*
       3. *Brung To Ewe By* (30 seconds)   *Down When Ed . . .*
       4. *Kenny Everett Interview With*   9. *Day Tripper*
           Cottonfields   10. *Brung To Ewe By* (60 seconds)
       5. *Brung To Ewe By* (30 seconds)   11. *Interview*
       6. *Bealir Mansion Interview With John* 12. *Houston Concert Medley*
           And Paul
       Cut 2: Recorded by Paul February 12, 1975 in New Orleans. It was to have been
            released on the VENUS AND MARS album.
       Cuts 3, 5, 10: From the RAM promo record.
       Cut 4: Recorded in January of 1968 by Kenny and John.
       Cut 6: Recorded March, 1965.
       Cut 7: Unknown.
       Cut 8: From the "Ed Sullivan Memorial" TV show.
       Cut 9: Recorded live at the Budokan Hall concert in Tokyo on July 2, 1966.
       Cut 11: Interview from the 1962 13–hour BBC Beatle special.

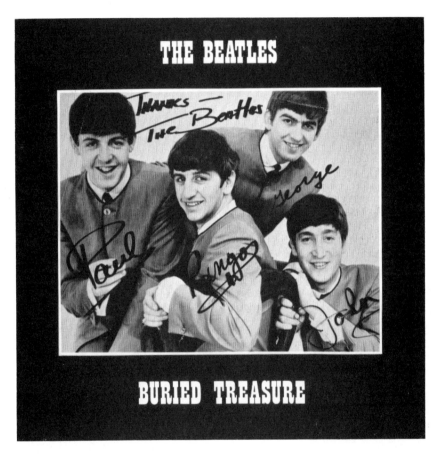

Buried Treasure (LP)   Wunderland W49001 (Entry 150)

Cut 12: From the Houston concert, August 19, 1966.
NOTES: Deluxe laminated cover. Cut 12 is not listed on the cover. Cut 1 is from a radio show.

145   BOTTOM APPLES; RENAISSANCE MINSTRELS III   Wizardo 404   (LP)

1. *Coochy--Coo*
2. *Deep Blue*
3. *Do The Oz*
4. *Down And Out*
5. *Miss O'Dell*
6. *Move Over Miss L*
7. *Blindman*
8. *Bangla Desh*
9. *God Save Us*
10. *I Don't Care Anymore*

Cuts 1--10: All original recordings. Numbers 1, 4 and 7 are by Ringo. Numbers 2, 5, 8 and 10 are by George. Numbers 3, 6 and 9 are by John.
SEE ALSO: **BOTTOM OF THE APPLE TAPES.**

146   BOTTOM OF THE APPLE TAPES   Wizardo 404   (LP)
NOTES: Same as **BOTTOM APPLES: RENAISSANCE MINSTRELS III.**

147   BRITISH COLUMBIA '64   Wizardo 340   (2 LPs)

1. *Twist And Shout*
2. *You Can't Do That*
3. *All My Loving*
4. *She Loves You*
5. *Things We Said Today*
6. *Roll Over Beethoven*

7. *Can't Buy Me Love*
8. *If I Fell*
9. *I Want To Hold Your Hand*
10. *Boys*
11. *A Hard Day's Night*
12. *Long Tall Sally*

Cuts 1--12: Recorded live at the Empire Stadium in Vancouver, British Columbia on August 22, 1964. There are also many interviews included on this album.
SEE ALSO: **B.C. '64; VANCOUVER 1964** (TMQ); **VANCOUVER 1964** (K&S).

148   BUG CRUSHER "LIVE"   TMOQ   (LP)
NOTES: Exact cuts unknown.

149   BUMBLE WORDS -- SUPER STUDIO SESSIONS NO. 2   CBM B203; Instant Analysis 3624/3626   (LP)

1. *L.S. Bumblebee*
2. *Don't Let Me Down*
3. *Maxwell's Silver Hammer*
4. *Two Of Us*
5. *I've Got A Feeling*
6. *One After 909*
7. *Across The Universe*
8. *I Dig A Pony*
9. *Have You Heard The Word*
10. *You Really Got A Hold On Me*
11. *Maxwell's Silver Hammer*
12. *Cha Cha*
13. *Octopus's Garden*
14. *I Me Mine*
15. *Don't Let Me Down*

Cut 1: Thought to be by the Beatles, but actually by Peter Cook and Dudley Moore.
Cuts 2--8, 10--15: Recorded during the **LET IT BE** sessions early in 1969. Recording took place at London's Twickenham Studios.
Cut 9: Recorded June, 1970. This is supposed to be John and at least a few of the Bee Gees. (For discussion, see footnote on pages xxiv-xxv.)
SEE ALSO: **HAVE YOU HEARD THE WORD** (side one); **L.S. BUMBLEBEE** (side one).

150   BURIED TREASURE   Wunderland W49001; Berkeley 10   (2 LPs)

1. *Soldier Of Love*
2. *I Got A Woman*
3. *Kansas City*
11. *Johnny B. Goode*
12. *Slow Down*
13. *Ain't Nothing Shakin' But The*

4. *Some Other Guy*
5. *Lend Me Your Comb*
6. *Carol*
7. *Lucille*
8. *Hippy Hippy Shake*
9. *Shout*
10. *Memphis*

Leaves On The Trees
14. *I'm Gonna Sit Right Down And Cry*
15. *Honey Don't*
16. *Rock And Roll Music*
17. *Dizzy Miss Lizzy*

18. *Murray The K Fan Club Message*
19. *I Saw Her Standing There*
20. *You Can't Do That*

21. *All My Loving*
22. *She Loves You*
23. *Till There Was You*
24. *Roll Over Beethoven*
25. *Can't Buy Me Love*
26. *This Boy*
27. *Long Tall Sally*

Cut 1: 1963 outtake, played to Ed Sullivan by transatlantic phone in 1964.
Cut 2: John Lennon outtake played on WABC radio in New York.
Cut 3: Recorded at the Granville Theatre, October 9, 1964. Tape was shown in the U.S.A. on "Shindig" on January 20, 1965.
Cut 4: Recorded at the Cavern Club by Granada TV on October 13, 1962. Shown on the "People And Places" show November 7, 1962.
Cuts 5–6: From a broadcast over radio Luxembourg on January 18, 1963.
Cut 7: Live unknown.
Cut 8: From a BBC radio broadcast in 1962.
Cut 9: Recorded for the Rediffusion TV show "Around The Beatles" on April 27–28, 1964. The show aired May 6, 1964.
Cuts 10–11: From the BBC radio show "Saturday Club" broadcast May 25, 1963.
Cuts 12–14: From a BBC radio broadcast of November, 1962.
Cut 15: 1963 outtake with John on lead.
Cut 16: Live 1966 (probably from the Japan concert).
Cut 17: BBC 1964.
Cut 18: Original Murray The K interviews with segments of *She Loves You* and *Shout*.
Cuts 19–27: Recorded live at the Melbourne, Australia, concert on June 16, 1964.
NOTES: Deluxe black--and--white cover.

151   BYE, BYE, BYE SUPERTRACKS VOL. 1   CBM 3922   (LP)

1. *You Really Got A Hold On Me*
2. *Have You Heard The Word*
3. *You Really Got A Hold On Me*
4. *What's The New Mary Jane*
5. *Teddy Boy*

6. *Dig It*
7. *L.S. Bumble Bee*
8. *Maxwell's Silver Hammer*
9. *Besame Mucho*
10. *Crying, Waiting, Hoping*
11. *Shake, Rattle And Roll*

Cut 1: Recorded for the Swedish TV show "Drop In" on October 30, 1963. The show aired November 3, 1963.
Cut 2: Recorded June, 1970. John and at least a few of the Bee Gees are supposed to have been involved. (For discussion, see footnote on pages xxiv-xxv.)
Cuts 3, 5–6, 8–9, 11: Recorded during the **LET IT BE** sessions early in 1969 at London's Twickenham Studios.
Cut 4: Recorded August 14, 1968 by John. This was to have been released by Apple, but never was.
Cut 7: This is Dudley Moore and Peter Cook, not the Beatles.
Cut 10: Recorded from a BBC radio broadcast of November, 1962.
SEE ALSO: **BACTRAX** (sides one and two); **SUPERTRACKS I** (CBM 3922); **SUPERTRACKS 1** (CBM).

152   BYE, BYE, BYE SUPERTRACKS VOL. 2   CBM 3923; TMOQ TB 1018 A/B
        (LP)

1. *Introduction*
2. *Paperback Writer*
3. *Rain*
4. *Peace Of Mind*
5. *Take 37*
6. *Tutty Fruity*
7. *Hey Jude*

8. *Get Back*
9. *Conversation*
10. *I Should Have Known Better*
11. *Conversation*
12. *If I Fell*
13. *Conversation*
14. *And I Love Her*
15. *Conversation*
16. *Tell Me Why*
17. *If I Fell*
18. *I Should Have Known Better*

Cuts 1–3: From the "Ed Sullivan Show" August, 1966.
Cuts 4–8: Recorded during the **LET IT BE** sessions, early 1969 at London's
    Twickenham Studio.
Cuts 9–18: From the movie soundtrack for "A Hard Day's Night."
SEE ALSO: **SUPERTRACKS 2; SUPERTRACKS II.**

153   CAUGHT OFF GUARD   Aftermath 4   (LP)

1. *Two Of Us*
2. *Don't Let Me Down*
3. *Suzy Parker*
4. *I've Got A Feeling*
5. *No Pakistanis*
6. *Get Back*
7. *Don't Let Me Down*

8. *Be Bop A Lula*
9. *She Came In Through The*
    Bathroom Window
10. *High–Heeled Sneakers*
11. *I Me Mine*
12. *I've Got A Feeling*
13. *One After 909*
14. *Norwegian Wood*
15. *She Came In Through The*
    Bathroom Window

Cuts 1–15: From the **LET IT BE** sessions. Recorded at London's Twickenham
    Studios in early 1969.
NOTES: This is the same as sides one and two of the album **HAHST AZ SUN.**
SEE ALSO: **SWEET APPLE TRAX** (Newsound, sides one and two); **SWEET
    APPLE TRAX VOL. 1.**

154   CAVERN CLUB   CBM 3906   (LP)

1. Medley:
    Love Me Do
    Please Please Me
    From Me To You
    She Loves You
    I Want To Hold Your Hand
2. *Can't Buy Me Love*
3. *Long Tall Sally*
4. *She Loves You*

5. *Introduction*
6. *Act Naturally*
7. *Can't Buy Me Love*
8. *Baby's In Black*
9. *I'm Down*
10. *Help*
11. *Twist And Shout*
12. *I Feel Fine*
13. *Dizzy Miss Lizzy*
14. *Ticket To Ride*

Cuts 1–4: Recorded April 27–28, 1964, for the Rediffusion TV show "Around
    The Beatles." The show was first aired May 6, 1964.
Cuts 5–14: Recorded live at the Shea Stadium concert on August 15, 1965.
SEE ALSO: **CAVERN DAYS -- SUPER STUDIO SERIES 5.**

155   CAVERN DAYS -- SUPER STUDIO SERIES 5   CBM B205; Shalom 3906/3907
        (LP)

1. Medley:

5. *You Really Got A Hold On Me*

Love Me Do
Please Please Me
From Me To You
She Loves You
I Want To Hold Your Hand
2. *Can't Buy Me Love*
3. *Long Tall Sally*
4. *She Loves You*

6. *Have You Heard The Word*
7. *Don't Let Me Down*
8. *Those Were The Days*
9. *Mean Mr. Mustard*
10. *All Together On The Wireless Machine*
11. *Dialogue*
12. *Step Inside Love*
13. *Bye Bye Bye*
14. *Cottonfields*
15. *Twist And Shout*

Cuts 1–4: Recorded April 27–28, 1964, for the Rediffusion TV show "Around The Beatles." The show first aired May 6, 1964.

Cuts 5, 15: Recorded October 30, 1963, for the Swedish TV show "Drop In." The show was aired November 3, 1963.

Cut 6: Recorded in June, 1970. Reportedly this is John and at least some of the Bee Gees. (For discussion, see footnote on pages xxiv-xxv.)

Cuts 7–8: Recorded in the fall of 1968, live at a press conference.

Cuts 9–10, 13: Depending on the source, these songs were either recorded in the spring of 1969 or 1970.

Cut 12: Demo cut by Paul in February, 1968. The song was later given to Cilla Black.

Cut 14: Recorded January, 1968, by John as a part of an interview with Kenny Everett.

NOTES: Side one of this LP is the same as side one of **CAVERN CLUB** (CBM 3906), while side two is the same as side one of **ABBEY ROAD REVISITED** (Wizardo 353).

SEE ALSO: **THOSE WERE THE DAYS.**

156   CHRISTMAS ALBUM -- FIRST AMENDMENT II   ZAP 7857   (LP)

1. *Christmas Message 1963*
2. *Christmas Message 1964*
3. *Christmas Message 1965*
4. *Christmas Message 1966*

5. *Christmas Message 1967*
6. *Christmas Message 1968*
7. *Christmas Message 1969*

Cuts 1–7: All original recordings.

SEE ALSO: **CHRISTMAS MEETINGS; CHRISTMAS MESSAGE FROM LIVERPOOL; COMPLETE CHRISTMAS ALBUM; COMPLETE CHRISTMAS ALBUM; 2ND AMENDMENT CHRISTMAS ALBUM; THEIR COMPLETE CHRISTMAS COLLECTION '63–69; WHITE CHRISTMAS.**

157   CHRISTMAS MEETINGS   Unknown   (LP)

1. *The Beatles – Christmas Record 1963*
2. *Another Christmas Record 1964*
3. *Third Christmas Record 1965*
4. *Pantomima, Everywhere It's Christmas 1966*

5. *Christmas Time Is Here Again 1967*
6. *Happy Christmas 1968*
7. *Happy Christmas 1969*

Cuts 1–7: All original recordings.

SEE ALSO: **CHRISTMAS ALBUM – FIRST AMENDMENT II; CHRISTMAS MESSAGE FROM LIVERPOOL; COMPLETE CHRISTMAS COLLECTION; COMPLETE CHRISTMAS COLLECTION; 2ND AMENDMENT – CHRISTMAS ALBUM; THEIR COMPLETE CHRISTMAS COLLECTION; WHITE CHRISTMAS.**

158   CHRISTMAS MESSAGE   I.C.R. 12   (LP)

1. *Christmas Message*
2. *The Long And Winding Road*
3. *When You Walk*
4. *Instant Karma*
5. *Two Of Us*

6. *Don't Let Me Down*
7. *Teddy Boy*
8. *Across The Universe*
9. *For You Blue*
10. *Let It Be*
11. *You Know My Name*

Cut 1: Interview with John and Yoko on December 15, 1969 – "War Is Over."
Cuts 2–3, 5–10: From the **LET IT BE** sessions recorded at Twickenham Studios early in 1969.
Cut 4: From the BBC TV show "Top Of The Pops." Recorded February 12, 1970.
Cut 11: Original recording.
SEE ALSO: **CHRISTMAS MESSAGE** (Unknown).

159   CHRISTMAS MESSAGE   Unknown   (LP)

1. *Christmas Message*
2. *The Long And Winding Road*
3. *When You Walk*
4. *Instant Karma*
5. *Two Of Us*

6. *Don't Let Me Down*
7. *Teddy Boy*
8. *Across The Universe*
9. *For You Blue*

NOTES: This album is the same as **CHRISTMAS MESSAGE** (I.C.R. 12), except *Let It Be* and *You Know My Name* have been left out.

160   CHRISTMAS MESSAGE FROM LIVERPOOL   Unknown   (LP)

1. *The Beatles -- Christmas Record 1963*
2. *Another Christmas Record 1964*
3. *Third Christmas Record 1965*
4. *Pantomima, Everywhere It's Christmas 1966*

5. *Christmas Time Is Here Again 1967*
6. *Happy Christmas 1968*
7. *Happy Christmas 1969*

Cuts 1–7: Original recordings.
SEE ALSO: **CHRISTMAS ALBUM – FIRST AMENDMENT II; CHRISTMAS MEETINGS; COMPLETE CHRISTMAS COLLECTION; COMPLETE CHRISTMAS COLLECTION; 2ND AMENDMENT CHRISTMAS ALBUM; THEIR COMPLETE CHRISTMAS COLLECTION; WHITE CHRISTMAS.**

161   CINELOGUE   CBM TB 4020   (2 LPs)

1. *Paul's Piano Theme*
2. *Don't Let Me Down*
3. *Maxwell's Silver Hammer*
4. *Maxwell's Silver Hammer*
5. *Two Of Us*
6. *I've Got A Feeling*
7. *I've Got A Feeling*
8. *Oh Darling*
9. *One After 909*
10. *Piano Boogie*
11. *Two Of Us*
12. *Across The Universe*
13. *Dig A Pony*
14. *Suzie Parker*
15. *I Me Mine*
16. *For You Blue*

17. *Besame Mucho*
18. *Octopusses' Garden*
19. *Octopusses' Garden*
20. *Octopusses' Garden*
21. *Octopusses' Garden*
22. *You Really Got A Hold On Me*
23. *Long And Winding Road*
24. *Cha Cha Cha*
25. *Long And Winding Road*
26. *Shake, Rattle And Roll*
27. *Kansas City*
28. *Good Golly Miss Molly*
29. *Dig It*

30. *Two Of Us*
31. *Let It Be*
32. *Long And Winding Road*
33. *Get Back*
34. *Don't Let Me Down*
35. *I've Got A Feeling*
36. *One After 909*
37. *Dig A Pony*
38. *Get Back*
39. *Get Back Reprise*

Cuts 1–39: The complete "Let It Be" soundtrack. Recorded in early 1969 at the Twickenham Studio in London.

162 **CINELOGUE COMPILATION** CBM B212 (2 LPs)
NOTES: Exact cuts unknown.

163 **CINELOGUE: LET IT BE** CBM 211 (2 LPs)
NOTES: Exact cuts are unknown, but this album is presumably the same as **CINELOGUE** (CBM TB 4020).

164 **CINELOGUE 2** CBM?; Instant Analysis? (2 LPs)

1. *Yellow Submarine*
2. *Penny Lane*
3. *All Together Now*
4. *When I'm 64*
5. *Nowhere Man*
6. *Lucy In The Sky*

7. *Sgt. Pepper*
8. *All You Need Is Love*
9. *Baby You're A Rich Man*
10. *It's All Too Much*
11. *All Together Now*

Cuts 1–11: Mostly from the soundtrack of "Yellow Submarine."

165 **CINELOGUE 3 – A HARD DAY'S NIGHT** CBM?; Instant Analysis?; King Kong 632 (2 LPs)

1. *A Hard Day's Night*
2. *I Should Have Known Better*
3. *I Wanna Be Your Man*
4. *All My Loving*
5. *If I Fell*
6. *Can't Buy Me Love*

7. *And I Love Her*
8. *I'm Happy Just To Dance With You*
9. *Instrumental*
10. *A Hard Day's Night*
11. *Can't Buy Me Love*
12. *Tell Me Why*
13. *If I Fell*
14. *I Should Have Known Better*
15. *She Loves You*
16. *A Hard Day's Night*

Cuts 1–16: The complete soundtrack to "A Hard Day's Night."
SEE ALSO: **A HARD DAY'S NIGHT; A HARD DAY'S NIGHT + SKINNIE MINNIE; COMPLETE SOUNDTRACK TO A HARD DAY'S NIGHT; HARD DAY'S NIGHT SOUNDTRACK.**

166 **CINELOGUE 4 -- HELP** Instant Analysis 1026; King Kong 633 (2 LPs)

1. *Help*
2. *Bitter End*
3. *You're Gonna Lose That Girl*
4. *You've Got To Hide Your Love Away*
5. *From Me To You Fantasy*
6. *Ticket To Ride*

7. *I Need You*
8. *The Night Before*
9. *Another Girl*
10. *Another Hard Day's Night*
11. *Help*

Cuts 1–11: The complete soundtrack to the movie "Help."

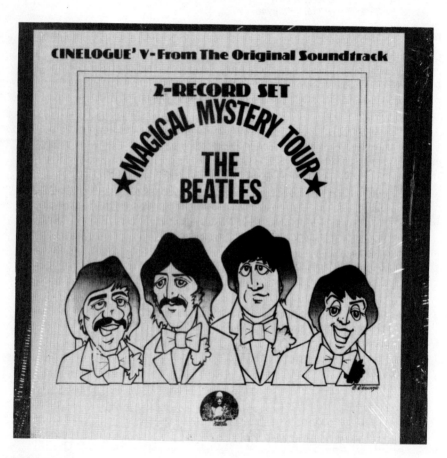

Cinelogue 5
—Magical Mystery Tour (2 LPs)   Instant Analysis 1028 (Entry 167)

167 **CINELOGUE 5 – MAGICAL MYSTERY TOUR** CBM?; Instant Analysis 1028;
King Kong 634 (2 LPs)

1. *Magical Mystery Tour*
2. *Fool On The Hill*

3. *Yesterday*
4. *La La La*
5. *All My Loving*

6. *I Am The Walrus*
7. *Blue Jay Way*

8. Medley:
Tu Tu Tutsy Goodbye
Happy Wanderer
When Irish Eyes Are Smiling
Never On Sunday
9. *Baby Don't Do It*
10. *Your Mother Should Know*
11. *Magical Mystery Tour*

Cuts 1--11: Mostly from the soundtrack of the TV film "Magical Mystery Tour."

168 **CINELOGUE 6** CBM 4022–C/3665A (2 LPs)

1. *Michelle*
2. *Heart Of The Country*
3. *Mary Had A Little Lamb*
4. *My Love*
5. *Uncle Albert*
6. Medley:
Pennies From Heaven
Pack Up Your Troubles
You Are My Sunshine

7. *Gotta Sing, Gotta Dance*
8. *Live And Let Die*
9. *The Mess*
10. *Maybe I'm Amazed*
11. *Long Tall Sally*
12. *Yesterday*

13. *Twist And Shout*
14. *Roll Over Beethoven*
15. *I Wanna Be Your Man*
16. *Long Tall Sally*
17. Medley:
Love Me Do
Please Please Me
From Me To You
She Loves You
I Want To Hold Your Hand
18. *Can't Buy Me Love*
19. *Shout*

20. *Attica State*
21. *Luck Of The Irish*
22. *Oh Sisters*

Cuts 1–12: From the ABC–TV special "James Paul McCartney," first shown
April 16, 1973.
Cuts 13--19: Recorded April 27--28, 1964 for the Rediffusion TV show "Around
The Beatles." The show first aired May 6, 1964.
Cuts 20--22: Recorded live at the John Sinclair benefit concert by John, Yoko
and others. The concert took place December 18, 1971.

169 **CINELOGUE SIX** King Kong 635 (2 LPs)

1. *Twist And Shout*
2. *Roll Over Beethoven*
3. *I Wanna Be Your Man*
4. *Long Tall Sally*
5. Medley:
Love Me Do
Please Please Me
From Me To You

8. *Kansas City*
9. *I'm A Loser*
10. *Boys*

Four By The Beatles (AKA Clarabella) (EP) Unknown (Entry 170)

Come Together/Something (45 sleeve)   Apple 2654 (Entry 171)

> *She Loves You*
> *I Want To Hold Your Hand*
> 6. *Can't Buy Me Love*
> 7. *Shout*

11. *Big Barn Bed*
12. *Little Woman Love*
13. *C Moon*
14. *My Love*
15. *The Mess*
16. *Maybe I'm Amazed*
17. *Long Tall Sally*
18. *Another Day*
19. *Oh Woman Oh Why*
20. *Hi Hi Hi*
21. *Gotta Sing, Gotta Dance*
22. *Live And Let Die*

23. Medley:
    Blackbird
    Blue Bird
    Michelle
    Heart Of The Country
    Yesterday

Cuts 1--7: Recorded April 27--28, 1964, for the Rediffusion TV show "Around The Beatles." The show first aired May 6, 1964.
Cuts 8--10: Recorded before a live audience at the Granville Theatre in London on October 9, 1964. The film was shown on the U.S. TV show "Shindig" on January 20, 1965.
Cuts 11--23: From the McCartney TV special "James Paul McCartney," shown on ABC--TV on April 16, 1973.

170 **CLARABELLA** Unknown (EP)

1. *Carol*
2. *Soldier Of Love*
3. *Lend Me Your Comb*
4. *Clarabella*

Cuts 1, 3: From a broadcast on radio Luxembourg, January 18, 1963.
Cut 2: 1963 outtake.
Cut 4: Unknown.
NOTES: Issued in mid--1980 with a full color sleeve.

171 *COME TOGETHER/SOMETHING* Apple 2654 (sleeve)
NOTES: This is a picture sleeve only. No sleeve was originally released with this record. Black--and--white picture from the "Let It Be" era showing Paul at the control board. Also in the picture are Ringo, George and Yoko. The same photo appears on both sides of the sleeve.

172 **COMPLETE CHRISTMAS ALBUM** Unknown (LP)

1. *The Beatles -- Christmas Record 1963*
2. *Another Christmas Record 1964*
3. *Third Christmas Record 1965*
4. *Pantomima, Everywhere It's Christmas 1966*
5. *Christmas Time Is Here Again 1967*
6. *Happy Christmas 1968*
7. *Happy Christmas 1969*

Cuts 1--7: Original recordings.
SEE ALSO: **CHRISTMAS ALBUM -- FIRST AMENDMENT II; CHRISTMAS MEETINGS; CHRISTMAS MESSAGE FROM LIVERPOOL; COMPLETE CHRISTMAS COLLECTION; 2ND AMENDMENT -- CHRISTMAS ALBUM; THEIR COMPLETE CHRISTMAS COLLECTION; WHITE CHRISTMAS.**

173 **COMPLETE CHRISTMAS COLLECTION** CBM 2 A/B (LP)
NOTES: Same as **BEST OF THE BEATLES AND JETHRO TULL.**
SEE ALSO: **DON'T PASS ME BY.**

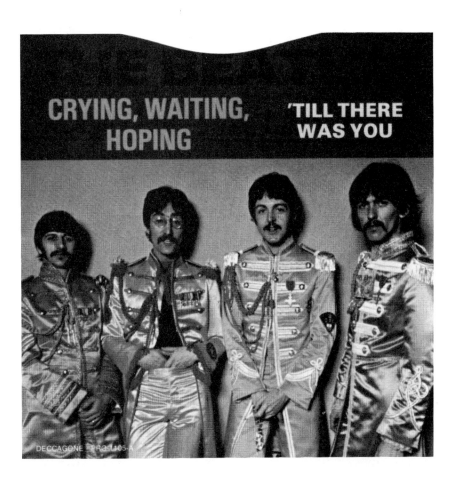

Crying, Waiting, Hoping/
  'Till There Was You (45)   Deccagone 1105 (Entry 179)

174   **COMPLETE CHRISTMAS COLLECTION**   TMOQ BCC 104; TMOQ 71015   (LP)

1. *The Beatles – Christmas Record*   5. *Christmas Time Is Here Again*
    1963   *1967*
2. *Another Christmas Record 1964*   6. *Happy Christmas 1968*
3. *Third Christmas Record 1965*   7. *Happy Christmas 1969*
4. *Pantomima, Everywhere It's*
    Christmas 1966

Cuts 1–7: Original recordings.
SEE ALSO: **CHRISTMAS ALBUM – FIRST AMENDMENT II; CHRISTMAS MEETINGS; CHRISTMAS MESSAGE FROM LIVERPOOL; COMPLETE CHRISTMAS COLLECTION; 2ND AMENDMENT – CHRISTMAS ALBUM; THEIR COMPLETE CHRISTMAS COLLECTION; WHITE CHRISTMAS.**

175   **COMPLETE ED SULLIVAN SHOWS**   CBM?
NOTES: Exact cuts unknown.

176   **COMPLETE "LET IT BE" SESSIONS**   Wizardo 315   (2 LPs)

1. *Instrumental*   9. *For You Blue*
2. *Save The Last Dance For Me*   10. *Teddy Boy*
3. *Don't Let Me Down*   11. *Two Of Us*
4. *Don't Let Me Down*   12. *Maggie May*
5. *Dig A Pony*   13. *Dig It*
6. *I Got A Feeling*   14. *Let It Be*
7. *Get Back*   15. *Get Back*
8. *One After 909*

16. *Waiting For The Man* (Lou Reed)   23. *Rock And Roll Music*
17. *She's A Woman*   24. *Baby's In Black*
18. *Ticket To Ride*   25. *I Feel Fine*
19. *Can't Buy Me Love*   26. *Yesterday*
20. *I'm A Loser*   27. *Nowhere Man*
21. *Everybody's Trying To Be My*   28. *I'm Down*
    Baby   29. *Money*
22. *Long Tall Sally*   30. *From Me To You*

Cuts 1–15: Recorded during the **LET IT BE** sessions early in 1969 at London's Twickenham Studios.
Cut 16: Not the Beatles, but Lou Reed.
Cuts 17–22: Recorded live in Paris June 20, 1965.
Cuts 23–28: 1966 concert, probably Tokyo (July 2, 1966).
Cuts 29–30: Unknown.
SEE ALSO: **THE "LET IT BE" PERFORMANCE.**

177   **COMPLETE SOUNDTRACK TO A HARD DAY'S NIGHT**   Wizardo 303   (2 LPs)
SEE ALSO: **A HARD DAY'S NIGHT; A HARD DAY'S NIGHT + SKINNIE MINNIE; CINELOGUE 3 – A HARD DAY'S NIGHT; HARD DAY'S NIGHT SOUNDTRACK.**

178   **COPENHAGEN 1964**   Wizardo 501
NOTES: Same as **THE BEATLES "JOHN, PAUL, GEORGE AND JIMMY" COPENHAGEN '64.**
SEE ALSO: **JOHN, PAUL, GEORGE AND JIMMY.**

179   *CRYING, WAITING, HOPING/TILL THERE WAS YOU*   Deccagone 1105   (45)
NOTES: This recording was originally released by one of the Beatle fan clubs.
The 45 came with a full color picture sleeve and was pressed on green vinyl.
It was later booted by another outfit. The songs are from the Decca audition tapes, recorded January 1, 1962.

180 *CRYING, WAITING, HOPING/TILL THERE WAS YOU* Deccagone 1105 (45)
> NOTES: This is a bootleg of the original Deccagone bootleg released by one of the Beatle fan clubs. Originals had a light green label with black printing, while these had a dark green label with silver printing. The original picture sleeve had a red space at the top with "THE BEATLES" in black, "CRYING, WAITING, HOPING" in yellow and "TILL THERE WAS YOU" in light blue. On this issue, the top area is green, "THE BEATLES" and "CRYING, WAITING, HOPING" are as on the original, but "TILL THERE WAS YOU" is in red. The records were pressed in several different colors of vinyl including blue, gold, orange, red and yellow.

181 **DAWN OF OUR INNOCENCE** BE 1001
> NOTES: Same as **BEATLES LIVE.**
> SEE ALSO: **EARLY BEATLES LIVE; LIVE.**

182 **DECADE RADIO SPOTS** MBRF 55551
> NOTES: This one–sided disc was originally issued by Capital to celebrate the Beatles' tenth year with that company. The record contains one 30–second and one 60–second spot. The boots appeared a short time after the original release, issued on gold vinyl.
> SEE ALSO: Listing in counterfeit section.

183 **DECCA AUDITION OUTTAKES** CBM 202 (2 LPs)
> NOTES: Exact cuts are unknown. Possibly the same as **DECCA AUDITION OUTTAKES -- SUPER STUDIO SESSIONS 2** (CBM 3640/3641).

184 **DECCA AUDITION OUTTAKES – SUPER STUDIO SESSIONS 2** CBM 3640/3641
(2 LPs)

1. *You Really Got A Hold On Me*		7. *Honey Don't*	
2. *Hippy Hippy Shake*		8. *Chains*	
3. *Misery*		9. *I Saw Her Standing There*	
4. *Money*		10. *I'm Sure To Fall*	
5. *Till There Was You*		11. *Lucille*	
6. *Do You Want To Know A Secret*		12. *Boys*	

13. *From Me To You*		19. *She Loves You*	
14. *Roll Over Beethoven*		20. *Words Of Love*	
15. *Love Me Do*		21. *Devil In Her Heart*	
16. *Kansas City*		22. *Anna*	
17. *Long Tall Sally*		23. *Money*	
18. *Please Please Me*		24. *There's A Place*	

Cuts 1, 3--9, 12--24: Probably originals or studio outtakes.
Cut 2: From BBC radio 1962.
Cut 10: From BBC radio broadcast of November, 1962.
Cut 11: From BBC, 1963.
SEE ALSO: **OUTAKES VOL. I** (sides one, three); **OUTAKES VOL. II** (sides two, four); **OUTAKES VOL. I/VOL. II; STUDIO SESSIONS VOL. I** (sides one, three); **STUDIO SESSIONS VOL. II** (sides two, four); **STUDIO SESSIONS NO. 1 AND NO. 2; WORDS OF LOVE.**

185 **DECCA AUDITION TAPE** Berkeley 03 (LP)

1. *I Got A Woman*		9. *Ain't Nothin' Shakin' But The*	
2. *I Got A Woman*		*Leaves On The Trees*	
3. *Glad All Over*		10. *I Forgot To Remember To Forget*	
4. *I Just Don't Understand*		11. *Bound By Love*	
5. *Hippy Hippy Shake*		12. *Lonesome Tears In My Eyes*	
6. *I'm Sure To Fall*		13. *Everyone Wants Someone*	

The Decca Audition Tapes (LP)   Berkeley 102 (Entry 186)

7. *Please Don't Ever Change*
8. *A Shot Of Rhythm And Blues*

14. *Love Of The Loved*
15. *Lucille*
16. *I'm Gonna Sit Right Down And Cry Over You*

Cuts 1--13, 16: From a BBC radio broadcast of November, 1962.
Cut 14: From the Decca audition tapes recorded January 1, 1962.
Cut 15: Unknown from 1962.

186   DECCA AUDITION TAPES   Berkeley 102   (LP)

1. *I Got A Woman*
2. *Glad All Over*
3. *I Just Don't Understand*
4. *Slow Down*
5. *Please Don't Ever Change*
6. *A Shot Of Rhythm And Blues*
7. *I'm Sure To Fall*
8. *There's Nothing Shakin'*
9. *Lonesome Tears In My Eyes*
10. *Everyone Wants Someone*
11. *I'm Gonna Sit Right Down And Cry Over You*
12. *Crying, Waiting, Hoping*
13. *To Know Her Is To Love Her*
14. *Bound By Love*

Cuts 1--14: Recorded from a BBC radio broadcast of November, 1962.

187   THE DECCAGONES   Cx369A/Cx369B   (LP)

1. *Money*
2. *Sheik Of Araby*
3. *Memphis*
4. *Three Cool Cats*
5. *Sure To Fall*
6. *September In The Rain*
7. *Take Good Care Of My Baby*
8. *Till There Was You*
9. *Crying, Waiting, Hoping*
10. *To Know Her Is To Love Her*
11. *Besame Mucho*
12. *Searchin'*
13. *Like Dreamers Do*
14. *Hello Little Girl*
15. *Love Of The Loved*

Cuts 1--15: From the Decca audition sessions of January 1, 1962.
NOTES: Issued in a plain white sleeve on purple vinyl.
SEE ALSO: **THE DECCA TAPES; THE DECCA TAPES; THE DECCA TAPES.**

188   DECCAGONE SESSIONS   Smilin' Ears 7701   (LP)

1. *Searchin'*
2. *Like Dreamers Do*
3. *Three Cool Cats*
4. *Hello Little Girl*
5. *How Do You Do It*
6. *Crying, Waiting, Hoping*
7. *Bound By Love*
8. *There's Nothing Shaking*
9. *Love Of The Loved*
10. *Memphis*
11. *September In The Rain*
12. *Sheik Of Araby*
13. *Revolution*
14. *Some Other Guy*
15. *Everyone Wants Someone*
16. *I'm Gonna Sit Right Down And Cry Over You*
17. *A Shot Of Rhythm And Blues*

Cuts 1--4, 6, 9--12: From the Decca audition tapes, recorded January 1, 1962.
Cut 5: Recorded November 26, 1962. Was to have been the follow--up to *Love Me Do*, but *Please Please Me* was released instead.
Cuts 7--8, 15--17: From a BBC radio broadcast in November, 1962.
Cut 14: Recorded at the Cavern Club October 13, 1962, by Granada TV. Shown on the "People And Places" show November 7, 1962.
Cut 13: From the BBC--TV show "Top Of The Pops." Shown September 19, 1968.
NOTES: Color laminated cover. A small bit of *White Power/Promenade* appears between cuts 5 and 6. It is not listed on the cover.

The Decca Tapes (LP)   **Circuit LK 4438 (Entry 189)**

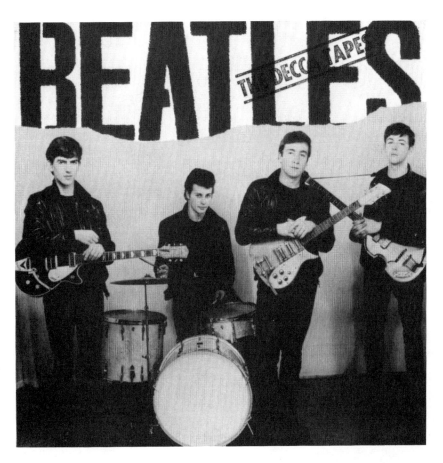

The Decca Tapes (LP)   **Circuit LK 4438 (Entry 190)**

The Decca Tapes (LP)   **Unknown (Entry 191)**

189   THE DECCA TAPES   Circuit Records LK 4438   (LP)

1. *Hello Little Girl*
2. *Three Cool Cats*
3. *Crying, Waiting, Hoping*
4. *Love Of The Loved*
5. *September In The Rain*
6. *Besame Mucho*
7. *Searchin'*
8. *Like Dreamers Do*
9. *Money*
10. *Till There Was You*
11. *Sheik Of Araby*
12. *To Know Him Is To Love Him*
13. *Take Good Care Of My Baby*
14. *Memphis*
15. *Sure To Fall*

Cuts 1--15: From the Decca audition tapes, recorded January 1, 1962.
NOTES: This is a picture record. The A--side has John and Paul and the B--side
has George and Pete Best. The picture is from their leather jacket days.
SEE ALSO: **THE DECCAGONES; THE DECCA TAPES; THE DECCA TAPES.**

190   THE DECCA TAPES   Circuit LK 4438   (LP)

1. *Hello Little Girl*
2. *Three Cool Cats*
3. *Crying, Waiting, Hoping*
4. *Love Of The Loved*
5. *September In The Rain*
6. *Besame Mucho*
7. *Searchin'*
8. *Like Dreamers Do*
9. *Money*
10. *Till There Was You*
11. *Sheik Of Araby*
12. *To Know Him Is To Love Him*
13. *Take Good Care Of My Baby*
14. *Memphis*
15. *Sure To Fall*

Cuts 1--15: All cuts are the same as those on **THE DECCA TAPES** (Circuit
4438, pic disc).
NOTES: This album is the same as **THE DECCA TAPES** picture disc (Circuit
4438), but is not a picture disc. It was released in a full--color, laminated
jacket. The back of the album jacket has "The Untold Story Of The Decca
Tapes." This is a false and funny look at what might have happened to
the Decca tapes.
SEE ALSO: **THE DECCAGONES; THE DECCA TAPES; THE DECCA TAPES.**

191   THE DECCA TAPES   Disc contains no label markings at all.   (LP)

1. *Like Dreamers Do*
2. *Money*
3. *Till There Was You*
4. *Sheik Of Araby*
5. *To Know Him Is To Love Him*
6. *Take Good Care Of My Baby*
7. *Memphis*
8. *Sure To Fall*
9. *Hello Little Girl*
10. *Three Cool Cats*
11. *Crying, Waiting, Hoping*
12. *Love Of The Loved*
13. *September In The Rain*
14. *Besame Mucho*
15. *Searchin'*

Cuts 1--15: All cuts the same as on **THE DECCA TAPES** (Circuit LK 4438),
except the sides have been switched.
NOTES: This is a picture disc, but a different picture has been used than the one
on the Circuit album. This one has a full--color picture on each side. Side
one shows the Beatles, John, Paul, George and Ringo, in the ocean. Side
two shows the four of them in "tank"--type swim suits. The Circuit disc was
the first to be released, this one came later.
SEE ALSO: **THE DECCAGONES; THE DECCA TAPES; THE DECCA TAPES.**

192   DIALOGUE FROM THE BEATLES' MOTION PICTURE "LET IT BE"
Beatles Promo--1970   (45)
NOTES: The original was released in May of 1970. This was booted in two colors
of vinyl, black and clear.
SEE ALSO: **LET IT BE -- DIALOGUE FROM THE BEATLES MOTION PICTURE.**

193   DISTRICT OF COLUMBIA   CBM 1100; CBM 3795   (LP)
NOTES: Same as **BEATLES LIVE IN WASHINGTON, D.C.**
SEE ALSO: **LIVE IN WASHINGTON, D.C.**

194   DISTRICT OF COLUMBIA   Unknown   (LP)

1. *Roll Over Beethoven*
2. *From Me To You*
3. *I Saw Her Standing There*
4. *This Boy*
5. *All My Loving*
6. *I Wanna Be Your Man*
7. *Please Please Me*
8. *Till There Was You*
9. *She Loves You*
10. *I Want To Hold Your Hand*

Cuts 1--10: From a live concert at the Washington, D.C. Coliseum on February 11, 1964.
SEE ALSO: **FIRST U.S. PERFORMANCE; FOUR YOUNG NOVICES.**

195   DR. ROBERT   Wizardo 378   (LP)

1. *I'm Only Sleeping*
2. *Dr. Robert*
3. *I'm Only Sleeping*
4. *Penny Lane*
5. *Blue Jay Way*
6. *Have You Heard The Word*
7. *What's Yer New Mary Jane*
8. *L.S. Bumblebee*
9. *Peace Of Mind*
10. *And Your Bird Can Sing*

Cuts 1--5, 10: Original recordings.
Cut 6: Recorded in June, 1970. This is supposed to be John Lennon and some of the Bee Gees. (For discussion, see footnote on pages xxiv-xxv.)
Cut 7: Recorded August 14, 1968. This was supposed to be released as Apple 1002, but it was never released.
Cut 8: Thought by many to be the Beatles, this song was actually done by Peter Cook and Dudley Moore.
Cut 9: The tape of this song was found in the Apple trash can.
NOTES: The originals were pressed on color vinyl.

196   DON'T PASS ME BY   CBM RI 3316   (2 LPs)

1. *Nothing Is Easy*
2. *Dig It*
3. *Christmas Record 1963*
4. *Christmas Record 1964*
5. *Christmas Record 1965*
6. *Christmas Record 1966*
7. *Christmas Record 1967*
8. *Christmas Record 1968*
9. *Christmas Record 1969*

10. *The Saints*
11. *Glad All Over*
12. *I Just Don't Understand*
13. *Slow Down*
14. *Please Don't Ever Change*
15. *A Shot Of Rhythm And Blues*
16. *I'm Sure To Fall*
17. *My Bonnie*
18. *I Got A Woman*
19. *Nothin' Shakin' But The Leaves On The Trees*
20. *Lonesome Tears In My Eyes*
21. *Everyone Loves Someone*
22. *I'm Gonna Sit Right Down And Cry Over You*
23. *Crying, Waiting, Hoping*
24. *To Know Her Is To Love Her*
25. *Bound By Love*

Cut 1: Jethro Tull, not the Beatles.
Cut 2: Recorded during the **LET IT BE** sessions early in 1969.
Cuts 3--9: Original fan club Christmas messages.
Cuts 10, 17: Original recordings.
Cuts 11--16, 18--25: Recorded from the BBC radio in November, 1962.
SEE ALSO: **AS SWEET AS YOU ARE; BEST OF BEATLES AND JETHRO**

TULL; COMPLETE CHRISTMAS COLLECTION; JUDY; YELLOW
MATTER CUSTARD (Shalom 3316C/3316D).

197   **DOUBLE ALBUM**   Unknown   (2 LPs)
      NOTES: Cuts unknown.

198   *DO YOU WANT TO KNOW A SECRET/THANK YOU GIRL*   Oldies 45 149   (45)
      NOTES: This is not an attempt to counterfeit the original Oldies 45 label. The
             label design and color here are different. This was pressed on orange vinyl.
      SEE ALSO: Listing under counterfeit section.

199   **DYLAN/BEATLES/STONES**   U 4089–92   (2 LPs)

1. *I Want To Hold Your Hand*
2. *Like A Rolling Stone*
3. *Satisfaction*
4. *She Loves You*
5. *Positively 4th Street*
6. *Get Off My Cloud*

7. *Love Me Do*
8. *Rainy Day Women*
9. *As Tears Go By*
10. *Help*
11. *Just Like A Woman*
12. *Paint It Black*

13. *Yesterday*
14. *Lay Lady Lay*
15. *Ruby Tuesday*
16. *Hey Jude*
17. *Times They Are A Changin'*
18. *Jumpin' Jack Flash*

19. *Get Back*
20. *Blowin' In The Wind*
21. *Honky Tonk Woman*
22. *Let It Be*
23. *Mr. Tambourine Man*
24. *19th Nervous Breakdown*

      Cuts 1, 4, 7, 10, 13, 16, 19, 22: All original recordings by the Beatles.
      Cuts 2, 5, 8, 11, 14, 17, 20, 23: All original recordings by Bob Dylan.
      Cuts 3, 6, 9. 12, 15, 18, 21, 24: All original recordings by the Rolling Stones.

200   **DYLAN/BEATLES/STONES**   IRC 741 AK/B–1   (LP)

1. *I Can't Be Satisfied*
2. *Stoned*
3. *Money*
4. *Wild Mountain Theme*
5. *It Ain't Me Babe*
6. *To Ramona*
7. *Let It Be*
8. *When You Walk*

9. *Teddy Boy*
10. *Long And Winding Road*
11. *Down In The Flood*
12. *You Ain't Going Nowhere*
13. *Million Dollar Bash*
14. *Midnight Rambler*

      Cuts 1–6, 11–14: All by Bob Dylan or the Rolling Stones, not the Beatles.
      Cuts 7–10: Recorded during the **LET IT BE** sessions at the Twickenham Studio
             in London early in 1969.

201   **EARLY BEATLES LIVE**   BE 1001   (LP)
      NOTES: Same as **BEATLES LIVE.**
      SEE ALSO: **DAWN OF OUR INNOCENCE; LIVE.**

202   **ED RUDY 1 -- TALK ALBUM**   LA Soot Records 346   (LP)
      NOTES: Same as original Ed Rudy interview album from 1964.
      SEE ALSO: **AMERICAN TOUR WITH ED RUDY 1964; ED RUDY VOL. I;
             1964 TALK ALBUM.**

203   **ED RUDY INTERVIEW VOL. I**   Wizardo 346   (LP)
      NOTES: Same as the original 1964 Ed Rudy interview album.
      SEE ALSO: **AMERICAN TOUR WITH ED RUDY 1964; ED RUDY I – TALK
             ALBUM; 1964 TALK ALBUM.**

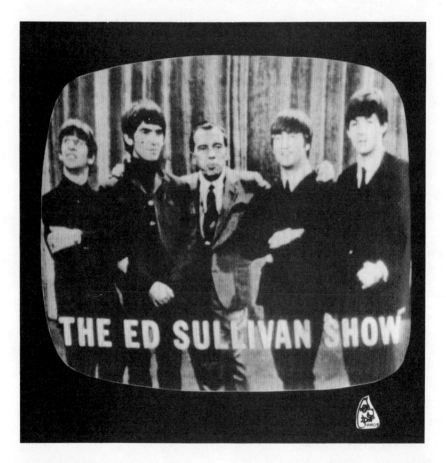

Ed's Really Big Beatle Blasts (LP)   **Melvin MM05 (Entry 205)**

204   ED RUDY INTERVIEW VOL. II   Wizardo 347   (LP)
NOTES: Same as the original Ed Rudy 1965 interview album.
SEE ALSO: **AMERICAN TOUR WITH ED RUDY 1964; 1965 TALK ALBUM.**

205   ED'S REALLY BIG BEATLE BLASTS   Melvin MM05   (LP)

1. *All My Loving*
2. *Till There Was You*
3. *She Loves You*
4. *I Saw Her Standing There*
5. *I Want To Hold Your Hand*
6. *She Loves You*
7. *This Boy*
8. *All My Loving*
9. *I Saw Her Standing There*
10. *From Me To You*
11. *I Want To Hold Your Hand*
12. *Twist And Shout*
13. *Please Please Me*
14. *I Want To Hold Your Hand*

Cuts 1–3, 7: From the "Ed Sullivan Show" of February 9, 1964.
Cuts 4–6, 10, 12–13: From the "Ed Sullivan Show" of February 16, 1964.
Cuts 8–9, 11, 14: Unknown.
NOTES: Also issued on pink vinyl.

206   ELVIS MEETS ... THE BEATLES   Best Seller Records ES--LP--50   (LP)

1. *My Way*
2. *One Sided Love Affair*
3. *I'm Counting On You*
4. *Blue Christmas*
5. *Can't Help Falling In Love*
6. *America*
7. *Long And Winding Road*
8. *My Bonnie*
9. *Money*
10. *Sweet Georgia Brown*
11. *You're Gonna Lose That Girl*
12. *Girl*

Cuts 1–6: Original recordings by Elvis Presley.
Cuts 7–12: Original recordings by the Beatles.

207   EMI OUTTAKES   TAKRL 1374; Phonygraf 1115   (LP)

1. *What A Shame Mary Jane Had A Pain At The Party*
2. *Penny Lane*
3. *Blue Jay Way*
4. *All My Loving*
5. *Sie Liebt Dich*
6. *Twist And Shout*
7. *Roll Over Beethoven*
8. *I Wanna Be Your Man*
9. *Long Tall Sally*
10. Medley:
   Love Me Do
   Please Please Me
   From Me To You
   She Loves You
   I Want To Hold Your Hand
11. *Can't Buy Me Love*

Cut 1: Recorded by John August 14, 1968. This was to have been released as Apple 1002.
Cut 2: Original DJ recording with the trumpet ending.
Cut 3: Studio outtake.
Cut 4: Original recording with hi--hat beginning.
Cut 5: Original recording.
Cuts 6–11: Recorded April 17–18, 1964, for Rediffusion TV show "Around The Beatles." The show aired May 6, 1964.

208   EUROPEAN CONCERT & U.S. TV CUTS   Unknown   (LP)

1. *Rock And Roll Music*
2. *Baby's In Black*
3. *Nowhere Man*
4. *Yesterday*
5. *Kansas City*

7. *Kansas City*
8. *Boys*
9. *I'm A Loser*
10. *Hey Jude*

Exclusive Beatles Interview (45)   **Beatles Interview 610 x 11 (Entry 209)**

5. *I Feel Fine*   11. *Revolution*
6. *I'm Down*

Cuts 1–6: Recorded at the Circus Krone in Munich, Germany, on June 24, 1966.
Cuts 7–9: Recorded October 9, 1964, at the Granville Theatre in London for
    later showing on "Shindig" (shown January 20, 1965).
Cut 10: From the British TV show "Frost On Sunday." Recorded September 4,
    1968 and shown September 8, 1968.
Cut 11: From the TV show "Top Of The Pops," September 19, 1968.
SEE ALSO: **LIVE GERMAN CONCERT & U.S. TELECASTS; LIVE IN
    EUROPE/U.S. TELECASTS; LIVE IN EUROPE/U.S. TV CASTS.**

209   **EXCLUSIVE BEATLES INTERVIEW**   Exclusive! Beatles Interview 610 x 11   (45)
    NOTES: Came with a black--and--white picture sleeve. The Beatles are interviewed
    on side one, while on side two there is an interview with the Dave Clark 5.
    They talk about the Beatles and other things.

210   **EXCLUSIVE! BEATLES INTERVIEWS 1966**   Exclusive Beatles Interview 66 x
    53A/66 x 53B   (45)
    NOTES: These interviews were done in Seattle during the American tour. A
    picture insert was included with this record.
    SEE ALSO: **INTERVIEWS; SEATTLE 66.**

211   **FAB FOUR**   M.A.K. S 1/2   (LP)

1. *Get Back*   7. *Don't Let Me Down*
2. *When You Walk*   8. *I've Got A Feeling*
3. *Let It Be*   9. *Long And Winding Road*
4. *One After 909*   10. *Dig It*
5. *Teddy Boy*   11. *For You Blue*
6. *Two Of Us*   12. *Dig A Pony*
                                  13. *Get Back Again*

Cuts 1–13: Recorded at Twickenham Studio, London in early 1969 during the
    LET IT BE sessions.
SEE ALSO: **KUM BACK** (M.A.K. S 1/2).

212   **FAB RAVER SHOW**   TMOQ   (LP)
    NOTES: Exact cuts unknown.

213   **FIRST U.S. PERFORMANCE**   RR 360; Wizardo 360   (LP)
    NOTES: Same as **DISTRICT OF COLUMBIA.**   (Unknown)
    SEE ALSO: **FIRST U.S. PERFORMANCE** (King Kong); **FOUR YOUNG
    NOVICES.**

214   **FIRST U.S. PERFORMANCE**   King Kong 1070   (LP)

1. *Roll Over Beethoven*   6. *I Wanna Be Your Man*
2. *From Me To You*   7. *Please Please Me*
3. *I Saw Her Standing There*   8. *Till There Was You*
4. *This Boy*   9. *She Loves You*
5. *All My Loving*   10. *I Want To Hold Your Hand*
                                  11. *Shout*

Cuts 1–10: Live concert at Washington, D.C. Coliseum on February 11, 1964.
Cut 11: Recorded April 27–28, 1964, for Rediffusion TV show "Around The
    Beatles." The show aired May 6, 1964.
NOTES: This album is the same as **FIRST U.S. PERFORMANCE** (RR 360;
    Wizardo 360), except for the addition of *Shout* at the end of side two.
SEE ALSO: **DISTRICT OF COLUMBIA; FOUR YOUNG NOVICES.**

215　**FIVE NIGHTS IN A JUDO ARENA**　CBM 1000　(LP)
　　　　NOTES: Cuts are unknown, but presumably from the Tokyo concert, July 2,
　　　　1966.

216　**FIVE NIGHTS IN A JUDO ARENA**　De Weintraub 426　(LP)

　　　1. *Rock And Roll Music*　　　　　7. *Yesterday*
　　　2. *She's A Woman*　　　　　　　　8. *I Wanna Be Your Man*
　　　3. *If I Needed Someone*　　　　　9. *Nowhere Man*
　　　4. *Day Tripper*　　　　　　　　10. *Paperback Writer*
　　　5. *Baby's In Black*　　　　　　11. *I'm Down*
　　　6. *I Feel Fine*

　　　Cuts 1--11: Recorded live at Budokan Hall, Tokyo, Japan, July 2, 1966.
　　　NOTES: Full--color laminated sleeve.
　　　SEE ALSO: **BEATLES ON STAGE IN JAPAN THE 1966 TOUR; BEATLES ON
　　　STAGE IN JAPAN 1966; FIVE NIGHTS IN A JUDO ARENA/SPICY
　　　BEATLES SONGS; LIVE AT THE JUDO ARENA** (picture disc).

217　**FIVE NIGHTS IN A JUDO ARENA/SPICY BEATLES SONGS**　FYG 7403　(LP)

　　　1. *Rock And Roll Music*　　　　12. *Have You Heard The Word*
　　　2. *She's A Woman*　　　　　　　13. *Don't Let Me Down*
　　　3. *If I Needed Someone*　　　　14. *Those Were The Days*
　　　4. *Day Tripper*　　　　　　　　15. *What's The New Maryjane*
　　　5. *Baby's In Black*　　　　　　16. *Cottonfields*
　　　6. *I Feel Fine*　　　　　　　　17. *Twist And Shout*
　　　7. *Yesterday*　　　　　　　　　18. *Dizzy Miss Lizzy*
　　　8. *I Wanna Be Your Man*　　　　19. *You Really Got A Hold On Me*
　　　9. *Nowhere Man*　　　　　　　　20. *Roll Over Beethoven*
　　10. *Paperback Writer*　　　　　　21. *All My Loving*
　　11. *I'm Down*　　　　　　　　　22. *I Want To Be Your Man*
　　　　　　　　　　　　　　　　　　23. *A Hard Day's Night*
　　　　　　　　　　　　　　　　　　24. *Things We Said Today*
　　　　　　　　　　　　　　　　　　25. *From Us To You*

　　　Cuts 1--11: Recorded live at the Budokan Hall in Tokyo, July 2, 1966.
　　　Cut 12: Recorded June, 1970. John and some of the Bee Gees are supposed to
　　　　have had a hand in this. (For discussion, see footnote on pages xxiv-xxv.)
　　　Cuts 13--14: From an interview in the fall of 1968.
　　　Cut 15: Recorded August 14, 1968. This was to have been Apple 1002, but it
　　　　was never released.
　　　Cut 16: From an interview with Kenny Everett in January,1968.
　　　Cuts 17--19: Live, unknown.
　　　Cuts 20--25: From various BBC radio shows from July and August, 1964.
　　　NOTES: European bootleg with a deluxe black--and--white cover.
　　　SEE ALSO: **FIVE NIGHTS IN A JUDO ARENA** (side one); **MARY JANE** (side
　　　two); **SPICY BEATLES SONGS** (side two).

218　**FOREST HILLS**　Wizardo?　(LP)

　　　1. *Ed Sullivan Introduction*　　　8. *Baby's In Black*
　　　2. *I Feel Fine*　　　　　　　　　9. *I Saw Her Standing There*
　　　3. *Dizzy Miss Lizzy*　　　　　　10. *From Me To You*
　　　4. *Lucille*　　　　　　　　　　11. *Money*
　　　5. *Help*　　　　　　　　　　　12. *Day Tripper*
　　　6. *Help*　　　　　　　　　　　13. *We Can Work It Out*
　　　7. *I'm Down*

　　　Cuts 1--7: Recorded from a radio broadcast on WBOX in September, 1965.
　　　Cuts 8--13: Unknown.

219 **FOREST HILLS/LONDON**   Shalom 4228/3687   (LP)

1. *Introduction*
2. *I Feel Fine*
3. *Dizzy Miss Lizzy*
4. *Lucille*
5. *Help*
6. *I'm Down*
7. *Baby's In Black*

8. *I Want To Hold Your Hand*
9. *This Boy*
10. *All My Loving*
11. *Money*
12. *Twist And Shout*

Cuts 1–7: Recorded from a radio broadcast on WBOX in September, 1965.
Cuts 8–12: From the TV show "Sunday Night At The London Palladium" which
was broadcast October 13, 1963.
SEE ALSO: **FOREST HILLS TENNIS STADIUM; LONDON PALLADIUM;
SUNDAY NIGHT AT THE LONDON PALLADIUM.**

220 **FOREST HILLS TENNIS STADIUM**   CBM 4228; King Kong 1058   (LP)

1. *Introduction*
2. *I Feel Fine*
3. *Dizzy Miss Lizzy*
4. *Lucille*
5. *Help*
6. *I'm Down*
7. *Baby's In Black*

8. *I Saw Her Standing There*
9. *From Me To You*
10. *Money*
11. *Day Tripper*
12. *We Can Work It Out*

Cuts 1–7: Recorded from a radio broadcast on WBOX in September, 1965.
Cuts 8–12: Unknown.
NOTES: Side one is the same as **FOREST HILLS/LONDON.**

221 **FOR THE LAST TIME**   Aftermath 10   (LP)

1. *Let It Be*
2. *Dizzy Miss Lizzy*
3. *Sie Liebt Dich*
4. *Honey Don't*
5. *I'm Sure To Fall*
6. *I Need You*
7. *For You Blue*

8. *Twist And Shout*
9. *You Can't Do That*
10. *All My Loving*
11. *If I Needed Someone*
12. *Day Tripper*
13. *She Loves You*
14. *Things We Said Today*
15. *Roll Over Beethoven*

Cuts 1–2, 4, 6–7: Unknown.
Cut 3: Original recording.
Cut 5: From a broadcast over the BBC radio in November, 1962.
Cuts 8–10, 13–15: Recorded live at the Hollywood Bowl, August 23, 1964.
Cuts 11–12: Recorded live in Tokyo at the Budokan Hall on July 2, 1966.

222 **14 UNRELEASED SONGS**   Dittolino Records 0001   (LP)
NOTES: Same as **AS SWEET AS YOU ARE.**
SEE ALSO: **DON'T PASS ME BY; JUDY.**

223 **FOUR YOUNG NOVICES**   Wizardo 361   (LP)
NOTES: Same as **DISTRICT OF COLUMBIA.**
SEE ALSO: **FIRST U.S. PERFORMANCE** (RR 360); **FIRST U.S. PERFOR–
MANCE** (King Kong).

224 **FROM THE BEGINNING**   Unknown   (LP)
NOTES: Same as **BATTLE.**

225 **FROM US TO YOU, A PARLOPHONE REHEARSAL SESSION**   Ruthless
Rhymes LMW–281F   (LP)

**From Us To You,
A Parlophone Rehearsal Session.**

From Us To You (LP)   Ruthless Rhymes LMW-281F (Entry 225)

1. *From Us To You* (Version 1)
2. *Kansas City*
3. *Long Tall Sally*
4. *If I Fell*
5. *Boys*
6. *I'm Happy Just To Dance With You* (Instrumental)
7. *I'm Happy Just To Dance With You* (Vocal)
8. *I Should Have Known Better* (False start)
9. *I Should Have Known Better* (Without Harmonica)
10. *I Should Have Known Better* (With Harmonica)
11. *Things We Said Today*
12. *A Hard Day's Night*
13. *From Us To You* (Version 2)

Cuts 1–13: All studio recordings.
NOTES: This is a ten–inch disc with a special cover. The records were pressed on various colors of vinyl, including green, orange, red (marbled with white/ purple), and yellow.

226   GET BACK   Amazon Etcetra 637; Lemon LRS 123   (LP)

1. *One After 909*
2. *When You Walk*
3. *Don't Let Me Down*
4. *Dig A Pony*
5. *I've Got A Feeling*
6. *Get Back*
7. *For You Blue*
8. *Teddy Boy*
9. *Two Of Us*
10. *Dig It*
11. *Let It Be*
12. *Long And Winding Road*
13. *Across The Universe*

Cuts 1–13: Recorded at Twickenham Studios in London early in 1969 during the **LET IT BE** sessions.
SEE ALSO: **GET BACK SESSIONS STEREO** (Pine Tree); **KUM BACK (ORIGINAL BOOTLEG "LET IT BE" ALBUM) STEREO.**

227   GET BACK   Wizardo 320   (LP)

1. *One After 909*
2. *The Walk*
3. *Don't Let Me Down*
4. *Dig A Pony*
5. *I've Got A Feeling*
6. *Get Back*
7. *For You Blue*
8. *Teddy Boy*
9. *Two Of Us*
10. *Dig It*
11. *Let It Be*
12. *Long And Winding Road*

Cuts 1–12: Recorded at the Twickenham Studios in London early in 1969 during the **LET IT BE** sessions.
SEE ALSO: **GET BACK SESSIONS STUDIO OUTTAKES.**

228   GET BACK   Unknown   (LP)

1. *Jam*
2. *Don't Let Me Down*
3. *I Dig A Pony*
4. *I Got A Feeling*
5. *Get Back*
6. *One After 909*
7. *For You Blue*
8. *Teddy Boy*
9. *Two Of Us*
10. *Maggie Mae*
11. *Dig It*
12. *Let It Be*
13. *Long And Winding Road*
14. *Get Back*

Cuts 1–14: Recorded during the **LET IT BE** sessions in early 1969 at London's Twickenham Studio.

229   GET BACK AND MORE   J.S.J. Records 1313   (LP)

1. *Get Back*
2. *When You Walk*
3. *Let It Be*
4. *On Our Way Home*
8. *Blah Blah Song*
9. *Across The Universe*
10. *Teddy Boy*
11. *Dig A Pony*

5. *Don't Let Me Down*
6. *I've Got A Feeling*
7. *Don't Keep Me Waiting*

Cuts 1–13: Recorded during the **LET IT BE** sessions early in 1969 at London's Twickenham Studio.

SEE ALSO: **J.S.J. PRESENTS GET BACK AND MORE.**

12. *Ballad Of John And Yoko*
13. *Across The Universe*

230   GET BACK SESSION   Michael & Allison Records; Dittolino Discs   (LP)

1. *One After 909*
2. *The Walk*
3. *Don't Let Me Down*
4. *Dig A Pony*
5. *I've Got A Feeling*
6. *Get Back*
7. *Get Back*
8. *Teddy Boy*
9. *On Our Way Home*
10. *All I Want Is You*
11. *For You Blue*
12. *Teddy Boy*
13. *Two Of Us*
14. *Dig It*
15. *Let It Be*
16. *Long And Winding Road*
17. *Across The Universe*
18. *Let It Be*
19. *Don't Let Me Down*
20. *Sunshine And Love Girl*
21. *Get Back*
22. *When You Walk*
23. *Christmas Message*

Cuts 1–17: Recorded during the **LET IT BE** sessions in early 1969 at London's Twickenham Studio.

Cuts 18–23: Listed on cover, but not on the album.

231   GET BACK SESSIONS   TMOQ BGB 111; TMOQ 71024; TMOQ 1801 A/B   (LP)

1. *One After 909*
2. *When You Walk*
3. *Don't Let Me Down*
4. *Dig A Pony*
5. *I've Got A Feeling*
6. *Get Back*
7. *For You Blue*
8. *Teddy Boy*
9. *Two Of Us*
10. *Dig It*
11. *Let It Be*
12. *Long And Winding Road*

Cuts 1–12: All recorded during the **LET IT BE** sessions early in 1969 at London's Twickenham Studio.

232   GET BACK SESSIONS ONE AND TWO   MARC   (2 LPs)

1. *One After 909*
2. *The Walk*
3. *Don't Let Me Down*
4. *Dig A Pony*
5. *I've Got A Feeling*
6. *Get Back*
7. *Get Back*
8. *Teddy Boy*
9. *On Our Way Home*
10. *All I Want Is You*
11. *For You Blue*
12. *Teddy Boy*
13. *Two Of Us*
14. *Dig It*
15. *Let It Be*
16. *Long And Winding Road*
17. *Across The Universe*

18. *Maxwell's Silver Hammer*
19. *Besame Mucho*
20. *Two Of Us*
21. *One After 909*
22. *Shake, Rattle and Roll*
23. *Get Back*
24. *Dig A Pony*
25. *Whole Lotta Shakin'*
26. *Suzie Parker*
27. *I Me Mine*
28. *Dig A Pony*
29. *Paul Talks*
30. *Let It Be*

Cuts 1–30: Recorded during the **LET IT BE** sessions in early 1969 at London's Twickenham Studio.
NOTES: Japanese bootleg.

233   GET BACK SESSIONS STEREO   Pine Tree Records S2131/2132   **(LP)**
NOTES: Same as **GET BACK** (Lemon 123).
SEE ALSO: **KUM BACK (ORIGINAL BOOTLEG "LET IT BE" ALBUM) STEREO.**

234   GET BACK SESSIONS STUDIO OUTTAKES   Wizardo 320   **(LP)**
NOTES: Same as **GET BACK** (Wizardo 320).

235   GET BACK SESSIONS 2   K&S 018   **(LP)**

1. *Maxwell's Silver Hammer*
2. *Maxwell's Silver Hammer*
3. *Besame Mucho*
4. *Two Of Us*
5. *One After 909*
6. *Shake, Rattle And Roll*
7. *Get Back*
8. *Dig A Pony*
9. *Whole Lotta Shakin'*
10. *Suzy Parker*
11. *I Me Mine*
12. *Dig A Pony*
13. *Paul Raps*
14. *Let It Be*

Cuts 1–14: Recorded at London's Twickenham Studio early in 1969 during the **LET IT BE** sessions.
NOTES: This is a re–issue of TMOQ 71068. It was pressed on green vinyl. The run was limited to 100 copies.

236   GET BACK SESSIONS VOL. 1   2102   **(LP)**

1. *One After 909*
2. *The Walk*
3. *Don't Let Me Down*
4. *I Dig A Pony*
5. *I've Got A Feeling*
6. *Get Back*
7. *For You Blue*
8. *Teddy Boy*
9. *Two Of Us*
10. *Dig It*
11. *Let It Be*
12. *The Long And Winding Road*
13. *Across The Universe*

Cuts 1–13: Recorded during the **LET IT BE** sessions early in 1969 at London's Twickenham Studio.

237   GET BACK SESSIONS VOL. 2   Amazon Etcetra 638; TMOQ BHB 118; TMOQ 71068; TMOQ 1892 A/B   **(LP)**

1. *Maxwell's Silver Hammer*
2. *Maxwell's Silver Hammer*
3. *Besame Mucho*
4. *Two Of Us*
5. *One After 909*
6. *Shake, Rattle And Roll*
7. *Get Back*
8. *Dig A Pony*
9. *Whole Lotta Shakin'*
10. *Suzy Parker*
11. *I Me Mine*
12. *Dig A Pony*
13. *Paul Raps*
14. *Let It Be*

Cuts 1--14: Recorded during the **LET IT BE** sessions at London's Twickenham Studio early in 1969.
SEE ALSO: **MORE GET BACK SESSIONS; VIRGIN AND THREE.**

238   GET BACK TO TORONTO   B.C. Records V36766   **(LP)**

1. *Peace Message*
2. *Get Back*
3. *Teddy Boy*
6. *I Got A Feeling*
7. *Don't Let Me Down*
8. *Sweet And Lovely Girl*

4. *On Our Way Home*
5. *All I Want Is You*
9. *When You Walk*
10. *Pantomima, Everywhere It's Christmas*

Cut 1: "War Is Over" interview with John and Yoko, December 15, 1969.
Cuts 2–9: Recorded at the Twickenham Studio in London during the **LET IT BE** sessions in early 1969.
Cut 10: Part of the 1966 Beatles Fan Club Christmas message.
SEE ALSO: **GET BACK TO TORONTO – HIGH STEREO RECORDING FROM JOHN AND YOKO.**

239 **GET BACK TO TORONTO**   CBM 209   (LP)

1. *Peace And Christmas Message From John And Yoko*
2. *Teddy Boy*
3. *Two Of Us*
4. *I Dig A Pony*
5. *I Got A Feeling*
6. *Let It Be*
7. *Don't Let Me Down*
8. *For You Blue*
9. *Get Back*
10. *The Walk*

Cut 1: "War Is Over" interview with John and Yoko, December 15, 1969.
Cuts 2–10: From the **LET IT BE** sessions recorded in early 1969 at the Twickenham Studio in London.

240 **GET BACK TO TORONTO**   I.P.F. 111; RP No. 23; CBM 3519   (LP)

1. *Let It Be*
2. *Christmas Message*
3. *Get Back*
4. *Teddy Boy*
5. *(Two Of Us) On Our Way Home*
6. *All I Want Is You*
7. *Get Back Again*
8. *I Got A Feeling*
9. *Don't Let Me Down*
10. *Sweet And Lovely Girl*
11. *When You Walk*
12. *Pantomima, Everywhere It's Christmas*

Cuts 1, 3–11: Recorded during the **LET IT BE** sessions early in 1969 at the Twickenham Studio in London.
Cut 2: "War Is Over" interview with John and Yoko, December 15, 1969.
Cut 12: Part of the 1966 Christmas Record from the Beatles to their fan club members.
SEE ALSO: **GET BACK TO TORONTO – STEREO** (CBM 3519).

241 **GET BACK TO TORONTO – HIGH STEREO RECORDING FROM JOHN AND YOKO**   Unknown   (LP)
NOTES: Same as **GET BACK TO TORONTO** (B.C. V36766).

242 **GET BACK TO TORONTO – STEREO**   I.P.F. – Glendale Records on CBM 3519 (LP)

1. *Peace Message*
2. *Get Back*
3. *Teddy Boy*
4. *On Our Way Back Home*
5. *All I Want Is You*
6. *I Got A Feeling*
7. *Let It Be*
8. *Don't Let Me Down*
9. *Sweet And Lovely Girl*
10. *When You Walk*
11. *Christmas Message*

Cut 1: "War Is Over" interview with John and Yoko, December 15, 1969.
Cuts 2–10: From the **LET IT BE** sessions recorded early in 1969 at the Twicken–ham Studio in London.
Cut 11: Part of the Beatles 1966 Fan Club Christmas record.
SEE ALSO: **GET BACK TO TORONTO** (CBM 3519).

243   GET BACK TO TORONTO – STEREO   Toronto Records LP 23 A/B   **(LP)**

1. *Peace Message*
2. *Get Back*
3. *Teddy Boy*
4. *On Our Way Home*
5. *All I Want Is You*
6. *I Got A Feeling*
7. *Let It Be*
8. *Don't Let Me Down*
9. *Sweet And Lovely Girl*
10. *Get Back*
11. *When You Walk*
12. *Christmas Message*

Cut 1: "War Is Over" interview with John and Yoko, December 15, 1969.
Cuts 2--11: From the **LET IT BE** sessions recorded at London's Twickenham
    Studio in early 1969.
Cut 12: Part of the 1966 Beatles Christmas record sent to fan club members.

244   GET 'CHER YEAH YEAHS OUT   Wizardo 316   **(2 LPs)**

1. *Twist And Shout*
2. *You Can't Do That*
3. *All My Loving*
4. *She Loves You*
5. *Things We Said Today*
6. *Roll Over Beethoven*
7. *Can't Buy Me Love*
8. *If I Fell*
9. *I Want To Hold Your Hand*
10. *Boys*
11. *A Hard Day's Night*
12. *Long Tall Sally*

13. *Rock And Roll Music*
14. *She's A Woman*
15. *If I Needed Someone*
16. *Day Tripper*
17. *Baby's In Black*
18. *I Feel Fine*
19. *Yesterday*
20. *I Wanna Be Your Man*
21. *Ain't She Sweet*
22. *P.S. I Love You*
23. *There's A Place*
24. *Misery*
25. *Dizzy Miss Lizzy*
26. *This Boy*
27. *From Me To You*
28. *Nowhere Man*
29. *Paperback Writer*
30. *I'm Down*

Cuts 1--12: Recorded live at the Hollywood Bowl August 23, 1964.
Cuts 13--20, 28–30: Recorded live in Tokyo at the Budokan Hall, July 2, 1966.
Cuts 21--27: Probably all originals.
SEE ALSO: **SP 602; VERY BEST OF THE BEATLES RAREST NO. 3** (sides
    three and four).

245   *GIRL/YOU'RE GONNA LOSE THAT GIRL*   Capitol 4506   **(45)**
NOTES: DJ copies of this record were mailed before Capitol decided not to re--
    lease it because it might interfere with the new McCartney release. The
    record was counterfeited, but a boot was also made. The boot was pressed
    on clear (with a gold tint) vinyl.

246   GOLDEN SLUMBERS   TMOQ   **(LP)**
NOTES: Exact cuts unknown.

247   GONE ARE THE DAYS   Unknown   **(LP)**
NOTES: Exact cuts and order of cuts are not known. However, it is known that
    the album contains cuts from the Royal Command Variety Show at the
    Prince of Wales Theatre November 4, 1963, *(From Me To You, She Loves
    You, Till There Was You, Twist And Shout)* and cuts from the BBC–TV
    show "Around The Beatles" which was recorded April 27--28, 1964 and
    broadcast May 6, 1964.

248   THE GOOD OLD DAYS   Shea S--2531   **(LP)**
NOTES: Exact cuts unknown. Possibly the same as **SHEA: THE GOOD OLD
    DAYS.**

Hahst Az Son (2 LPs)   **Phoenix 44784 (Entry 253)**

249 **GREATEST HITS BY JOHN, PAUL, GEORGE AND RINGO** FL 1178 (LP)

1. *Long Tall Sally*
2. *Sie Liebt Dich*
3. *Anna*
4. *Matchbox*
5. *You Really Got A Hold On Me*
6. *She's A Woman*
7. *Ask Me Why*
8. *I Feel Fine*
9. *Komm, Gib Mir Deine Hand*
10. *Chains*
11. *Slow Down*
12. *All I've Got To Do*
13. *I Call Your Name*
14. *This Boy*

Cuts 1–14: Original recordings.

250 **GREATEST HITS: COLLECTOR'S EDITION** Sunshine Music 501–4 (4 LPs)
NOTES: Same as **ALPHA OMEGA VOL. I.**
SEE ALSO: **BEATLES VOL. I; VOLUME ONE.**

251 **THE GREATEST SHOW ON EARTH** Eagle Records 1832 (LP)

1. *My Way* (with Frank Sinatra)
2. *Hurt* (with Timi Yuro)
3. *Sweet Caroline* (with Neil Diamond)
4. *You Don't Know Me* (with Bette Midler)
5. *Something* (with Beatles)
6. *Let Me Be There* (with Olivia Newton-John)
7. *Green Green Grass Of Home* (with Tom Jones)
8. *Bridge Over Troubled Water* (with Simon and Garfunkel)
9. *Shake A Hand* (with Little Richard)
10. *I Got Stung* (with Jonny Hallyday)
11. *You Gave Me A Mountain* (with Frankie Laine)
12. *Love Me Tender* (with Linda Ronstadt)

Cuts 1–12: All cuts are Elvis Presley records mixed together with the records of the performers mentioned after each cut. The mixing is bad and many of the duos are unintelligible.
NOTES: The LP was pressed on green vinyl.

252 **THE GREAT TAKEOVER** Wizardo 502 (LP)
NOTES: Same as **BEATLES TOUR -- THE GREAT TAKEOVER.**

253 **HAHST AZ SON** Phoenix 44784 (2 LPs)

1. *Two Of Us*
2. *Don't Let Me Down*
3. *When You Get To Suzy Parker Everybody Gets Well Done*
4. *I've Got A Feeling*
5. *No Pakistanis*
6. *Get Back*
7. *Be Bop A Lula*
8. *She Came In Through The Bathroom Window*
9. *High--Heeled Sneakers*
10. *I Me Mine*
11. *I've Got A Feeling*
12. *One After 909*
13. *Norwegian Wood*
14. *She Came In Through The Bathroom Window*

15. *Let It Be*
16. *Shakin' In The Sixties*
17. *Good Rockin' Tonight*
18. *Across The Universe*
19. *Two Of Us*
20. *Momma, You've Been On My Mind*
21. *Tennessee*
22. *House Of The Rising Sun*
23. *Back To Commonwealth*
24. *White Power/Promenade*
25. *Hi Ho Silver*
26. *For You Blue*
27. *Let It Be*

NOTES: Full–color laminated jacket. Full label information is given. Jacket says that it was manufactured by Phoenix Records, Sydney, Australia. This

looks like a legitimate release, but when you look at the run–off wax you can see TAKRL 2950, the original bootleg label and number.
SEE ALSO: **CAUGHT OFF GUARD; HAHST AZ SUN; HOT AS SUN; SWEET APPLE TRAX** (Newsound); **SWEET APPLE TRAX VOL. I** (Image Disc); **SWEET APPLE TRAX VOL. II** (Image Disc).

254   HAHST AZ SUN   TAKRL 2950   (2 LPs)

1. *Two Of Us*
2. *Don't Let Me Down*
3. *When You Get To Suzy Parker's Everybody Gets Well Done*
4. *I've Got A Feeling*
5. *No Pakistanis*
6. *Get Back*
7. *Don't Let Me Down (Reprise)*
8. *Practice And Stage Check*
9. *Be Bop A Lula*
10. *She Came In Through The Bathroom Window*
11. *High Heeled Sneakers*
12. *I Me Mine*
13. *I've Got A Feeling*
14. *One After 909*
15. *Norwegian Wood*
16. *She Came In Through The Bathroom Window*

17. *Let It Be (By The Numbers)*
18. *Shakin' In The Sixties*
19. *Good Rockin' Tonight*
20. *Across The Universe*
21. *Two Of Us*
22. *Momma You've Been On My Mind*
23. *Tennessee*
24. *House Of The Rising Sun*
25. *Back To Commonwealth*
26. *White Power Promenade*
27. *Hi Ho Silver*
28. *For You Blue*
29. *Let It Be*

Cuts 1–29: Recorded during the **LET IT BE** sessions at the London Twickenham Studio early in 1969.
NOTES: The album was re–issued in 1978 with a black–and–white deluxe laminated cover.
SEE ALSO: **CAUGHT OFF GUARD; HAHST AZ SON; HOT AS SUN; SWEET APPLE TRAX** (Newsound); **SWEET APPLE TRAX VOL. I** (Image Disc); **SWEET APPLE TRAX VOL. II** (Image Disc).

255   HAPPY BIRTHDAY   CBM TB 5030   (LP)

1. *Johnny B. Goode*
2. *Happy Birthday*
3. *You Really Got A Hold On Me*
4. *Memphis*
5. *This Boy*
6. *Twist And Shout*
7. *I Want To Hold Your Hand*
8. *Roll Over Beethoven*
9. *All My Loving*
10. *I Wanna Be Your Man*
11. *Tell Me Why*
12. *If I Fell*
13. *I Should Have Known Better*

Cuts 1–4: From the BBC radio show "Saturday Club," May 25, 1963.
Cuts 5–7: Recorded for the Granada TV show "Scene At 6:30." Shown August 19, 1963.
Cuts 8–10: From the BBC radio show "From Us To You," broadcast December 26, 1963.
Cuts 11–13: From the soundtrack of "A Hard Day's Night."
SEE ALSO: **BEATLES HAPPY BIRTHDAY; RARE BEATLES; RARE SESSIONS.**

256   HAPPY BIRTHDAY   Wizardo 345   (LP)

1. *Johnny B. Goode*
2. *Shout*
3. *Pop Goes The Beatles*
4. *You Really Got A Hold On Me*
12. *Murray The K 1964 Interview With: She Loves You, Shout*
13. *I'll Be On My Way*
14. *Soldier Of Love*

5. *Memphis*
6. *Happy Birthday*
7. *Some Other Guy*
8. *Lucille*
9. *Boys*
10. *Act Naturally*
11. *Shout No. 3*

Cuts 1, 4–6: From the BBC radio show "Saturday Club" broadcast May 25, 1963.

Cuts 2, 11: Unknown for sure, but could be from BBC radio shows in July and August, 1964 or from the Rediffusion TV show "Around The Beatles" which aired May 6, 1964. Could possibly be one from each source.

Cut 3: Theme from the Beatles' BBC radio series which ran for 15 weeks beginning June 4, 1963. Each show was 30 minutes long.

Cut 7: Recorded October 13, 1962, at the Cavern Club by Granada TV. The clip was later shown on the "People And Places" show on November 7, 1962.

Cut 8: BBC radio 1963.

Cuts 9–10: Unknown.

Cut 12: Original Murray The K interviews with all four Beatles. Also includes the songs *She Loves You* and *Shout*.

Cut 13: From a BBC radio broadcast in the fall of 1962.

Cut 14: 1963 outtake.

NOTES: Same as **HAPPY BIRTHDAY/SOLDIER OF LOVE** (Wizardo 345) except for title and song distribution.

257 **HAPPY BIRTHDAY/SOLDIER OF LOVE**   Wizardo 345   (LP)

1. *Johnny B. Goode*
2. *Shout*
3. *Pop Goes The Beatles*
4. *You Really Got A Hold On Me*
5. *Memphis*
6. *Happy Birthday*
7. *Some Other Guy*
8. *Lucille*
9. *Boys*
10. *Shout*
11. *Act Naturally*
12. *Murray The K Fan Club*
13. *I'll Be On My Way*
14. *Soldier Of Love*

NOTES: This is the same as **HAPPY BIRTHDAY** (Wizardo 345), except for song order and title.

258 **HARD DAY'S NIGHT SOUNDTRACK**   Wizardo 303 ABCD   (2 LPs)

NOTES: Same as **A HARD DAY'S NIGHT** (Wizardo 303).
SEE ALSO: **A HARD DAY'S NIGHT + SKINNIE MINNIE; COMPLETE SOUNDTRACK TO A HARD DAY'S NIGHT.**

259 **HAVE YOU HEARD THE WORD**   Amazon Etcetra 600   (LP)

NOTES: Exact cuts included here are unknown.

260 **HAVE YOU HEARD THE WORD**   Berkeley   (LP)

1. *Have You Heard The Word*
2. *Fut*
3. *I Forgot To Remember*
4. *Twist And Shout*
5. *Roll Over Beethoven*
6. *Long Tall Sally*
7. *Dizzy Miss Lizzy*
8. *Lucille*
9. *You Really Got A Hold On Me*
10. *Long And Winding Road*
11. *Boogie Piano*
12. *I Me Mine*
13. *Besame Mucho*
14. *Octopus's Garden*

Cuts 1–2: Recorded in June, 1970. John and a few of the Bee Gees are supposed to have been involved. (For discussion, see footnote on pages xxiv-xxv.)

Cut 3: From a BBC radio broadcast in November, 1962.

Cut 4: Recorded for the Swedish TV show "Drop In" on October 30, 1962. The show was aired November 3, 1962.

Cuts 5, 8: From a BBC broadcast from the summer of 1963.

Have You Heard The Word (LP)   **CBM WEC 3624 (Entry 262)**

Cut 6: Recorded August 1963 at the Top Ten Club in London.
Cut 7: Original recording.
Cuts 9–14: From the **LET IT BE** sessions held at Twickenham Studio in London, early in 1969.

261   HAVE YOU HEARD THE WORD   CBM 3620   (LP)

1. *Have You Heard The Word*
2. *You Really Got A Hold On Me*
3. *Long And Winding Road Cha Cha Cha*
4. *Two Of Us*
5. *Piano Boogie*
6. *I Me Mine*
7. *Besame Mucho*
8. *Octopusses' Garden*
9. *I Forgot To Remember*
10. *Twist And Shout*
11. *Long Tall Sally*
12. *From Us To You*
13. *Dizzy Miss Lizzy*
14. *Lucille*

Cut 1: Recorded in June, 1970. John and a few of the Bee Gees were supposed to have been involved. (For discussion, see footnote on pages xxiv-xxv.)
Cuts 2–8: From the **LET IT BE** sessions held at Twickenham Studio in early 1969.
Cut 9: From a BBC radio broadcast in November 1962.
Cut 10: Recorded for the Swedish TV show "Drop In" on October 30, 1963. The show aired November 3, 1963.
Cut 11: Recorded April 1963 at the Top Ten Club in London.
Cut 12: From a BBC radio broadcast in August of 1964.
Cut 13: Original recording.
Cut 14: From a BBC broadcast, November 1963.

262   HAVE YOU HEARD THE WORD   CBM WEC 3624; Kustom Records No. 002
       (LP)

1. *Have You Heard The Word*
2. *You Really Got A Hold On Me*
3. *The Long And Winding Road*
4. *Cha Cha Cha*
5. *Maxwell's Silver Hammer*
6. *Piano Boogie*
7. *Besame Mucho*
8. *Octopusses' Garden*
9. *I Me Mine*
10. *Don't Let Me Down*
11. *I Forgot To Remember To Forget Her*
12. *Twist And Shout*
13. *Roll Over Beethoven*
14. *Long Tall Sally*
15. *Dizzy Miss Lizzy*
16. *Lucille*

Cut 1: Recorded in June, 1970, supposedly by John and some members of the Bee Gees. (For discussion, see footnote on pages xxiv-xxv.)
Cuts 2–10: Recorded during the **LET IT BE** sessions in early 1969 at London's Twickenham Studio.
Cut 11: From a BBC radio broadcast in November of 1962.
Cut 12: Listed as being recorded at the Indra Club in 1962.
Cut 13: Listed as being recorded at the Kaiserkeller in 1962.
Cut 14: Recorded at the Top Ten Club in London in August, 1963.
Cut 15: Original recording.
Cut 16: From a BBC broadcast from the summer of 1963.
SEE ALSO: **BUMBLE WORDS – SUPER STUDIO SESSIONS NO. 3** (side two).

263   HAVE YOU HEARD THE WORD   SXTT–979   (LP)

1. *Have You Heard The Word*
2. *I Forgot To Remember*
3. *Twist And Shout*
4. *Roll Over Beethoven*
8. *You Really Got A Hold On Me*
9. *Long And Winding Road*
10. *Two Of Us*
11. *Piano Boogie*

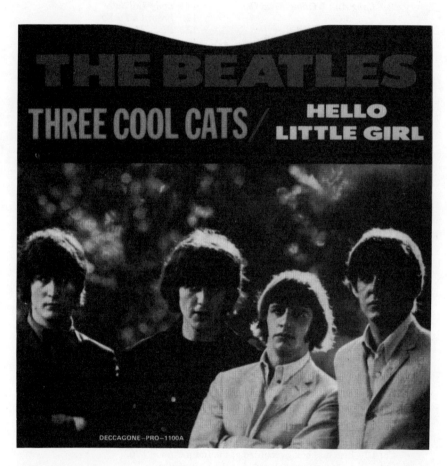

**Hello Little Girl/
Three Cool Cats (45)**   **Deccagone 1100 (Entry 266)**

Hello Little Girl/Three Cool Cats/
   Love Of The Loved/Memphis (EP)   Beacon 508 (Entry 269)

    5. *Long Tall Sally*   12. *I Me Mine*
    6. *Dizzy Miss Lizzy*   13. *Besame Mucho*
    7. *Lucille*   14. *Octopusses' Garden*

Cut 1: Recorded in June, 1970. John and a few of the Bee Gees are supposed to have been involved. (For discussion, see footnote on pages xxiv-xxv.)

Cut 2: From a BBC radio broadcast in November of 1962.

Cut 3: Recorded for the Swedish TV show "Drop In" on October 30, 1962. The show aired November 3, 1962.

Cuts 4, 7: From a BBC broadcast from the summer of 1963.

Cut 5: Recorded August 1963 at the Top Ten Club in London.

Cut 6: Original recording.

Cuts 8–14: From the **LET IT BE** sessions recorded in early 1969 at London's Twickenham Studios.

264   *HAVE YOU HEARD THE WORD/FUTTING AROUND*   Fut 160   (45)
       NOTES: Recorded June, 1970. John and at least some of the Bee Gees were supposedly involved. (For discussion, see footnote on pages xxiv-xxv.)

265   **HELLO–GOODBYE AMERICA TOUR**   TMOQ   (LP)
       NOTES: Exact cuts unknown.

266   *HELLO LITTLE GIRL/THREE COOL CATS*   Deccagone 1100   (45)
       NOTES: These are two cuts from the Decca sessions held January 1, 1962. This 45 was originally released by one of the Beatle fan clubs and came with a full–color picture sleeve. The originals were pressed on blue vinyl and had a purple label with silver printing.

267   *HELLO LITTLE GIRL/THREE COOL CATS*   Deccagone 1100   (45)
       NOTES: This is a counterfeit of the original Deccagone series issued by one of the Beatle fan clubs. The counterfeit also came with a picture sleeve and was pressed on blue vinyl. However, its label was green with black printing, unlike the originals.

268   *HELLO LITTLE GIRL/THREE COOL CATS*   Pye 106   (45)
       NOTES: Yet another copy of the Deccagone series singles. This was issued with a black--and--white picture sleeve.

269   **HELLO LITTLE GIRL/THREE COOL CATS/LOVE OF THE LOVED/MEMPHIS**
       Beacon 508   (EP)
       NOTES: From the Decca audition tapes, recorded January 1, 1962. This EP contains songs from the Deccagone series. Came with a full color picture sleeve which was printed by Queens Litho Graphing Corp., the same company who did picture sleeve for Capitol and Apple records.

270   **HELP: SOUNDTRACK**   Wizardo 317; Wizardo 102--202   (2 LPs)
       NOTES: Same as **CINELOGUE 4.**

271   **HELP: SOUNDTRACK AND '65 OUTTAKES**   Unknown   (2 LPs)
       NOTES: Exact cuts unknown.

272   **HEY JUDE & TOP OF THE POPS**   Unknown   (LP)

    1. *Hey Jude*   5. *A Hard Day's Night*
    2. *Revolution*   6. *Things We Said Today*
    3. *Long Tall Sally*   7. *Shout*
    4. *Interview*   8. *People Say*
                          9. *I'm Walking*

Cut 1: From the British TV show "Frost On Sunday." Show was recorded September 4, 1968 and broadcast September 8, 1968.

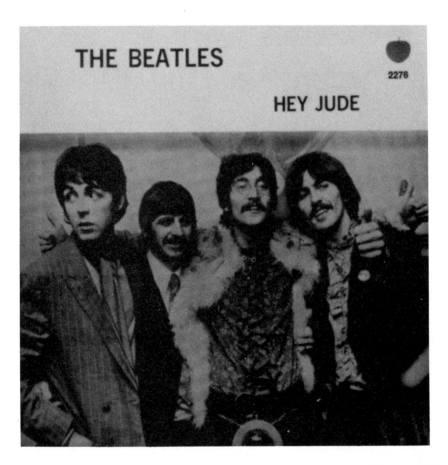

Hey Jude/Revolution (45)   **Apple 2276 (Entry 273)**

Cut 2: From the BBC–TV show "Top Of The Pops" which was broadcast September 19, 1968.

Cuts 3–6: From the BBC radio show "Brian Matthews Introduces" on "Top Of The Pops." Originally broadcast July 8, 1964.

Cut 7: From the Rediffusion TV show "Around The Beatles." Show was recorded April 27–28, 1964 and aired May 6, 1964.

Cuts 8–9: Not the Beatles. Thought by some to be by Pete Best or by the Nurk Twins.

273   *HEY JUDE/REVOLUTION*   Apple 2276   (45)
NOTES: This is a picture sleeve only. No picture sleeve was issued with the original single. The same picture appears on both sides of this two–tone (blue/yellow) sleeve.

274   **HEY JUDE WHITE**   Unknown   (LP)
NOTES: Exact cuts unknown, but probably all from the **LET IT BE** sessions.

275   **HI HO SILVER**   CBM 4438; CBM B201; Shalom 8410   (LP)

1. *Get Back*	9. *Hi Ho Silver*
2. *Tennessee Credit*	10. *Suzy Parker*
3. *House Of The Rising Sun*	11. *Pakistani Song*
4. *Commonwealth Song*	12. *Don't Let Me Down*
5. *Enoch Powell*	13. *I've Got A Feeling*
6. *White Power*	14. *For You Blue*
7. *Momma You've Been On My Mind*	15. *Everybody's Rockin' Tonight*
8. *Across The Universe*	16. *Two Of Us*
	17. *Let It Be*

Cuts 1–17: All cuts from the **LET IT BE** sessions held early in 1969 at the Twickenham Studio in London.
NOTES: Deluxe color cover.

276   **THE HISTORY OF SYRACUSE MUSIC VOLS. 8/9**   Unknown   (2 LPs)
NOTES: These two volumes contain various music and talk, plus the "Everson" interview of John and Yoko and an interview with Wings' drummer Joe English.

277   **HIT HEARD ROUND THE WORLD NO. 1**   Hit 001   (EP)

1. *Early Beatles, Appearances, Club Dates, Composing*	4. *Strawberry Fields Forever*
2. *Love Me Do*	
3. *Fool On The Hill*	

NOTES: This is a U.S. Army recruiting program. The interviewer is American Fred Robbins. He talks to Jimmy Sable of the BBC. This particular show was set to air September 30, 1968. This is the complete program, including the Army propaganda spots. Came with a special hard cover picture sleeve.

278   **HIT HEARD ROUND THE WORLD NO. 2**   Hit 002   (EP)

1. *Interview With John Lennon*	3. *Think* (Aretha Franklin)
2. *Beatle Music Montage*	

NOTES: This is a U.S. Army recruiting program. The host is Fred Robbins. His guest is Kenny Everett (BBC DJ). The show aired October 14, 1968. This is the complete show, including the Army recruiting spots. Came with a special hard cover picture sleeve.

279   HIT HEARD ROUND THE WORLD NO. 3   Hit 003   (EP)

1. *Hey Jude And Beatle Talk*
2. *House That Jack Built* (Aretha Franklin)
3. *Those Were The Days* (Mary Hopkin)

NOTES: This is a U.S. Army recruiting program. The host is Fred Robbins. His guest is Alan Freeman (radio Luxembourg). The show aired November 6, 1968. This is the complete show, including Army recruiting spots. Came with a special hard cover picture sleeve.

280   HIT HEARD ROUND THE WORLD NO. 4   Hit 004   (EP)

1. *Liverpool Accent*
2. *Apple Label*
3. *Sour Milk Sea* (Jackie Lomax)
4. *Thingumybob* (Black Dyke Mills Band)
5. *I Started A Joke* (Bee Gees)

NOTES: This is a U.S. Army recruiting program. The host is Fred Robbins. His guest is Kenny Everett. The show aired November 18, 1968. This is the complete show, including Army recruiting spots. Came with a special hard cover picture sleeve.

281   HIT HEARD ROUND THE WORLD NO. 5   Hit 005   (EP)

1. *Angel Of The Morning* (Merrilee Rush)
2. *Sour Milk Sea* (Jackie Lomax)
3. *Times Were* (Cats)

NOTES: This is a U.S. Army recruiting program. The host is Fred Robbins. His guest is Yon Van Vien (radio Veronica). The show aired November 21, 1968. This is the complete show, including all the Army recruiting spots. Came with a special hard cover picture sleeve.

282   *HIT HEARD ROUND THE WORLD NO. 6*   Hit 006   (45)

1. *Yellow Submarine LP & Music*
2. *Hey Bulldog*

NOTES: This is a U.S. Army recruiting program. The host is Fred Robbins. His guest is Kenny Everett. The show aired February 3, 1969. This is the complete show, including all Army recruiting spots. Came with a special hard cover picture sleeve.

283   HIT HEARD ROUND THE WORLD   Hit 007   (LP)

1. *Early Beatles, Appearances, Club Dates, Composing*
2. *Love Me Do*
3. *Fool On The Hill*
4. *Strawberry Fields Forever*
5. *Interview With John*
6. *Beatle Song Montage*
7. *Think* (Aretha Franklin)
8. *Hey Jude And Beatle Talk*
9. *House That Jack Built* (Aretha Franklin)
10. *Those Were The Days* (Mary Hopkin)
11. *Liverpool Accent*
12. *Apple Label*
13. *Sour Milk Sea* (Jackie Lomax)
14. *Thingumybob* (Black Dyke Mills Band)
15. *I Started A Joke* (Bee Gees)
16. *Angel Of The Morning* (Merrilee Rush)
17. *Sour Milk Sea* (Jackie Lomax)
18. *Times Were* (Cats)
19. *Yellow Submarine: LP & Movie*
20. *Hey Bulldog*

NOTES: The cuts on this LP are taken from six Army recruiting shows of the late 60's. Each show also appears on an EP or 45, also listed in this discography. See those listings for full details. This album lacks the Army recruiting spots. It came with a special sleeve.

284   HOLLAND/SWEDEN -- SUPER LIVE CONCERT SERIES 1   Shalom 8430A/
3795A   (LP)

1. *I Saw Her Standing There*
2. *From Me To You*
3. *Money*
4. *Roll Over Beethoven*
5. *You Really Got A Hold On Me*
6. *She Loves You*
7. *Twist And Shout*
8. *She Loves You*
9. *All My Loving*
10. *Twist And Shout*
11. *Roll Over Beethoven*
12. *Long Tall Sally*
13. *Can't Buy Me Love*

Cuts 1–7: From the Swedish TV show "Drop In." Recorded October 30, 1963
and aired November 3, 1963.
Cuts 8--13: From the Hollywood Bowl concert, August 23, 1964.
NOTES: This is obviously not Holland, but Hollywood.
SEE ALSO: **SUPER LIVE CONCERT SERIES VOL. I HOLLAND/SWEDEN;
SWEDEN 1963; SWEDEN; WASHINGTON; SWEDEN; WORLDWIDE.**

285   HOLLYWOOD BOWL   Berkeley   (LP)

1. *Twist And Shout*
2. *You Can't Do That*
3. *All My Loving*
4. *She Loves You*
5. *Things We Said Today*
6. *Roll Over Beethoven*
7. *Can't Buy Me Love*
8. *If I Fell*
9. *I Want To Hold Your Hand*
10. *Boys*
11. *A Hard Day's Night*
12. *Long Tall Sally*

Cuts 1–12: Recorded during the live concert at the Hollywood Bowl, August 23,
1964.

286   HOLLYWOOD BOWL 1964   TMOQ BHB 115   (LP)
NOTES: Exact cuts unknown. Possibly the same as **LIVE AT THE HOLLYWOOD
BOWL** (TMQ 115).

287   HOLLYWOOD BOWL '64   Wizardo, Dittolino   (LP)
NOTES: Same as **BACK IN 1964 AT THE HOLLYWOOD BOWL** (Lemon 143).
SEE ALSO: **BACK IN 1964 AT THE HOLLYWOOD BOWL** (CBM); **BEATLES
1964; LIVE AT HOLLYWOOD BOWL; LIVE AT THE HOLLYWOOD
BOWL; L.A.; LIVE AT SHEA; THE ONLY LIVE RECORDINGS** (Kustom);
THE ONLY LIVE RECORDINGS (Unknown); **THE SHEA STADIUM
CONCERT 1964; THE SHEA STADIUM "MORE OR LESS" STEREO;
SHEA: THE GOOD OLD DAYS** (Kustom); **SHEA: THE GOOD OLD
DAYS** (Pine Tree).

288   HOLLYWOOD BOWLS VOL. II   (Mushroom)   (LP)
NOTES: Exact cuts unknown.

289   HOT AS SUN   Instant Analysis 4216/4217   (2 LPs)

1. *Old Hillbilly Way*
2. *House Of The Rising Sun*
3. *Commonwealth Song*
4. *Get Off White Power*
5. *Winston, Richard, John*
6. *Yackety Yack*
7. *For You Blue*
8. *Let It Be*
9. *Get Back*
10. *Don't Let Me Down*
11. *On Our Way Home*
12. *Ba Ba Black Sheep*
13. *Encore*
14. *Suzy Parker*
15. *I Got A Feeling*
16. *No Pakistanis*

17. *Let It Be*
18. *Be Bop A Lula*
26. *A Long Road*
27. *Shakin' In The 60's*

How Do You Do It/Revolution (45)   SFF/SOK 21 (Entry 292)

19. *She Came In Through The
    Bathroom Window*
20. *Tuesday Speaking*
21. *High Heeled Sneakers*
22. *I Me Mine*
23. *One After 909*
24. *Norwegian Wood*
25. *She Came In Through The
    Bathroom Window*

28. *Everybody's Rockin'*
29. *Across The Universe*
30. *On Our Way Home*
31. *Momma You've Been On My
    Mind*
32. *Domino*

Cuts 1–32: All recorded at Twickenham Studio in London early in 1969 during
the **LET IT BE** sessions.
SEE ALSO: **CAUGHT OFF GUARD; HAHST AZ SON; HAHST AZ SUN;
SWEET APPLE TRAX** (Newsound); **SWEET APPLE TRAX VOL. I** (Image
Disc); **SWEET APPLE TRAX VOL. II** (Image Disc).

290   **HOW DO YOU DO IT**   Wizardo 381   (LP)

1. *Money*
2. *How Do You Do It*
3. *Misery*
4. *Love Of The Loved*
5. *Slow Down*
6. *Dizzy Miss Lizzy*
7. *I Got A Woman*

8. *Seattle Interviews*
9. *Revolution*

Cuts 1, 3–7: Unknown.
Cut 2: Recorded November 26, 1962. This was to have been a Beatle single, but
was never released.
Cut 8: Interviews from the Seattle concert in 1966.
Cut 9: From the BBC–TV show "Top Of The Pops" broadcast September 19,
1968.

291   *HOW DO YOU DO IT/KOMM, GIB MIR DEINE HAND*   Swan 4197   (45)
     NOTES: *How Do You Do It* was recorded by the Beatles November 26, 1962.
Komm, Gib Mir Deine Hand is the original recording. This single, on a fake
Swan label, was issued in 1977.

292   *HOW DO YOU DO IT/REVOLUTION*   SFF/SOK 21   (45)
     NOTES: *How Do You Do It* was recorded by the Beatles, November 26, 1962.
It was to have been the follow–up to *Love Me Do,* but that plan was scrapped
and it was never released. Side two is from the David Frost TV show in
September, 1968. This is the "doo whops" version. The single came with
a black–and–white picture sleeve and was released around the time
of the third annual Magical Mystery Tour Beatles' Convention in 1976.
The record came with an insert explaining the origins of *How Do You
Do It* and was issued in several colors of vinyl, including blue, green,
red, yellow, and clear.

293   **I APOLOGIZE**   Beat–L 008   (LP)
     NOTES: Recorded at a press conference at the Astor Tower in Chicago by Bill
Bender and Barney Sterling, this was originally released as a one–sided
album on Sterling 8895–6481. The album came with a deluxe black–and–
white cover. The interview was mainly John apologizing for his statement
that the Beatles were bigger than God, but the other three Beatles also join
in at the end. The boot came in a plain white sleeve and was two–sided.

294   **I FORGOT TO REMEMBER**   Unknown   (LP)

1. *I Forgot To Remember To Forget*
2. *Love Of The Loved*

11. *I Just Don't Understand*
12. *Slow Down*

Indian Rope Trick (LP)   **Beat 1 (Entry 297)**

Intervista Con I Beatles (45)   Apple DPR 108 (Entry 299)

3. *Lend Me Your Comb*	13. *Please Don't Ever Change*
4. *Carol*	14. *Ain't Nothing Shakin'*
5. *I Got A Woman*	15. *Lonesome Tears In My Eyes*
6. *A Shot Of Rhythm And Blues*	16. *Everyone Wants Someone*
7. *Hippy Hippy Shake*	17. *I'm Gonna Sit Right Down And*
8. *Lucille*	*Cry*
9. *I Got A Woman*	18. *Crying, Waiting, Hoping*
10. *Glad All Over*	19. *To Know Her Is To Love Her*
	20. *Bound By Love*

Cuts 1, 5–6, 9–20: From a BBC radio broadcast in November, 1962.
Cut 2: From the Decca audition sessions January 1, 1962.
Cuts 3–4: From a broadcast over Radio Luxembourg, January 18, 1963.
Cut 7: From the BBC radio in 1962.
Cut 8: From the BBC radio, 1962.

295 *I'M YOUR SINGER/MAXWELL'S SILVER HAMMER*   Beat–L 004   (45)
NOTES: These are the original recordings with comments by Alan Parsons, the
Beatles former engineer. These are taken from the DJ album **AUDIO GUIDE
TO THE ALAN PARSONS' PROJECT** (Arista SP 68) released in 1979.

296 **IN ATLANTA WHISKEY FLAT**   TMOQ ODP 79; TMOQ ODP 67–2/70418F;
TMOQ 1704; TMOQ 71007   (LP)
NOTES: See cuts and comments under **ALIVE AT LAST IN ATLANTA.**

297 **INDIAN ROPE TRICK**   Beat 1; Idle Mind 1162   (LP)

1. *Mein Bonnie*	9. *Fool On The Hill*
2. *I Love You Too*	10. *I Am The Walrus*
3. *It's Only Love*	11. *Watching Rainbows*
4. *Indian Rope Trick*	12. *Mean Mr. Mustard*
5. *Happy Birthday Mike Love*	13. *All Things Must Pass*
6. *Not Guilty*	14. *Cheese And Onions*
7. *Hey Bulldog*	15. *Oriental Nightfish*
8. *Savoy Truffle*	16. *The Pirate Song*

Cut 1: Original slow version from 1961.
Cut 2: The Fourmost.
Cut 3: 1965 outtake featuring John.
Cuts 4–5: Recorded March 15, 1968, in Rishikesh, India.
Cut 6: This is actually *Frenzy And Distortion* from **RAGA.**
Cuts 7–8: 1968 outtakes.
Cuts 9–10: 1967 demos.
Cut 11: From a 1969 studio jam.
Cut 12: 1969 outtake with an extra verse.
Cut 13: 1969 Beatle version of a George Harrison song.
Cut 14: Listed as a Lennon outtake, this is actually early Rutles.
Cut 15: A 1973 Paul and Linda demo.
Cut 16: Recorded in 1975, this George Harrison song is about his *My Sweet Lord*
law suit. From the Rutland Weekend Television Christmas Show. Written
by George and Eric Idle.
NOTES: **INDIAN ROPE TRICK** is also known as **SPIRITUAL REGENERATION.**

298 **INTERVIEWS**   Unknown   (45)
NOTES: Same as **EXCLUSIVE! BEATLES INTERVIEWS 1966.**
SEE ALSO: **SEATTLE 66.**

299 *INTERVISTA CON I BEATLES*   Apple DPR 108   (45)
NOTES: This seven–inch disc came with a picture sleeve. This is a copy of a
legitimate Italian Apple release. The interview is the 1968 Kenny Everett

interview with John doing *Cottonfields* and many other bits of songs are also included. The record was pressed on several colors of vinyl, including blue and green.

300   IN THE LAPS OF THE GODS AND THE HANDS OF THE BEATLES
Wizardo 325   (LP)

1. *Have You Heard The Word*
2. *Futting Around*
3. *Don't Bring Me Down*
4. *Those Were The Days*
5. *Cottonfields*
6. *Twist And Shout*
7. *Dizzy Miss Lizzy*
8. *You Really Got A Hold On Me*
9. *Roll Over Beethoven*
10. *All My Loving*
11. *I Wanna Be Your Man*
12. *Long Tall Sally*
13. *A Hard Day's Night*
14. *Things We Said Today*
15. *From Me To You*
16. *Hey Jude*

Cuts 1–2: Recorded in June, 1970. John and a few of the Bee Gees are supposed to have been involved in this recording. (For discussion, see footnote on pages xxiv-xxv.) *Futting Around* is an instrumental.
Cuts 3–4: From a press conference interview in the fall of 1968.
Cut 5: From a Kenny Everett interview from January, 1968.
Cuts 6–8: Unknown.
Cuts 9–11: From the BBC radio show "From Us To You," broadcast December 26, 1963.
Cuts 12–14: From the BBC radio show "Top Of The Pops" hosted by Brian Matthews. Show was broadcast July 8, 1964. Brian's interviews with the Beatles are also included, although not listed on the jacket.
Cut 15: Unknown.
Cut 16: From the David Frost Show. Song was recorded September 4, 1968, and the show aired September 8, 1968.

301   *INTRODUCING THE BEATLES/FROM ME TO YOU*   Swan S–4182–1   (45)
NOTES: In Mark Shipper's book, "Paperback Writer," he talks of this record. Although the book, and the record, were spoofs of the Beatles, someone obviously took it seriously enough to put out this bootleg. *Introducing The Beatles* consists of John, Paul, George and Ringo introducing themselves. Clips from various interview records are used to achieve this effect. *From Me To You* is the original recording.

302   I SHOULD HAVE KNOWN BETTER   Orfeh 276   (EP)

1. *I Should Have Known Better*
2. *Ringo* (Lorne Greene)
3. *Theme From Come September* (Dick Jacobs)
4. *The Villa* (No artist listed)

NOTES: This EP was released in 1964. No song writer or publisher credit is given on the label. This has to be one of the earliest, if not the earliest, Beatle bootleg to appear.

303   ITALY   Instant Analysis 4178   (LP)

1. *Boys*
2. *Do You Want To Know A Secret*
3. *All My Loving*
4. *Please Please Me*
5. *Misery*
6. *Twist And Shout*
7. *You Can't Do That*
8. *Twist And Shout*
9. *You Can't Do That*
10. *All My Loving*
11. *Can't Buy Me Love*

Cuts 1–7: Unknown, presumably studio originals.
Cuts 8–11: Recorded live in concert at the Paris Sports Palais on June 20, 1965.

NOTES: This LP was supposedly recorded live in Italy, but it consists mostly
of studio cuts.
SEE ALSO: **ITALY/PARIS** (side one); **LIVE IN ITALY**.

304   **ITALY/PARIS**   Shalom 4178A/3688A   (LP)

1. *Boys*
2. *Do You Want To Know A Secret*
3. *All My Loving*
4. *Please Please Me*
5. *Misery*
6. *Twist And Shout*
7. *You Can't Do That*

8. *Twist And Shout*
9. *She's A Woman*
10. *Ticket To Ride*
11. *Can't Buy Me Love*
12. *I'm A Loser*

Cuts 1–7: Unknown, but presumably studio originals.
Cuts 8–12: Recorded live in concert at the Paris Sports Palace on June 20, 1965.
SEE ALSO: **ITALY; LIVE AT THE PARIS OLYMPIA** (CBM); **LIVE AT THE
PARIS OLYMPIA** (Shalom); **LIVE AT THE PARIS OLYMPIA JANUARY
1964; LIVE IN ITALY; PARIS AGAIN**.

305   **JOHN, PAUL, GEORGE AND JIMMY**   Wizardo 501   (LP)

1. *I Wanna Be Your Man*
2. *All My Loving*
3. *She Loves You*
4. *Till There Was You*
5. *Roll Over Beethoven*
6. *Can't Buy Me Love*
7. *This Boy*

8. *Twist And Shout*
9. *She Loves You*
10. *All My Loving*
11. *Twist And Shout*
12. *Roll Over Beethoven*
13. *Long Tall Sally*
14. *Can't Buy Me Love*

Cuts 1, 6, 9–13: Unknown.
Cuts 2–5, 7–8, 14: Recorded live in Copenhagen, June 4, 1964, with Jimmy Nicol
replacing Ringo on the drums.
SEE ALSO: **THE BEATLES "JOHN, PAUL, GEORGE AND JIMMY" COPEN–
HAGEN '64; COPENHAGEN 1964**.

306   **J.S.J. PRESENTS GET BACK AND MORE**   J.S.J. 1313   (LP)
NOTES: Same as **GET BACK AND MORE** (J.S.J. 1313).

307   **JUDY**   Kustom Rekords ASC 003   (LP)

1. *Judy! Judy!*
2. *Lady Mother*
3. *Ballad*
4. *Rain*
5. *Brown Shoes*
6. *This Guy*

7. *All You Need*
8. *Inner Lightnin'*
9. *I'm An Opulent Man*
10. *I'm Laid*
11. *Copper Path*
12. *Raspberry Gardens*

NOTES: Has a special laminated cover. These are all original records. Cut 1 is
really *Hey Jude*, cut 2 is *Lady Madonna*, cut 3 is *Ballad Of John And Yoko*,
cut 5 is *Old Brown Shoe*, cut 6 is *This Boy*, cut 7 is *All You Need Is Love*,
cut 8 is *The Inner Light*, cut 9 is *Baby You're A Rich Man*, cut 10 is *I'm
Down*, cut 11 is *Penny Lane*, and cut 12 is *Strawberry Fields Forever*.

308   **JUDY**   Unknown   (LP)
NOTES: Same as **AS SWEET AS YOU ARE**, except *Till There Was You* and
Twist And Shout are added here.
SEE ALSO: **DON'T PASS ME BY; 14 UNRELEASED SONGS; YELLOW
MATTER CUSTARD** (Shalom); **YELLOW MATTER CUSTARD** (TMQ).

309 *KOMM GIB MIR DEINE HAND/SIE LIEBT DICH* Swan? (45)
NOTES: These are original recordings of the Beatles singing *I Want To Hold Your Hand* and *She Loves You* in German.

310 **KUM BACK** CBM No. 15 (LP)

1. *Get Back*	6. *Don't Let Me Down*
2. *The Walk*	7. *I've Got A Feeling*
3. *Let It Be*	8. *Long And Winding Road*
4. *Teddy Boy*	9. *For You Blue*
5. *Two Of Us*	10. *I Dig A Pony*

Cuts 1–10: From the **LET IT BE** sessions. Recorded at London's Twickenham Studio early in 1969.

311 **KUM BACK** KB 10 (LP)

1. *Get Back*	6. *Don't Let Me Down*
2. *Can It Walk*	7. *I've Got A Feeling*
3. *Let It Be*	8. *Sweet And Lovely Girl*
4. *Teddy Don't Worry*	9. *Who Knows*
5. *On Our Way Home*	10. *Tojo Was A Loner*

Cuts 1–10: From the **LET IT BE** sessions. Recorded early in 1969 at London's Twickenham Studio.
SEE ALSO: **KUM BACK – STEREO.**

312 **KUM BACK** Kum Back No. 1 (LP)

1. *Get Back*	7. *I've Got A Feeling*
2. *When You Walk*	8. *Long And Winding Road*
3. *Let It Be*	9. *For You Blue*
4. *Teddy Boy*	10. *Dig A Pony*
5. *Two Of Us*	11. *Get Back*
6. *Don't Let Me Down*	12. *Dig It*

Cuts 1–12: Recorded during the **LET IT BE** sessions held at London's Twickenham Studio early in 1969.

313 **KUM BACK** M.A.K. 5 S1/2 (LP)
NOTES: Same as **FAB FOUR** (M.A.K. S1/2).

314 **KUM BACK (ORIGINAL BOOTLEG "LET IT BE" ALBUM) STEREO** Unknown (LP)
NOTES: Same as **GET BACK** (Lemon 123).
SEE ALSO: **GET BACK SESSIONS STEREO** (Pine Tree).

315 **KUM BACK STEREO** CBM? (LP)

1. *Get Back*	5. *Don't Let Me Down*
2. *Let It Be*	6. *I've Got A Feeling*
3. *Teddy Boy*	7. *Long And Winding Road*
4. *Two Of Us*	8. *For You Blue*
	9. *Dig A Pony*

Cuts 1–9: Recorded early in 1969 at London's Twickenham Studio during the **LET IT BE** sessions.

316 **KUM BACK STEREO** KB 10 (LP)

1. *Get Back*	6. *Don't Let Me Down*
2. *Can He Walk*	7. *I've Got A Feeling*
3. *Let It Be*	8. *Long And Winding Road*

4. *Teddy Boy*   9. *For You Blue*
5. *Two Of Us*   10. *I Dig A Pony*
                                  11. *Get Back Medley*

Cuts 1–11: From the **LET IT BE** sessions. Recorded early in 1969 at London's Twickenham Studio.

SEE ALSO: **KUM BACK** (KB10).

---

317   THE LAST BEETLE RECORD   Wizardo 393   (LP)

1. *Do You Want To Know A Secret*   11. *Long Tall Sally*
2. *You Really Got A Hold On Me*   12. *Please Please Me*
3. *Hippy Hippy Shake*   13. *Honey Don't*
4. *Misery*   14. *Chains*
5. *Money*   15. *I Saw Her Standing There*
6. *Till There Was You*   16. *I'm Sure To Fall*
7. *From Me To You*   17. *Lucille*
8. *Roll Over Beethoven*   18. *Boys*
9. *Love Me Do*   19. *She Loves You*
10. *Kansas City*   20. *Words Of Love*

Cuts 1–2, 4–15, 17–20: Unknown, many are no doubt originals.
Cut 3: From a BBC radio broadcast in 1962.
Cut 16: From a BBC radio broadcast in November, 1962.
NOTES: This record was not released by the real Wizardo company, but by someone using their name and logo.

---

318   LAST LIVE SHOW   Dittolino Discs?   (LP)

1. *Twist And Shout*   7. *Can't Buy Me Love*
2. *You Can't Do That*   8. *If I Fell*
3. *All My Loving*   9. *I Want To Hold Your Hand*
4. *She Loves You*   10. *Boys*
5. *Things We Said Today*   11. *A Hard Day's Night*
6. *Roll Over Beethoven*   12. *Long Tall Sally*

Cuts 1–12: Recorded live at the Hollywood Bowl August 23, 1964.
NOTES: This was not the Beatles last live show.

---

319   LAST LIVE SHOW   TMOQ LL 5101; TMOQ 501; TMOQ 71012; TMOQ 1800;
                   Live Records 101   (LP)

1. *I'm Down*   8. *Act Naturally*
2. *Interview*   9. *Can't Buy Me Love*
3. *Introducing The Group*   10. *Baby's In Black*
4. *Twist And Shout*   11. *A Hard Day's Night*
5. *I Feel Fine*   12. *Help*
6. *Dizzy Miss Lizzy*   13. *I'm Down*
7. *Ticket To Ride*

Cuts 1–13: Live at Shea Stadium August 15, 1965.
NOTES: Issued on red vinyl.
SEE ALSO: **SHEA STADIUM.**

---

320   LAST LIVE SHOW (LIVE AT SHEA)   WCF 501   (LP)

1. *I'm Down*   8. *Baby's In Black*
2. *Twist And Shout*   9. *A Hard Day's Night*
3. *I Feel Fine*   10. *Help*
4. *Dizzy Miss Lizzy*   11. *I'm Down*
5. *Ticket To Ride*   12. *Introductions By Ed Sullivan And*
6. *Act Naturally*   *Murray The K*

7. *Can't Buy Me Love*   13. *Interviews With Brian Epstein*
                                              And The Beatles
Cuts 1–13: Live at Shea Stadium August 15, 1965.
NOTES: This was not really the Beatles' last live show.

321   L.B. IN TORONTO   Cumbat?   (LP)

1. *Get Back*   5. *I've Got A Feeling*
2. *Teddy Boy*   6. *Let It Be*
3. *Two Of Us*   7. *Don't Let Me Down*
4. *I Want You*   8. *Sweet And Lovely Girl*
                                     9. *Christmas Message*
Cuts 1–3, 5–8: Recorded early in 1969 at London's Twickenham Studio during
   the **LET IT BE** sessions.
Cut 4: Unknown.
Cut 9: Part of the Beatles 1964 Christmas record for their fan club members.

322   LET IT BE   Underground Sounds 101   (LP)

1. *I've Got A Feeling*   7. *Christmas Message*
2. *Let It Be*   8. *Teddy Boy*
3. *Don't Let Me Down*   9. *On Our Way Home*
4. *For You Blue*   10. *All I Want Is You*
5. *Get Back*   11. *Instant Karma*
6. *When You Walk*   12. *You Know My Name*
Cuts 1–6, 8–10: Recorded early in 1969 at London's Twickenham Studio during
   the **LET IT BE** sessions.
Cut 7: Part of the 1964 Beatles Christmas record to their fan club.
Cut 11: From the BBC TV show "Top Of The Pops" broadcast February 12,
   1970.
Cut 12: Original recording.

323   LET IT BE: BEFORE PHIL SPECTOR   Wizardo 315   (LP)
NOTES: Same as **A/B SINGLE ACETATE**.
SEE ALSO: **THE BEATLES LET IT BE; ORIGINAL "GET BACK" ACETATE;
   ORIGINAL STEREO ACETATE FOR LET IT BE (BEFORE PHIL
   SPECTOR).**

324   *LET IT BE – DIALOGUE FROM THE BEATLES MOTION PICTURE*
          Beatles Promo 1970   (45)
NOTES: Same as *DIALOGUE FROM THE BEATLES MOTION PICTURE –
   LET IT BE.*

325   LET IT BE – LIVE   Amazon Etcetra 659   (LP)

1. *Don't Let Me Down*   7. *Let It Be*
2. *Dig A Pony*   8. *Long And Winding Road*
3. *Get Back*   9. *One After 909*
4. *For You Blue*   10. *Dig A Pony*
5. *Two Of Us*   11. *Get Back*
6. *Dig It*
Cuts 1–11: Recorded early in 1969 during the **LET IT BE** sessions at London's
   Twickenham Studio.

326   LET IT BE LIVE   Berkeley 11; Silver Greatest Records LB 1   (LP)

1. *Don't Let Me Down*   6. *You Can Dig It*
2. *All I Want Is You*   7. *Let It Be*
3. *Get Back*   8. *Don't Keep Me Waiting*

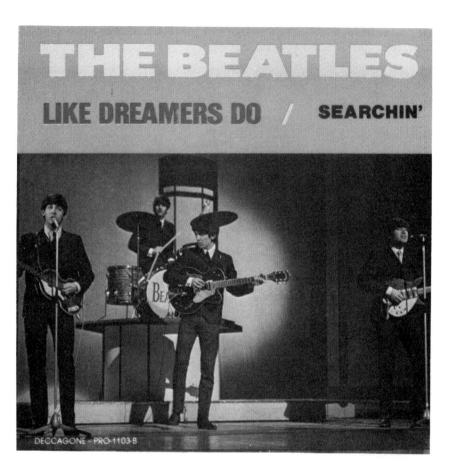

Like Dreamers Do/Searchin' (45)   Deccagone 1103 (Entry 330)

4. *For You Blue*   9. *One After 909*
5. *On Our Way Home*   10. *Across The Universe*
Cuts 1–10: Recorded during the **LET IT BE** sessions early in 1969 at London's
Twickenham Studio.
SEE ALSO: **LIVE ON SILVER.**

327 **THE "LET IT BE" PERFORMANCE**   Wizardo 315   (2 LPs)
     NOTES: Same as **COMPLETE "LET IT BE" SESSIONS.**

328 **LET IT BE: SOUNDTRACK**   Unknown   (2 LPs)
     NOTES: Exact cuts unknown, but presumably similar to **CINELOGUE: LET IT BE.**

329 **LET THEM BEATLES BE**   Unknown   (2 LPs)

     1. *Don't Let Me Down*   5. *Oh Darling*
     2. *Maxwell's Silver Hammer*   6. *One After 909*
     3. *Two Of Us*   7. *Across The Universe*
     4. *I've Got A Feeling*   8. *Dig A Pony*

      9. *Suzy Parker*   16. *Shake, Rattle And Roll*
     10. *I Me Mine*   17. *Lawdy Miss Clawdy*
     11. *For You Blue*   18. *Dig It*
     12. *Besame Mucho*   19. *Two Of Us*
     13. *Octopusses' Garden*   20. *Don't Let Me Down*
     14. *You Really Got A Hold On Me* 21. *Long And Winding Road*
     15. *Long And Winding Road*   22. *Some Other Guy*
     Cuts 1–22: From the **LET IT BE** sessions recorded early in 1969 at London's
     Twickenham Studio.

330 *LIKE DREAMERS DO/SEARCHIN'*   Deccagone 1103   (45)
     NOTES: This recording was originally released by one of the Beatle fan clubs.
     Both songs are from the Decca auditions, January 1, 1962. It was issued
     with a color picture sleeve. The originals were pressed on red vinyl. It
     was later copied.

331 *LIKE DREAMERS DO/SEARCHIN'*   Deccagone 1103   (45)
     NOTES: This is a copy of the original which was released by the Beatle fan club
     mentioned above. Like the original, it came with a color picture
     sleeve. This one was pressed on blue vinyl, not red like the originals. The
     label was also pink, not orange like the originals.

332 *LIKE DREAMERS DO/SEARCHIN'*   Pye 306   (45)
     NOTES: Yet another copy of the original Deccagone single released by the Beatle
     fan club above. This one came with a black-and-white picture sleeve.

333 **LIVE**   BE 1001   (LP)
     NOTES: Same as **BEATLES LIVE.**
     SEE ALSO: **DAWN OF OUR INNOCENCE; EARLY BEATLES LIVE.**

334 **LIVE AT A.B.C. MANCHESTER**   Wizardo 360   (LP)
     NOTES: Same as **BEATLES LIVE AT A.B.C. MANCHESTER.**
     SEE ALSO: **A.B.C. MANCHESTER 1964.**

335 **LIVE AT HOLLYWOOD BOWL**   CBM 1103; Mushroom 4; TMOQ 1704   (LP)
     NOTES: See cuts and comments under **ALIVE AT LAST IN ATLANTA.**

Live At Sam Houston Colosseum (2 LPs)   **Audifon BVP 006 (Entry 339)**

336   **LIVE AT HOLLYWOOD BOWL**   TMOQ 71065   (LP)
NOTES: Same as **BACK IN 1964 AT THE HOLLYWOOD BOWL** (CBM).
SEE ALSO: **BACK IN 1964 AT THE HOLLYWOOD BOWL** (Lemon);
    **BEATLES 1964; LIVE AT HOLLYWOOD BOWL; LIVE AT THE
    HOLLYWOOD BOWL; L.A.; LIVE AT SHEA; THE ONLY LIVE
    RECORDINGS** (Kustom); **THE ONLY LIVE RECORDINGS** (Unknown);
    **HOLLYWOOD BOWL 1964; THE SHEA STADIUM CONCERT 1964;
    THE SHEA STADIUM "MORE OR LESS" STEREO; SHEA: THE GOOD
    OLD DAYS** (Kustom); **SHEA: THE GOOD OLD DAYS** (Pine Tree).

337   **LIVE AT NASSAU COLLOSEUM**   CBM 2999; Zapple Records 999   (LP)

1. *People Say*	7. *Interview*
2. *I'm Walking*	8. *A Hard Day's Night*
3. *Hey Jude*	9. *Things We Said Today*
4. *Revolution*	10. *Shout*
5. *Happy Christmas Song*	11. *Everywhere It's Christmas*
6. *Long Tall Sally*	12. *Christmas Time Is Here Again*
	13. *Sie Liebt Dich*

Cuts 1–2: Not the Beatles. Original label says John and Paul. Thought by some
    to be by the Nurk Twins or Pete Best.
Cut 3: Shown on the David Frost TV show on September 8, 1968. This was
    recorded for that show on September 4, 1968.
Cut 4: Shown on the British TV show, "Top Of The Pops" September 19, 1968.
Cut 5: From the 1969 Christmas record issued to fan club members.
Cuts 6–9: From the BBC radio show "Top Of The Pops" with Brian Matthews.
    Aired July 8, 1964.
Cut 10: Unknown.
Cut 11: From the 1966 Christmas record issued to fan club members.
Cut 12: From the Beatles 1967 Christmas record issued to fan club members.
Cut 13: Original recording.
SEE ALSO: **LIVE FROM GERMANY; LIVE IN GERMANY.**

338   **LIVE AT SAM HOUSTON COLISEUM**   Tobe–Milo 5Q 1/2   (EP)

1. *Introduction*	3. *Ticket To Ryde*
2. *Dizzy Miss Lizzy*	4. *New York Telephone Commercial*
	(Phony)

NOTES: Same as **BEATLES LIVE IN HOUSTON.**

339   **LIVE AT SAM HOUSTON COLOSSEUM**   Audifon BVP 006   (2 LPs)

1. *Twist And Shout*	7. *Can't Buy Me Love*
2. *She's A Woman*	8. *Baby's In Black*
3. *I Feel Fine*	9. *I Wanna Be Your Man*
4. *Dizzy Miss Lizzy*	10. *A Hard Day's Night*
5. *Ticket To Ride*	11. *Help*
6. *Everybody's Trying To Be My Baby*	12. *I'm Down*
13. *Twist And Shout*	19. *Can't Buy Me Love*
14. *She's A Woman*	20. *Baby's In Black*
15. *I Feel Fine*	21. *I Wanna Be Your Man*
16. *Dizzy Miss Lizzy*	22. *A Hard Day's Night*
17. *Ticket To Ride*	23. *Help*
18. *Everybody's Trying To Be My Baby*	24. *I'm Down*

Cuts 1–12: Recorded at the Sam Houston Colosseum August 19, 1965, during
    the afternoon show.
Cuts 13–24: Recorded at the Sam Houston Colosseum August 19, 1965, during
    the evening show.

NOTES: Deluxe, laminated color cover showing an alternate take of the "butcher" picture.

340   LIVE AT SAN FRANCISCO CANDLESTICK PARK   Unknown   (LP)

1. *Rock And Roll Music*
2. *She's A Woman*
3. *If I Needed Someone*
4. *Day Tripper*
5. *Baby's In Black*
6. *I Feel Fine*
7. *Yesterday*
8. *I Wanna Be Your Man*
9. *Nowhere Man*
10. *Paperback Writer*
11. *I'm Down*

Cuts 1–11: Recorded live in concert at Candlestick Park August 29, 1966. Recorded by Tony Barrow.

341   LIVE AT SHEA   Figa   (LP)
NOTES: Same as **BACK IN 1964 AT THE HOLLYWOOD BOWL** (Lemon 143). SEE ALSO: **BACK IN 1964 AT THE HOLLYWOOD BOWL** (CBM); **BEATLES 1964; HOLLYWOOD BOWL '64; LIVE AT HOLLYWOOD BOWL; LIVE AT THE HOLLYWOOD BOWL; L.A.; THE ONLY LIVE RECORDINGS** (Kustom); **THE ONLY LIVE RECORDINGS** (Unknown); **THE SHEA STADIUM CONCERT 1964; THE SHEA STADIUM "MORE OR LESS" STEREO; SHEA: THE GOOD OLD DAYS** (Kustom); **SHEA: THE GOOD OLD DAYS** (Pine Tree).

342   LIVE AT SHEA, 1964   Unknown   (2 EPs)

1. *Twist And Shout*
2. *You Can't Do That*
3. *All My Loving*
4. *She Loves You*
5. *Things We Said Today*
6. *Roll Over Beethoven*

7. *Can't Buy Me Love*
8. *If I Fell*
9. *I Want To Hold Your Hand*
10. *Boys*
11. *A Hard Day's Night*
12. *Long Tall Sally*

Cuts 1–12: Recorded at the Hollywood Bowl Concert August 23, 1964.

343   LIVE AT SHEA 1964 1   1A/1B   (EP)

1. *Twist And Shout*
2. *You Can't Do That*
3. *All My Loving*
4. *She Loves You*
5. *Things We Said Today*
6. *Roll Over Beethoven*

Cuts 1–6: Recorded live at the Hollywood Bowl August 23, 1964.
NOTES: This European EP was released with a picture sleeve.

344   LIVE AT SHEA 1964 2   2A/2B   (EP)

1. *Can't Buy Me Love*
2. *If I Fell*
3. *I Want To Hold Your Hand*
4. *Boys*
5. *A Hard Day's Night*
6. *Long Tall Sally*

Cuts 1–6: Recorded live at the Hollywood Bowl August 23, 1964.
NOTES: This European EP was released with a picture sleeve.

345   LIVE AT SHEA STADIUM   Benbecula Records P24 2813   (LP)
NOTES: Same as **BEATLES LIVE AT SHEA STADIUM**.

346   LIVE AT SHEA STADIUM   Berkeley 01   (LP)

1. *I'm Down*
2. *Interviews*
3. *Twist And Shout*
7. *Act Naturally*
8. *Can't Buy Me Love*
9. *Baby's In Black*

Live At The Judo Arena (LP)   **Image Disc 2043/526 (Entry 351)**

4. *I Feel Fine*   10. *A Hard Day's Night*
5. *Dizzy Miss Lizzy*   11. *Help*
6. *Ticket To Ride*   12. *I'm Down*

Cuts 1--12: Recorded August 15, 1965, at Shea Stadium.

347   **LIVE AT SHEA STADIUM 1964**   Unknown   (LP)

1. *Twist And Shout*   7. *Can't Buy Me Love*
2. *You Can't Do That*   8. *A Hard Day's Night*
3. *All My Loving*   9. *Long Tall Sally*
4. *She Loves You*   10. *Please Don't Bring That Banjo*
5. *Things We Said Today*   *Back*
6. *Roll Over Beethoven*   11. *Everywhere It's Christmas*
                                    12. *What's The News Mary Jane*

Cuts 1--9: Recorded live at the Hollywood Bowl August 23, 1965.
Cuts 10--11: From the 1966 Beatles Christmas record to their fan club members.
Cut 12: Recorded by John August 14, 1968, this was to have been released by
       Apple but it never was.

348   **LIVE AT THE ATLANTA WHISKEY FLAT**   CBM 1001; TMOQ OPD 67--2/70418F;
          TMOQ OPD 19; TMOQ 71007; Amazon Etcetera 619   (LP)
          NOTES: See cuts and comments under **ALIVE AT LAST IN ATLANTA.**

349   **LIVE AT THE HOLLYWOOD BOWL**   TMOQ 115   (LP)
          NOTES: Same as **HOLLYWOOD BOWL 1964** (TMQ 115).

350   **LIVE AT THE HOLLYWOOD BOWL, LOS ANGELES**   Unknown   (LP)
          NOTES: Same as **BACK IN 1964 AT THE HOLLYWOOD BOWL** (Lemon 143).
          SEE ALSO: **BACK IN 1964 AT THE HOLLYWOOD BOWL** (CBM); **BEATLES
          1964; HOLLYWOOD BOWL 1964; LIVE AT HOLLYWOOD BOWL; LIVE
          AT SHEA; THE ONLY LIVE RECORDINGS** (Kustom); **THE ONLY LIVE
          RECORDINGS** (Unknown); **THE SHEA STADIUM CONCERT 1964; THE
          SHEA STADIUM "MORE OR LESS" STEREO; SHEA: THE GOOD OLD
          DAYS** (Kustom); **SHEA: THE GOOD OLD DAYS** (Pine Tree).

351   **LIVE AT THE JUDO ARENA**   Image Disc Inc. 2043/526   (LP)

1. *Rock And Roll Music*   7. *Yesterday*
2. *She's A Woman*   8. *I Wanna Be Your Man*
3. *If I Needed Someone*   9. *Nowhere Man*
4. *Day Tripper*   10. *Paperback Writer*
5. *Baby's In Black*   11. *I'm Down*
6. *I Feel Fine*

Cuts 1--11: Recorded at the Budokan Hall concert in Tokyo, July 2, 1966.
NOTES: This is a picture record with photos from the Japanese concert. It was
       pressed from De Weintraub (**FIVE NIGHTS IN A JUDO ARENA**) masters.
       Only 1000 were pressed. The record was produced by Monique Corriveau
       and designed by Michel Vermeer.

352   **LIVE AT THE PARIS OLYMPIA**   Shalom 3688   (LP)

1. *I Feel Fine*   7. *I Wanna Be Your Man*
2. *Twist And Shout*   8. *A Hard Day's Night*
3. *She's A Woman*   9. *Baby's In Black*
4. *Ticket To Ride*   10. *Rock And Roll Music*
5. *Can't Buy Me Love*   11. *Everybody's Trying To Be My*
6. *I'm A Loser*   *Baby*
                                   12. *Long Tall Sally*

Cuts 1–12: Recorded live at the Palais de Sports, Paris, June 20, 1965.
SEE ALSO: **LIVE AT THE PARIS OLYMPIA** (CBM); **LIVE AT THE PARIS OLYMPIA JAN. 1964; PARIS AGAIN.**

353   **LIVE AT THE PARIS OLYMPIA**   CBM 3688   (LP)

1. *Twist And Shout*
2. *She's A Woman*
3. *Ticket To Ride*
4. *Can't Buy Me Love*
5. *I'm A Loser*
6. *I Wanna Be Your Man*
7. *A Hard Day's Night*
8. *Baby's In Black*
9. *Rock And Roll Music*
10. *Everybody's Trying To Be My Baby*
11. *Long Tall Sally*

Cuts 1–11: Recorded live at the Palais de Sports, Paris, June 20, 1965.
SEE ALSO: **LIVE AT THE PARIS OLYMPIA** (Shalom); **LIVE AT THE PARIS OLYMPIA JAN. 1964; PARIS AGAIN.**

354   **LIVE AT THE PARIS OLYMPIA JANUARY 1964**   Shalom Records on CBM WEC
            3688   (LP)
         NOTES: Same as **LIVE AT THE PARIS OLYMPIA** (CBM 3688).
         SEE ALSO: **LIVE AT THE PARIS OLYMPIA** (Shalom); **PARIS AGAIN.**

355   **LIVE CONCERT ATLANTA**   CBM 3552   (LP)
         NOTES: See cuts and comments under **ALIVE AT LAST IN ATLANTA.**

356   **LIVE CONCERT ATLANTA, GEORGIA**   CBM 3552   (LP)
         NOTES: See cuts and comments under **ALIVE AT LAST IN ATLANTA.**

357   **LIVE CONCERT AT WHISKEY FLATS**   Lemon 510A; WCF 510   (LP)
         NOTES: See cuts and comments under **ALIVE AT LAST IN ATLANTA.**

358   **LIVE FROM GERMANY**   CBM 2999   (LP)
         NOTES: Same as **LIVE AT NASSAU COLOSEUM.**
         SEE ALSO: **LIVE IN GERMANY.**

359   **LIVE GERMAN CONCERT AND U.S. TELECASTS**   CBM 1002   (LP)
         NOTES: Same as **EUROPEAN CONCERT AND U.S. TV CUTS.**
         SEE ALSO: **LIVE IN EUROPE/U.S. TELECASTS; LIVE IN EUROPE/U.S. TV CASTS.**

360   **LIVE IN ANYTOWN**   Highway Records High Fi HHCER 110 (a TMOQ label)
            (LP)

1. *Twist And Shout*
2. *You Can't Do That*
3. *All My Loving*
4. *If I Needed Someone*
5. *Day Tripper*
6. *She Loves You*
7. *Things We Said Today*
8. *Roll Over Beethoven*
9. *Can't Buy Me Love*
10. *If I Fell*
11. *I Want To Hold Your Hand*
12. *Boys*
13. *Yesterday*
14. *Nowhere Man*
15. *Paperback Writer*
16. *A Hard Day's Night*
17. *Long Tall Sally*

Cuts 4–5, 13–15: Recorded live at the Budokan Hall in Tokyo, July 2, 1966.
Cuts 1–3, 6–12, 16–17: Recorded live at the Hollywood Bowl, August 23, 1964.

361   **LIVE IN ATLANTA WHISKEY FLAT**   TMOQ S–201; TMOQ 70417/70418;
            Whiskey 510 A/B   (LP)
         NOTES: See cuts and comments under **ALIVE AT LAST IN ATLANTA.**

362   LIVE IN AUSTRALIA AND WASHINGTON   Wizardo 314   (LP)

1. *I Saw Her Standing There* (two versions)
2. *You Can't Do That*
3. *All My Loving* (two versions)
4. *She Loves You* (two versions)
5. *Till There Was You* (two versions)
6. *Roll Over Beethoven* (two versions)
7. *Can't Buy Me Love* (two versions)
8. *This Boy* (two versions)
9. *From Me To You*
10. *I Wanna Be Your Man*
11. *Please Please Me*
12. *I Want To Hold Your Hand*

Cuts 1–12: All cuts are from either the Washington, DC concert of February 11, 1964, or the Melbourne, Australia, concert of June 15, 1964. Where two versions of a particular song are listed, there is one from each concert.
SEE ALSO: **ON STAGE IN MELBOURNE; AUSTRALIA AND WASHINGTON, D.C.**

363   LIVE IN EUROPE   Unknown   (LP)
NOTES: Exact cuts unknown.

364   LIVE IN EUROPE/U.S. TV CASTS   CBM 3571   (LP)
NOTES: Same as **EUROPEAN CONCERT AND U.S. TV CUTS.**
SEE ALSO: **LIVE GERMAN CONCERT AND U.S. TELECASTS; LIVE IN EUROPE/U.S. TELECASTS.**

365   LIVE IN GERMANY   CBM 2999; Zapple Records 999   (LP)
NOTES: This album is the same as **LIVE AT NASSAU COLLOSEUM** (CBM 2999; Zapple Records 999) except for the title.
SEE ALSO: **LIVE FROM GERMANY.**

366   LIVE IN GERMANY   MARC 75112   (EP)

1. *Rock And Roll Music*
2. *I Feel Fine*
3. *Yesterday*
4. *Nowhere Man*
5. *I'm Down*

Cuts 1–5: Recorded live at the Circus Krone in Munich, Germany on June 24, 1966.
NOTES: This EP came with a special picture sleeve and was issued in Japan.

367   LIVE IN GERMANY AND TOP OF THE POPS   Berkeley 206   (LP)

1. *Mary Jane*
2. *People Say*
3. *I'm Walking*
4. *Sie Liebt Dich*
5. *Long Tall Sally*
6. *Hard Day's Night*
7. *Things We Said Today*
8. *You Know My Name*

Cut 1: Recorded August 14, 1968 by John. This was to have been released as Apples 1002, but it was never released.
Cuts 2–3: Not the Beatles. The label on the original single of these songs lists the artists as John and Paul. Thought by some to be by the Nurk Twins or Pete Best.
Cuts 4, 8: Original recordings.
Cuts 5–7: From the BBC radio show "Top Of The Pops" with Brian Matthews from July 8, 1964.

368   LIVE IN HOLLYWOOD   CBM A110   (LP)
NOTES: See cuts and comments under **ALIVE AT LAST IN ATLANTA.**

369   LIVE IN ITALY   CBM 4178/Instant Analysis 1038   (LP)
NOTES: Same as **ITALY.**
SEE ALSO: **ITALY/PARIS.**

370   **LIVE IN MALMO**   Unknown   (LP)

1. *I Saw Her Standing There*
2. *From Me To You*
3. *Money*
4. *Roll Over Beethoven*
5. *You Really Got A Hold On Me*
6. *She Loves You*
7. *Twist And Shout*
8. *Till There Was You*
9. *I Want To Hold Your Hand*
10. *Roll Over Beethoven*
11. *All My Loving*
12. *I Wanna Be Your Man*
13. *From Us To You*

Cuts 1–7: From the Swedish TV show "Drop In." Recorded October 30, 1963, and aired November 3, 1963.
Cut 8: From the "Ed Sullivan Show," February 9, 1964.
Cut 9: From the "Ed Sullivan Show," February 16, 1964.
Cuts 10–13: From the BBC radio show "From Us To You" which was broadcast December 26, 1963.

371   **LIVE IN MELBOURNE AUSTRALIA 7/16/64**   CBM 4162; Instant Analysis 1034 (LP)

1. *I Saw Her Standing There*
2. *Ringo's Back*
3. *You Can't Do That*
4. *All My Loving*
5. *She Loves You*
6. *Till There Was You*
7. *Roll Over Beethoven*
8. *Can't Buy Me Love*
9. *This Boy*
10. *Farewell And Dedication*

Cuts 1–10: Recorded live at the Melbourne, Australia Concert on June 16, 1964.
SEE ALSO: **MELBOURNE 1964; MELBOURNE/VANCOUVER – SUPER LIVE CONCERT SERIES 4.**

372   **LIVE IN MUNICH 1966**   ZAP 7870   (LP)

1. *Can't Buy Me Love*
2. *If I Fell*
3. *I Want To Hold Your Hand*
4. *Twist And Shout*
5. *You Can't Do That*
6. *All My Loving*
7. *Long Tall Sally*
8. *Rock And Roll Music*
9. *Baby's In Black*
10. *I Feel Fine*
11. *Yesterday*
12. *Nowhere Man*
13. *I'm Down*

Cuts 1–7: From the Hollywood Bowl Concert August 23, 1964.
Cuts 8–13: Recorded at the Cirkus Krone in Munich, Germany, June 24, 1966.
SEE ALSO: **MUNICH AT LEAST -- 7TH AMENDMENT; TOUR ALBUM.**

373   **LIVE IN PARIS OLYMPIA, JUNE 1965**   Unknown   (LP)
NOTES: This LP is the same as **LIVE AT THE PARIS OLYMPIA** (Shalom 3688).
SEE ALSO: **LIVE AT THE PARIS OLYMPIA** (CBM); **PARIS AGAIN.**

374   **LIVE IN SWEDEN**   Unknown   (LP)
NOTES: Exact cuts unknown, but possibly the same as **SWEDEN 1963.**

375   **LIVE IN TOKYO, JULY 1ST, 1966**   Wizardo 501   (LP)

1. *Documentary*
2. *E.H. Eric Interview*
3. *Mr. Moonlight*
4. *Welcome To the Beatles*
5. *Rock And Roll Music*
6. *She's A Woman*
7. *If I Needed Someone*
8. *Day Tripper*
9. *Baby's In Black*
10. *I Feel Fine*
11. *Yesterday*
12. *I Wanna Be Your Man*
13. *Nowhere Man*
14. *Paperback Writer*
15. *I'm Down*

116

Liverpool Flash – Sixth Amendment (LP) ZAP 7869 (Entry 383)

Cuts 1–15: From the Tokyo concert at Budokan Hall on July 1, 1966. This is a different show than appears on **FIVE NIGHTS IN A JUDO ARENA**.

376   **LIVE IN TOKYO '66**   Mushroom 12   (LP)

1. *Rock And Roll Music*
2. *She's A Woman*
3. *If I Needed Someone*
4. *Day Tripper*
5. *Baby's In Black*
6. *I Feel Fine*
7. *Yesterday*
8. *I Wanna Be Your Man*
9. *Nowhere Man*
10. *Paperback Writer*
11. *I'm Down*

Cuts 1–11: Recorded live at the Budokan Hall concert in Tokyo, July 2, 1966.

377   **LIVE IN VANCOUVER**   CBM 4162   (LP)

1. *Twist And Shout*
2. *You Can't Do That*
3. *All My Loving*
4. *She Loves You*
5. *Things We Said Today*
6. *Roll Over Beethoven*
7. *Can't Buy Me Love*
8. *Boys*
9. *A Hard Day's Night*
10. *Long Tall Sally*
11. *She Loves You*
12. *Things We Said Today*
13. *Roll Over Beethoven*
14. *If I Fell*
15. *I Want To Hold Your Hand*
16. *Boys*
17. *A Hard Day's Night*
18. *Long Tall Sally*

Cuts 1–10: Recorded live in Vancouver, British Columbia on August 22, 1964.
Cuts 1–18: Recorded live at the Hollywood Bowl on August 23, 1964.
SEE ALSO: **LIVE IN VANCOUVER, CANADA; MELBOURNE/VANCOUVER – SUPER LIVE CONCERT SERIES 4.**

378   **LIVE IN VANCOUVER, CANADA**   Instant Analysis VN 1032   (LP)
NOTES: Same as **LIVE IN VANCOUVER** (CBM 4162).
SEE ALSO: **MELBOURNE/VANCOUVER – SUPER LIVE CONCERT SERIES 4.**

379   **LIVE IN WASHINGTON, D.C.**   CBM 3795 C1/3571 B   (LP)
NOTES: Same as **THE BEATLES LIVE IN WASHINGTON, D.C.**
SEE ALSO: **DISTRICT OF COLUMBIA.**

380   **LIVE ON SILVER**   Silver Greatest Records LB1   (LP)
NOTES: Same as **LET IT BE LIVE.**

381   **LIVE PERFORMANCE AT SHEA 8--15--65**   Unknown   (LP)
NOTES: Same as **LAST LIVE SHOW** (TMOQ LL 5101).

382   **LIVERPOOL ALIVE '65**   TMOQ   (LP)
NOTES: Exact cuts unknown.

383   **LIVERPOOL FLASH -- SIXTH AMENDMENT**   ZAP 7869   (LP)

1. *Paperback Writer*
2. *A Hard Day's Night*
3. *From Me To You*
4. *From Us To You*
5. *Have You Heard The Word*
6. *Get Back*
7. *I Want To Hold Your Hand*
8. *Long Tall Sally*
9. *Words Of Love*
10. *Hi Ho Silver*
11. *Johnny B. Goode*
12. *Act Naturally*
13. *I'm Down*
14. *Love Me Do*
15. *I Dig A Pony*
16. *Hippy Hippy Shake*
17. *She Loves You*

Cuts 1–2: 1966 live, unknown.
Cut 3: 1964 studio, unknown.
Cut 4: From the BBC radio show "From Us To You" which aired December 26, 1963.
Cut 5: Recorded June, 1970. John and at least some of the Bee Gees were supposedly involved. (For discussion, see footnote on pages xxiv-xxv.)
Cuts 6, 10, 15: From the LET IT BE sessions early in 1969 at London's Twickenham Studio.
Cuts 7–8: 1963, unknown.
Cut 9: Original.
Cut 11: From the BBC radio show "Saturday Club" broadcast May 25, 1963.
Cut 12: Ringo on the Cilla Black show February 6, 1968. This was a duo by Ringo and Cilla.
Cut 13: 1966 live, unknown.
Cuts 14, 17: 1964, unknown.
Cut 16: BBC radio 1963.

384   LONDON PALLADIUM   CBM 3687   (LP)

1. *I Want To Hold Your Hand*
2. *This Boy*
3. *All My Loving*
4. *Money*
5. *Twist And Shout*
6. *Please Mr. Postman*
7. *All My Loving*
8. *I Wanna Be Your Man*
9. *Till There Was You*
10. *Please Mr. Postman*
11. *I Want To Hold Your Hand*

Cuts 1–5: From the TV show "Sunday Night At The London Palladium." Shown October 13, 1963.
Cuts 6–9: From the TV show "Big Night Out" recorded February 23, 1964, and shown February 29, 1964.
Cuts 10–11: From the show "Sunday Night At The London Palladium" of January 12, 1964.
SEE ALSO: **SUNDAY NIGHT AT THE LONDON PALLADIUM; FOREST HILLS/LONDON.**

385   *LONG AND WINDING ROAD/DIALOGUE FROM THE BEATLES*
Apple Beatles Promo–1964   (45)
NOTES: Contains the Music City/KFW Beatles interviews and a version of *The Long And Winding Road* from the LET IT BE sessions in early 1969. This is not the versions released commercially.

386   *LONG AND WINDING ROAD/MY SWEET LORD*   Beat–L: 009   (45)
NOTES: Both cuts are originals. *Long And Winding Road* is from the "Weekly Top–30 Show" of May 17, 1980. Host Mark Elliot talks about Phil Spector's production and the fact that Paul was not too happy with the finished song. *My Sweet Lord* is from the "Weekly Top–30 Show" of May 31. 1980.

387   LOOSE CABOOSE -- BONZO DOG BAND   TAKRL 1922   (LP)

1. *Button Up Your Overcoat*
2. *Shirt*
3. *Hello Mabel*
4. *Fiddle About; Tommy's Holiday Camp*
5. *The Young Ones*
6. *Ooo–Chuck–A–Moo–Moo*
7. *I'm Gonna Bring A Watermelon To My Girl Tonight*
11. *My Brother Makes The Noises For The Talkies*
12. *Da Story Of Da Bonzo Itself*
13. *Ready Mades*
14. *Canyons Of Your Mind*
15. *Trouser Freak*
16. *Dropout*
17. *Paper Round*
18. *Are You Havin' Any Fun*

Love Of The Loved/Reunion (45) Club No. 3 (Entry 390)

8. *Alley Oop*   19. *Urban Spaceman*
9. *What Noise Annoys A Noisy Oyster*
10. *Death Cab For Cutie*
NOTES: This LP is by the Bonzo Dog Band, not the Beatles. It contains
Death Cab For Cutie which the band did in the Beatles' film "Magical
Mystery Tour" and *Urban Spaceman* which Paul produced for them.

388   **LOVE ME DO/TWIST AND SHOUT/THERE'S A PLACE/P.S. I LOVE YOU**
Vee Jay VJ–103   (EP)
NOTES: This is a copy of the phony Tollie EP, but on the VJ label. No sleeve
was issued with this disc.

389   *LOVE OF THE LOVED/LOVE OF THE LOVED*   PR–100   (45)
NOTES: Has two different lengths of the same song. Side one is 1:42 in length,
while side two is 1:48 long. Issued with a black–and–white picture sleeve.

390   *LOVE OF THE LOVED/REUNION*   Club No. 3   (45)
NOTES: This was issued by a fan club. *Love Of The Loved* is the 1:48 length
version. *Reunion* is a break–in novelty of the Dickie Goodman type. For
more information on it see its entry in the novelty section of this book.
Came with a black–and–white picture sleeve.

391   **L.S. BUMBLEBEE**   CBM 1005; Cumbat Label on CBM 3626   (LP)

1. *L.S. Bumblebee*   10. *Save The Last Dance For Me*
2. *Don't Let Me Down*   11. *Don't Let Me Down*
3. *Maxwell's Silver Hammer*   12. *Suzy Parker*
4. *Two Of Us*   13. *Yesterday*
5. *I've Got A Feeling*   14. *Love Of The Loved*
6. *Oh Darling*   15. *Hey Jude*
7. *One After 909*   16. *All You Need Is Love*
8. *Across The Universe*
9. *Dig A Pony*

Cut 1: Not the Beatles, but Dudley Moore and Peter Cook.
Cuts 2–12: From the **LET IT BE** sessions recorded early in 1969 at London's
Twickenham Studio.
Cut 13: Recorded August 14, 1965. Shown on the "Ed Sullivan Show" on
September 12, 1965.
Cut 14: From the Decca audition tapes January 1, 1962.
Cut 15: Recorded for the "David Frost" British TV show September 4, 1968.
Aired September 8, 1968.
Cut 16: From the "Our World" TV broadcast of June 25, 1967.
SEE ALSO: **BUMBLEWORDS -- SUPER STUDIO SESSIONS 3** (side one).

392   **L.S. BUMBLEBEE**   Unknown   (LP)

1. *L.S. Bumblebee*   8. *Maxwell's Silver Hammer*
2. *Love Of The Loved*   9. *Two Of Us*
3. *Save The Last Dance For Me*   10. *Oh Darling*
4. *Don't Let Me Down*   11. *Suzy Parker*
5. *All You Need Is Love*   12. *One After 909*
6. *Hey Jude*   13. *I've Got A Feeling*
7. *Yesterday*   14. *Across The Universe*
                                   15. *Dig A Pony*
                                   16. *Don't Let Me Down*

NOTES: Same as **L.S. BUMBLEBEE** (CBM 1005) except the order of the songs
has been changed.

393 MAGICAL MYSTERY TOUR, PLUS BEATLES RARITIES AND TRUE COLLECTOR'S ITEMS   Wizardo 310   (2LPs)

1. *Magical Mystery Tour*
2. *The Fool On The Hill*
3. *Shirley's Wild Accordian*
4. *She Loves You (Instrumental)*
5. *Race Music*
6. *Flying*
7. *All My Loving (Instrumental)*
8. *I Am The Walrus*
9. *Jessie's Dream*
10. *Blue Jay Way*
11. *Sing Along Medley*
12. *Death Cab For Cutie* (Bonzo Dog Band)
13. *Your Mother Should Know*
14. *Magical Mystery Tour*

15. *Mean Mr. Mustard*
16. *All Together On The Wireless Machine*
17. *Step Inside Love*
18. *Bye Bye Bye*
19. *Peace Of Mind*
20. *Move Over Ms. Clawdy*
21. *Mary Jane*
22. *The Way I Feel About You*
23. *If You Can't Get Her*
24. *Boys*
25. *Kansas City*
26. *People Say*
27. *I'm Walking*
28. *I'll Be On My Way*
29. *Soldier Of Love*
30. *Interviews*

Cuts 1–14: From the film "Magical Mystery Tour."
Cuts 15–16, 18: Recorded in the spring of 1969.
Cut 17: February, 1968, demo by Paul of a song later given to Cilla Black.
Cut 19: Taken from the Apple trash can in 1970.
Cut 20: Twickenham Studio, 1969.
Cut 21: Recorded by John August 14, 1968. This was to have been released as Apple 1002, but it was never released.
Cuts 22–23: Not the Beatles, but Pete Best.
Cuts 24–25: Recorded at the Granville Theatre, London, on October 9, 1964. The film was shown on "Shindig" on January 20, 1965.
Cuts 26–27: Not the Beatles. Some say these are by Pete Best while others claim them to be by the Nurk Twins.
Cut 28: From a BBC radio broadcast from the fall of 1962.
Cut 29: 1963 outtake.
Cut 30: Unknown.
SEE ALSO: **MEAN MR. MUSTARD.**

394 MANUAL EXCITATIONS   Aftermath 12   (LP)

1. *Let It Be*
2. *Shakin' In The 60s*
3. *Good Rockin' Tonight*
4. *Across The Universe*
5. *Two Of Us*
6. *Momma You're Just On My Mind*
7. *Tennessee*
8. *House Of The Rising Sun*
9. *Back To Commonwealth*
10. *White Power Promenade*
11. *Hi Ho Silver*
12. *For You Blue*
13. *Let It Be*

Cuts 1–13: Recorded during the **LET IT BE** sessions early in 1969 at London's Twickenham Studio.
NOTES: This is the same as sides three and four of **HAHST AZ SUN.**

395 THE MAN WHO GAVE THE BEATLES AWAY   Unknown   (LP)
NOTES: This is an interview with Allan Williams, the Beatles first manager. Williams talks about the Beatles' early days, especially the time they spent in Germany. This was issued for a fan club in very limited quantities.

396   MARY JANE   CBM 3626; TMOQ MJ 543; TMOQ 71076   (LP)

1. *Have You Heard The Word*
2. *Don't Let Me Down*
3. *Those Were The Days*
4. *What's The New Mary Jane*
5. *Cottonfields*
6. *Twist And Shout*
7. *Dizzy Miss Lizzy*
8. *You Really Got A Hold On Me*
9. *Roll Over Beethoven*
10. *All My Loving*
11. *I Wanna Be Your Man*
12. *A Hard Day's Night*
13. *Things We Said Today*
14. *From Us To You*

Cut 1: Recorded June, 1970. John and some of the Bee Gees are supposed to have been involved. (For discussion, see footnote on pages xxiv-xxv.)
Cuts 2–3: From an interview in the fall of 1968.
Cut 4: Recorded August 14, 1968. This was to have been Apple 1002, but it was not released.
Cut 5: From an interview with Kenny Everett in January, 1968.
Cuts 6–8: Live, unknown.
Cuts 9–14: From various BBC radio shows July and August, 1964.
SEE ALSO: **SPICY BEATLES SONGS** (TMQ 543).

397   MARY JANE   Cumbat Production on CBM 3585   (LP)

1. *Mary Jane*
2. *Shout*
3. *Interview*
4. *People Say*
5. *You Know*
6. *Top Of The Pops Interview*
7. *Long Tall Sally*
8. *A Hard Day's Night*
9. *Things We Said Today*
10. *I'm Walking*
11. *Sie Liebt Dich*

Cut 1: Recorded August 14, 1968. This was to have been Apple 1002, but it was never released.
Cut 2: Recorded April 27–28, 1964, for the Rediffusion TV show "Around The Beatles." The show aired May 6, 1964.
Cut 3: Unknown.
Cuts 4, 10: Not the Beatles. This is thought by some to be by the Nurk Twins or Pete Best. The label on the original single shows the artists as John and Paul.
Cuts 5, 11: Original recordings. Cut 5 is *You Know My Name (Look Up My Number)*.
Cuts 6–9: From the BBC radio show "Tops Of The Pops" with Brian Matthews from July 8, 1964.
SEE ALSO: **MARY JANE 2ND VERSION; THE NEVER RELEASED MARY JANE; THE NEW MARY JANE; THEIR NEVER RELEASED MARY JANE; THEIR NEVER RELEASED THE NEW MARY JANE; WHAT'S THE NEW MARY JANE; RETURN OF MARY JANE.**

398   MARY JANE 2ND VERSION   Unknown   (LP)
NOTES: Same as **MARY JANE** (CBM 3585).
SEE ALSO: **THE NEVER RELEASED MARY JANE; THE NEW MARY JANE; THEIR NEVER RELEASED MARY JANE; THEIR NEVER RELEASED THE NEW MARY JANE; WHAT'S THE NEW MARY JANE; RETURN OF MARY JANE.**

399   MEAN MR. MUSTARD   Unknown   (LP)
NOTES: Same as sides three and four of **MAGICAL MYSTERY TOUR, PLUS THE BEATLES RARITIES AND TRUE COLLECTOR'S ITEMS.** The order of the songs is changed somewhat.

Memphis/Love Of The Loved (45)   Deccagone 1102 (Entry 404)

400   MEET THE BEATLES OPEN–END INTERVIEW   Capitol PRO 2549   (EP)

1. *Interview*   3. *This Boy*
2. *I Want To Hold Your Hand*   4. *It Won't Be Long*
Cuts 2–4: Original recordings.
NOTES: Issued with a black–and–white picture sleeve with the printed interview
    included. Not an exact copy of the original Capitol promo. This has a plain
    black label and does not have the rainbow swirl around the edge. Issued on
    several colors of vinyl, including black and gold (yellow).

401   MELBOURNE AND WASHINGTON   Wizardo 314   (LP)

1. *I Saw Her Standing There*   10. *Roll Over Beethoven*
2. *You Can't Do That*   11. *From Me To You*
3. *All My Loving*   12. *I Saw Her Standing There*
4. *She Loves You*   13. *This Boy*
5. *Till There Was You*   14. *All My Loving*
6. *Roll Over Beethoven*   15. *I Wanna Be Your Man*
7. *Can't Buy Me Love*   16. *Please Please Me*
8. *This Boy*   17. *She Loves You*
9. *Farewell and Dedication*   18. *I Want To Hold Your Hand*
Cuts 1–9: From the Melbourne, Australia concert, June 15, 1964.
Cuts 10–18: From the Washington, DC concert February 11, 1964.

402   MELBOURNE 1964   Unknown   (LP)
NOTES: Same as **LIVE IN MELBOURNE, AUSTRALIA 7/16/64.**
SEE ALSO: **MELBOURNE/VANCOUVER – SUPER LIVE CONCERT SERIES 4.**

403   MELBOURNE/VANCOUVER – SUPER LIVE CONCERT SERIES 4
Instant Analysis 1032A/1034A   (LP)

1. *I Saw Her Standing There*   5. *Twist And Shout*
2. *You Can't Do That*   6. *You Can't Do That*
3. *All My Loving*   7. *All My Loving*
4. *She Loves You*   8. *She Loves You*
                                 9. *Things We Said Today*
                                 10. *Roll Over Beethoven*
                                 11. *Can't Buy Me Love*
                                 12. *Boys*
                                 13. *A Hard Day's Night*
                                 14. *Long Tall Sally*
Cuts 1–4: From the Melbourne, Australia concert June 15, 1964.
Cuts 5–14: From the Vancouver, British Columbia, concert August 22, 1964.
SEE ALSO: **LIVE IN MELBOURNE, AUSTRALIA 7/16/64; LIVE IN
VANCOUVER; CANADA; MELBOURNE 1964.**

404   *MEMPHIS/LOVE OF THE LOVED*   Deccagone 1102   (45)
NOTES: Originally released by one of the Beatle fan clubs, these two
    cuts are from the Decca auditions of January 1, 1962. This original record
    was released with a full--color picture sleeve. The label was light blue and
    the record was pressed on green vinyl. It was later copied.

405   *MEMPHIS/LOVE OF THE LOVED*   Deccagone 1102   (45)
NOTES: This is a copy of the original Deccagone single released by the Beatle
    fan club mentioned above. The copy also came with a full-color
    picture sleeve, but was pressed on yellow vinyl instead of green like the
    original.

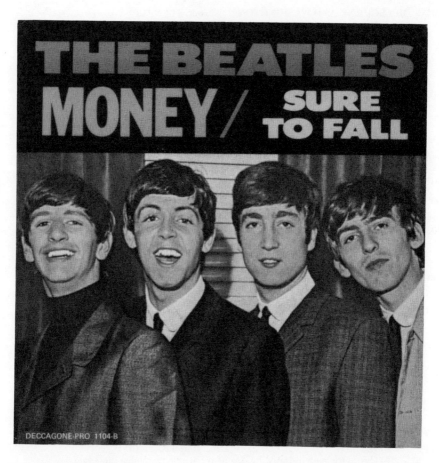

Money/Sure To Fall (45)   Deccagone 1104 (Entry 409)

406 *MEMPHIS/LOVE OF THE LOVED*   Pye 406   (45)
   NOTES: Another copy of the original Deccagone single issued by the Beatle fan
      club Strawberry Fields Forever. This one came with a black–and–white
      picture sleeve.

407 **THE MEN WHO MAKE THE MUSIC**   Unknown   (2 LPs)
   NOTES: The album was released in mid–1980, too late to include full information
      here. It is known that it is a double album and has a deluxe color cover.

408 **MISCELLANEOUS**   Speed Records 3001   (LP)

   1. *Let It Rock*
   2. *Cops And Robbers*
   3. *Don't Lie To Me*
   4. *Ain't That Loving You*
   5. *Snake Drive*
   6. *West Coast Idea*
   7. *Shades Of Orange*
   8. *Loving Sacred Loving*
   9. *Con Le Mie Lacrine*
   10. *Memo From Turner*
   11. *Wild Colonial Boy*

   Cuts 1–11: Not the Beatles, but the Rolling Stones.
   Cuts 7–8: There is supposed to have been some Beatle involvement on these
      two cuts, but there really wasn't.

409 *MONEY/SURE TO FALL*   Deccagone 1104   (45)
   NOTES: Originally issued by one of the Beatle fan clubs. This is from
      the Decca audition tapes from January 1, 1962. Original was issued with a
      full–color picture sleeve and was pressed on clear vinyl. It was later copied.

410 *MONEY/SURE TO FALL*   Deccagone 1104   (45)
   NOTES: This is a copy of the original single issued by the Beatle fan club
      mentioned above. Like the original, it came with a full-color picture
      sleeve. The Deccagone print on the label is of a script type, while the original
      was block. It was issued in several colors of vinyl, including blue and clear.

411 **MORE FROM THE FAB FOUR**   Wizardo 390   (LP)
   NOTES: Side one is the same as side two of **LIVERPOOL FLASH – SIXTH
      AMENDMENT**. Side two is the same as side one of **BACK UPON US ALL**
      (ZAP 7864). This album was not released by Wizardo, but another company
      using their name and logo.

412 **MORE GET BACK SESSIONS**   Michael & Allyson HH 1/2; Mushroom 13;
      TMOQ 71068   (LP)
   NOTES: Same as **GET BACK SESSIONS 2**. Originals were released on color
      vinyl.
   SEE ALSO: **VIRGIN AND THREE.**

413 **MUNICH AT LEAST – 7TH AMENDMENT**   ZAP 7870   (LP)
   NOTES: Same as **LIVE IN MUNICH 1966.**
   SEE ALSO: **TOUR ALBUM.**

414 **MURRAY THE K AND THE BEATLES AS IT HAPPENED**   IBC F4KM–0082/3
      (EP)
   NOTES: Issued with a black–and–white picture sleeve. Label says 1976, but it
      wasn't in general release until 1980.
   SEE ALSO: **AS IT HAPPENED: THE BEATLES AND MURRAY THE K.**

415 **MUSIC CITY/KWF BEATLES/THE BEATLES TALKING/YOU CAN'T DO THAT**
      Custom RB–2637/RB–2638   (45)
   NOTES: Originals were released June 5, 1964 by KWFB radio and the Music
      City Record Store in Los Angeles. Wink Martindale does the interview.

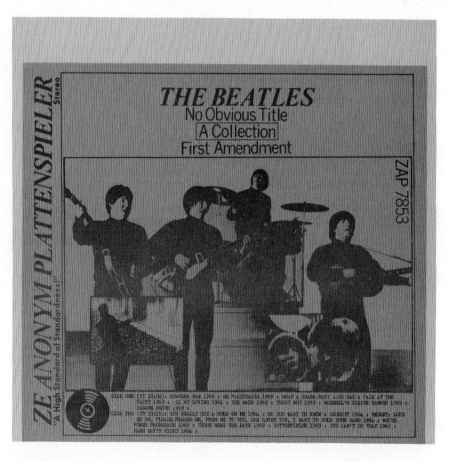

No Obvious Title – 1st Amendment (LP)   **ZAP 7853 (Entry 422)**

416 *MY BONNIE/THE SAINTS*   Decca 31382   (45)
> NOTES: This is a copy of the DJ version of this record with a pink label. This one has the German opening version on one side and the English version on the other side.

417 **THE NEVER RELEASED MARY JANE**   Cumbat Productions on CBM 3585   (LP)
> NOTES: Same as **MARY JANE (CBM 3585)**.
> SEE ALSO: **MARY JANE 2ND VERSION; THEIR NEVER RELEASED MARY JANE; THEIR NEVER RELEASED THE NEW MARY JANE; THE NEW MARY JANE; RETURN OF MARY JANE.**

418 **THE NEW MARY JANE**   CBM 3585   (LP)
> NOTES: Same as **MARY JANE (CBM 3585)**.
> SEE ALSO: **MARY JANE 2ND VERSION; THE NEVER RELEASED MARY JANE; THE NEW MARY JANE; THEIR NEVER RELEASED MARY JANE; THEIR NEVER RELEASED THE NEW MARY JANE; WHAT'S THE NEW MARY JANE; RETURN OF MARY JANE.**

419 **NEXT TO LAST RECORDING SESSION -- 5TH AMENDMENT**   ZAP 7866   (LP)
> NOTES: Same as **BEATLES RAREST NO. 6**.
> SEE ALSO: **VERY BEST OF THE BEATLES RAREST NO. 6.**

420 **1964 TALK ALBUM**   Funky Soul Jive Records 347   (LP)
> NOTES: Original 1964 Ed Rudy interviews with all four Beatles.
> SEE ALSO: **AMERICAN TOUR WITH ED RUDY 1964; ED RUDY I -- TALK ALBUM; ED RUDY VOL. I.**

421 **1965 TALK ALBUM**   Funky Soul Jive Records 347   (LP)
> NOTES: Original 1965 Ed Rudy interviews with the Beatles.
> SEE ALSO: **AMERICAN TOUR WITH ED RUDY 1965; ED RUDY VOL. II.**

422 **NO OBVIOUS TITLE -- 1ST AMENDMENT**   ZAP 7853   (LP)

1. *Nowhere Man*
2. *No Pakistanis*
3. *Mary Jane*
4. *All My Loving*
5. *The Walk*
6. *Teddy Boy*
7. *Maxwell's Silver Hammer*
8. *Besame Mucho*
9. *You Really Got A Hold On Me*
10. *Do You Want To Know A Secret*
11. Medley:
    Love Me Do
    Please Please Me
    From Me To You
    She Loves You
    I Want To Hold Your Hand
12. *White Power Promenade*
13. *Those Were The Days*
14. *Cottonfields*
15. *You Can't Do That*
16. *Hard Day's Night*

Cut 1: From the Tokyo concert at Budokan Hall July 2, 1966.
Cuts 2, 5–8, 12: From the **LET IT BE** sessions in early 1969.
Cut 3: Recorded by John, August 14, 1968.
Cut 4: Recorded live at the Hollywood Bowl August 23, 1964.
Cuts 9–10: 1964 studio versions.
Cut 11: From the Rediffusion TV show "Around the Beatles." Recorded April 27–28, 1964, and shown May 6, 1964.
Cut 13: From a press conference in the fall of 1968.
Cut 14: From an interview with Kenny Everett in January 1968.
Cut 15: 1965 live unknown.
Cut 16: From the BBC radio show "Top Of The Pops" July 8, 1964.

No. 3 Abbey Road (LP)   NW 8 AR8-69 (Entry 423)

423   **NO. 3 ABBEY ROAD**   NW 8 AR 8–69   (LP)

1. *Golden Slumbers*
2. *Carry That Weight*
3. *Her Majesty*
4. *You Never Give Me Your Money*
5. *Octopus's Garden*
6. *Maxwell's Silver Hammer*
7. *Oh Darling*
8. *Something*
9. *How Do You Do*
10. *Blackbird*
11. *The Unicorn*
12. *Lalena*
13. *Heather*
14. *Mr. Wind*
15. *The Walrus And The Carpenter*
16. *Land Of Gisch*

Cuts 1–8: Outtakes from the **ABBEY ROAD** sessions.
Cuts 9–16: Paul and Donovan.
NOTES: Issued with full--color laminated jacket.

424   **NO TURNING BACK**   Unknown   (2 LPs)

1. *Besame Mucho*
2. *Octopusses' Garden*
3. *You Really Got A Hold On Me*
4. *Shake, Rattle And Roll*
5. *Kansas City*
6. *Lawdy Miss Clawdy*
7. *Miss Ann*
8. *Dig It*
9. *I Me Mine*
10. *Suzy Parker*

11. *Dig A Pony*
12. *Across The Universe*
13. *Jazz Piano Theme*
14. *One After 909*
15. *Oh Darling*
16. *I've Got A Feeling*
17. *Two Of Us*
18. *Maxwell's Silver Hammer*
19. *Don't Let Me Down*
20. *Paul On Piano*

Cuts 1–20: From the **LET IT BE** sessions held at London's Twickenham Studio early in 1969.

425   **ONCE UPON A . . .**   Unknown   (LP)

1. *She Loves You*
2. *Till There Was You*
3. *Ain't She Sweet*
4. *Cry For A Shadow*
5. *My Bonnie*
6. *Lucille*
7. *Christmas Records 1968–69*
8. *Across The Universe*
9. *Love Me Do*
10. *P.S. I Love You*
11. *Bad Boy*
12. *Twist And Shout*
13. *There's A Place*

Cuts 1–2: Live, unknown.
Cuts 3–5, 9–13: Original recordings.
Cut 6: BBC radio 1963.
Cut 7: Parts of the 1968–69 Christmas records to fan club members.
Cut 8: Original recording from the Wildlife Fund LP **NO ONE'S GONNA CHANGE OUR WORLD**.

426   **ONCE UPON A TIME . . .**   Napoleon 11044   (LP)
NOTES: Same as **AND THE BEATLES WERE BORN**. Full title is: **ONCE UPON A TIME A FAROUT SOUND ECHOED 'ROUND A CAVERN WHERE FOUR BOYS SANG: THAT'S HOW THE BEATLES WERE BORN.**
SEE ALSO: **BEATLES WERE BORN.**

427   **THE ONLY LIVE RECORDS**   Kustom Records ASC 002   (LP)
NOTES: Same as **BACK IN 1964 AT THE HOLLYWOOD BOWL** (Lemon).
SEE ALSO: **BACK IN 1964 AT THE HOLLYWOOD BOWL** (CBM); **BEATLES 1964; HOLLYWOOD BOWL '64; LIVE AT HOLLYWOOD BOWL; LIVE AT THE HOLLYWOOD BOWL; L.A.; LIVE AT SHEA; THE ONLY LIVE RECORDINGS** (unknown); **THE SHEA STADIUM CONCERT 1964; THE**

SHEA STADIUM "MORE OR LESS" STEREO; SHEA: THE GOOD OLD DAYS (Kustom); SHEA: THE GOOD OLD DAYS (Pine Tree).

428   **THE ONLY LIVE RECORDINGS**   Unknown   (LP)
NOTES: Same as **BACK IN 1964 AT THE HOLLYWOOD BOWL** (Lemon).
SEE ALSO: **BACK IN 1964 AT THE HOLLYWOOD BOWL** (CBM); **BEATLES 1964; HOLLYWOOD BOWL '64; LIVE AT HOLLYWOOD BOWL; LIVE AT THE HOLLYWOOD BOWL; L.A.; LIVE AT SHEA; THE ONLY LIVE RECORDINGS** (Kustom); **THE SHEA STADIUM CONCERT 1964; THE SHEA STADIUM "MORE OR LESS" STEREO; SHEA: THE GOOD OLD DAYS** (Kustom); **SHEA: THE GOOD OLD DAYS** (Pine Tree).

429   **ON STAGE**   Wizardo 328   (LP)

1. *Yesterday*	7. *Day Tripper*
2. *Nowhere Man*	8. *We Can Work It Out*
3. *Rock And Roll Music*	9. *I Saw Her Standing There*
4. *Baby's In Black*	10. *From Me To You*
5. *I Feel Fine*	11. *Money*
6. *I'm Down*	12. *Roll Over Beethoven*
	13. *You Really Got A Hold On Me*
	14. *She Loves You*
	15. *Twist And Shout*

Cuts 1–6: From the concert at the Circus Krone in Munich, Germany, June 24, 1966.
Cuts 7–8: From the BBC TV show "Top Of The Pops" from December 2, 1965.
Cuts 9–15: Live, unknown.
SEE ALSO: **ON STAGE IN EUROPE.**

430   **ON STAGE IN EUROPE**   Wizardo 328   (LP)
NOTES: Same as **ON STAGE.** Issued on color vinyl.

431   **ON STAGE IN JAPAN**   Wizardo 318   (LP)
NOTES: Exact cuts unknown, but presumably the Tokyo 1966 concert.

432   **ON STAGE IN JAPAN 1966**   TAKRL 1900; Pigs Eye PE No. 1   (LP)
NOTES: Same as **BEATLES ON STAGE IN JAPAN THE 1966 TOUR.**
SEE ALSO: **FIVE NIGHTS IN A JUDO ARENA; ON STAGE IN JAPAN – 1966 TOUR; TOKYO 1966.**

433   **ON STAGE IN JAPAN – 1966 TOUR**   ZAP 1900   (LP)
NOTES: Same as **BEATLES ON STAGE IN JAPAN THE 1966 TOUR.**
SEE ALSO: **FIVE NIGHTS IN A JUDO ARENA; ON STAGE IN JAPAN 1966; TOKYO 1966.**

434   **ON STAGE IN MELBOURNE, AUSTRALIA AND WASHINGTON, D.C.**
     Wizardo 314   (LP)
NOTES: Same as **LIVE IN AUSTRALIA AND WASHINGTON.**

435   **ON TOUR**   Unknown   (LP)
NOTES: Exact cuts are unknown.

436   **ORIGINAL AUDITION TAPE – CIRCA 1962**   Wizardo 308   (LP)

1. *I Got A Woman*	12. *Bound By Love*
2. *I Got A Woman*	13. *Lonesome Tears In My Eyes*
3. *Glad All Over*	14. *Everyone Wants Someone*
4. *I Just Don't Understand*	15. *Love Of The Loved*

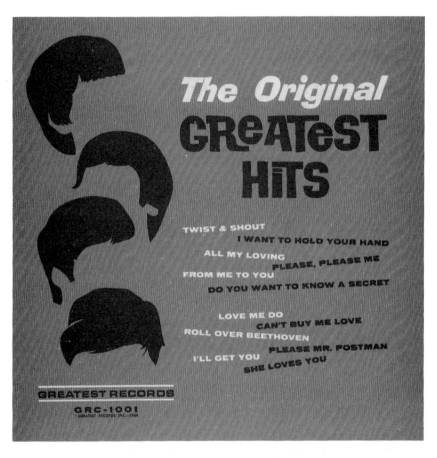

Original Greatest Hits (LP)   GRC 1001 (Entry 439)

5. *Hippy Hippy Shake*
6. *I'm Sure To Fall*
7. *Please Don't Ever Change*
8. *A Shot Of Rhythm And Blues*
9. *A Shot Of Rhythm And Blues*
10. *There's Nothin' Shakin'*
11. *I Forgot To Remember*

16. *Lucille*
17. *Crying, Waiting, Hoping*
18. *To Know Her Is To Love Her*
19. *Lend Me Your Comb*
20. *Oh Carol*
21. *I'm Gonna Sit Right Down And Cry*

Cuts 1, 3--4, 6--8, 10, 12--14, 17--18, 21: From a BBC radio broadcast in November of 1962.
Cuts 2, 9, 11: Unknown.
Cut 5: From a BBC radio broadcast in March, 1963.
Cut 15: From the Decca auditions, January 1, 1962.
Cut 16: From a BBC radio broadcast in the summer of 1963.
Cuts 19--20: From a broadcast on Radio Luxembourg on January 18, 1963.
SEE ALSO: **ORIGINAL DEMO SESSIONS.**

437 **ORIGINAL DEMO SESSIONS**   Wizardo 308   (LP)
   NOTES: Same as **ORIGINAL DECCA AUDITION TAPE -- CIRCA 1962** (Wizardo 308).

438 **ORIGINAL "GET BACK" ACETATE**   Wizardo 315   (LP)
   NOTES: Same as **A/B SINGLE ACETATE.**
   SEE ALSO: **THE BEATLES LET IT BE; LET IT BE: BEFORE PHIL SPECTOR; ORIGINAL STEREO ACETATE FOR LET IT BE (BEFORE PHIL SPECTOR).**

439 **ORIGINAL GREATEST HITS**   GRC 1001   (LP)

1. *Twist And Shout*
2. *I Want To Hold Your Hand*
3. *All My Loving*
4. *Please Please Me*
5. *From Me To You*
6. *Do You Want To Know A Secret*

7. *Love Me Do*
8. *Can't Buy Me Love*
9. *Roll Over Beethoven*
10. *Please Mr. Postman*
11. *I'll Get You*
12. *She Loves You*

Cuts 1--12: Original cuts.
NOTES: This is one of the first Beatle bootlegs from the 60's. Has a laminated cover.

440 **ORIGINAL GREATEST HITS BY THE BEATLES**   Sutra 6667   (LP)

1. *Strawberry Fields Forever*
2. *Twist And Shout*
3. *I Want To Hold Your Hand*
4. *All My Loving*
5. *Please Please Me*
6. *From Me To You*

7. *Love Me Do*
8. *Do You Want To Know A Secret*
9. *Can't Buy Me Love*
10. *Roll Over Beethoven*
11. *Please Mr. Postman*
12. *I'll Get You*

Cuts 1--12: Original recordings.
NOTES: Laminated cover.

441 **ORIGINAL STEREO ACETATE FOR LET IT BE (BEFORE PHIL SPECTOR)**
   Wizardo 315   (LP)
   NOTES: Same as **A/B SINGLE ACETATE.**
   SEE ALSO: **THE BEATLES LET IT BE; LET IT BE: BEFORE PHIL SPECTOR; ORIGINAL "GET BACK" ACETATE.**

442 **OUTAKES VOL. I**   TMOQ B0519; TMOQ 71048   (LP)

1. *Do You Want To Know A Secret*
2. *You Really Got A Hold On Me*

7. *From Me To You*
8. *Roll Over Beethoven*

3. *Hippy Hippy Shake*
4. *Misery*
5. *Money*
6. *Till There Was You*
9. *Love Me Do*
10. *Kansas City*
11. *Long Tall Sally*
12. *Please Please Me*

Cuts 1–2, 4–12: Unknown, but probably studio outtakes or originals.
Cut 3: From the BBC radio, 1962.
SEE ALSO: **DECCA AUDITION OUTTAKES – SUPER STUDIO SESSIONS 2;
OUTAKES VOL. I/OUTAKES VOL. II; STUDIO SESSIONS VOL. I;
STUDIO SESSIONS NO. 1 AND NO. 2.**

443   OUTAKES VOL.II   TMOQ 71049   (LP)

1. *She Loves You*
2. *Words Of Love*
3. *She's Got The Devil In Her Heart*
4. *Anna*
5. *Money*
6. *There's A Place*
7. *Honey Don't*
8. *Chains*
9. *I Saw Her Standing There*
10. *I'm Sure To Fall*
11. *Lucille*
12. *Boys*

Cuts 1–9, 12: Unknown, probably studio outtakes or originals.
Cut 10: From a BBC radio broadcast of November, 1962.
Cut 11: From the BBC, 1963.
SEE ALSO: **DECCA AUDITION OUTTAKES – SUPER STUDIO SESSIONS 2;
OUTAKES VOL. I/OUTAKES VOL. II; STUDIO SESSIONS VOL. II;
STUDIO SESSIONS NO. 1 AND NO. 2.**

444   OUTAKES VOL. I/OUTAKES VOL. II   TMOQ 7508   (2 LPs)
NOTES: This is the same as **OUTAKES VOL. 1** (TMOQ 71048) and **OUTAKES
VOL. II** (TMOQ 71049).
SEE ALSO: **DECCA AUDITION OUTTAKES – SUPER STUDIO SESSIONS 2;
STUDIO SESSIONS VOL. I; STUDIO SESSIONS VOL. II; STUDIO
SESSIONS NO. 1 AND NO. 2.**

445   OUTTAKES 1   TMQ–WIZ D–207   (LP)
NOTES: Exact cuts unknown.

446   PARIS AGAIN   CBM 3688   (LP)
NOTES: Same as **LIVE AT THE PARIS OLYMPIA** (CBM 3688).
SEE ALSO: **LIVE AT THE PARIS OLYMPIA** (Shalom); **LIVE AT THE PARIS
OLYMPIA JAN. 1964; ITALY/PARIS.**

447   PARIS 65   Wizardo 335   (LP)

1. *Twist And Shout*
2. *She's A Woman*
3. *Ticket To Ride*
4. *Can't Buy Me Love*
5. *I'm A Loser*
6. *A Hard Day's Night*
7. *Baby's In Black*
8. *Rock And Roll Music*
9. *Everybody's Trying To Be My
   Baby*
10. *Long Tall Sally*
11. *Twist And Shout*
12. *She's A Woman*
13. *I'm A Loser*
14. *I Wanna Be Your Man*
15. *A Hard Day's Night*
16. *Everybody's Trying To Be My
    Baby*
17. *Rock And Roll Music*
18. *I Feel Fine*
19. *Ticket To Ride*
20. *Long Tall Sally*

Cuts 1–20: From both Paris concerts, June 20, 1965.

448   PARIS SPORTS PALAIS   CBM LPPA 77; Wizardo 335   (LP)

1. *Twist And Shout*
2. *She's A Woman*
6. *I Wanna Be Your Man*
7. *A Hard Day's Night*

135

3. *I'm A Loser*
4. *Can't Buy Me Love*
5. *Baby's In Black*

8. *Everybody's Trying To Be My Baby*
9. *Rock And Roll Music*
10. *I Feel Fine*
11. *Ticket To Ride*
12. *Long Tall Sally*

Cuts 1–12: From the Paris concert June 20, 1965.
SEE ALSO: **PARIS SPORTS PALAIS 1965** (Wizardo 335); **SPORTS PALACE -- FRANCE -- SECOND SHOW.**

449 **PARIS SPORTS PALAIS 1965**   Wizardo 335   (LP)
NOTES: Same as **PARIS SPORTS PALAIS** (Wizardo 335).
SEE ALSO: **SPORTS PALACE -- FRANCE – SECOND SHOW.**

450 **PEACE OF MIND**   Berkeley 2009; CBM 3670   (LP)

1. *Peace Of Mind*
2. *Lend Me Your Comb*
3. *Carol*
4. *Lawdy Miss Clawdy*
5. *Shake, Rattle And Roll*

6. *I Feel Fine*
7. *I'm Down*
8. *Act Naturally*
9. *Ticket To Ride*
10. *Yesterday*
11. *Help*

Cut 1: From the Apple trash can. Recorded June, 1967.
Cuts 2–3: From Radio Luxembourg January 18, 1963.
Cuts 4–5: From the **LET IT BE** sessions held at London's Twickenham Studios in early 1969.
Cuts 6–11: Recorded August 14, 1965. Shown on the "Ed Sullivan Show" September 12, 1965.
NOTES: *Kansas City* appears between cuts 3 and 4, but is not listed. This is from the **LET IT BE** sessions of early 1969.

451 *PENNY LANE/STRAWBERRY FIELDS FOREVER*   Capitol 5810   (45)
NOTES: This is a boot of the DJ version of *Penny Lane.* It was released in several colors of vinyl, including red, green, yellow and gold.

452 **PETE BEST STORY – BEST . . . OF THE BEATLES**   BRB 100   (LP)

1. *The Way I Feel About You*
2. *If You Can't Get Her*
3. *Last Night*
4. *Why Did You Leave Me Baby*
5. *Shimmy Like My Sister Kate*
6. *I Need Your Loving*
7. *Nobody But You*
8. *I Can't Do Without You*

9. *Boys*
10. *Kansas City*
11. *Casting My Spell*
12. *Wait And See*
13. *Some Other Guy*
14. *I'm Blue*
15. *She's Alright*
16. *Keys To My Heart*

Cuts 1–16: Not the Beatles, but former Beatle member Pete Best.
NOTES: Originals were pressed on red vinyl.

453 **POP GOES THE BEATLES**   Unknown   (LP)

1. *Pop Goes The Beatles*
2. *Boys*
3. *There's A Place*
4. *Lend Me Your Comb*
5. *Pop Goes The Beatles*
6. *A Shot Of Rhythm And Blues*
7. *Till There Was You*

8. *Chains*
9. *Twist And Shout*
10. *Crying, Waiting, Hoping*
11. *Do You Want To Know A Secret*
12. *I'm Gonna Sit Right Down And Cry Over You*
13. *Pop Goes The Beatles*

Cuts 1, 5, 13: From the BBC radio show "Pop Goes The Beatles." This half hour

show ran for 15 weeks beginning June 4, 1963.
Cuts 2–3, 7–9, 11: Unknown.
Cut 4: From a broadcast on Radio Luxembourg, January 18, 1963.
Cuts 6, 10, 12: From a BBC radio broadcast of November, 1962.

454   **POWER BROKERS** Wizardo 392 (LP)

1. *Nowhere Man*	9. *Let It Be*
2. *No Pakistanis*	10. *Dizzy Miss Lizzy*
3. *What A Shame Mary Jane* . . .	11. *Sie Liebt Dich*
4. *All My Loving*	12. *Honey Don't*
5. *The Walk*	13. *I'm Sure To Fall*
6. *Teddy Boy*	14. *I Need You*
7. *Maxwell's Silver Hammer*	15. *For You Blue*
8. *Besame Mucho*	

Cut 1: From the Tokyo concert at Budokan Hall, July 2, 1966.
Cuts 2, 5–9, 15: From the **LET IT BE** sessions early in 1969.
Cut 3: Recorded by John August 14, 1968.
Cut 4: Recorded live at the Hollywood Bowl, August 23, 1964.
Cut 10: Live, unknown.
Cut 11: Original recording.
Cut 12: From a BBC radio show in 1963 with John singing lead.
Cut 13: From a BBC radio broadcast in November, 1962.
Cut 14: From the soundtrack of "Help." Some dialogue is also included.
NOTES: These were not released by Wizardo, but some company using the
        Wizardo name and logo.
SEE ALSO: **BACK UPON US ALL** (Zap); **BACK UPON US ALL** (Kornyphone);
      **MORE FROM THE FAB FOUR; NO OBVIOUS TITLE -- 1ST AMEND--
      MENT; UPON US ALL -- 4TH AMENDMENT.**

455   **PROSPECTOR** Unknown (LP)

1. *Let It Be*	6. *Teddy Boy*
2. *Get Back*	7. *Two Of Us*
3. *Don't Let Me Down*	8. *For You Blue*
4. *I've Got A Feeling*	9. *Across The Universe*
5. *I Dig A Pony*	

Cuts 1–9: From the **LET IT BE** sessions held at London's Twickenham Studios
      early in 1969.

456   **THE QUARRYMEN** Unknown (LP)
      NOTES: Exact cuts unknown.

457   **RADIO LONDON'S LAST HOUR** Unknown (LP)
      NOTES: Disc contains an interview with Ringo from June, 1967.

458   **RARE BEATLES** CBM TB5030 (LP)
      NOTES: Same as **HAPPY BIRTHDAY.**
      SEE ALSO: **RARE SESSIONS.**

459   **RARE BEATLES/HAPPY BIRTHDAY – STUDIO SERIES NO. 13** CBM B213 (LP)
      NOTES: Exact cuts unknown, but probably the same as **HAPPY BIRTHDAY.**

460   **RARE SESSIONS** CBM (LP)
      NOTES: Same as **HAPPY BIRTHDAY.**
      SEE ALSO: **RARE BEATLES.**

461   **REMEMBER, WE DON'T LIKE THEM WE LOVE THEM**   ZTSC 97436/7   (EP)
       NOTES: This is the official IBBB interview of John, Paul, George and Ringo by
       DJ Tom Clay which was released in 1964. The boot has a plain white label,
       showing the title only.

462   **RENAISSANCE MINSTRELS VOL. I**   Amazon Etcetra 612; KO 401; R.R. GM
       725; RR 1002; TMOQ 1852; TMOQ 73001; TMOQ 71026   (LP)

    1. *From Me To You*   6. *I Want To Hold Your Hand*
    2. *Twist And Shout*   7. *Please Please Me*
    3. *This Boy*   8. *All My Loving*
    4. *I Saw Her Standing There*   9. *She Loves You*
    5. *She Loves You*
    Cuts 3, 5, 8: From the "Ed Sullivan Show" February 9, 1964.
    Cuts 1–2, 4, 6–7, 9: From the "Ed Sullivan Show" February 16, 1964.
    SEE ALSO: **ABBEY ROAD REVISITED** (Wizardo 353, side two).

463   **RENAISSANCE MINSTRELS VOL. II**   KO 402; R.R. 726; RR 1001; TMOQ
       73002; Wizardo 358   (LP)

    1. *The Walk*   8.   *Across The Universe*
    2. *Teddy Boy*   9.   *Inner Light*
    3. *Two Of Us On Our Way Home*   10. *Don't Let Me Down*
    4. *I've Got A Feeling*   11. *Get Back*
    5. *Long And Winding Road*   12. *I'm Down*
    6. *For You Blue*   13. *Instant Karma*
    7. *Dig A Pony*
    Cuts 1–7: From the **LET IT BE** sessions in early 1969 at London's Twickenham
    Studios.
    Cut 8: From the Wildlife Fund LP **NO ONE'S GONNA CHANGE OUR WORLD**.
    Cuts 9–13: Original recordings.

464   **RENAISSANCE MINSTRELS VOL. III**   Amazon Etcetra 625; Berkeley 2033;
       KO 404; TMOQ 1702; TMOQ 73032   (LP)

    1. *It Don't Come Easy*   7.   *Blind Man*
    2. *Cold Turkey*   8.   *Happy Christmas (War Is Over)*
    3. *Deep Blue*   9.   *Bangla Desh*
    4. *Another Day*   10. *Give Ireland Back To The Irish*
    5. *Instant Karma*   11. *Give Peace A Chance*
    6. *Back Off Boogaloo*   12. *Early 1970*
    Cuts 1–12: Original recordings by the solo Beatles.

465   **RENAISSANCE MINSTRELS 3**   CBM   (LP)

    1. *Beaucoups Of Blues*   8.   *It Don't Come Easy*
    2. *Happy Christmas (War Is Over)*   9.   *Cold Turkey*
    3. *Bangla Desh*   10. *Deep Blue*
    4. *Give Ireland Back To The Irish*   11. *Another Day*
    5. *Give Peace A Chance*   12. *Instant Karma*
    6. *Early 1970*   13. *Back Off Boogaloo*
    7. *Blindman*
    Cuts 1–13: Original recordings by the solo Beatles.

466   **RENAISSANCE MINSTRELS VOL. IV**   Cumquat on CBM TB 5020; KO 405   (LP)

    1. *I'm Down*   6. *Happy Christmas (War Is Over)*
    2. *Coochy Coochy*   7. *Bangla Desh*
    3. *Step Inside Love*   8. *You Know My Name*

4. *You've Got To Hide Your Love Away*
5. *That Means A Lot*
9. *Sie Liebt Dich*
10. *Give Peace A Chance*
11. *Cold Turkey*

Cuts 1–11: Original recordings. Cut 3 is by Cilla Black; cut 4 by the Silkie; and cut 5 by P.J. Proby.

467   **RETURN OF MARY JANE**   Unknown   (LP)
NOTES: Same as **MARY JANE** (CBM 3585).
SEE ALSO: **MARY JANE SECOND VERSION; THE NEVER RELEASED MARY JANE; THE NEW MARY JANE; THEIR NEVER RELEASED MARY JANE; THEIR NEVER RELEASED THE NEW MARY JANE; WHAT'S THE NEW MARY JANE.**

468   **REUNION NONSENSE -- A COLLECTION – NINTH AMENDMENT**   ZAP 7873   (LP)

1. *All My Loving*
2. *She Loves You*
3. *Till There Was You*
4. *Roll Over Beethoven*
5. *Can't Buy Me Love*
6. *This Boy*
7. *Long Tall Sally*
8. *Soldier Of Love*
9. *I Got A Woman*
10. *Kansas City*
11. *Some Other Guy*
12. *Carol*
13. *Lucille*
14. *Hippy Hippy Shake*
15. *Shout*
16. *Lend Me Your Comb*
17. *Memphis*

Cuts 1–7: From the Melbourne, Australia concert June 16, 1964.
Cuts 8–9: 1963 outtakes.
Cut 10: 1964 outtake.
Cut 11: Recorded by Granada TV at the Cavern Club on October 13, 1962. Shown on "People And Places" on November 7, 1962.
Cuts 12, 16: Recorded from a broadcast over Radio Luxembourg on January 18, 1963.
Cut 13: Recorded from a BBC radio show in the summer of 1963.
Cut 14: Recorded from the BBC radio in 1962.
Cut 15: From the TV show "Around The Beatles," which was recorded April 27–28. 1964, and aired May 6, 1964.
Cut 17: From the BBC radio show "Saturday Club," May 25, 1963.

469   **ROCK 'N' ROAD**   C320A/C320B   (LP)

1. *John On "How Do You Do It"*
2. *How Do You Do It*
3. *Long Tall Sally*
4. *Things We Said Today*
5. *A Hard Day's Night*
6. *Octopus's Garden*
7. *Her Majesty (with last chord)*
8. *Golden Slumbers/Carry That Weight*
9. *You Never Give Me Your Money*
10. *Sun King*
11. *Oh Darling*
12. *Maxwell's Silver Hammer*
13. *Something*
14. *Instrumental*

Cut 1: Unknown date; John talking about why they recorded *How Do You Do It*.
Cut 2: Recorded by the Beatles November 26, 1962. It was to have been their second single, but it was never released.
Cuts 3–5: Outtakes.
Cuts 6–13: Outtakes from the **ABBEY ROAD** album.
Cut 14: Unknown.
NOTES: Issued on purple vinyl.

470   **ROCK 'N' ROLL**   Unknown   (LP)
NOTES: Exact cuts unknown, but it is known to contain *She Loves You* and *Twist And Shout* recorded at the Ardwick Apollo in Manchester, England

on November 20, 1963. Also has *Rain* and *Paperback Writer* from the BBC–TV show "Top Of The Pops" on June 16, 1966.

471   ROLLING STONES ROCK AND ROLL CIRCUS   Unknown   (LP)

1. *Route 66*
2. *Confessin' The Blues*
3. *Jumpin' Jack Flash*
4. *Parachute Woman*
5. *You Can't Always Get What You Want*
6. *Sympathy For The Devil*
7. *No Expectations*
8. *Salt Of The Earth*
9. *Yer Blues*

NOTES: From the soundtrack of the Rolling Stones' "Rock & Roll Circus". John and Yoko do *Yer Blues*. No Beatles appear on any of the other cuts.

472   RUTLAND SPECIAL   Rut 547   (EP)

1. *Get Up And Go*
2. *Goose Step Momma*
3. *Made For Each Other (Between Us)*
4. *You Need Feet*

NOTES: Not the Beatles, but the Rutles. These four songs are from the TV special "All You Need Is Cash" which was shown March 22, 1978. These songs did not appear on the regular release album by the Rutles.

473   SCRAPS   Reign 001   (LP)

1. *It's For You*
2. *How Do You Do It*
3. *Love Of The Loved*
4. *I'll Be On My Way*
5. *Hippy Hippy Shake*
6. *Some Other Guy*
7. *I Forgot To Remember To Forget Her*
8. *Lend Me Your Comb*
9. *Lucille*
10. *Shout*
11. *I Don't Want To See You Again*
12. *Across The Universe*
13. *What's The New Mary Jane*
14. *Dig It*
15. *Maxwell's Silver Hammer*
16. *Besame Mucho*
17. *Long And Winding Road*
18. *Jazz Piano Theme*
19. *Rip It Up*
20. *Shake And Roll*

Cut 1: Not the Beatles, but Cilla Black.
Cut 2: Recorded by the Beatles, November 26, 1962. This was to have been their second single, but it was not released.
Cut 3: From the Decca auditions, January 1, 1962.
Cut 4: From a BBC radio show in the fall of 1962.
Cut 5: Recorded from the BBC radio in 1962.
Cut 6: Recorded by Granada TV at the Cavern Club on October 13, 1962. The clip was shown on "People And Places" on November 7, 1962.
Cut 7: From the BBC radio in 1962.
Cut 8: Recorded from Radio Luxembourg on January 18, 1963.
Cut 9: From the BBC radio 1963.
Cut 10: From the Rediffusion TV show "Around The Beatles" which was filmed April 27--28, 1964, and aired May 6, 1964.
Cut 11: Not the Beatles, but Peter and Gordon.
Cuts 12--20: From the **LET IT BE** sessions early in 1969 at London's Twickenham Studios.
NOTES: Only 200 copies of this album were pressed.

474   SEATTLE 66   66 x 53   (EP)
NOTES: Same as **EXCLUSIVE! BEATLES INTERVIEWS 1966.**
SEE ALSO: **INTERVIEWS.**

September In The Rain/
   Sheik of Araby (45)   Deccagone 1101 (Entry 478)

475 **SECOND AMENDMENT CHRISTMAS ALBUM** ZAP 7857 (LP)
NOTES: Same as **CHRISTMAS ALBUM – 1ST AMENDMENT II.**
SEE ALSO: **CHRISTMAS MEETINGS; CHRISTMAS MESSAGE FROM
LIVERPOOL; COMPLETE CHRISTMAS COLLECTION; COMPLETE
CHRISTMAS COLLECTION; THEIR COMPLETE CHRISTMAS
COLLECTION '63–69; WHITE CHRISTMAS.**

476 **SECOND TO NONE** SODD 009 (2 LPs)

1. *Twist And Shout*
2. *You Can't Do That*
3. *All My Loving*
4. *She Loves You*
5. *Things We Said Today*
6. *Roll Over Beethoven*
7. *Love Me Do*
8. *Please Please Me*
9. *Can't Buy Me Love*

10. *If I Fell*
11. *I Want To Hold Your Hand*
12. *Boys*
13. *A Hard Day's Night*
14. *Long Tall Sally*
15. *Till There Was You*
16. *I Saw Her Standing There*
17. *Rock And Roll Music*

18. *She's A Woman*
19. *If I Needed Someone*
20. *Day Tripper*
21. *Baby's In Black*
22. *I Feel Fine*
23. *Yesterday*
24. *I Wanna Be Your Man*
25. *Ain't She Sweet*
26. *P.S. I Love You*

27. *There's A Place*
28. *Misery*
29. *Dizzy Miss Lizzy*
30. *This Boy*
31. *From Me To You*
32. *Nowhere Man*
33. *Paperback Writer*
34. *I'm Down*

Cuts 1–6, 9–14: Recorded live at the Hollywood Bowl, August 23, 1964.
Cuts 7–8, 25–31: Unknown, probably original.
Cuts 17–24, 32–34: Recorded live at Budokan Hall in Tokyo, July 2, 1966.
Cuts 15–16: Recorded live in Melbourne, Australia June 16, 1964.

477 **SECRET** Wizardo 359 (LP)
NOTES: Same as **AROUND THE BEATLES** (Wizardo 349).

478 *SEPTEMBER IN THE RAIN/SHEIK OF ARABY* Deccagone 1101 (45)
NOTES: Originally released by one of the Beatle fan clubs. Both cuts
are from the Decca auditions January 1, 1962. Issued with a full-color
picture sleeve. Originals were pressed on yellow vinyl. This was later
copied.

479 *SEPTEMBER IN THE RAIN/SHEIK OF ARABY* Deccagone 1101 (45)
NOTES: This is a copy of the original Deccagone release which was released by
one of the Beatle fan clubs. The recording also came with a full-color
picture sleeve. Unlike the original, the copies were pressed on blue vinyl.

480 *SEPTEMBER IN THE RAIN/SHEIK OF ARABY* Pye 206 (45)
NOTES: Copy of the Deccagone single. This came with a black–and–white
picture sleeve.

481 **SHADES OF ORANGE** RS 2597 (LP)

1. *Cops And Robbers*
2. *Don't You Lie To Me*
3. *Ain't That Loving You*
4. *Look What You've Done*
5. *Con Le Mie La Crime*

8. *Loving Sacred Loving*
9. *Child Of The Moon*
10. *Memo From Turner*
11. *Snake Drive*
12. *West Coast Idea*

6. *We Love You*　　　　　　　　13. *Let It Rock*
7. *Shades of Orange*
NOTES: These songs are done by the Rolling Stones, not the Beatles. There was involvement by John and Paul on *We Love You* and the Beatles were also supposed to have been involved in *Shades Of Orange*.

482　SHEA . . . AT LAST　Ruthless Rhyme　(LP)

1. *Twist And Shout*　　　　　5. *Act Naturally*
2. *I Feel Fine*　　　　　　　　6. *Can't Buy Me Love*
3. *Dizzy Miss Lizzy*　　　　　7. *Baby's In Black*
4. *Ticket To Ride*　　　　　　8. *A Hard Day's Night*
　　　　　　　　　　　　　　　9. *Help*
　　　　　　　　　　　　　　　10. *I'm Down*

Cuts 1--10: From the Shea Stadium concert, August 15, 1965.
NOTES: This is a re–issue of the TMOQ 71012 album. In fact, the insert has that label and number on it. Issued on colored vinyl.

483　SHEA STADIUM　Unknown　(LP)
NOTES: Same as **LAST LIVE SHOW.**

484　THE SHEA STADIUM CONCERT　Unknown　(LP)

1. *Twist And Shout*　　　　　7. *Can't Buy Me Love*
2. *You Can't Do That*　　　　8. *If I Fell*
3. *All My Loving*　　　　　　9. *I Want To Hold Your Hand*
4. *She Loves You*　　　　　　10. *Boys*
5. *Things We Said Today*　　11. *A Hard Day's Night*
6. *Roll Over Beethoven*　　　12. *Long Tall Sally*

Cuts 1–12: Recorded at the Hollywood Bowl concert August 23, 1964.

485　THE SHEA STADIUM CONCERT 1964　Unknown　(LP)
NOTES: Same as **BACK IN 1964 AT THE HOLLYWOOD BOWL** (Lemon).
SEE ALSO: **BACK IN 1964 AT THE HOLLYWOOD BOWL** (CBM); **BEATLES 1964; HOLLYWOOD BOWL '64; LIVE AT HOLLYWOOD BOWL; LIVE AT THE HOLLYWOOD BOWL; L.A.; LIVE AT SHEA; THE ONLY LIVE RECORDINGS** (Kustom); **THE ONLY LIVE RECORDINGS** (Unknown); **THE SHEA STADIUM "MORE OR LESS" STEREO; SHEA: THE GOOD OLD DAYS** (Kustom); **SHEA: THE GOOD OLD DAYS** (Pine Tree).

486　THE SHEA STADIUM "MORE OR LESS" STEREO　Unknown　(LP)
NOTES: Same as **BACK IN 1964 AT THE HOLLYWOOD BOWL** (Lemon).
SEE ALSO: **BACK IN 1964 AT THE HOLLYWOOD BOWL** (CBM); **BEATLES 1964; HOLLYWOOD BOWL '64; LIVE AT HOLLYWOOD BOWL; LIVE AT THE HOLLYWOOD BOWL; L.A.; LIVE AT SHEA; THE ONLY LIVE RECORDINGS** (Kustom); **THE ONLY LIVE RECORDINGS** (Unknown); **THE SHEA STADIUM CONCERT 1964; SHEA: THE GOOD OLD DAYS** (Kustom); **SHEA: THE GOOD OLD DAYS** (Pine Tree).

487　SHEA THE GOOD OLD DAYS　CBM 2315　(LP)

1. *I'm Down*　　　　　　　　8. *Can't Buy Me Love*
2. *Interview*　　　　　　　　9. *Baby's In Black*
3. *Introduction*　　　　　　10. *A Hard Day's Night*
4. *Twist And Shout*　　　　11. *Help*
5. *I Feel Fine*　　　　　　　12. *I'm Down*
6. *Dizzy Miss Lizzy*
7. *Ticket To Ride*

Cuts 1–12: Shea Stadium August 15, 1965.

488   **SHEA: THE GOOD OLD DAYS**   Kustom Records ASC 002   (LP)

1. *Twist*
2. *All Lovin'*
3. *You She Loves*
4. *Things Today*
5. *Roll Over*
6. *Can't Purchase Me*
7. *Fallin' In Love*
8. *Holding Hands*
9. *Boys*
10. *Hard Knights*
11. *Sally*

NOTES: Titles are different, but this is the same as **BACK IN 1964 AT THE HOLLYWOOD BOWL** (Lemon).
SEE ALSO: **BACK IN 1964 AT THE HOLLYWOOD BOWL** (CBM); **BEATLES 1964; HOLLYWOOD BOWL '64; LIVE AT HOLLYWOOD BOWL; LIVE AT THE HOLLYWOOD BOWL; L.A.; LIVE AT SHEA; THE ONLY LIVE RECORDINGS** (Kustom); **THE ONLY LIVE RECORDINGS** (Unknown); **SHEA STADIUM CONCERT 1964; SHEA STADIUM "MORE OR LESS" STEREO; SHEA: THE GOOD OLD DAYS** (Pine Tree).

489   **SHEA: THE GOOD OLD DAYS**   Pine Tree Records S 2531/2532   (LP)
NOTES: Same as **BACK IN 1964 AT THE HOLLYWOOD BOWL** (Lemon).
SEE ALSO: **BACK IN 1964 AT THE HOLLYWOOD BOWL** (CBM); **BEATLES 1964; HOLLYWOOD BOWL '64; LIVE AT HOLLYWOOD BOWL; LIVE AT THE HOLLYWOOD BOWL; L.A.; LIVE AT SHEA; THE ONLY LIVE RECORDINGS** (Kustom); **THE ONLY LIVE RECORDINGS** (Unknown); **THE SHEA STADIUM CONCERT 1964; THE SHEA STADIUM "MORE OR LESS" STEREO; SHEA: THE GOOD OLD DAYS** (Kustom).

490   *SHE LOVES YOU/I'LL GET YOU*   Swan 4152   (45)
NOTES: Issued with the black Swan label with silver printing. This was pressed in several colors of vinyl including blue, red, violet and yellow.

491   **SHOUT**   Unknown   (LP)

1. *Shout*
2. *Some Other Guy*
3. *Johnny B. Goode*
4. *Memphis*
5. *You Really Got A Hold On Me*
6. *She's A Woman*
7. *Everybody's Trying To Be My Baby*
8. *Rock And Roll Music*
9. *I Feel Fine*
10. *Ticket To Ride*
11. *Yesterday*
12. *Nowhere Man*
13. *Till There Was You*
14. *I Want To Hold Your Hand*
15. *This Boy*
16. *All My Loving*

Cut 1: From the Rediffusion TV show "Around The Beatles." Show was taped April 27–28, 1964 and aired May 6, 1964.
Cut 2: Recorded by Granada TV at the Cavern Club on October 13, 1962. The tape was shown on "People And Places" on November 7, 1962.
Cuts 3–5: From the BBC radio show "Saturday Club" from May 25, 1963.
Cuts 6–10: Recorded at the Paris Sports Palais on June 20, 1965.
Cuts 11–12: Recorded at the Cirkus Krone in Munich, Germany, June 24, 1966.
Cuts 13–14: From the Washington, DC concert February 11, 1964.
Cuts 15–16: From the "Ed Sullivan Show" of February 9, 1964.

492   *SIE LIEBT DICH/KOMM, GIB MIR DEINE HAND*   Capitol 444   (12–inch 45)
NOTES: This twelve–inch 45 was issued for the first time in 1978. Both songs are original recordings done in Germany. It was issued on several colors of vinyl including clear and red.

493   SILVER ALBUM OF WORLD'S GREATEST   Jarris 0020   (LP)

1. *Don't Let Me Down*
2. *Everything You Are*
3. *Get Back Tojo Go Home*
4. *Sweet And Lovely Girl*
5. *On Our Way Home*
6. *If You Want It You Can Dig It*
7. *Let It Be*
8. *Don't Leave Me Waiting Here*
9. *Move Over Honey*
10. *Nothing's Gonna Change My Life*

Cuts 1–10: From the **LET IT BE** sessions recorded at London's Twickenham Studios early in 1969.
NOTES: Released before the **LET IT BE** album, so the bootleggers made up the titles themselves.

494   SING THIS ALL TOGETHER   Smilin' Ears 7700–2   (2 LPs)

1. *Sing This All Together*
2. *Jagger Interview*
3. *The Lantern*
4. *In Another Land No. 1*
5. *Brian Jones Studio Interview*
6. *The Gompher*
7. *2000 Light Years From Home*
8. *Citadel*
9. *Shades Of Orange*
10. *Stones Street Interview*
11. *The Gompher*
12. *In Another Land No. 2*
13. *She's A Rainbow*
14. *Ride On Baby*

15. *Too Many Cooks*
16. *That Place*
17. *2120 S. Michigan Ave.*
18. *Cops And Robbers*
19. *Paint It Black*
20. *Satisfaction*
21. *Little Queenie*
22. *I Want To Be Loved*
23. *Ain't That Lovin' You Baby*
24. *Through The Lonely Nights*
25. *Everybody Needs Somebody*
26. *Look What You Done*
27. *Meet Me In The Bottom*
28. *We Got A Good Thing Goin'*
29. *We Love You*

NOTES: Laminated cover. All cuts by the Rolling Stones except cut 15 and cut 23. Cut 15 is an unreleased Apple single with Mick Jagger singing lead, Ringo on drums and John producing. Cut 29 has John and Paul singing background vocals.
SEE ALSO: **BEATLES/STONES.**

495   SOLDIER OF LOVE   CBM 1022   (LP)

1. *I'll Be On My Way*
2. *Till There Was You*
3. *Do The Oz*
4. *Sentimental Journey*
5. *I Got A Woman*
6. *Soldier Of Love*
7. *Murray The K Fan Club*
   She Loves You
   Shout

Cut 1: From a BBC radio broadcast in the fall of 1962.
Cut 2: From the "Ed Sullivan Show" February 9, 1964.
Cut 3: Original recording, by Bill Elliot and the Elastic Oz Band.
Cut 4: Ringo on the "Ed Sullivan Show" May 17, 1970.
Cut 5: 1963 outtake.
Cut 6: 1963 outtake.
Cut 7: Original Murray The K interviews.

496   SOLDIER OF LOVE   CBM B208   (LP)
NOTES: Exact cuts unknown, but probably the same as **SOLDIER OF LOVE** (CBM 1022).

497   SOLDIER OF LOVE   King Kong TB1022   (LP)

1. *Soldier Of Love*
2. *Murray The K Fan Club*

3. *I Got A Woman*
4. *Till There Was You*
5. *Sentimental Journey*
6. *Do The Oz*

NOTES: Same as **SOLDIER OF LOVE** (CBM 1022), except for the order of the songs and *I'll Be On My Way* has been left off.

498   SOME LIKE IT HOT   MARC   (LP)

1. *Dialogue*
2. *Don't Let Me Down*
3. *Maxwell's Silver Hammer*
4. *Two Of Us*
5. *Oh Darling*
6. *Whole Lotta Shakin'*
7. *Across The Universe*
8. *I Dig A Pony*
9. *Suzy Parker*
10. *I Me Mine*
11. *For You Blue*

12. *Besame Mucho*
13. *Octopusses' Garden*
14. *Long And Winding Road*
15. *Shake, Rattle And Roll*
16. *Miss Ann*
17. *Lawdy Miss Clawdy*
18. *Dig It*
19. *Message From Paul*
20. *Let It Be*
21. *Long And Winding Road*

Cuts 1–21: From the **LET IT BE** sessions recorded early in 1969 at London's Twickenham Studios.
NOTES: Japanese bootleg.

499   SOME OTHER GUY   Berkeley 2008; CBM WEC 3813   (LP)

1. *Some Other Guy*
2. *Lucille*
3. *Boys*
4. *Instant Karma*
5. *Act Naturally*
6. *Butcher Cover Radio Rap*

7. *From Us To You*
8. *Shout*
9. *Mary Jane*
10. *Hop On The Bus*
11. *Across The Universe*
12. *Twist And Shout*
13. *Roll Over Beethoven*
14. *I Wanna Be Your Man*
15. *Long Tall Sally*

Cut 1: Recorded by Granada TV at the Cavern Club on October 13, 1962. Shown on "People And Places" on November 7, 1962.
Cuts 2–3: From the BBC radio, 1963.
Cut 4: From the BBC TV show "Top Of The Pops" which aired February 12, 1970.
Cut 5: Ringo with Cilla Black on the "Cilla Black" TV show February 6, 1968.
Cut 6: Interview with Tony Barrow about the Butcher cover in June, 1966.
Cut 7: From the BBC radio show "From Us To You," December 26, 1963.
Cut 8: From a BBC radio show in the summer of 1964.
Cut 9: Recorded by John, August 14, 1968. This was to have been released by Apple, but never was.
Cut 10: From the film "Magical Mystery Tour."
Cut 11: From the Wildlife Fund LP **NO ONE'S GONNA CHANGE OUR WORLD**.
Cuts 12–15: From the Rediffusion TV show "Around The Beatles." The show was taped April 27–28, 1964, and shown May 6, 1964.

500   SOME OTHER GUY   Unknown   (LP)

1. *Some Other Guy*
2. *What's Yer New Mary Jane*
3. *Lucille*
4. *Boys*

8. *From Us To You*
9. *Shout*
10. *Twist And Shout*
11. *Roll Over Beethoven*

Sound Of The Stars (EP)   **Lyn 996 (Entry 502)**

5. *Instant Karma*
6. *Act Naturally*
7. *Tony Barrow Discusses The Butcher Cover*
12. *I Wanna Be Your Man*
13. *Long Tall Sally*
14. *Dialogue From Magical Mystery Tour*

NOTES: See **SOME OTHER GUY** (Berkeley) for origins of songs. Both albums are the same, except this one does not contain *Across The Universe*.

501 **SOME OTHER GUY/CAVERN CLUB '63** CBM B215 (LP)
NOTES: Exact cuts unknown, but presumably contains cuts from **SOME OTHER GUY** (CBM) and **CAVERN CLUB** (CBM).

502 **SOUND OF THE STARS** Lyn 996 (EP)
NOTES: Contains a radio Caroline interview of the Beatles by DJ Tom Lodge. Disc also contains Cilla Black with the Bachelors, Cliff Richard with Hank Melvin and Bruce Welch, Judith Durham with Penny Valentine, Cathy McGowan with the Hollies, Dusty Springfield with Spencer Davis, the Walker Brothers with Pete Townshend and Penny Valentine, and Sandie Shaw with Adam Faith. Came with a special black--and--white picture sleeve.

503 **SOUVENIR OF THEIR VISIT TO AMERICA** Vee Jay EP1–903 (EP)

1. *Misery*
2. *Taste Of Honey*
3. *Ask My Why*
4. *Anna*

NOTES: This is a picture disc, released in 1980. It uses the same picture as was on the picture cover to the original EP. This was the first seven--inch Beatles picture disc boot.

504 **SPICY BEATLES SONGS** TMOQ MJ 543; TMOQ 1892; TMOQ 71076 (LP)
NOTES: Same as **MARY JANE** (TMOQ MJ 543).
SEE ALSO: **SPICY BEATLES SONGS/MARY JANE.**

505 **SPICY BEATLES SONGS/MARY JANE** Amazon Etcetra 635 (LP)
NOTES: Same as **MARY JANE** (TMOQ MJ 543).
SEE ALSO: **SPICY BEATLES SONGS.**

506 **SPORTS PALACE FRANCE -- SECOND SHOW** CBM 1101 (LP)
NOTES: Same as **PARIS SPORTS PALAIS** (CBM).
SEE ALSO: **PARIS SPORTS PALAIS 1965.**

507 **SP 602** Wizardo 316 (2 LPs)
NOTES: Same as **GET 'CHER YEAH YEAHS OUT.**

508 **STARS OF 63** Gamma Alpha Records -- CBM 4779/4750 (2 LPs)

1. *I Saw Her Standing There*
2. *Roll Over Beethoven*
3. *Hippy Hippy Shake*
4. *Sweet Little Sixteen*
5. *Lend Me Your Comb*
6. *Your Feets Too Big*
7. *Twist And Shout*
8. *Mr. Moonlight*
9. *A Taste Of Honey*
10. *Besame Mucho*
11. *Reminiscing*
12. *Kansas City*

13. *Ain't Nothing Shakin'*
14. *To Know Her Is To Love Her*
15. *Little Queenie*
16. *Falling In Love Again*
17. *Ask Me Why*
18. *Be--Bop--A--Lula*
20. *Red Sails In The Sunset*
21. *Everybody's Trying To Be My Baby*
22. *Matchbox*
23. *Talkin' 'bout You*
24. *Shimmy Shake*

19. *Hallelujah I Love Her So*

25. *Long Tall Sally*
26. *I Remember You*

NOTES: This is a pirate of **LIVE AT THE STAR CLUB**, the German version.

509   STOCKHOLM 1964   Instant Analysis 4179   (LP)

1. *A Shot Of Rhythm And Blues*
2. *There's A Place*
3. *Twist And Shout*
4. *She Loves You*
5. *Twist And Shout*
6. *Long Tall Sally*
7. *I Saw Her Standing There*

8. *I Feel Fine*
9. *I'm Down*
10. *Act Naturally*
11. *Ticket To Ride*
12. *Yesterday*
13. *Help*

Cuts 1--3: From the BBC radio in 1963.
Cuts 4--7: Recorded for the Swedish TV show "Drop In" on October 30, 1963. The show aired November 3, 1963.
Cuts 8--13: From the TV show "Blackpool Night Out." The show was taped on July 7, 1965, and aired August 1, 1965.

510   STRAWBERRY FIELDS FOREVER 1975 FIRST ANNUAL CHRISTMAS RECORD
Eva-Tone 10207521 A&B   (Flexidisc EP)

1. *Joe Pope -- Introduction*
2. *Butcher Cover Auction*
3. *Jurgen Volmer (Guest Speaker)*
4. *Peter McCabe (Speaker)*
5. *Richard Dilello*

6. *Joe Pope Again*
7. *Call Me Back Again* -- Bernice & Rippers
8. *Band On The Run* -- Bernice & Rippers
9. *Live And Let Die* -- Bernice & Rippers
10. *Hi Hi Hi* -- Bernice & Rippers
11. *Joe Pope Again*

NOTES: Many of the cuts on this disc were recorded at the Magical Mystery Tour '75 -- Boston Beatles Convention held at the Bradford Hotel. This is a square, red flexidisc.

511   STRAWBERRY FIELDS FOREVER 1976 SECOND ANNUAL CHRISTMAS RECORD   Eva-Tone 12877A&B   (10--inch flexidisc)

1. *Joe Pope*
2. *Here Comes The Sun*
3. *Homeward Bound*
4. *Slippin' And Slidin'*
5. *Imagine*
6. *Joe Pope*

7. *Think For Yourself*
8. *Storm In A Teacup* (Badfinger)
9. *Spiritual Regeneration a/k/a Indian Rope Trick*
10. *Happy Birthday To Mike Love*
11. *No No Song*
12. *Angel Baby*
13. *Joe Pope*
14. *Mine For Me*
15. *Strawberry Fields Forever*

Cut 1: Fan club president Joe Pope talking about this record.
Cuts 2--3: George Harrison and Paul Simon on the TV show "Saturday Night Live." Show was taped November 16, 1976 and aired November 18, 1976.
Cuts 4--5: John Lennon on the TV show "Salute To Sir Lew Grade," which aired June 13, 1975.
Cut 7: Just a short clip from the film "Yellow Submarine."
Cut 8: Not the Beatles, but Badfinger. This is a cut never released in the U.S.
Cuts 9--10: Recorded in Rishikesh, India, March 15, 1968.
Cut 11: Ringo on the "Smothers Brothers" TV show April 28, 1975.
Cut 12: Outtake from John's **ROCK AND ROLL** album.

149

Cut 14: Paul and Linda harmonizing with Rod Stewart on a song written for Rod by Paul.
Cut 15: Just a small bit of the original single.
NOTES: This was issued as Audio Issue No. 24 of the fan club magazine Strawberry Fields Forever. Issued as a ten--inch red flexidisc.

512 **STRAWBERRY FIELDS FOREVER 1977 A HARD DAY'S NIGHT BEFORE CHRISTMAS** Eva--Tone 1123772 A&B (10--inch flexidisc)

1. *I Want A Beatle For Christmas*
2. *Bye Bye Love*
3. *Blackbird*
4. *Heather*
5. *Fool On The Hill*

6. *Penina*
7. *Ringo, I Love You*
8. *Things We Said Today*
9. *Her Majesty*
10. *Oh Darling*

Cut 1: Beatle novelty by Becky Lee Beck.
Cut 2: From the taping sessions for "Saturday Night Live" by George and Paul Simon, November 16, 1976. This one was not aired.
Cuts 3--4: Paul and Donovan in 1968.
Cut 5: Outtake from "Magical Mystery Tour."
Cut 6: Listed as by Jotta Herre.
Cut 7: Beatle novelty by Bonnie Jo Mason, now better known as Cher.
Cut 8: Outtake.
Cut 9: Full version with last chord.
Cut 10: Studio outtake.
NOTES: This was issued as Audio Issue No. 27 of the fan club magazine Strawberry Fields Forever. Issued as a ten--inch red flexidisc.

513 **STRAWBERRY FIELDS FOREVER 1978 CHRISTMAS RECORD**
Eva--Tone 128781 A&B (10--inch flexidisc)

1. *Little Beatle Boy*
2. *Oriental Nightfish*
3. *Interview*
4. *John Reading Poetry:*
   The National Health Cow
   The Fat Budgie
   I Sat Belonely
5. *Ringo Suit Commercial*
6. *Ding Dong*
7. *"Shout" Contest*

8. *Soilie*
9. *A Hard Day's Night Spot*
10. *Hi Hi Hi/C Moon Spot*
11. *Imagine*
12. *Interview*
13. *Strawberry Fields Forever*

Cut 1: Beatle novelty by the Angels.
Cut 2: Paul and Linda 1973 demo.
Cut 3: From a 1964 interview . . . Ringo on Beethoven.
Cut 4: John reading his own poetry.
Cut 5: Ringo for leisure suits on Japanese TV.
Cut 6: George demo.
Cut 7: This was a special contest for club members. It consists of shouting from various Beatle records. The object is to guess which songs were used.
Cut 8: Studio version, not live.
Cut 9: A radio commercial for the movie.
Cut 10: A radio commercial by Paul and Linda for their single.
Cut 11: An acoustic outtake by John.
Cut 12: John and Paul talk about songwriting.
Cut 13: A short bit of the original single.
NOTES: This was issued as Audio Issue No. 32 of the fan club magazine Strawberry Fields Forever. Issued as a ten--inch blue flexidisc.

514 **STRAWBERRY FIELDS FOREVER 1979 CHRISTMAS RECORD**
Eva–Tone 117801   (10–inch flexidisc)

1. *Christmas With The Beatles*
2. *Living In A Pet Shop*
3. *That's My Life*
4. *Interview*
5. *Devil In His Heart*
6. *Soundstage Of My Mind*
7. *The Kids Are Alright*
8. *I Saw Her Standing There*
9. *The Heart That You Broke*
10. *Wonderful Christmas Time/
    Happy Christmas (War Is Over)*

Cut 1: Beatle novelty by Judy & The Duets.
Cut 2: Ringo from the soundtrack of "Scouse The Mouse."
Cut 3: Not the Beatles, but John's father Freddie Lennon.
Cut 4: Interview of George and Ringo by Jackie Stewart on ABC–TV's "Wide
World Of Sports" at Monaco.
Cut 5: The Donays doing their original version of the song later recorded by the
Beatles.
Cut 6: From George's 1974 tour.
Cut 7: Ringo doing a commercial for the Who movie.
Cut 8: Unknown, possibly the Who.
Cut 9: 1975 outtake from Paul in Nashville.
Cut 10: Just bits of Paul's and John's Christmas records.
NOTES: This was issued as Audio Issue No. 36 of the fan club magazine
Strawberry Fields Forever. Issued as a ten–inch black flexidisc.

515 **STUDIO OUTTAKE RECORDINGS 1962–64**   Wizardo 326   (LP)

1. *Love Me Do*
2. *Please Please Me*
3. *From Me To You*
4. *I Saw Her Standing There*
5. *Misery*
6. *Do You Want To Know A Secret*
7. *There's A Place*
8. *Anna*
9. *Chains*
10. *Boys*
11. *She Loves You*
12. *Till There Was You*
13. *Roll Over Beethoven*
14. *You Really Got A Hold On Me*
15. *Devil In Her Heart*
16. *Money*
17. *Long Tall Sally*
18. *Honey Don't*
19. *Kansas City*
20. *Words Of Love*

Cuts 1–20: Listed at outtakes from 1962–64, these are more likely original
recordings.
SEE ALSO: **WORDS OF LOVE.**

516 **STUDIO SESSIONS VOL. I**   CBM 3640   (LP)
NOTES: Same as sides one and three of **DECCA AUDITION OUTTAKES –**
SUPER STUDIO SESSIONS 2.
SEE ALSO: **OUTAKES VOL. I; OUTAKES VOL. I/OUTAKES VOL. II;**
STUDIO SESSIONS NO. 1 AND NO. 2.

517 **STUDIO SESSIONS VOL. II**   Berkeley 11; CBM 3641   (LP)
NOTES: Same as sides two and four of **DECCA AUDITION OUTTAKES –**
SUPER STUDIO SESSIONS 2.
SEE ALSO: **OUTAKES VOL. II; OUTAKES VOL. I/OUTAKES VOL. II;**
STUDIO SESSIONS NO. 1 AND NO. 2.

518 **STUDIO SESSIONS NO. 1 & NO. 2**   Unknown (probably CBM 3640/3641)
(2 LPs)
NOTES: Same as **DECCA AUDITION OUTTAKES – SUPER STUDIO**
SESSIONS 2.
SEE ALSO: **OUTAKES VOL. I; OUTAKES VOL. II; OUTAKES VOL. I/**
OUTAKES VOL. II; STUDIO SESSIONS VOL. I; STUDIO SESSIONS
VOL. II.

519   **SUNDAY NIGHT AT THE LONDON PALLADIUM**   CBM WEC 3687   (LP)
      NOTES: Same as **LONDON PALLADIUM.**
      SEE ALSO: **FOREST HILLS/LONDON** (side two).

520   **SUPER LIVE CONCERT SERIES VOL. 1 HOLLAND/SWEDEN**   CBM A101   (LP)
      NOTES: Same as **HOLLAND/SWEDEN -- SUPER LIVE CONCERT SERIES I.**

521   **SUPER LIVE CONCERT SERIES VOL. 2 BUDOKAN HALL, TOKYO**
          CBM A102   (LP)
      NOTES: Exact cuts unknown.

522   **SUPER LIVE CONCERT SERIES VOL. 3 ITALY/PARIS**   CBM A103   (LP)
      NOTES: Same as **ITALY/PARIS** (Shalom).

523   **SUPER LIVE CONCERT SERIES VOL. 4 VANCOUVER/MELBOURNE**
          CBM A104   (LP)
      NOTES: Same as **MELBOURNE/VANCOUVER -- SUPER LIVE SERIES 4.**

524   **SUPER LIVE CONCERT SERIES VOL. 5 HOLLYWOOD BOWL**   CBM A105   (LP)
      NOTES: Exact cuts unknown.

525   **SUPER LIVE CONCERT SERIES VOL. 6 FOREST HILLS/LONDON**
          CBM A106   (LP)
      NOTES: Same as **FOREST HILLS/LONDON** (Shalom).

526   **SUPER LIVE CONCERT SERIES VOL. 7 AUDITORIUM THEATRE, U.S.A.**
          CBM A107   (LP)
      NOTES: Exact cuts unknown.

527   **SUPERTRACKS**   CBM 207; HHCER 102   (LP)
      NOTES: Same as **SUPERTRACKS 2** (HHCER 102).
      SEE ALSO: **BACTRAX.**

528   **SUPERTRACKS**   CBM 1018   (LP)

     1. *Paperback Writer*   7. *Get Back*
     2. *Rain*   8. *I Should Have Known Better*
     3. *Peace Of Mind*   9. *If I Fell*
     4. *Take 37*   10. *And I Love Her*
     5. *Tutty Frutty*   11. *Tell Me Why*
     6. *Hey Jude*

      Cuts 1–2: From the BBC–TV show "Top Of The Pops" shown June 16, 1966.
          Later shown on "Thank Your Lucky Stars" and the "Ed Sullivan Show."
      Cut 3: Recorded in June 1967, and found in the Apple trash can in 1970. Also
          known as *The Candle Burns.*
      Cuts 4–7: From the **LET IT BE** sessions in early 1969.
      Cuts 8–11: From the soundtrack of "A Hard Day's Night."

529   **SUPERTRACKS I**   CBM 3922   (LP)
      NOTES: Same as **BYE BYE BYE SUPERTRACKS VOL. I.**
      SEE ALSO: **BACTRAX; SUPERTRACKS 1** (CBM).

530   **SUPERTRACKS 1**   CBM   (LP)
      NOTES: Sames as sides one and two of **BACTRAX.**
      SEE ALSO: **BYE BYE BYE SUPERTRACKS VOL. I; SUPERTRACKS I.**

531   **SUPERTRACKS 2**   CBM TB1018   (LP)
      NOTES: Same as **BYE BYE BYE SUPERTRACKS 2.**
      SEE ALSO: **SUPERTRACKS II.**

532   SUPERTRACKS 2   Highway Hi Fi 102   (LP)

1. *Let It Be*
2. *Dialogue*
3. *Rain*
4. *Paperback Writer*
5. *Get Back*
6. *The Candle Burns*
7. *Hey Jude*
8. *I Should Have Known Better*
9. *If I Fell*
10. *And I Love Her*
11. *Tell Me Why*

Cuts 1–2, 5, 7: From the **LET IT BE** sessions early in 1969 at London's
    Twickenham Studios.
Cuts 3–4: From the BBC–TV show "Top Of The Pops" shown June 16, 1966.
    Also later shown on "Thank Your Lucky Stars" and the "Ed Sullivan Show."
Cut 6: Also known as *Peace Of Mind*. Recorded June, 1967, and discovered in
    1970 in the Apple trash can.
Cuts 8–11: From the soundtracks to "A Hard Day's Night."
SEE ALSO: **BACTRAX; SUPERTRACKS** (HHCER 102).

533   SUPERTRACKS II   Unknown   (LP)

1. *Let It Be*
2. *Dialogue*
3. *Rain*
4. *Paperback Writer*
5. *Dialogue*
6. *Get Back*
7. *Peace Of Mind*

Cuts 1–2, 5–6: From the **LET IT BE** sessions held in early 1969 at London's
    Twickenham Studios.
Cuts 3–4: From the BBC–TV show "Top Of The Pops" shown June 16, 1966.
    also later shown on "Thank Your Lucky Stars" and the "Ed Sullivan Show."
Cut 7: Recorded in June, 1967 and found in the Apple trash can in 1970. This
    is also known as *The Candle Burns.*

534   SUPERTRACKS II   Unknown   (LP)
NOTES: Same as **BYE BYE BYE SUPERTRACKS 2.**
SEE ALSO: **SUPERTRACKS 2.**

535   SWEDEN 1963   CBM 3795 C1/3571   (LP)

1. *I Saw Her Standing There*
2. *From Me To You*
3. *Money*
4. *Roll Over Beethoven*
5. *You Really Got A Hold On Me*
6. *She Loves You*
7. *Twist And Shout*
8. *Till There Was You*
9. *I Want To Hold Your Hand*
10. *Roll Over Beethoven*
11. *All My Loving*
12. *I Wanna Be Your Man*
13. *From Us To You*
14. *Interview*

Cuts 1–7: Recorded for the Swedish TV show "Drop In" on October 30, 1963.
    The show aired November 3, 1963.
Cuts 8–9: Recorded live at the Washington, DC concert February 11, 1964.
Cuts 10–14: From the BBC radio show "From Us To You" broadcast December
    26, 1963.
SEE ALSO: **HOLLAND/SWEDEN; SWEDEN, WASHINGTON, SWEDEN;
    WORLDWIDE.**

536   SWEDEN, WASHINGTON, SWEDEN   CBM 3795   (LP)
NOTES: Same as **SWEDEN 1963.**
SEE ALSO: **HOLLAND/SWEDEN; WORLDWIDE.**

537   SWEET APPLE TRAX   Newsound Records NR 909–1   (2 LPs)

1. *Two Of Us*
2. *Don't Let Me Down*
8. *Be Bop A Lula*
9. *She Came In Through The*

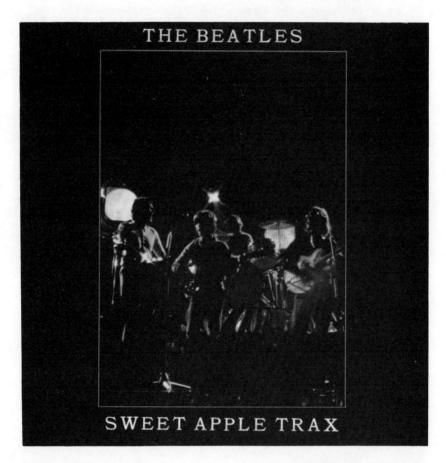

Sweet Apple Trax (2 LPs)   **Newsound NR 909-1 (Entry 537)**

3. *Suzy Parker*
4. *I've Got A Feeling*
5. *No Pakistanis*
6. *Get Back*
7. *Don't Let Me Down*
    Bathroom Window
10. *High Heeled Sneakers*
11. *I Me Mine*
12. *I've Got A Feeling*
13. *One After 909*
14. *Norwegian Wood*
15. *She Came In Through The Bathroom Window*

16. *Let It Be*
17. *Shakin' In The 60's*
18. *Good Rockin' Tonight*
19. *Across The Universe*
20. *Two Of Us*
21. *Momma, You're Just On My Mind*
22. *Tennessee*
23. *House Of The Rising Sun*
24. *Back To Commonwealth*
25. *White Power/Promenade*
26. *Hi Ho Silver*
27. *For You Blue*
28. *Let It Be*

Cuts 1–28: Recorded during the **LET IT BE** sessions at London's Twickenham Studios early in 1969.
NOTES: Deluxe, full color, laminated cover.
SEE ALSO: **CAUGHT OFF GUARD; HAHST AZ SON; HAHST AZ SUN; HOT AS SUN; SWEET APPLE TRAX VOL. I** (Image Disc); **SWEET APPLE TRAX VOL. II** (Image disc).

538   SWEET APPLE TRAX   Wizardo 343   (2 LPs)

1. *Old Hillbilly Way*
2. *House Of The Rising Sun*
3. *Commonwealth Song*
4. *Get Off White Power*
5. *Winston, Richard, John*
6. *Yackety Yack*
7. *For You Blue*
8. *Let It Be*
9. *Get Back*
10. *Don't Let Me Down*
11. *On Our Way Home*
12. *Ba Ba Black Sheep*
13. *Encore*
14. *Suzy Parker*
15. *Oh Yeah (I've Got A Feeling)*
16. *No Pakistanis*

17. *Let It Be*
18. *Be Bop A Lula*
19. *Silver Spoon*
20. *Tuesday Speaking*
21. *High Heeled Sneakers*
22. *I Me Mine*
23. *One After 909*
24. *Norwegian Wood*
25. *Bathroom Window*
26. *A Long Road*
27. *Shakin' in the 60's*
28. *Everybody's Rockin'*
29. *Across The Universe*
30. *On Our Way Home*
31. *Momma, You've Been On My Mind*
32. *Da Da Da*

Cuts 1–31: Recorded at Twickenham Studios in London early in 1969 during the **LET IT BE** sessions.
NOTES: Pressed on colored vinyl.
SEE ALSO: **APPLE TRAX ONE '69; APPLE TRAX TWO '69; SWEET APPLE TRAX VOL. ONE** (CBM); **SWEET APPLE TRAX VOL. TWO** (CBM).

539   SWEET APPLE TRAX VOL. I   APP 001   (LP)
NOTES: Exact cuts unknown, but presumably the same as **SWEET APPLE TRAX VOL. I.**

540   SWEET APPLE TRAX I   Berkeley 05   (2 LPs)

1. *Hillbilly Way*
2. *House Of The Rising Sun*
3. *Commonwealth Song*
4. *Get Off White Power*
5. *Winston, Richard and John*
6. *Yackety Yack*
7. *For You Blue*
8. *Let It Be*

Sweet Apple Trax Vol. 1 (LP)   **Image Disc 909 1A/B (Entry 541)**

9. *Get Back*
10. *Don't Let Me Down*
11. *On Our Way Home*
12. *Ba Ba Black Sheep*
13. *Encore*

14. *Suzy Parker*
15. *Oh Yeah (I've Got A Feeling)*
16. *No Pakistanis*

Cuts 1–16: Recorded during the **LET IT BE** sessions early in 1969 at London's Twickenham Studios.

SEE ALSO: **APPLETRAX ONE '69.**

541   **SWEET APPLE TRAX VOL. 1**   Image Disc Inc. 909 1A/1B   (LP)

1. *Two Of Us*
2. *Don't Let Me Down*
3. *Suzy Parker*
4. *I've Got A Feeling*
5. *No Pakistanis*
6. *Get Back*
7. *Don't Let Me Down*

8. *Be Bop A Lula*
9. *She Came In Through The Bathroom Window*
10. *High Heeled Sneakers*
11. *I Me Mine*
12. *I've Got A Feeling*
13. *One After 909*
14. *Norwegian Wood*
15. *She Came In Through The Bathroom Window*

Cuts 1–15: Recorded during the **LET IT BE** sessions held at London's Twickenham Studios in early 1969.

NOTES: This disc contains sides one and two of the Newsound masters. This is a picture disc. The color picture shows the famous Apple rooftop concert. The album was produced by Monique Corriveau and designed by Michel Vermeer. Only 1,000 were pressed.

SEE ALSO: **CAUGHT OFF GUARD; HAHST AZ SON; HAHST AZ SUN; HOT AS SUN.**

542   **SWEET APPLE TRAX VOL. ONE**   CBM 4182   (2 LPs)

1. *Old Hillbilly Way*
2. *House Of The Rising Sun*
3. *Commonwealth Song*
4. *Get Back White Power*

5. *Winston, Richard And John*
6. *Yackety Yack*
7. *For You Blue*
8. *Let It Be*

9. *Get Back*
10. *Don't Let Me Down*
11. *On Our Way Home*
12. *Ba Ba Black Sheep*
13. *Encore*

14. *Suzy Parker*
15. *Oh Yeah (I've Got A Feeling)*
16. *No Pakistanis*

Cuts 1–16: From the **LET IT BE** sessions held at London's Twickenham Studios early in 1969.

NOTES: Deluxe laminated cover.

SEE ALSO: **APPLETRAX ONE '69; SWEET APPLE TRAX I** (Berkeley); **SWEET APPLE TRAX** (Wizardo 343).

543   **SWEET APPLE TRACKS 2**   Unknown   (LP)

1. *I Threw It All Away*
2. *Momma, You've Been On My Mind*
3. *Untitled*
4. *Let It Be*
5. *I Me Mine*
6. *One After 909*
7. *I Got A Feeling*

8. *Norwegian Wood*
9. *She Came In Through The Bathroom Window*
10. *Shakin' In The 60's*
11. *Everybody's Rockin' Tonight*
12. *Be Bop A Lula*

Cuts 1–12: Recorded during the **LET IT BE** sessions at London's Twickenham Studios early in 1969.

Sweet Apple Trax Vol. II (LP)   **Image Disc 909 K/1D (Entry 545)**

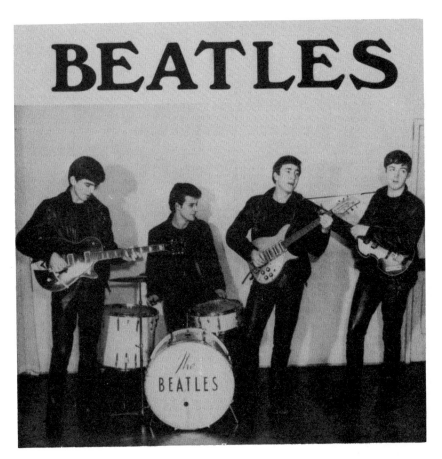

Take Good Care Of My Baby (45)   Demo Disc L-1389 (Entry 548)

544   SWEET APPLE TRAX VOL. II   APP 002   (LP)
      NOTES: Exact cuts unknown, but presumably the same as **SWEET APPLE TRAX VOL. II.**

545   SWEET APPLE TRAX VOL. II   Image Disc Inc. 909 K/1D   (LP)

1. *Let It Be*
2. *Shakin' In The Sixties*
3. *Good Rockin' Tonight*
4. *Across The Universe*
5. *Two Of Us*
6. *Momma, You're Just On My Mind*
7. *Tennessee*
8. *House Of The Rising Sun*
9. *Back To Commonwealth*
10. *White Power/Promenade*
11. *Hi Ho Silver*
12. *For You Blue*
13. *Let It Be*

Cuts 1–13: Recorded at London's Twickenham Studios early in 1969 during the **LET IT BE** sessions.
NOTES: This is recorded from the Newsound masters. This is a picture disc with the same photo on both sides. The photo shows Paul at the console pointing and John, Yoko, George and Ringo looking on. Disc was produced by Monique Corriveau and designed by Michel Vermeer. Only 1,000 copies were pressed.
SEE ALSO: **HAHST AZ SON; HAHST AZ SUN; HOT AS SUN; SWEET APPLE TRAX** (Newsound).

546   SWEET APPLE TRAX VOL. TWO   CBM 4181   (2 LPs)

1. *Let It Be*
2. *Be Bop A Lula*
3. *Silver Spoon*
4. *Tuesday Speaking*
5. *Hi Heeled Sneakers*
6. *I'll Be Mine*
7. *One After 909*
8. *Norwegian Wood*
9. *Bathroom Window*

10. *A Long Road*
11. *Shakin' In The 60's*
12. *Everybody's Rockin'*
13. *Across The Universe*
14. *On Our Way Home*
15. *Momma, You've Been On My Mind*
16. *Da De Da*

Cuts 1–16: From the **LET IT BE** sessions in early 1969. Recorded at the Twickenham Studios in London.
NOTES: Came with a deluxe yellow cover.
SEE ALSO: **APPLETRAX TWO '69; SWEET APPLE TRAX** (Wizardo 343).

547   *SWEET GEORGIA BROWN/TAKE OUT SOME INSURANCE ON ME BABY*
      Atco 6302   (45)
      NOTES: This is a picture sleeve only. No sleeve was issued with the original record. The sleeve is made to look like the *Ain't She Sweet* sleeve, except these new titles have been substituted.

548   *TAKE GOOD CARE OF MY BABY*   Demo Disc L–1389   (45)
      NOTES: This is a one–sided disc with a black–and–white picture sleeve, made to look like a test pressing. One side of the sleeve has the full shot of John, Paul, George and Pete as used on the picture disc of **THE DECCA TAPES** (Circuit 4438) while the other side features another picture from that same session.

549   TANKS FOR THE MAMMARIES   TAKRL ANTHOL A/B/C/D BOZO 1   (2 LPs)

1. *Nowhere Man*
2. *If You Wanna Be Me* (Cat Stevens)
3. *Purple Danger* (Fleetwood Mac)
8. *Baby Don't Do It* (The Band)
9. *You Don't Know Where Your Interest Lies* (Simon & Garfunkel)

4. *Dallas* (Steely Dan)
5. *Toujours L'Amour* (Procol Harum)
6. *Rest In Peace* (Mott The Hoople)
7. *Rebel, Rebel* (David Bowie)

10. *Summer Day Sand* (Jethro Tull)
11. *Red Light Roll On* (Spirit)
12. *Grow Pins, Diddy Wah Diddy* (Capt. Beefheart)
13. *So You Want To Be A Rock & Roll Star* (Move)

14. *The Fever* (Bruce Springsteen)
15. *Long May You Run* (Crosby, Stills, Nash & Young)
16. *Little Drummer Boy, Silent Night, Auld Lang Syne* (Jimi Hendrix)
17. *Deadly Jaws* (Frank Zappa)
18. *Get Up And Go* (Rutles)
19. *No Pakistanis*

20. *The Lion Sleeps Tonight* (Brian Eno)
21. *The Runaway* (Gentle Giant)
22. *Lay Down* (Strawbs)
23. *The Twelve Drugs of Christmas* (Mushroom Tabernacle Choir)
24. *You Just Want Meat* (Jackson Browne)
25. *All That You Dream* (Little Feat)
26. *Hooray For Capt. Spaulding* (Groucho Marx)

NOTES: Only cut 1 and cut 19 are by the Beatles. Cut 1 is from the Japanese concert July 2, 1966 and cut 19 is from the **LET IT BE** sessions from early 1969. Cut 18 is by the Rutles and may be of interest to Beatle fans.

550   *THANK YOU GIRL/FROM ME TO YOU*   Vee Jay 522   (45)
NOTES: This item is a picture sleeve only. No sleeve was issued with the original record. Made like the counterfeit sleeve for *Please Please Me*, except "THE BEATLES" is in red instead of green.

551   **THEIR BIGGEST HITS**   Tollie EP1--8091   (EP)

1. *Love Me Do*
2. *Twist And Shout*

3. *There's A Place*
4. *P.S. I Love You*

NOTES: This may be one of the rarest bootlegs. Issued in 1975 with a hard sleeve, there are as few as 15 copies of this disc in existence. At first, it was passed off as a real release.

552   **THEIR COMPLETE CHRISTMAS COLLECTION '63–69**   CBM 206   (LP)

1. *The Beatles Christmas Record 1963*
2. *Another Christmas Record 1964*
3. *Third Christmas Record 1965*
4. *Pantomima, Everywhere It's Christmas 1966*

5. *Christmas Time Is Here Again 1967*
6. *Happy Christmas 1968*
7. *Happy Christmas 1969*

Cuts 1–7: All original recordings released to fan club members.

553   **THEIR NEVER RELEASED MARY JANE**   A.J.C. Cumquat Prod. on CBM 3585 (LP)
NOTES: Same as **MARY JANE** (CBM 3585).
SEE ALSO: **MARY JANE 2ND VERSION; THE NEVER RELEASED MARY JANE; THE NEW MARY JANE; THEIR NEVER RELEASED THE NEW MARY JANE; WHAT'S THE NEW MARY JANE; RETURN OF MARY JANE.**

554   **THEIR NEVER RELEASED "THE NEW MARY JANE"**   CBM 3585   (LP)
NOTES: Same as **MARY JANE** (CBM 3585).
SEE ALSO: **MARY JANE 2ND VERSION; THE NEVER RELEASED MARY JANE; THE NEW MARY JANE; THE NEVER RELEASED MARY JANE; WHAT'S THE NEW MARY JANE; RETURN OF MARY JANE.**

555   THIRTY NOSTALGIA HITS   Wizardo 102–232   (2 LPs)

1. *Twist And Shout*
2. *You Can't Do That*
3. *All My Loving*
4. *She Loves You*
5. *Things We Said Today*
6. *Roll Over Beethoven*

7. *Can't Buy Me Love*
8. *If I Fell*
9. *I Want To Hold Your Hand*
10. *Boys*
11. *A Hard Day's Night*
12. *Long Tall Sally*

13. *Rock And Roll Music*
14. *She's A Woman*
15. *If I Needed Someone*
16. *Day Tripper*
17. *Baby's In Black*
18. *I Feel Fine*
19. *Yesterday*
20. *I Wanna Be Your Man*

21. *Ain't She Sweet*
22. *P.S. I Love You*
23. *There's A Place*
24. *Misery*
25. *Dizzy Miss Lizzy*
26. *This Boy*
27. *From Me To You*
28. *Paperback Writer*
29. *I'm Down*

Cuts 1–12: From the Hollywood Bowl concert August 23, 1964.
Cuts 13–20, 28–29: From the concert at Budokan Hall in Tokyo, July 2, 1966.
Cuts 21–24: Original recordings.
Cut 25: 1962 outtake.
Cut 26: From the "Ed Sullivan Show" February 9, 1964.
Cut 27: From the "Ed Sullivan Show" February 16, 1964.

556   THOSE WERE THE DAYS   CBM 3907   (LP)

1. *You Really Got A Hold On Me*
2. *Have You Heard The Word*
3. *Don't Let Me Down*
4. *Those Were The Days*
5. *Mean Mr. Mustard*
6. *All Together On The Wireless Machine*
7. *Step Inside Love*
8. *Bye Bye Bye*
9. *Cottonfields*
10. *Twist And Shout*
11. *Dizzy Miss Lizzy*

12. *From Me To You*
13. *Twist And Shout*
14. *This Boy*
15. *I Saw Her Standing There*
16. *She Loves You*
17. *I Want To Hold Your Hand*
18. *Please Please Me*
19. *All My Loving*

Cuts 1, 10: Recorded October 30, 1963, for the Swedish TV show "Drop In." The show was aired November 3, 1963.
Cut 2: Recorded June of 1970. Reportedly this is John and at least some of the Bee Gees. (For discussion, see footnote on pages xxiv-xxv.)
Cuts 3–4: Recorded in the fall of 1968, live at a press conference.
Cuts 5–6, 8: Depending on the source, these three songs were recorded either in the spring of 1969 or the spring of 1970.
Cut 7: Demo cut by Paul in February 1968. The song was later given to Cilla Black.
Cut 9: Recorded January, 1968, by John, as a part of an interview with Kenny Everett.
Cut 11: Original recording.
Cuts 12–13, 15–18: From the Beatles second appearance on the "Ed Sullivan Show." Broadcast live from the Deauville Hotel in Miami Beach on February 16, 1964. There were 3,400 fans in attendance.
Cuts 14, 19: From the Beatles first appearance on the "Ed Sullivan Show." Recorded in New York City on February 7, 1964. Shown on February 9, 1964.
SEE ALSO: **ABBEY ROAD REVISITED** (CBM); **ABBEY ROAD REVISITED** (Wizardo); **CAVERN DAYS – SUPER STUDIO SERIES 5.**

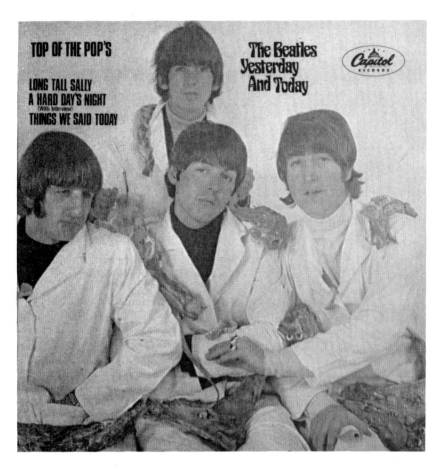

Top Of The Pops (EP) Capitol P9431 (Entry 561)

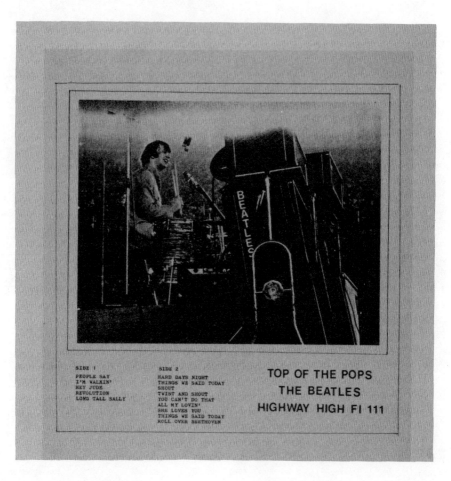

SIDE 1

PEOPLE SAY
I'M WALKIN'
HEY JUDE
REVOLUTION
LONG TALL SALLY

SIDE 2

HARD DAYS NIGHT
THINGS WE SAID TODAY
SHOUT
TWIST AND SHOUT
YOU CAN'T DO THAT
ALL MY LOVIN'
SHE LOVES YOU
THINGS WE SAID TODAY
ROLL OVER BEETHOVEN

TOP OF THE POPS
THE BEATLES
HIGHWAY HIGH FI 111

Top Of The Pops (LP)   **Highway HHCER 111 (Entry 562)**

557   TOKYO   Unknown   (LP)

1. *Day Tripper*
2. *Paperback Writer*
3. *If I Needed Someone*
4. *Nowhere Man*
5. *Yesterday*
6. *Rock And Roll Music*
7. *Can't Buy Me Love*
8. *Baby's In Black*
9. *I Feel Fine*
10. *I'm Down*
11. *She's A Woman*
12. *I Wanna Be Your Man*

Cuts 1–12: Recorded live at the Budokan Hall concert in Tokyo on July 2, 1966.

558   TOKYO EXPRESS   Unknown   (LP)

NOTES: Exact cuts unknown, but presumably from the concert at Budokan Hall in Tokyo on July 2, 1966.

559   TOKYO JULY 1ST 1966   Wizardo   (LP)

1. *Documentary*
2. *E.H. Eric Interview*
3. *Mr. Moonlight*
4. *Welcome To The Beatles*
5. *Rock And Roll Music*
6. *She's A Woman*
7. *If I Needed Someone*
8. *Day Tripper*
9. *Baby's In Black*
10. *I Feel Fine*
11. *Yesterday*
12. *I Wanna Be Your Man*
13. *Nowhere Man*
14. *Paperback Writer*
15. *I'm Down*

Cuts 1–15: Recorded during the 1966 tour of Japan. This was recorded at the Budokan Hall on July 1, 1966.

560   TOKYO 1966   CBM 1900   (LP)

1. *Rock And Roll Music*
2. *She's A Woman*
3. *If I Needed Someone*
4. *Day Tripper*
5. *Baby's In Black*
6. *I Feel Fine*
7. *Yesterday*
8. *I Wanna Be Your Man*
9. *Nowhere Man*
10. *Paperback Writer*
11. *I'm Down*

Cuts 1–11: Recorded live at the Budokan Hall concert in Tokyo on July 2, 1966.

561   TOP OF THE POPS   Capitol P 9431   (EP)

1. *A Hard Day's Night*
2. *Things We Said Today*
3. *Top Of The Pops Interview*
4. *Long Tall Sally*

Cuts 1–4: From the BBC radio show "Top Of The Pops" with Brian Matthews. Broadcast July 8, 1964.

NOTES: Capitol never issued such an EP. Comes with a hard picture cover. Front shows an alternate take of the "butcher" cover session. Back shows an alternate of the cover finally used for the **YESTERDAY AND TODAY** album.

562   TOP OF THE POPS   Highway Records Hi Fi HHCER 111   (LP)

1. *People Say*
2. *I'm Walking*
3. *Hey Jude*
4. *Revolution*
5. *Long Tall Sally*
6. *A Hard Day's Night*
7. *Things We Said Today*
8. *Shout*
9. *Twist And Shout*
10. *You Can't Do That*
11. *All My Lovin'*

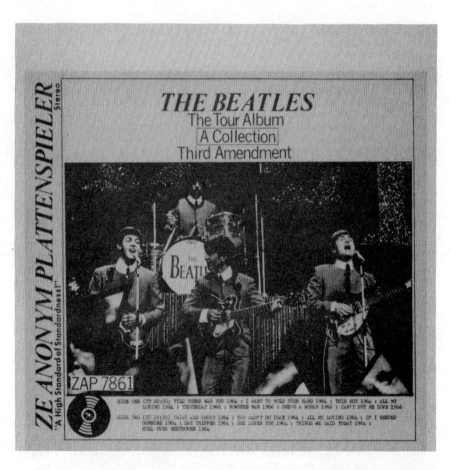

Tour Album – Third Amendment (LP)   **ZAP 7861 (Entry 567)**

12. *She Loves You*
13. *Things We Said Today*
14. *Roll Over Beethoven*

Cuts 1–2: Not the Beatles. Thought by some to be Pete Best or the Nurk Twins.
Cut 3: From the British TV show "Frost On Sunday." Recorded September 4,
1968, and aired September 8, 1968.
Cut 4: From the BBC radio show "Top Of The Pops" which aired September 19,
1968.
Cuts 5–7: From the BBC radio show "Top Of The Pops." The show aired July 8,
1964.
Cut 8: From the **MURRAY THE K** fan club record.
Cuts 9–14: From the Hollywood Bowl concert August 23, 1964.

563   TOP OF THE POPS   01971 4A/B   (LP)
NOTES: Unknown, but possibly the same as **TOP OF THE POPS** (HHCER 111).

564   TOP OF THE POPS   713   (LP)

1. *A Hard Day's Night*	7. *People Say*
2. *Things We Said Today*	8. *I'm Walking*
3. *Shout*	9. *Hey Jude*
4. *Everywhere It's Christmas*	10. *Revolution*
5. *Christmas Time Is Here Again*	11. *This Is To Wish You*
6. *Sie Liebt Dich*	12. *Long Tall Sally*

Cuts 1–2, 12: From the BBC radio show "Top Of The Pops" which aired July 8,
1964.
Cut 3: From the **MURRAY THE K** fan club record.
Cuts 4–5, 11: From various Beatles' Christmas records ('66, '67 & '69 respectively).
Cut 6: Original recording.
Cuts 7–8: Not the Beatles. Thought to be by Pete Best or the Nurk Twins.
Cut 9: From the British TV show "Frost On Sunday." Show taped September 4,
1968, and aired September 8, 1968.
Cut 10: From the BBC–TV show "Top Of The Pops" which aired September
19, 1968.

565   TOUR ALBUM   ZAP 7870   (LP)
NOTES: Same as **LIVE IN MUNICH 1966.**
SEE ALSO: **MUNICH AT LEAST -- 7TH AMENDMENT.**

566   TOUR ALBUM   Unknown   (LP)

1. *Till There Was You*	9. *Twist And Shout*
2. *I Want To Hold Your Hand*	10. *You Can't Do That*
3. *This Boy*	11. *All My Loving*
4. *All My Loving*	12. *If I Needed Someone*
5. *Yesterday*	13. *Day Tripper*
6. *Nowhere Man*	14. *She Loves You*
7. *She's A Woman*	15. *Things We Said Today*
8. *Can't Buy Me Love*	

Cuts 1–4: From the Washington, DC concert February 11, 1964.
Cuts 5–7, 12–13: From the Cirkus Krone concert in Munich, Germany, June 24,
1966.
Cuts 8–11, 14–15: From the Hollywood Bowl concert August 23, 1964.
SEE ALSO: **TOUR ALBUM -- 3RD AMENDMENT.**

567   TOUR ALBUM – 3RD AMENDMENT   ZAP 7861   (LP)
NOTES: Same as **TOUR ALBUM** (Unknown), except *Roll Over Beethoven* is
added here. It's from the Hollywood Bowl concert.

20 x 4

The Beatles

SIDE ONE:
1) OH DARLING outtake from Abbey Road LP 1969; 2) CANDLE BURNS (Peace of Mind), unreleased track from Sgt. Pepper sessions 1967; 3) BLACKBIRD, acoustic outtake from White Album with Donovan Leitch 1968; 4) THINGS WE SAID TODAY outtake version from A Hard Days Night recording sessions 1964; 5) HELP! demo version (recorded with hand held recorder by journalist in studio) 1965; 6) EVERY LITTLE THING outtake recording from 1965; 7) PENNY O'DELL unreleased track from McCartneys Nashville recording sessions in 1974.

SIDE TWO:
8) IMAGINE live version from Lennon's appearance on "Salute To Sir Lew" TV special from 1975; 9) SIMPLE LIFE Ringo's song for Simple Life leisure suits from Japanese TV 1977; 10) BYE BYE LOVE outtake taping of Harrison's appearance on "Saturday Night" with Paul Simon 1976; 11) MY CARNIVAL unreleased track from Wings recording session live from studio in New Orleans 1975; 12) HEATHER unreleased track from White Album recording sessions with Donovan Leitch 1968; 13) HER MAJESTY outtake from Abbey Road Lp with missing chord 1969; 14) WHEN EVERYBODY COMES TO TOWN — I'D HAVE YOU ANYTIME George Harrison & Bob Dylan recorded at Dylan's Woodstock home 1970; 16) BLUEBIRD, MOMAS LITTLE GIRL, MICHELLE, HEART OF THE COUNTRY outtakes from the acoustic taping of "James Paul McCartney" 1973.

20 X 4 (LP)   **Ruthless Rhymes (Entry 569)**

568   TUESDAY NIGHT AT THE WASHINGTON COLLOSSEUM   1070 A/B   (LP)

1. *Roll Over Beethoven*
2. *From Me To You*
3. *I Saw Her Standing There*
4. *This Boy*
5. *All My Loving*
6. *I Wanna Be Your Man*
7. *Please Please Me*
8. *Till There Was You*
9. *She Loves You*
10. *I Want To Hold Your Hand*
11. *Shout*

Cuts 1–10: From the Washington, DC concert February 11, 1964.
Cut 11: Recorded April 27–28, 1964, for the Rediffusion TV show "Around The
Beatles." Show aired May 6, 1964.

569   20 X 4   Idle Mind 1176; Ruthless Rhymes Ltd.   (LP)

1. *Oh Darling*
2. *Candle Burns (Peace Of Mind)*
3. *Blackbird*
4. *Things We Said Today*
5. *Help*
6. *Every Little Thing*
7. *Penny O'Dell*
8. *Imagine*
9. *Simple Life*
10. *Bye Bye Love*
11. *My Carnival*
12. *Heather*
13. *Her Majesty*
14. *When Everybody Comes To
Town–I'd Have You Anytime*
15. *Bluebird, Mommas Little Girl,
Michelle, Heart Of The Country*
16. *Hi, Hi, Hi/C Moon Commercial*

Cut 1: Abbey Road outtake, 1969.
Cut 2: Recorded June, 1967 and found in the Apple trash can in 1970.
Cuts 3, 12: Paul and Donovan.
Cut 4: Outtake.
Cut 5: Demo.
Cut 6: 1965 outtake.
Cut 7: Allegedly a Paul McCartney outtake from 1974; probably not.
Cut 8: John of the TV show, "Salute To Sir Lew Grade" on June 13, 1975.
Cut 9: Ringo doing a Japanese commercial for leisure suits.
Cut 10: Outtake from the taping of "Saturday Night Live" with George and
Paul Simon. The taping was done November 16, 1976.
Cut 11: Outtake recorded in New Orleans in 1975 by Wings.
Cut 13: Full version with the last chord.
Cut 14: George and Bob Dylan at Dylan's Woodstock home in 1970.
Cut 15: Outtakes from the **JAMES PAUL McCARTNEY** TV special.
Cut 16: Paul and Linda with a radio commercial for their single.

570   "21"   Melvin MM02   (LP)
NOTES: Cuts unknown.

571   21 BIG ONES   Unknown   (LP)

1. *Hippy Hippy Shake*
2. *To Know Her Is To Love Her*
3. *I'm Gonna Sit Right Down
And Cry*
4. *Some Other Guy*
5. *Love Of The Loved*
6. *Lucille*
7. *Crying, Waiting, Hoping*
8. *A Shot Of Rhythm And Blues*
9. *I'm Sure To Fall*
10. *Shout*
11. *Have You Heard The Word*
12. *Yakety Yack*
13. *Commonwealth*
14. *White Power*
15. *Suzy Parker*
16. *Besame Mucho*
17. *Cottonfields*
18. *Everybody's Rockin' Tonight*
19. *Whole Lotta Shakin' Goin' On*
20. *The Walk*
21. *What's The New Mary Jane*

21 (The New 21) (LP)   **Melvin MM06 (Entry 572)**

Cut 1: From the BBC radio 1963.
Cuts 2–3, 7–9: From a BBC radio broadcast in November, 1962.
Cut 4: Recorded by Granada TV at the Cavern Club on October 13, 1962.
The tape was shown on "People And Places" on November 7, 1962.
Cut 5: From the Decca auditions, January 1, 1962.
Cut 6: From the BBC radio in the summer of 1963.
Cut 10: From the Rediffusion TV show "Around The Beatles" which aired May 6, 1964.
Cut 11: Recorded June, 1970. Supposedly John and some of the Bee Gees were involved in the recording. (For discussion, see footnote on pages xxiv-xxv.)
Cuts 12–16, 18–20: From the LET IT BE sessions early in 1969.
Cut 17: From an interview with Kenny Everett in January, 1968.
Cut 21: Recorded by John on August 14, 1968. This was to have been released as Apple 1002, but it never was.

572   21 (THE NEW 21)   Melvin MM06   (LP)

1. *Three Cool Cats*
2. *How Do You Do It*
3. *Like Dreamers Do*
4. *Lucille*
5. *Glad All Over*
6. *Hello Little Girl*
7. *Ain't Nothing Shakin'*
8. *Lonesome Tears In My Eyes*
9. *Honeymoon Song (Bound By Love)*
10. *Spiritual Regeneration*
11. *The Abduction (Help Film Finale)*
12. *Watching Rainbows*
13. *Momma You've Been On My Mind*
14. *Ready, William And Able (Instrumental)*
15. *Save The Last Dance For Me*
16. *Shake, Rattle And Roll*
17. *The Walk*
18. *Commonwealth Song*
19. *White Power/Promenade*
20. *Honey Hush (Hi Ho Silver)*
21. *Youngblood*

Cuts 1, 3, 6: From the Decca auditions, January 1, 1962.
Cut 2: Recorded November 26, 1962. This was to have been the second Beatle single, but it was not released.
Cut 4: From the BBC radio in 1963.
Cuts 5, 7–9: From a BBC radio broadcast in November, 1962.
Cut 10: Also known as *Indian Rope Trick*. Recorded in Rishikesh, India on March 15, 1968.
Cut 11: From the film "Help."
Cut 12: 1969 outtake.
Cuts 13–20: From the LET IT BE sessions early in 1969 at London's Twickenham Studios.
Cut 21: From the BBC radio in 1962.
NOTES: This album was released with several variations. The original release had a blue front and a brown back cover. The second version had a brown front and a black back cover. It may also have been released on gold vinyl.

573   TWICKENHAM JAMS   PRO 909   (EP)

1. *Early In The Morning – Hi Ho Silver*
2. *Stand By Me*
3. *Hare Krsna Mantra*
4. *All Things Must Pass*
5. *A Fool Like Me*
6. *You Win Again*

Cuts 1–6: From the LET IT BE sessions filmed at London's Twickenham Studios early in 1969.
NOTES: This special EP was issued with a picture sleeve. They were pressed on green vinyl.

Twickenham Jams (LP)   **Smilin' Ears SE7702 (Entry 574)**

Twist And Shout/There's A Place (45 sleeve)   Tollie 9001 (Entry 576)

574   TWICKENHAM JAMS   Smilin' Ears SE 7702   (LP)

1. *Early In The Morning -- Hi Ho*
   Silver
2. *Stand By Me*
3. *Hare Krsna Mantra*
4. *All Things Must Pass*
5. *A Fool Like Me*
6. *You Win Again*

7. *Slippin' And Slidin'*
8. *Ed Sullivan Memorial TV Show*
9. *Cottonfields*

Cuts 1--6: From the **LET IT BE** sessions early in 1969.
Cut 7: John on the TV show "Salute To Sir Lew Grade" on June 13, 1975.
Cut 8: From the "Memorial Ed Sullivan Show."
Cut 9: Sung by John during a Kenny Everett interview, January, 1968.
NOTES: Laminated jacket. *When Everybody Comes To Town* by George
   Harrison and Bob Dylan appears after *Cottonfields.* but is not listed on the
   cover. Ringo on the "Smothers Brothers Show" singing the *No No Song* is
   listed as being on the album, but it does not appear.

575   TWICKENHAM STUDIOS   CBM B210   (2 LPs)
   NOTES: Exact cuts unknown, but presumably contains cuts from **TWICKENHAM
   JAMS** and **WATCHING RAINBOWS.**

576   *TWIST AND SHOUT/THERE'S A PLACE*   Tollie 9001   (45 sleeve)
   NOTES: This is a picture sleeve. There was no sleeve issued with the original
   record. The black--and--white sleeve shows the Beatles on stage playing on
   one side and simply has "The Beatles," the song titles and the label and
   number.

577   ULTIMATE RADIO BOOTLEG   Mercury MK2--121   (2 LPs)

1. *The Three Big B's Ultimate Radio*
   Interviews: Beatles With Art
   Roberts And Ron Riley; Steve
   Allen With Al Jolson
2. *The Magic Of San Diego On KMJC*
3. *The Seattle Reunion Of Radio*
   Crazies On KYYX

2. *Good Morning America*
   Dick Purtan -- CKLW
   "Crazy" Dave Otto -- KOPA
   Rick Dees -- KHJ
5. *Rescue Off Charity Mountain*
   On KYYX

NOTES: This is not really a bootleg, but real radio shows pressed onto discs.
   The discs were sent to radio stations only in 1979.
SEE ALSO: **WLS INTERVIEW.**

578   UNITED   Unknown   (LP)
   NOTES: Cuts unknown.

579   UPON US ALL -- 4TH AMENDMENT   ZAP 7864   (LP)
   NOTES: Same as **BACK UPON US ALL** (ZAP).
   SEE ALSO: **BACK UPON US ALL** (Kornyphone); **MORE FROM THE FAB
   FOUR; POWER BROKERS.**

580   VANCOUVER 1964   TMOQ D--211; TMOQ 72012   (2 LPs)
   NOTES: Same as **B.C. 64** (Wizardo 340). Re--issued in 1980 with a full--color
   sleeve.
   SEE ALSO: **BRITISH COLUMBIA 64; VANCOUVER 1964** (K&S).

581   VANCOUVER 1964   K&S   (2 LPs)
   NOTES: This is the same as **VANCOUVER 1964** (TMOQ 72012), except it was
   pressed in color vinyl. One record in yellow and one in blue. Only 150
   were pressed.
   SEE ALSO: **B.C. 64; BRITISH COLUMBIA 64.**

582   VANCOUVER +   Unknown   (LP)

1. *Press Conference*
2. *Interviews*
3. *Radio Plugs And Description*
4. *Twist And Shout*
5. *You Can't Do That*
6. *All My Loving*
7. *She Loves You*
8. *Things We Said Today*
9. *Roll Over Beethoven*
10. *Can't Buy Me Love*
11. *If I Fell*
12. *I Want To Hold Your Hand*
13. *Boys*
14. *A Hard Day's Night*
15. *Long Tall Sally*

Cuts 1–15: Recorded at the Vancouver, British Columbia concert August 22, 1964.

583   VERY BEST OF THE BEATLES RAREST NO. 1   TKRWM 1985   (LP)
NOTES: Same as **BEATLES RAREST NO. 1** (TAKRL 1985).

584   VERY BEST OF THE BEATLES RAREST NO. 2   TKRWM 1986   (LP)

1. *Twist And Shout*
2. *You Can't Do That*
3. *All My Loving*
4. *She Loves You*
5. *Things We Said Today*
6. *Roll Over Beethoven*
7. *Love Me Do*
8. *Please Please Me*
9. *Can't Buy Me Love*
10. *If I Fell*
11. *I Want To Hold Your Hand*
12. *Boys*
13. *A Hard Day's Night*
14. *Long Tall Sally*
15. *Till There Was You*
16. *I Saw Her Standing There*

Cuts 1–16: All recorded live at various concerts, including Washington, DC, Hollywood Bowl and Shea Stadium.

585   VERY BEST OF THE BEATLES RAREST NO. 3   TKRWM 1987   (LP)

1. *Rock And Roll Music*
2. *She's A Woman*
3. *If I Needed Someone*
4. *Day Tripper*
5. *Baby's In Black*
6. *I Feel Fine*
7. *Yesterday*
8. *I Wanna Be Your Man*
9. *Ain't She Sweet*
10. *P.S. I Love You*
11. *There's A Place*
12. *Misery*
13. *Dizzy Miss Lizzy*
14. *This Boy*
15. *From Me To You*
16. *Nowhere Man*
17. *Paperback Writer*
18. *I'm Down*

Cuts 1–8, 16–18: Recorded live in Tokyo, Japan, at the Budokan Hall concert on July 2, 1966.
Cut 9: Original recording.
Cuts 10–12: EMI outtakes from 1963. Probably original.
Cuts 13–15: Unknown, probably original.

586   VERY BEST OF THE BEATLES RAREST NO. 4   TKRWM 1988   (LP)
NOTES: Same as **BEATLES RAREST NO. 4** (TAKRL 1988).

587   VERY BEST OF THE BEATLES RAREST NO. 5   TKRWL 1989   (LP)
NOTES: Same as **BEATLES RAREST NO. 5** (TAKRL 1989).

588   VERY BEST OF THE BEATLES RAREST VOL. 6   TKRWM 1995   (LP)
NOTES: Same as **BEATLES RAREST NO. 6** (TAKRL 1995).
SEE ALSO: **NEXT TO LAST RECORDING SESSION -- 5TH AMENDMENT.**

589   VERY BEST OF THE BEATLES RAREST VOL. SEVEN   TKRWM 1998   (LP)
NOTES: Same as **BEATLES RAREST NO. 7** (TAKRL 1998).

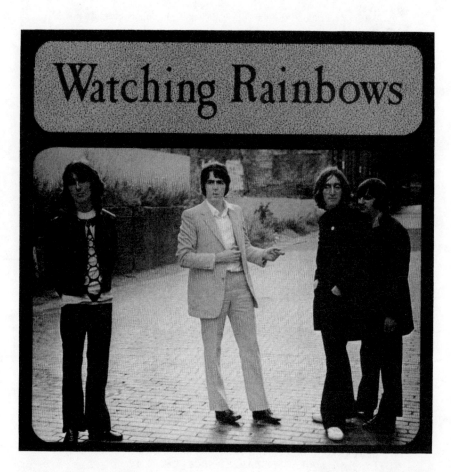

Watching Rainbows (LP)   **Audifon L-7 (Entry 596)**

590 **VIEWS** BV 1966 (LP)
    NOTES: Same as **BEATLE VIEWS** (BV 1966).

591 **VIRGIN & THREE** TMOQ 71068 (LP)
    NOTES: Same as **GET BACK SESSIONS VOL. 2** (TMOQ 71068).
    SEE ALSO: **MORE GET BACK SESSIONS.**

592 **VISIT TO MINNEAPOLIS** Melvin MMEP 001–A/B (EP)

1. *Press Conference*   4. *Jerk With A Badge*
2. *She's A Woman*   5. *Everybody's Trying To Be My*
3. *Twist And Shout*   *Baby*
    Cuts 1–5: From the Minneapolis concert August 21, 1965.
    Cut 4: This is a policeman talking about Beatle security, etc.
    NOTES: The EP came with a picture sleeve.

593 **VOLUME ONE** TV Products ATRBH DCT 2 ART BH 101 1–8 (4 LPs)
    NOTES: This is the same as **ALPHA OMEGA VOL. 1** (ATRBH 3583).
    SEE ALSO: **BEATLES VOL. I; GREATEST HITS: COLLECTOR'S EDITION.**

594 **VOLUME TWO** Record Promotions ATRBH TVP 9–16 (4 LPs)
    NOTES: Same as **ALPHA OMEGA VOL. 2** (Audio Tape ATRB 4).
    SEE ALSO: **BEATLES VOL. 2.**

595 **VOLUME THREE** Unknown (2 LPs)
    NOTES: Same as **ALPHA OMEGA VOL. 3** (Audio Tape 1–4).

596 **WATCHING RAINBOWS** Audifon L–7 (LP)

1. *Watching Rainbows*   9. *Too Bad About The Sorrows/*
2. *Mean Mr. Mustard*   *She Said, She Said*
3. *Blackbird*   10. *Mean Mr. Mustard*
4. *Early In The Morning/Hi Ho* 11. *Don't Let Me Down*
    Silver   12. *All Things Must Pass*
5. *Stand By Me*   13. *A Fool Like Me*
6. *Hare Krsna Mantra* (Harry Driscol?) 14. *You Win Again*
7. *Two Of Us*   15. *She Came In Through The*
8. *One After 909*   *Bathroom Window*
                             16. *Golden Slumbers/Carry That*
                                 Weight
                             17. *A Quick One He's Away/Feedback*
                                 Guitar
    Cut 1: Recorded at Apple Studios in March of 1969.
    Cut 2: Recorded June, 1969.
    Cut 3: Recorded at Elmstree Studios.
    Cuts 4–15: From the **LET IT BE** sessions at London's Twickenham Studios in
        early 1969.
    Cut 16: Demo recorded at the Abbey Road Studios in August, 1969.
    Cut 17: John, George and others at Abbey Road Studios on July 23, 1969.
    NOTES: The order of the songs on the album is slightly different than listed on
        the jacket. Also, *Her Majesty*, with the last chord, appears after cut 17 on
        the album. The album has a full–color laminated jacket.

597 **WATCHING RAINBOWS** 77132M/77133M (EP)

1. *Watching Rainbows*   3. *Too Bad About Sorrows*
2. *She Came In Through The*   4. *She Said She Said*
    Bathroom Window   5. *Mean Mr. Mustard*

6. *Don't Let Me Down*
7. *Golden Slumbers/Carry That Weight*

Cut 1: Recorded at Apple in March, 1969.
Cuts 2–6: Recorded during the **LET IT BE** sessions at Twickenham Studios in early 1969.
Cut 7: Recorded at Abbey Road Studios in August, 1969.
NOTES: This seven–inch EP was released with a picture sleeve and on multi–color vinyl.

598   **WELCOME THE BEATLES**   MARC TB 76057   (LP)

1. *Documentary*
2. *Welcome To The Beatles*
3. *Rock And Roll Music*
4. *She's A Woman*
5. *If I Needed Someone*
6. *Day Tripper*
7. *Baby's In Black*
8. *I Feel Fine*
9. *Yesterday*
10. *I Wanna Be Your Man*
11. *Nowhere Man*
12. *Paperback Writer*
13. *I'm Down*

Cuts 1–13: Recorded live in Japan at Budokan Hall on July 1, 1966.
NOTES: Japanese bootleg with a deluxe cover.

599   **WHAT'S THE NEW MARY JANE**   CBM 3585   (LP)
NOTES: Same as **MARY JANE** (CBM 3585).
SEE ALSO: **MARY JANE 2ND VERSION; THE NEVER RELEASED MARY JANE; THE NEW MARY JANE; THEIR NEVER RELEASED MARY JANE; THEIR NEVER RELEASED THE NEW MARY JANE; RETURN OF MARY JANE.**

600   **WHITE CHRISTMAS**   Unknown   (LP)
NOTES: Same as **CHRISTMAS ALBUM – 1ST AMENDMENT II.**
SEE ALSO: **CHRISTMAS MEETINGS; CHRISTMAS MESSAGE FROM LIVER-POOL; COMPLETE CHRISTMAS COLLECTION; COMPLETE CHRISTMAS COLLECTION; SECOND AMENDMENT CHRISTMAS ALBUM; THEIR COMPLETE CHRISTMAS COLLECTION '63–69.**

601   **WIZARDO'S GREATEST HITS**   Wizardo 391   (LP)

1. *Twist And Shout*
2. *You Can't Do That*
3. *All My Loving*
4. *She Loves You*
5. *Things We Said Today*
6. *Roll Over Beethoven*
7. *Can't Buy Me Love*
8. *A Hard Day's Night*
9. *Boys*
10. *Long Tall Sally*
11. *Rock And Roll Music*
12. *She's A Woman*
13. *If I Needed Someone*
14. *Day Tripper*
15. *Yesterday*
16. *I Wanna Be Your Man*
17. *Nowhere Man*
18. *Paperback Writer*
19. *I'm Down*

Cuts 1–10: Recorded live at the Hollywood Bowl, August 23, 1964.
Cuts 11–19: Recorded live at Budokan Hall in Tokyo, Japan, July 2, 1966.
NOTES: This was not released by Wizardo, but by persons using their name and logo.

602   **WLS INTERVIEW**   Unknown   (LP)
NOTES: This interview was done by Art Roberts and Ron Riley via transcontin-ental phone. All four Beatles are interviewed.
SEE ALSO: **ULTIMATE RADIO BOOTLEG.**

Yellow Matter Custard (LP)   **YMC 101/102 (Entry 606)**

603 **WORDS OF LOVE**   Wizardo 326   (LP)
NOTES: Same as **STUDIO OUTTAKE RECORDINGS 1962–64.**

604 **WORLDWIDE**   CBM 3795   (LP)
NOTES: Same as **SWEDEN 1963.**
SEE ALSO: **SWEDEN, WASHINGTON, SWEDEN; HOLLAND/SWEDEN.**

605 **WQAM–560–MIAMI "TIGER RADIO"**   WQ 1096 A/B   (EP)

I. *Introductions (Rick Shaw & Lee Sherwood)*
II. *Beatles At Miami International Airport (Lee Sherwood, Charlie Murdock, Jack Sorbi)*
III. *Beatles at the Deauville Hotel (Robert Kaye)*
IV. *George Harrison Interview (Charlie Murdock)*
V. *Beatles Farewell To Miami*

Cuts I–V: Recorded in Miami Beach February, 1964 during the Beatles visit there.

606 **YELLOW MATTER CUSTARD**   Berkeley 02; TMOQ BB 513; TMOQ 71032; YMC 101/102   (LP)
NOTES: Same as **AS SWEET AS YOU ARE.**
SEE ALSO: **DON'T PASS ME BY; 14 UNRELEASED SONGS; YELLOW MATTER CUSTARD** (Shalom).

607 **YELLOW MATTER CUSTARD**   CBM 2 C1/D1; CBM 204; Shalom 3316C/3316D (LP)

1. *The Saints*
2. *Glad All Over*
3. *I Just Don't Understand*
4. *Slow Down*
5. *Please Don't Ever Change*
6. *A Shot Of Rhythm And Blues*
7. *I'm Sure To Fall*
8. *My Bonnie*
9. *I Got A Woman*
10. *Nothin' Shakin' But The Leaves In The Trees*
11. *Lonesome Tears In My Eyes*
12. *Everyone Wants Someone*
13. *I'm Gonna Sit Right Down And Cry Over You*
14. *Crying, Waiting, Hoping*
15. *To Know Her Is To Love Her*
16. *Bound By Love*

Cuts 1, 8: Original recordings.
Cuts 2–7, 9–16: From a BBC radio broadcast in November, 1962.
SEE ALSO: **AS SWEET AS YOU ARE; DON'T PASS ME BY; 14 UNRELEASED SONGS; YELLOW MATTER CUSTARD** (TMOQ 513).

608 **YELLOW MATTER CUSTARD 2ND HELPING**   Unknown   (LP)
NOTES: Cuts unknown.

609 **YELLOW SUBMARINE**   Unknown   (LP)
NOTES: Cuts unknown, but presumably the same as **CINELOGUE 2.**

610 **YELLOW SUBMARINE**   YS A1B1C2D2   (2 LPs)
NOTES: Same as **CINELOGUE 2 (CBM).**

611 **YESTERDAY**   Unknown   (LP)
NOTES: Cuts unknown.

Youngblood (LP)   **Audifon BVP 005 (Entry 612)**

1. *Too Much Monkey Business*
2. *Hippy Hippy Shake*
3. *Sweet Little 16*
4. *Devil In Her Heart*
5. *A Shot Of Rhythm And Blues*
6. *Memphis*
7. *Sure To Fall*
8. *Youngblood*
9. *Crying, Waiting, Hoping*
10. *Kansas City*
11. *I Forgot To Remember*
12. *From Me To You*
13. *I Saw Her Standing There*
14. *All My Loving*
15. *Roll Over Beethoven*
16. *Boys*
17. *Till There Was You*
18. *She Loves You*
19. *This Boy*
20. *I Want To Hold Your Hand*
21. *Money*
22. *Twist And Shout*

Cuts 1-11: From the BBC radio in 1962. The shows were "Light And Popular" and "Stramash."

Cuts 12--22: From the Beatles Christmas Show at the Liverpool Empire on December 22, 1963.

George Harrison

613 BANGLA DESH Bang Records 4022 (LP)

1. *My Sweet Lord*
2. *Beware Of Darkness*
3. *My Guitar Gently Weeps*
4. *Here Comes The Sun*
5. *Something*
6. *Bangla Desh*
7. *A Hard Rain's Gonna Fall*
8. *It Takes A Lot To Laugh*
9. *Blowing In The Wind*
10. *Mr. Tambourine Man*
11. *Just Like A Man*

Cuts 1-11: From the Concert For Bangla Desh held at Madison Square Garden, August 1, 1971.
SEE ALSO: **BANGLA DESH** (Instant Analysis); **GEORGE HARRISON, BOB DYLAN, LEON RUSSELL, ERIC CLAPTON; GREATEST SHOW ON EARTH; MADISON SQUARE GARDEN, AUGUST 1ST, 1971.**

614 BANGLA DESH Bangla Records 1001--A1/1001 B--1 (LP)

1. *My Sweet Lord*
2. *It Ain't Easy*
3. *Beware Of Darkness*
4. *While My Guitar Gently Weeps*
5. *Jumpin' Jack Flash Medley*
6. *The Way God Planned It*
7. *Mr. Tambourine Man*
8. *Just Like A Woman*
9. *Something*
10. *Bangla Desh*

Cuts 1-10: From the Bangla Desh Concert, Madison Square Garden, August 1, 1971. Cut 2 is Ringo. Cut 3 is George and Leon Russell. Cut 4 is George and Eric Clapton. Cut 5 is Leon Russell. Cut 6 is Billy Preston. Cuts 7--8 are Bob Dylan.

615 BANGLA DESH Instant Analysis/SAD Productions (LP)
NOTES: Same as **BANGLA DESH** (Bang).
SEE ALSO: **GEORGE HARRISON, BOB DYLAN, LEON RUSSELL, ERIC CLAPTON; GREATEST SHOW ON EARTH; MADISON SQUARE GARDEN, AUGUST 1ST, 1971.**

616 BANGLA DESH EVENING King Kong 422 (LP)
NOTES: Exact cuts unknown.

617 BEST OF THREE Frenia Records (LP)

1. *Ballad Of Sir Frankie Crisp*
2. *Apple Scruffs*
3. *What Is Life*
4. *I'd Have You Anytime*
5. *My Sweet Lord*
6. *Art Of Dying*
7. *I Dig Love*
8. *Beware Of Darkness*
9. *Hear Me Lord*

Cuts 1-9: Original recordings.

618 CHICAGO CBM 1044 (LP)

1. *While My Guitar Gently Weeps*
2. *Something*
3. *Sue Me Sue You Blues*
4. *For You Blue*
5. *Give Me Love*

6. *In My Life*
7. *Dark Horse*
8. *What Is Life*
9. *My Sweet Lord*

Cuts 1--9: Recorded at the Chicago concert November 30, 1974.

619 CHICAGO AFTERNOON CBM 1168 (LP)
NOTES: Exact cuts unknown, possibly the same as **CHICAGO**.

620 CONCERT FOR BANGLA DESH FRT Records 1001 (LP)

1. *My Sweet Lord*
2. *Beware Of Darkness*
3. *While My Guitar Gently Weeps*
4. *Something*
5. *Bangla Desh*
6. *Mr. Tambourine Man*

7. *Just Like A Woman*
8. *That's The Way God Planned It*
9. *It Don't Come Easy*
10. *Jumpin' Jack Flash*

Cuts 1--10: From the Bangla Desh concert at Madison Square Garden, August 1, 1971. This is marked as the afternoon show, not the evening show.
NOTES: Cut 7 by Bob Dylan; cut 8 by Billy Preston; cut 9 by Ringo Starr; and, cut 10 by Leon Russell.

621 CONVERSATION WITH GEORGE HARRISON Dark Horse (LP)

1. *Interview With George*
2. *Gravy Train -- Splinter*
3. *Interview With George*
4. *Costafine Town -- Splinter*
5. *Interview With George*

6. *I Am Missing You -- Ravi Shankar*
7. *Interview With George*
8. *The Dawn -- Ravi Shankar*
9. *Interview With George*

NOTES: This was a special release from Dark Horse Records on their first two artists and records. Originally released to radio stations only.
SEE ALSO: **THE TANNED EQUINE INTERVIEW**.

622 CRACKERBOX PALACE Dark Horse 8313 (LP)
NOTES: This is a picture sleeve only. No sleeve was originally issued. The black--and--white sleeve shows a picture of George and the song title. Both sides are the same.

623 CRY FOR A SHADOW Unknown (2 LPs)

1. *The Lord Loves The One That Loves The Lord*
2. *Who Can See It*
3. *What Is Life*
4. *All Right As A Lumberjack*

5. *Something*
6. *While My Guitar Gently Weeps*
7. *Sue Me Sue You Blues*
8. *For You Blue*

9. *Give Me Love*
10. *Sound Stage Of The Mind*
11. *In My Life*
12. *Maya Love*

13. *Dark Horse*
14. *What Is Life*
15. *My Sweet Lord*

Cuts 1--15: From the 1974 tour.

624 DALLAS Instant Analysis (LP)

1. *Jam*
2. *While My Guitar Gently Weeps*

6. *Give Me Love*
7. *Soundstage '74*

3. *Something*   8. *In My Life*
4. *Sue Me Sue You Blues* 9. *Dark Horse*
5. *For You Texas (For You Blue)*
Cuts 1–9: Recorded live at Fort Worth, Texas, November 22, 1974.
NOTES: This is the original from which **A DARK HORSE IN 74** was made.

625 **DARK HORSE IN '74** Wizardo 374 (LP)
   NOTES: Same as **DALLAS** (Instant Analysis), except this one was pressed on
   colored vinyl.

626 **DEAD STICK** ZAP 7879 (LP)

   1. *While My Guitar Gently Weeps* 5. *Give Me Love*
   2. *Something*   6. *In My Life*
   3. *Baltke*   7. *I Shot The Sheriff*
   4. *Layla*   8. *Let It Grow*
   Cuts 1–2, 5--6: George Harrison.
   Cuts 3–4, 7–8: Eric Clapton.

627 **EXCERPTS FROM THREE MAJOR CONCERTS** Instant Analysis 4183/2044
   (2 LPs)

   1. *While My Guitar Gently Weeps* 4. *For You Blue*
   2. *Something*   5. *Give Me Love*
   3. *Sue Me Sue You Blues*   6. *Something*
                7. *Give Me Love & More*

   8. *In My Life*   12. *While My Guitar Gently Weeps*
   9. *Maya Love*   13. *My Sweet Lord & More*
   10. *Nothing From Nothing*
   11. *My Sweet Lord*
   NOTES: Excerpts from the Long Beach concert (December 10, 1974), Madison
   Square Garden and an unidentified concert. Cut 10 is Billy Preston.

628 **FALKONER CENTER, COPENHAGEN** CBM 403; CBM 4450; Shalom 8420
   (LP)

   1. *Oh Lord*   6. *Someone*
   2. *I Don't Know Why*   7. *Coming Home*
   3. *Those Who Will*   8. *Tutti Frutti*
   4. *Special Life*   9. *Long Tall Sally*
   5. *You're My Girl*
   Cuts 1–9: Recorded during the 1969 tour with Delaney & Bonnie & Friends.
   NOTES: The actual songs played on this date were:

   1. *Things Get Better*   7. *Coming Home*
   2. *Poor Elijah -- Tribute to* 8. Medley:
     Johnson   *Long Tall Sally*
   3. *Only You Know And I Know* *Jenny Jenny*
   4. *I Don't Want To Discuss It* *The Girl Can't Help It*
   5. *That's What My Man Is For* *Tutti Frutti*
   6. *Where There's A Will There's A Way*
   NOTES: Delaney and Bonnie were in Denmark on December 10–12, 1969. The
   band included: Delaney Bramlett – rhythm guitar; Bonnie Bramlett –
   vocals; George Harrison -- guitar; Eric Clapton – lead guitar; Dave Mason –
   guitar; Carl Radle -- bass; John Gordon – drums; Tex Johnson -- conga and
   bongo; Bobby Whitlock -- organ; Jim Price – trumpet; Bobby Keys – sax;
   Rita Coolidge -- vocals.

629   FORT WORTH   Unknown   (LP)

1. *Hari's On Tour*
2. *While My Guitar Gently Weeps*
3. *Something*
4. *Sue Me Sue You Blues*
5. *For You Blue*
6. *Give Me Love*
7. *In My Life*
8. *Dark Horse*

Cuts 1–8: Recorded live at the Fort Worth concert, November 22, 1974.

630   FORT WORTH TEXAS   King Kong 659   (2 LPs)
NOTES: Exact cuts unknown, but probably from the Fort Worth concert of
November 22, 1974.

631   THE GREATEST SHOW ON EARTH   Share 6699   (LP)
NOTES: Same as **BANGLA DESH** (Bang).
SEE ALSO: BANGLA DESH (Instant Analysis); GEORGE HARRISON, BOB
DYLAN, LEON RUSSELL, ERIC CLAPTON; MADISON SQUARE
GARDEN, AUGUST 1ST, 1971.

632   HARRISON, GEORGE   92444 C/D   (EP)
NOTES: This is a seven–inch picture record. There were six different Harrison
pictures used on these one–of–a–kind test pressings. At least one used the
cover art for the **GREATEST HITS** album. The songs on the record are
not by Harrison, but rather are a tribute to Elvis Presley by Paul Lichter.
This same recording was used for the following picture records: BEATLES;
DENNY LAINE; JOHN LENNON; JOHN LENNON/ELVIS PRESLEY;
PAUL McCARTNEY; RINGO STARR; WINGS.

633   GEORGE HARRISON, BOB DYLAN, LEON RUSSELL, ERIC CLAPTON
BRK 1001; CBM; Carnaby   (LP)
NOTES: Same as **BANGLA DESH** (Bang).
SEE ALSO: BANGLA DESH (Instant Analysis); GREATEST SHOW ON
EARTH; MADISON SQUARE GARDEN, AUGUST 1ST, 1971.

634   GEORGE HARRISON LIVE   CBM 7879   (LP)
NOTES: Exact cuts unknown.

635   GEORGE HARRISON 1974   Baby Moon Records   (2 LPs)

1. *The Lord Loves The One That*
   Loves The Lord
2. *Who Can See It?*
3. *What Is Life*

4. *All Right As A Lumberjack*
5. *Something*
6. *While My Guitar Gently Weeps*
7. *Sue Me Sue You Blues*

8. *For You Blue*
9. *Give Me Love*
10. *Soundstage Of My Mind*
11. *In My Life*

12. *Maya Love*
13. *Dark Horse*
14. *What Is Life*
15. *My Sweet Lord*

Cuts 1–3: From the Vancouver concert November 2, 1974.
Cuts 4–15: From the Seattle concert November 4, 1974.

636   *HARRISON SHOW*   GH 1110   (45)

1. *Promo*
2. *Interview With George*
3. *My Sweet Lord*

NOTES: From the "Weekly Top–30" show of November 10, 1979 with host
Mark Elliott.

637   HARRISON vs DYLAN/HARRISON vs EVERLY BROTHERS
Original Rock EP--1008   (EP)

1. *If Not For You*
2. *If Not For You*
3. *Bye Bye Love*
4. *Bye Bye Love*

Cuts 1, 3: Harison originals.
Cut 2: Bob Dylan original.
Cut 4: Everly Brothers original.

638   HELP   CBM 3587   (LP)

1. *Instrumental*
2. *I Wish I Was In London*
3. *Talkin' Teenage Blues*
4. *Gypsy Lou*
5. *Love Minus Zero; No Limit*
6. *Help*
7. *With God On Our Side*
8. *Ye Playboys And Playgirls*
9. *She's Your Lover Now*
10. *Killing Me Alive*
11. *She Belongs To Me*

NOTES: All cuts are by Bob Dylan. Cut 5 is from the Bangla Desh concert, August 1, 1971 with George.

639   LET'S HEAR ONE FOR LORD BUDDAH   Unknown   (LP)

1. *Opening Jam*
2. *While My Guitar Gently Weeps*
3. *Something*
4. *Sue Me Sue You Blues*
5. *For You Blue*
6. *Give Me Love*
7. *In My Life*
8. *Maya Love*
9. *Nothing From Nothing*
10. *My Sweet Lord*

Cuts 1–10: From the Long Beach concert December 10, 1974.
NOTES: Cut 9 is by Billy Preston.
SEE ALSO: **U.S. TOUR 1974.**

640   LIVE IN CALGARY   SODD 005   (2 LPs)

1. *Tom Cat*
2. *Maya Love*
3. *Outta Space*
4. *Give Me Love*
5. *Soundstage*
6. *In My Life*

7. *Dark Horse*
8. *Nothing From Nothing*
9. *What Is Life*
10. *While My Guitar Gently Weeps*
11. *My Sweet Lord*

Cuts 1--11: This is probably the Vancouver concert, November 2, 1974. Cut 1 is Tom Scott. Cuts 3 and 8 are Billy Preston.
SEE ALSO: **RECORDED LIVE IN VANCOUVER.**

641   LIVE IN CONCERT   Unknown   (LP)

1. *My Sweet Lord*
2. *Beware Of Darkness*
3. *While My Guitar Gently Weeps*
4. *Here Comes The Sun*
5. *Something*
6. *Bangla Desh*
7. *A Hard Rain's Gonna Fall*
8. *It Takes A Lot To Laugh*
9. *Blowin' In The Wind*
10. *Mr. Tambourine Man*
11. *Just Like A Woman*

Cuts 1--11: From the Concert For Bangla Desh at Madison Square Garden, August 1, 1971.
NOTES: Cuts 7–11 are by Bob Dylan.

642   LONG BEACH   Unknown   (LP)

1. *Hari's On Tour*
2. *While My Guitar Gently Weeps*
3. *Something*
4. *Sue Me Sue You Blues*
5. *For You Blue*
6. *Give Me Love*
7. *In My Life*
8. *Maya Love*
9. *Nothing From Nothing*
10. *My Sweet Lord*

Cuts 1–10: From the Long Beach concert, December 10, 1974.
NOTES: Cut 9 is by Billy Preston.

643   MADISON SQUARE GARDEN, AUGUST 1ST, 1971   Carnaby SAD 1/2   (LP)
NOTES: Same as **BANGLA DESH** (Bang).
SEE ALSO: **BANGLA DESH** (Instant Analysis); **GEORGE HARRISON, BOB
     DYLAN, LEON RUSSELL, ERIC CLAPTON; THE GREATEST SHOW
     ON EARTH.**

**644   MORE FROM THE '74 TOUR   CBM 4184; Instant Analysis 1048; King Kong 400
     (LP)**

1. *Hari's On Tour*
2. *While My Guitar Gently Weeps*
3. *Something*
4. *Sue Me Sue You Blues*
5. *For You Blue*
6. *Give Me Love*
7. *Nothing From Nothing*
8. *In My Life*
9. *Dark Horse*

Cuts 1–9: All from the 1974 U.S. tour.
NOTES: Cut 7 is by Billy Preston.

645   ON TOUR 1974   TAKRL 1373   (LP)

1. *Opening Jam*
2. *While My Guitar Gently Weeps*
3. *Something*
4. *Sue Me Sue You Blues*
5. *For You Blue*
6. *Give Me Love*
7. *In My Life*
8. *Maya Love*
9. *Nothing From Nothing*
10. *My Sweet Lord*

Cuts 1–10: All from the 1974 U.S. tour.
NOTES: Cut 9 is by Billy Preston.

646   RECORDED LIVE IN VANCOUVER   SODD 005   (2 LPs)
NOTES: Same as **LIVE IN CALGARY** (SODD 005).

647   THE TANNED EQUINE INTERVIEW   Cx321A/Cx321B
NOTES: Same as **CONVERSATION WITH GEORGE HARRISON.** Issued on
     purple vinyl.

648   TELEVISION OUTTAKES   Tobe–Mila 4Q 3–4   (EP)

1. *Ringo On The Smothers Bros. Show
     Jokes, No No Song, Jokes*
2. *Slippin' And Slidin'*
3. *And The House Came Down When . . .*
4. *Here Comes The Sun*
5. *Homeward Bound*
6. *Interview*

Cut 1: Ringo on the "Smothers Brothers Show" April 28, 1975.
Cut 2: John on the TV show "Salute To Sir Lew Grade" on June 13, 1975.
Cut 3: From the "Ed Sullivan Memorial" TV show.
Cuts 4–5: George and Paul Simon on "Saturday Night Live." Show was taped
     November 16, 1976 and aired November 18, 1976.
Cut 6: From the open–ended interview for the **BEATLES SECOND ALBUM**
     with a bit of *Roll Over Beethoven.*
NOTES: Came with a special hard–cover, color picture sleeve.

649 TOM THUMB BLUES/DYLAN–HARRISON//PLEASE CRAWL OUT YOUR
WINDOW   Rolling Thunder Records 695–EP–1   (EP)
NOTES: The Dylan–Harrison cut is *When Everybody Comes To Town* and *I'd
Have You Anytime.* The EP was also issued on colored vinyl, but had no
picture sleeve.

650 U.S. TOUR 1974   Phonygraf 1114   (LP)
NOTES: Same as **LET'S HEAR ONE FOR LORD BUDDAH.**

651 VANCOUVER   Unknown   (LP)

1. *Tom Cat*
2. *Maya Love*
3. *Outer Space*
4. *Give Me Love*
5. *Soundstage*
6. *In My Life*
7. *Dark Horse*
8. *Nothing From Nothing*
9. *What Is Life*
10. *While My Guitar Gently Weeps*
11. *My Sweet Lord*

Cuts 1–11: From the Vancouver concert November 2, 1974. Cut 1 is Tom
Scott. Cuts 3 and 8 are by Billy Preston.

A Guitar's All Right John, . . . (LP)   Audifon R6015 (Entry 652)

John Lennon

**652   A GUITAR'S ALL RIGHT JOHN, BUT YOU'LL NEVER EARN YOUR LIVING
        BY IT**   Audifon R6015   (LP)

1. *Whatever Gets You Through The*
   Night
2. *Lucy In The Sky With Diamonds*
3. *I Saw Her Standing There*

4. *Slippin' And Sliddin'*
5. *Stand By Me*
6. *Oh My Love*
7. *Lady Marmalade*
8. *Working Class Hero*
9. *Day Tripper*

Cuts 1–3: Recorded live on stage at Madison Square Garden with Elton John
     on November 25, 1974.
Cuts 4–5: From the BBC TV show "Old Grey Whistle Test" from April 18,
     1975.
Cut 6: Recorded at John's home at Weybridge, England in July, 1975.
Cut 7: Recorded at John's Dakota apartment by a French journalist in 1975.
Cut 8: Recorded at a party in New York in the spring of 1972.
Cut 9: John with Jimi Hendrix on London Radio One's "Top Gear" October,
     1967.
NOTES: This is a ten-inch LP with a special picture cover. Originals came with
     an insert made to look like the stationery of Dr. Winston O. Boogie and Dr.
     Reginald Dwight. This listed the songs and said where they were recorded.
     It does not match the songs listed on the cover or the label. It was pressed
     on several colors of vinyl, including blue, clear, orange and red.

**653   A GUITAR'S ALL RIGHT JOHN, BUT YOU'LL NEVER EARN YOUR LIVING
        BY IT**   Audifon R6015; Ruthless Rhymes   (LP)
NOTES: This is the same as the original of which it is a copy, except for a few
     minor things. First, the cover picture is reversed. On the original, John is
     on the right and Stu is in the background on the left. On the copies, John
     is on the left hand and Stu on the right. The label is sometimes different on
     the copies, being Ruthless Rhymes instead of Audifon. This also came in
     colors, including black, orange, green and rainbow.

654   ANGEL BABY   Unknown   (LP)

1. *Angel Baby*
2. *Be My Baby*
3. *Attica State*
4. *Luck Of The Irish*
5. *Imagine*

6. *Give Peace A Chance*
7. *What's Yer New Mary Jane*
8. *Yer Blues*
9. *Peace Of Mind*
10. *Interview*

Cuts 1–2: From the Adam VIII LP **JOHN LENNON SINGS THE GREAT ROCK
     AND ROLL HITS.**
Cuts 3–4: From the John Sinclair benefit rally of December 18, 1971.
Cuts 5–6: From the Willowbrook One To One concert August 30, 1972.
Cut 7: Recorded by John August 14, 1968. It was to have been released as
     Apple 1002, but it never was.
Cut 8: Recorded for the Rolling Stones' TV show "Rock And Roll Circus" on

December 11, 1968.
Cut 9: Recorded in June, 1967 and found in the Apple trash can in 1970.
Cut 10: Interview from September, 1974.

655 **ANGEL BABY/JOHN WINSTON LENNON**   Wizardo 362   (LP)
NOTES: Same as **ANGEL BABY** except for the order of the songs. Released
on colored vinyl.

656 **BRITISH BLUES JAM**   BBJ 1 A/B; CBM 3426   (LP)

1. *Yer Blues*   3. *Midnight Rambler*
2. *Love In Vain*   4. *Dead Flowers*
                             5. *Honky Tonk Woman*
                             6. *Satisfaction*
Cut 1: From the Rolling Stones' "Rock And Roll Circus" December 11, 1968.
John and Yoko with Rick Gretch, Keith Richard, Mitch Mitchell, Eric
Clapton and Klaus Voorman.
Cuts 2–6: By the Rolling Stones.

657 *COLD TURKEY/DON'T WORRY KYOKO*   Apple 1813   (45)
NOTES: This is a picture sleeve only. A black–and–white copy of the original
sleeve, this one has the colors reversed.

658 **COME BACK JOHNNY**   Melvin MM09   (LP)

1. *Introduction: A Comment To A*   9. *With Howard Cosell*
   Bleary Eyed Bob Dylan 1965   10. *Mother*
2. *New York City*   11. *Come Together*
3. *It's So Hard*   12. *Cold Turkey*
4. *Woman Is The Nigger Of The World* 13. *Hound Dog*
5. *Station Break: Walls And Bridges* 14. Medley:
6. *Well, Well, Well*   *Baby Please Don't Go*
7. *Instant Karma*   *Rock Island Line*
8. *Station Break: Goodnight Vienna*   *Maybe Baby*
                                          Peggy Sue
                                      15. *Johnny B. Goode*
                                      16. *Imagine*
                                      17. *Lennon–McCartney Feud*
Cut 1: As listed above.
Cuts 2–4, 7, 10–13: From the Willowbrook One To One concert August 30,
    1972.
Cuts 5–6, 8: John on WNEW radio as a guest DJ.
Cut 9: John on "Monday Night Football" with Howard Cosell.
Cut 14: Unknown.
Cuts 15–16: From the "Mike Douglas Show" the week of February 14–18, 1972.
    Cut 15 is with Chuck Berry.
Cut 17: Unknown.
NOTES: Laminated cover. Picture label, with a different picture of John on each
    side.

659 **DAY TRIPPER JAM**   CBM 4242; Instant Analysis 1056; King Kong   (LP)

1. *Give Peace A Chance*   5. *Luck Of The Irish*
2. *What's The New Mary Jane* 6. *Attica State*
3. *Day Tripper Jam*   7. *Imagine*
4. *God Save Us*   8. *Give Peace A Chance*
Cut 1: Listed as Holland, unknown.
Cut 2: Recorded by John, August 14, 1968. It was to have been released as

Apple 1002, but wasn't.

Cut 3: John with Jimi Hendrix on London Radio One's "Top Gear" in October, 1967.

Cut 4: Original.

Cuts 5–6: From the John Sinclair Rally on December 18, 1971.

Cut 7: From the "Jerry Lewis Telethon" September 6, 1972.

Cut 8: Same as cut 1.

660   DAY TRIPPIN' WITH HENDRIX   Unknown   (LP)

1. *Day Tripper*
2, *What's Yer New Mary Jane*
3. *Give Peace A Chance*
4. *Luck Of The Irish*

5. *Attica State*
6. *Imagine*
7. *Give Peace A Chance*

NOTES: Similar to **DAY TRIPPER JAM**. See that listing for song origins.

661   DR. WINSTON O'BOOGIE ON THE TOMORROW SHOW   Cx297A/Cx297B   (LP)

NOTES: NBC–TV's "Tomorrow" show (April 28, 1975), hosted by Tom Snyder. There are just a few bits of some of John's songs, including *Imagine, No. 9 Dream, Whatever Gets You Through The Night, How Do You Sleep*, and *Mind Games*. Leon Wildes, John's attorney in his fight to remain in the U.S., also appears on the show. The album was issued on purple vinyl.

662   THE GREAT ROCK AND ROLL CIRCUS   Idle Mind 1134; Mushroom 4   (LP)

NOTES: Contains *Yer Blues* recorded for the Rolling Stones' "Rock And Roll Circus" December 11, 1968. Has John and Yoko with Rick Gretch, Keith Richard, Mitch Mitchell, Eric Clapton and Klaus Voorman. Contains other cuts by the Who, Cream, Led Zeppelin and Buffalo Springfield.

SEE ALSO: **(VOL. 4 THE) ROCK AND ROLL CIRCUS.**

663   GUITAR HERO   Stoned 3; K&S 011   (LP)

1. *Radio One Theme*
2. *Experiencing The Blues*
3. *Can You Please Crawl Out Your Window*
4. *I'm Your Hoochie Coochie Man*
5. *Drivin' South*
6. *Spanish Castle Music*
7. *Day Tripper*

8. *Wait Until Tomorrow*
9. *Stone Free*
10. *Foxy Lady*
11. *Little Miss Lover*
12. *Burning Of The Midnight Lamp*
13. *Hound Dog*
14. *Hey Joe*
15. *Getting My Heart Back Together Again*

NOTES: This album is by Jimi Hendrix, but cut 7 is Jimi with John Lennon on Radio One's "London Top Gear" in 1976. The Stoned version has a full–color, laminated sleeve and the K&S version has a black–and–white laminated sleeve.

664   GULP   RL007   (LP)

1. *Yer Blues*
2. *Mini Opera* (Who)

3. *Blue Bird* (Buffalo Springfield)
4. *Diddy Wah Diddy* (Capt. Beefheart)
5. *Who Do You Think You Are* (Capt. Beefheart)
6. *Moon Child* (Capt. Beefheart)
7. *Frying Pan* (Capt. Beefheart)

Cut 1: From the Rolling Stones' "Rock And Roll Circus" December 11, 1968 with John, Yoko, Rick Gretch, Keith Richard, Mitch Mitchell, Eric Clapton, and Klaus Voorman.

SEE ALSO: **YER BLUES** (unknown).

Hound Dog/Long Tall Sally (45)   **Heavy 101 (Entry 666)**

665   **HOUND DOG**   CBM 5040; King Kong 638   (LP)

1. *Come Together*
2. *Instant Karma*
3. *Cold Turkey*
4. *Hound Dog*
5. *Give Peace A Chance*

6. *It's So Hard*
7. *Move On Fast*
8. *Woman Is The Nigger Of The World*

Cuts 1–8: From the Willowbrook One To One concert held at Madison Square Garden the evening of August 30, 1972.
SEE ALSO: **HOUND DOG/MORE FROM THE WILLOWBROOK ONE TO ONE CONCERT; JOHN LENNON/HOUND DOG.**

666   *HOUND DOG/LONG TALL SALLY*   Heavy 101   (45)
NOTES: *Hound Dog* was recorded by John with the Elephant's Memory Band on August 30, 1972. *Long Tall Sally* is by Paul and Wings and was recorded March 18, 1973. Issued with a black–and–white picture sleeve.

667   **HOUND DOG/MORE FROM THE WILLOWBROOK ONE TO ONE CONCERT**
CBM JL 5040   (LP)
NOTES: Same as **HOUND DOG** (CBM 5040).
SEE ALSO: **JOHN LENNON/HOUND DOG.**

668   **JOSHUA TREE TAPES**   TKBWM 1803   (LP)

1. *Imagine*
2. *Mother*
3. *Come Together*
4. *Give Peace A Chance*

5. *Yer Blues*
6. *John Sinclair*
7. *It's So Hard*
8. *The Luck Of The Irish*
9. *Woman Is The Nigger Of The World*
10. *Johnny B. Goode*

Cuts 1–4: From the Willowbrook One To One concert August 30, 1972.
Cut 5: From the Rolling Stones TV show "Rock And Roll Circus," taped December 11, 1968.
Cuts 6–10: From the "Mike Douglas Show" for the week of February 14–18, 1972. Cut 9 is with Chuck Berry.

669   *KYA 1969 PEACE TALK*   KYA 69A/69B   (45)
NOTES: John talks with KYA's Tom Campbell and Bill Holley. KYA is a San Francisco station, 1260 on the dial. This is also known as the 1969 peace talk or "war is over" interview. Issued on blue vinyl.

670   **LENNON, JOHN**   92444 C/D   (EP)
NOTES: This is a special picture disc. There are 15 different such discs available. All are one–of–a–kind test pressings. John does not sing on the record; instead it is an Elvis tribute by Paul Lichter. This same recording was also used to make the following picture discs: **BEATLES; GEORGE HARRISON; DENNY LAINE; JOHN LENNON/ELVIS PRESLEY; PAUL McCARTNEY; RINGO STARR; WINGS.**

671   **LENNON, JOHN & ELVIS PRESLEY**   92444 C/D   (EP)
NOTES: This is a special one–of–a–kind test pressing picture disc. Shows a black–and–white drawing of John and Elvis. John doesn't sing on the record; instead it contains a tribute to Elvis by Paul Lichter. This same recording was also used on the following picture records: **BEATLES; GEORGE HARRISON; DENNY LAINE; JOHN LENNON; PAUL McCARTNEY; RINGO STARR; WINGS.**

672   **JOHN LENNON/CHUCK BERRY TELECASTS**   Unknown   (LP)

1. *John Sinclair*
2. *It's Hard To Wait*
3. *The Luck Of The Irish*
4. *Sisters Oh Sisters*
5. *We All Wake Up*
6. *Woman Is The Nigger Of The World*
7. *Attica State*
8. *Johnny B. Goode*
9. *Memphis*
10. *Shake It*
11. *Sakura*
12. *Imagine*

Cuts 1–5, 7–12: From the "Mike Douglas Show" the week of February 14–18, 1972 when John served as co–host. Cuts 8 and 9 are with Chuck Berry.
Cut 6: From the "Dick Cavett Show" of May 11, 1972.

673   **JOHN LENNON – HOUND DOG**   CBM JL 5040   (LP)
NOTES: Same as **HOUND DOG** (CBM 5040).
SEE ALSO: **HOUND DOG/MORE FROM THE WILLOWBROOK ONE TO ONE CONCERT.**

674   *JOHN LENNON ON RONNIE HAWKINS: THE SHORT RAP/THE LONG RAP*
Cotillion 104/105   (45)
NOTES: This is a boot of the original disc which John made to help promote Ronnie Hawkins' record *Down In The Alley.*

675   *JOHN LENNON ROCK AND ROLL*   Quaye/Trident Spots SK 3419   (45)
NOTES: This one–sided disc consists of a sixty–second radio spot for the **ROCK 'N' ROLL** album.

676   *LENNON SHOW*   JL 1979   (45)

1. *Promo*
2. *Interview With John*
3. *Imagine*

NOTES: From the "Weekly Top–30" show of November 3, 1979 with host Mark Elliott.

677   **LENNON vs THE WORLD VOL. I**   Original Rock 1009   (LP)

1. *Be Bop A Lula*
2. *Be Bop A Lula*
3. *Ain't That A Shame*
4. *Ain't That A Shame*
5. *Bring It On Home To Me*
6. *Bring It On Home To Me*
7. *Do You Want To Dance*
8. *Do You Want To Dance*
9. *Just Because*
10. *Just Because*
11. *Peggy Sue*
12. *Peggy Sue*

Cuts 1, 3, 5, 7, 9, 11: John Lennon originals.
Cut 2: Original by Gene Vincent.
Cut 4: Original by Fats Domino.
Cut 6: Original by Sam Cooke.
Cut 8: Original by Bobby Freeman.
Cut 10: Original by Lloyd Price.
Cut 12: Original by Buddy Holly.

678   **LENNON vs THE WORLD VOL. II**   Original Rock 1010   (LP)

1. *Reddy Teddy*
2. *Reddy Teddy*
3. *Rip It Up*
4. *Rip It Up*
5. *Send Me Some Lovin'*
6. *Send Me Some Lovin'*
7. *Slippin' And Sliddin'*
8. *Slippin' And Sliddin'*
9. *Stand By Me*
10. *Stand By Me*
11. *Well (Baby Please Don't Go)*
12. *Well (Baby Please Don't Go)*

Cuts 1, 3, 5, 7, 9, 11: John Lennon originals.
Cuts 2, 4, 6, 8: Originals by Little Richard.
Cut 10: Original by Ben E. King.
Cut 12: Original by the Olympics.

679   LENNON vs THE WORLD VOL. III   Original Rock 1011   (LP)

1. *Sweet Little Sixteen*   7. *Angel Baby*
2. *Sweet Little Sixteen*   8. *Angel Baby*
3. *You Can't Catch Me*   9. *Be My Baby*
4. *You Can't Catch Me*   10. *Be My Baby*
5. *Ya Ya*   11. *Bony Moronie*
6. *Ya Ya*   12. *Bony Moronie*

Cuts 1, 3, 5, 7, 9, 11: Originals by John Lennon.
Cuts 2, 4: Originals by Chuck Berry.
Cut 6: Original by Lee Dorsey.
Cut 8: Original by Rosie and The Originals.
Cut 10: Original by the Ronettes.
Cut 12: Original by Larry Williams.

680   LIFE WITH THE LIONS   Tobe–Milo 4Q13/14   (EP)

1. *Song For John*   3. *Radio Play*
   Let's Go Flying
   Snow Is Falling All The Time
   Mummy's Only Looking For
      Her Hand In The Snow
2. *No Bed For Beatle John*

Cut 1: Recorded at the Cambridge Jazz Festival March 2, 1969 and included on
   the album **UNFINISHED MUSIC NO. 2: LIFE WITH THE LIONS.**
Cuts 2–3: Recorded at Queen Charlotte Hospital, London, November 4–25,
   1968 and included on the album **UNFINISHED MUSIC NO. 2: LIFE WITH
   THE LIONS.**
NOTES: Came with a cardboard picture sleeve. Only 1,000 numbered copies were
   issued.

681   MAN OF THE DECADE   MOTD1269   (LP)

1. *Give Peace A Chance*
2. *Reporter*
3. *If I Fell*
4. *Lennon*
5. *Reporter*
6. *A Hard Day's Night Train Scene*
7. *Reporter*
8. *Alive At Shea*
9. *Lennon On Acid*
10. *All You Need Is Love*
11. *Lennon*
12. *More Give Peace A Chance*
13. *Lennon*
14. *Lennon From Bed Interview*
15. *Reporter*
16. *Lennon*
17. *Reporter*
18. *Lennon*
19. *More All You Need Is Love*
20. *Reporter*
21. *Studio Toga*

One To One Concert And More (LP)   **Wizardo 301 (Entry 684)**

NOTES: This is a one-sided disc made to look like a test pressing. From some of the information on the album itself, it appears to be from a TV show (Allistar Cooke had something to do with it) which was shown December 31, 1979, the end of the decade. The LP was issued in a black–and–white laminated cover. *Give Peace A Chance* is live and unknown. *If I Fell* and *All You Need Is Love* are original recordings. The bit from Shea Stadium contains a portion of *I'm Down*. The last cut, *Studio Toga*, contains bits of several songs, including *Three Cool Cats, Blowin' In The Wind, Lucille, I'm So Tired, Ob La Di, Third Man Theme, Don't Let Me Down,* and *One After 909. Lucille, I'm So Tired* and *Ob La Di* appear to be studio outtakes. The remaining songs are from the **LET IT BE** sessions of early 1969.

682   ONE TO ONE CONCERT   CBM   (LP)

1. *Mother*
2. *Yoko Sings*
3. *Come Together*
4. *Give Peace A Chance*
5. *Imagine*
6. *Attica State*
7. *Luck Of The Irish*
8. *Oh Sisters*

Cuts 1–5: From the Willowbrook Children's concert at Madison Square Garden on August 30, 1972. Cut 2 is really *Midsummer New York.*
Cuts 6–8: From the concert for the benefit of John Sinclair held in Ann Arbor, Michigan on December 18, 1972.

683   ONE TO ONE CONCERT & ANN ARBOR   King Kong 641   (LP)
NOTES: Exact cuts unknown.

684   ONE TO ONE CONCERT AND MORE   Wizardo 301   (LP)

1. *Imagine*
2. *Come Together*
3. *Instant Karma*
4. *Cold Turkey*
5. *Mother*
6. *Give Peace A Chance*
7. *Attica State*
8. *Luck Of The Irish*
9. *John Sinclair*
10. *Do The Oz*
11. *God Save Us*
12. *Power To The People*

Cuts 1–6: From the Willowbrook One To One concert held at Madison Square Garden on August 30, 1972.
Cuts 7–9: From the benefit concert for John Sinclair held in Ann Arbor, Michigan, December 18, 1971.
Cuts 10–12: Original recordings. Cut 10 is Bill Elliot & The Elastic Oz Band.

685   ONE TO ONE CONCERT/MADISON SQUARE GARDEN & ANN ARBOR
Unknown   (LP)

1. *Mother*
2. *Imagine*
3. *Come Together*
4. *Give Peace A Chance*
5. *John Sinclair*
6. *Attica State*
7. *Sisters Oh Sisters*
8. *Luck Of The Irish*

Cuts 1–4: From the Willowbrook One To One concert at Madison Square Garden on August 30, 1972.
Cuts 5–8: From the benefit concert for John Sinclair held in Ann Arbor, Michigan, December 18, 1971.

686   PLOP PLOP . . . FIZZ FIZZ   Sean Mark HAR 170   (LP)

1. *Mother*
2. *Imagine*
3. *Come Together*
4. *Give Peace A Chance*
5. *Cold Turkey*
6. *Hound Dog*
7. *Slippin' And Slidin'*

199

4. *Give Peace A Chance*   8. *Imagine*
                                      9. *Whatever Gets You Through The Night*
                                  10. *Move Over Ms. L*

Cuts 1–4: From the Willowbrook One To One concert at Madison Square Garden on August 30, 1972. Afternoon show.

Cuts 5–6: Same as 1–4, but evening show.

Cuts 7–8: From the "Salute To Sir Lew Grade" TV special which aired June 13, 1975.

Cut 9: On stage with Elton John at Madison Square Garden on November 25, 1974.

Cut 10: Original recording.

NOTES: Issued on multi-color blue vinyl.

---

687   ROCK & ROLL CIRCUS   Unknown   (LP)
NOTES: Contains *Yer Blues* from the Rolling Stones' "Rock And Roll Circus" December 11, 1968. Features John, Yoko, Rick Gretch, Keith Richard, Mitch Mitchell, Eric Clapton and Klaus Voorman. Other cuts by Led Zeppelin, Cream, the Who and Buffalo Springfield. Issued on color vinyl.

---

688   THE ROCK AND ROLL CIRCUS   King Kong; Phonygraf Vinyl; TMOQ GRC 1383; Wizardo   (LP)

1. *Yer Blues*   4. *A Quick One While He's Away* (Who)
2. *Instrumental* (Cream)   5. *Everybody* (Cream)
3. *Riverside Blues* (Led Zeppelin) 6. *We'll See* (Buffalo Springfield)
                                7. *Down To The Wire* (Buffalo Springfield)
                                8. *Come On* (Buffalo Springfield)

NOTES: From the Rolling Stones' "Rock And Roll Circus" December 11, 1968. Features John and Yoko with Rick Gretch, Keith Richard, Mitch Mitchell, Eric Clapton and Klaus Voorman.

---

689   ROLLING STONES ROCK AND ROLL CIRCUS   Unknown   (LP)

1. *Route 66*   6. *Sympathy For The Devil*
2. *Confessin' The Blues*   7. *No Expectations*
3. *Jumping Jack Flash*   8. *Salt Of The Earth*
4. *Parachute Woman*   9. *Yer Blues*
5. *You Can't Always Get What You Want*

NOTES: All cuts are the Rolling Stones except cut 9 which is Lennon.

---

690   ROOTS   RTS A/B   (LP)

1. *Be Bop A Lula*   9. *Bony Moronie*
2. *Ain't That A Shame*   10. *Peggy Sue*
3. *Stand By Me*   11. *Bring It On Home To Me*
4. *Sweet Little Sixteen*   12. *Slippin' And Sliddin'*
5. *Rip It Up*   13. *Be My Baby*
6. *Angel Baby*   14. *Ya Ya*
7. *Do You Want To Dance*   15. *Just Because*
8. *You Can't Catch Me*

NOTES: This is a pirate of the Adam VIII album.

SEE ALSO: "ROOTS": THE ROCK AND ROLL OUTTAKES (CBM); "ROOTS": THE ROCK AND ROLL OUTTAKES (King Kong).

691 "ROOTS": THE ROCK AND ROLL OUTTAKES   CBM 404   (LP)
     NOTES: Same as **ROOTS**.
     SEE ALSO: "ROOTS": THE ROCK AND ROLL OUTTAKES.

692 "ROOTS": THE ROCK AND ROLL OUTTAKES   King Kong 636   (LP)

1. *Be Bop A Lula*
2. *Ain't That A Shame*
3. *Stand By Me*
4. *Sweet Little 16*
5. *Gonna Shake It Up Tonight*
6. *Angel Baby*
7. *Do You Wanna Dance*
8. *Can't Catch Me*
9. *Bony Morony*
10. *Peggy Sue*
11. *Bring Your Sweet Loving Home To Me*
12. *Slippin' And Sliddin'*
13. *Be My Baby*
14. *Ya Ya*
15. *Darling I Would Rather Let You Go*

     NOTES: Pirate of the Adam VIII album. Same as **ROOTS**, except for title of
        cut 15.
     SEE ALSO: "ROOTS": THE ROCK AND ROLL OUTTAKES.

693 TELECASTS   CBM 3711; TMOQ JL 517; TMOQ 1834; TMOQ 71046   (LP)

1. *John Sinclair*
2. *It's So Hard*
3. *The Luck Of The Irish*
4. *Sisters Oh Sisters*
5. *We All Woke Up*
6. *Woman Is The Nigger Of The World*
7. *Attica State*
8. *Shake It*
9. *Sakura*
10. *Memphis*
11. *Johnny B. Goode*
12. *Imagine*

     Cuts 1–5, 7–12: From the "Mike Douglas Show" from the week of February 14,
        1972. Cut 5 is really *We're All Water*. Cuts 10 and 11 are with Chuck
        Berry.
     Cut 6: From the "Dick Cavett Show" of May 11, 1972.
     NOTES: Re–issued in 1980 with a full–color, deluxe sleeve.

694 TELECASTS   King Kong 642   (LP)
     NOTES: Exact cuts unknown, but probably the same as **TELECASTS** (CBM).

695 TELEVISION OUT–TAKES   Tobe–Milo 4Q 3–4   (EP)
     NOTES: See comments for this EP under the listings for George Harrison.

696 UNKNOWN, WELL KNOWN   Unknown   (LP)

1. *Star Spangled Banner*
2. *Purple Haze*
3. *Instrumental Solo*
4. *Hear My Train A–Comin'*
5. *Day Tripper*
6. *Hound Dog*

     NOTES: All cuts are by Jimi Hendrix, except cut 5 which is Lennon and
        Hendrix on "Top Gear" October, 1967.

697 (VOL. 4 THE) ROCK AND ROLL CIRCUS   Mushroom Vol. 4; Slipped Disc 979
        (LP)
     NOTES: Reissue of **THE ROCK AND ROLL CIRCUS** (TMOQ 1383), only this
        one is on colored vinyl. Slipped Disc issue uses the Mushroom cover picture
        and number.
     SEE ALSO: **THE GREAT ROCK AND ROLL CIRCUS**.

698 YER BLUES   Unknown   (LP)
     NOTES: Same as **BRITISH BLUES JAM** (CBM 3426).

699   **YER BLUES**   Unknown   (LP)
        NOTES: Same as **GULP** (RL007).

700   **YER BLUES JAM**   King Kong 639   (LP)
        NOTES: Exact cuts unknown.

Lennon/McCartney

701   ANN ARBOR; NOW HEAR THIS   Unknown   (LP)

    1. *John Sinclair*   4. *Luck Of The Irish*
    2. *Attica State*   5. *Now Hear This Song Of Mine*
    3. *Sisters Oh Sisters*
    Cuts 1–4: From the concert for the benefit of John Sinclair held in Ann Arbor,
        Michigan on December 18, 1971.
    Cut 5: From the **RAM** promo disc.

702   JOHN AND PAUL IN MICHIGAN   Unknown   (LP)
    NOTES: Exact cuts unknown, but probably the same as **ANN ARBOR: NOW
    HEAR THIS.**

703   LENNON/McCARTNEY   CBM WEC R1 3665   (LP)
    NOTES: Same as **ANN ARBOR: NOW HEAR THIS.**

704   LENNON--McCARTNEY   King Kong 648   (LP)
    NOTES: Exact cuts unknown, but probably the same as **ANN ARBOR: NOW
    HEAR THIS.**

705   JOHN LENNON/PAUL McCARTNEY – ANN ARBOR "NOW HEAR THIS"
    Unknown   (LP)
    NOTES: Same as **ANN ARBOR: NOW HEAR THIS.**

706   NOW HEAR THIS   Unknown   (LP)
    NOTES: Same as **ANN ARBOR: NOW HEAR THIS.**

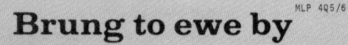

Brung to ewe by

MLP 4Q5/6

Here are some introductions you might like to use before
RAM album tracks.

We made them while we were doing RAM, and they're designed
to play straight into an album track, or out of it for that
matter.

Anyway, if you'd enjoy using them, we'd enjoy having you.

Ram On!

Paul & Linda McCartney

LIMITED EDITION

COMPACT 33⅓ R.P.M.

TOBE MILO

Brung To Ewe By (EP)   **Tobe-Milo 4Q 5/6 (Entry 713)**

Paul McCartney/Wings

707   **AN AFTERNOON WITH PAUL McCARTNEY**   RAM 103   (LP)
NOTES: This is a 50--minute interview broadcast April 1, 1979, on NBC radio
stations.

708   **BAND ON THE RUN -- OPEN END INTERVIEW WITH WINGS TO PROMOTE LP**
CO 8447 A/B   (LP)
NOTES: Interviews with Paul and Wings' members, complete with script. Also
has the songs *Helen Wheels, Band On The Run, Jet* and *Picasso's Last Words.*
Pressed on deep purple vinyl (has to be held to the light to see it's not black).
SEE ALSO: **OPEN END INTERVIEW.**

709   **BELGIUM**   King Kong 645   (LP)

1. *Lucille*
2. *Blue Moon Of Kentucky*
3. *Give Ireland Back To The Irish*
4. *Smile Away*
5. *Some People Never Know*

6. *Bip Bop*
7. *My Love*
8. *The Mess*
9. *Oh Darling*

Cuts 1--9: Recorded during Wings' tour of Belgium in August, 1972.

710   **BELGIUM**   Wizardo 370   (LP)

1. *Lucille (2 versions)*
2. *Blue Moon Of Kentucky*
3. *Give Ireland Back To The Irish*
   (2 versions)
4. *Smile Away*
5. *Some People Never Know*

6. *Bip Bop*
7. *My Love*
8. *The Mess (2 versions)*
9. *Say Darling*
10. *Green Acorn*

Cuts 1--10: Recorded live at the Cine Roma in Antwerp, Belgium August 22,
1972.
SEE ALSO: **WINGS AT HULL UNIVERSITY.**

711   **BELGIUM 1972**   CBM 1016   (LP)

1. *Lucille*
2. *Give Ireland Back To The Irish*
3. *Blue Moon*
4. *Some People Never Know*

5. *The Mess*
6. *Bip Bop*
7. *Say Darling*
8. *Smile Away*
9. *My Love*

Cuts 1--9: Recorded live at the Cine Roma in Antwerp, Belgium, August 22,
1972.
SEE ALSO: **LIVE IN BELGIUM.**

712   **BELGIUM 1972**   TMOQ 1016   (LP)

1. *Lucille*
2. *Give Ireland Back To The Irish*

6. *The Mess*
7. *Bip Bop*

3. *Blue Moon Of Kentucky*
4. *If You Don't Help Me Darling*
   (Henry's Blues)
5. *Some People Never Know*

8. *Say Darling*
9. *Smile Away*
10. *My Love*

Cuts 1–10: Although called **BELGIUM 1972**, some sources say this was recorded at York University on February 10, 1972.

713   **BRUNG TO EWE BY**   Tobe–Milo 4Q 5/6   (EP)
NOTES: This EP came with a black–and–white hard picture cover. The record is a copy of the **RAM** promo disc. Only 1,000 copies were made.

714   **BRUNG TO EWE BY**   SPRO–6210   (EP)
NOTES: A copy of the **RAM** promo disc. Contains twelve 30–second and three 60–second intros for the **RAM LP** tracks. Includes two letters, one by Paul and Linda and one by Diane Brooks of McCartney Productions, Inc.

715   **CAN YOU PLEASE CRAWL OUT YOUR WINDOW**   Jimi 1/Dragonfly Records;
Slipped Disc SX–TT 979   (LP)

1. *Auld Lang Syne*
2. *Interview: Alan Douglas*
3. *Little Drummer Boy*
4. *Silent Night*
5. *Mother Earth*
6. *Interview: Paul McCartney*

7. *Burning The Midnight Lamp*
8. *Can You Please Crawl Out Your Window*
9. *Drivin' South*
10. *Tobacco Road*

NOTES: All songs on this album are by Jimi Hendrix, but there is a short interview featuring Paul talking about Jimi at the end of side one.

716   *CHRISTMAS*   Ryde 5226   (45)
NOTES: This is really *WONDERFUL CHRISTMASTIME*. It is a one–sided disc made to look like a test pressing. Only 200 were pressed. It was recorded live at the Wings' concert in Brighton, England, on December 2, 1979. It came with the Columbia sleeve issued with the regular single. If the sleeve is a copy, it is a very good one.

717   *"COMING UP" TO NO. 1*   RAM 110   (45)

1. *Promo*
2. *Interview With Paul*

3. *Coming Up*

NOTES: From the "Weekly Top–30 Show" of June 7, 1980 with host Mark Elliott. This was the week that *Coming Up* hit number 1 on their charts.

718   **COPENHAGEN**   TMOQ 8205/6   (2 LPs)

1. *Venus And Mars Rock Show*
2. *Jet*
3. *Let Me Roll It*
4. *Spirits Of Ancient Egypt*
5. *Maybe I'm Amazed*
6. *Call Me Back Again*

7. *Lady Madonna*
8. *Long And Winding Road*
9. *Live And Let Die*
10. *Picasso's Last Words*
11. *Richard Cory*

12. *Bluebird*
13. *Yesterday*
14. *You Gave Me The Answer*

18. *Silly Love Songs*
19. *Beware My Love*
20. *Letting Go*

15. *Magneto And Titanium Man*   21. *Hi Hi Hi*
16. *My Love*   22. *Soilie*
17. *Let 'Em In*
Cuts 1–22: Recorded live at the Falkoner Theatre in Copenhagen, Denmark on
March 21, 1976.
SEE ALSO: **GREAT DANE; WINGS GREAT DANE–LIVE IN COPENHAGEN.**

719 **COPENHAGEN CONCERT 76** TKWRM 2807 (LP)
NOTES: Same as **COPENHAGEN** (TMOQ 8205/6).

720 *DID WE MEET SOMEWHERE BEFORE/DID WE MEET SOMEWHERE BEFORE*
RAM 108 (45)
NOTES: These two cuts of the same song are from the movie "Rock And Roll
High School." Side one is longer (1:22) and is from the opening credits
and introduction to the film. The second version (1:09) is from about a
third of the way through the film. There is dialogue heard over both
versions. McCartney has yet to release this song in any other form.

721 **1882** Wizardo 500 A/B (LP)

1. *1882*   5. *The Best Friend I've Ever Had*
2. *Blue Moon Of Kentucky*   6. *I Would Only Smile*
3. *Seaside Woman*   7. *Say You Don't Mind*
4. *I Am Your Singer*   8. *Take Me For A Ride Momma*
Cuts 1–8: Recorded live in Hanover, Germany, August 16, 1972.
SEE ALSO: **LIVE IN HANOVER, GERMANY 1972; McCARTNEY LIVE IN
HANOVER, GERMANY 1972.**

722 **ENCORE** CBM A109 (LP)
NOTES: Exact cuts unknown, but does include parts of the Seattle concert of
June 10, 1976.

723 **FIRST AMERICAN CONCERT 1976** King Kong 644 (LP)
NOTES: Exact cuts unknown, but contains parts of the Fort Worth, Texas
concert of May 3, 1976.

724 **FIRST AMERICAN CONCERT 1976** Shalom 4598 (2 LPs)

1. *Venus And Mars*   7. *Maybe I'm Amazed*
2. *Rock Show*   8. *Call Me Back Again*
3. *Jet*   9. *Lady Madonna*
4. *Let Me Roll It*   10. *Long And Winding Road*
5. *Spirits Of Ancient Egypt*   11. *Live And Let Die*
6. *Medicine Jar*

12. *Picasso's Last Words*   18. *Magneto And Titanium Man*
13. *Bluebird*   19. *My Love*
14. *I've Just Seen A Face*   20. *Listen To What The Man Said*
15. *Blackbird*   21. *Let 'Em In*
16. *Yesterday*   22. *Time To Hide*
17. *You Gave Me The Answer*
Cuts 1–22: From the Fort Worth, Texas concert, May 3, 1976.

725 **FIRST LIVE SHOW SPRING 1972** Wizardo 371 (2 LPs)

1. *Lucille*   6. *Some People Never Know*
2. *Give Ireland Back To The Irish* 7. *The Mess*
3. *Blue Moon Of Kentucky*   8. *Bip Bop*

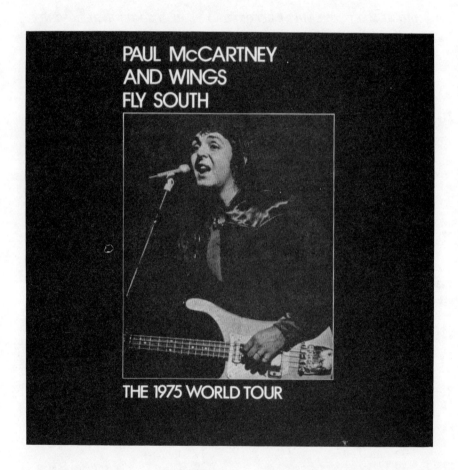

Fly South — 1975 World Tour (2 LPs)   Wunderland W49000 (Entry 727)

4. *Seaside Woman*
5. *Help Me Darling*

9. *Thank You (Say Darling)*
10. *Smile Away*
11. *My Love*
12. *Henry's Blues*

13. *Wildlife*
14. *Give Ireland Back To The Irish*
15. *The Mess*
16. *Long Tall Sally*

Cuts 1–16: Exact concert unknown. Wings toured various universities in England from February 9 through February 23, 1972. This is most likely from one of those concerts, possibly Hull University.
NOTES: Issued on colored vinyl.

726   FLASH BOMB   TWM 1807   (LP)

1. *Listen To What The Man Said*
2. *Let 'Em In*
3. *Time To Hide*
4. *Silly Love Songs*
5. *Beware My Love*

6. *Letting Go*
7. *Band On The Run*
8. *Hi Hi Hi*
9. *Soily*

Cuts 1–9: Recorded live at the L.A. Forum June 23, 1976.
NOTES: This is sides five and six of **WINGS FROM THE WINGS** (Idle Mind 1117–1119).

727   FLY SOUTH -- 1975 WORLD TOUR   Berkeley 46; Wunderland W49000   (2 LPs)

1. *Venus And Mars*
2. *Rock Show*
3. *Jet*
4. *Let Me Roll It*
5. *Maybe I'm Amazed*
6. *I've Just Seen A Face*

7. *Blackbird*
8. *Waltzing Matilda/Yesterday*
9. *Listen To What The Man Said*
10. *Call Me Back Again*
11. *Letting Go*
12. *Warmup/Batman*

13. *Long And Winding Road*
14. *Yesterday*
15. *Band On The Run*
16. *Hi Hi Hi*

17. *My Love*
18. *Blackbird Once More*
19. *Paul Talks After Concert*
20. *A Final Letting Go*
21. *Interview: Paul On Beatle Break–Up And Possible Reunion*

Cuts 1–21: Recorded live during the Australian tour in November, 1975.
NOTES: Deluxe, laminated cover.
SEE ALSO: **FLY SOUTH '75.**

728   FLY SOUTH '75   Wizardo 380   (LP)
NOTES: This one–record set is the same as **FLY SOUTH -- 1975 WORLD TOUR** (Wunderland W49000), except two songs are left off the album -- *Yesterday* and *A Final Letting Go*. Pressed on colored vinyl.

729   FORT WORTH & SEATTLE   King Kong 4599   (LP)

1. *Silly Love Songs*
2. *Beware My Love*
3. *Letting Go*

4. *Band On The Run*
5. *Hi Hi Hi*
6. *Silly Love Songs (Studio And Interview)*
7. *Band On The Run*
8. *Interview*
9. *Yesterday*

Cuts 1–9: From the Fort Worth (May 3, 1976) and Seattle (June 10, 1976) concerts.
SEE ALSO: **McCARTNEY & WINGS/FORT WORTH AND SEATTLE LIVE.**

730   GOODNIGHT AMERICA   RAM 102   (LP)

NOTES: From an ABC-TV broadcast of June 28, 1976 with Geraldo Rivera as host. Interviews with Paul, Linda, Denny, Jimmy, etc. There are excerpts from the Seattle concert (June 10), but only the song *Yesterday* is heard in its entirety.

731   GOTTA SING--GOTTA DANCE   Wizardo 342   (LP)

1. *Be My Friend (Big Barn Red)*
2. *My Little Woman Love*
3. *My Love*
4. *Uncle Albert*
5. *Live And Let Die*
6. *Gotta Sing–Gotta Dance*
7. *The Mess*
8. *Maybe I'm Amazed*
9. *Long Tall Sally*
10. *Another Day*
11. *Oh Woman Oh Why*
12. Medley:
    Bluebird
    Michelle
    Heart Of The Country
    Mary Had A Little Lamb
    Yesterday
13. *Hi Hi Hi*

Cuts 1--13: From the TV special "James Paul McCartney" which first aired April 16, 1972.

SEE ALSO: **GOTTA SING--GOTTA DANCE.**

732   GOTTA SING--GOTTA DANCE   Wizardo 342   (LP)

1. *Big Barn Red*
2. *C Moon*
3. *Little Woman Love*
4. *The Mess*
5. *Maybe I'm Amazed*
6. *Long Tall Sally*
7. *Gotta Sing–Gotta Dance*
8. *Live And Let Die*
9. *Now Hear This Song Of Mine -- Letting Go*
10. *Woman Oh Why*
11. *The Mess*
12. *Country Dreamer*
13. *I Lie Around*

Cuts 1--8, 10--11: From the "James Paul McCartney" TV special, April 16, 1972.

Cut 9: From the promo for the **RAM** album.

Cut 12--13: Original.

SEE ALSO: **GOTTA SING--GOTTA DANCE.**

733   GREAT DANE   TMOQ 8205/6   (2 LPs)

1. *Venus And Mars*
2. *Rock Show*
3. *Jet*
4. *Let Me Roll It*
5. *Maybe I'm Amazed*
6. *Call Me Back Again*
7. *Lady Madonna*
8. *Long And Winding Road*
9. *Picasso's Last Words*
10. *Richard Cory*
11. *Bluebird*
12. *I've Just Seen A Face*
13. *Blackbird*

14. *Yesterday*
15. *You Gave Me The Answer*
16. *Live And Let Die*
17. *My Love*
18. *Silly Love Songs*
19. *Beware My Love*
20. *Letting Go*
21. *Magneto And Titanium Man*
22. *Band On The Run*
23. *Hi Hi Hi*
24. *Soilie*

Cuts 1--24: Recorded live in Copenhagen on March 21, 1976.

SEE ALSO: **COPENHAGEN; WINGS GREAT DANE--LIVE IN COPENHAGEN.**

734   HOT HITS AND COLD CUTS   Wizardo 405   (LP)

1. *Mary Had A Little Lamb*
2. *Hi Hi Hi*
3. *Little Woman Love*
4. *The Mess*
5. *Give Ireland Back To The Irish*
6. *Sally G*
7. *C Moon*
8. *Junior's Farm*
9. *I Lie Around*
10. *Country Dreamer*

Cuts 1–10: Original recordings.

735   IN CONCERT IN COPENHAGEN   Unknown   (2 LPs)
NOTES: Reissued as **COPENHAGEN CONCERT 76** (TKWRM 2807). Has a color fold–out cover.

736   IN CONCERT UNDERNEATH THE CRUX TWINKLING   Unknown   (LP)

1. *Venus And Mars*
2. *Rock Show*
3. *Jet*
4. *Let Me Roll It*
5. *Maybe I'm Amazed*
6. *I've Just Seen A Face*
7. *Blackbird*
8. *Yesterday*
9. *Call Me Back Again*
10. *Listen To What The Man Said*
11. *Letting Go*
12. *Band On The Run*
13. *Hi Hi Hi*
14. *Paul's Apology For Cancelling The Japanese Tour*
15. *Bluebird*

Cuts 1–15: Recorded live in Australia during the November, 1975 concert tour.

737   IN SCOTLAND   Wizardo 302   (LP)

1. *Soilie*
2. *Big Barn Red*
3. *When The Night*
4. *Wild Life*
5. *Seaside Woman*
6. *Little Woman Love*
7. *C Moon*
8. *Live And Let Die*
9. *Maybe I'm Amazed*
10. *My Love*
11. *Go Now*
12. *Say You Didn't Mean It*
13. *The Mess*
14. *Long Tall Sally*

Cuts 1–15: Recorded live in Edinburgh, Scotland, May 23, 1973.

738   JAMES PAUL McCARTNEY   Berkeley 45; CBM 401; TMOQ 1882; TMOQ 73018
(LP)

1. *Big Barn Red*
2. Medley:
   Little Woman Love
   C Moon
   My Love
3. *The Mess*
4. *Maybe I'm Amazed*
5. *Long Tall Sally*
6. *Another Day*
7. *Oh Woman Oh Why*
8. *Hi Hi Hi*
9. *Gotta Sing–Gotta Dance*
10. *Live And Let Die*
11. Medley:
    Blackbird
    Bluebird
    Michelle
    Heart Of The Country
12. *Yesterday*

Cuts 1–12: From the "James Paul McCartney" TV special from April 16, 1973.

739   JAMES PAUL McCARTNEY   CBM 1882   (LP)

1. *Be My Friend*
2. *My Little Woman Mine*
3. *My Love Does It Good*
4. *Uncle Albert*
10. *Another Day*
11. *Oh Woman Oh Why*
12. Medley:
    I'm A Bluebird

5. *Live And Let Die*	*Michelle*
6. *Gotta Sing–Gotta Dance*	*Heart Of The Country*
7. *What A Mess I'm In*	13. *Mary Had A Little Lamb*
8. *Maybe I'm Amazed*	14. *Yesterday*
9. *Long Tall Sally*	15. *Hi Hi Hi*
	16. *Uncle Albert*

Cuts 1--16: From the TV special "James Paul McCartney" shown April 16, 1973.

740   *JET*   RAM 109   (45)

1. *Interview With Paul*   2. *Jet*

NOTES: From the "Weekly Top–30 Show" of April 19, 1980, with host Mark Elliott.

741   KINGDOME 6--10--76   Unknown   (2 LPs)
NOTES: Exact cuts unknown.

742   L.A. FORUM   TKRWM 2805   (2 LPs)

1. *Venus And Mars*	6. *Medicine Jar*
2. *Rock Show*	7. *Maybe I'm Amazed*
3. *Jet*	8. *Call Me Back Again*
4. *Let Me Roll It*	9. *Live And Let Die*
5. *Spirits Of Ancient Egypt*	

10. *Listen To What The Man Said*	15. *Letting Go*
11. *Let 'Em In*	16. *Band On The Run*
12. *Time To Hide*	17. *Hi Hi Hi*
13. *Silly Love Songs*	18. *Soily*
14. *Beware My Love*	

Cuts 1--18: Recorded at the Los Angeles concert June 21, 1976.
SEE ALSO: **WINGS L.A. 1976.**

743   LAINE, DENNY   92444 C/D   (EP)
NOTES: This is a picture disc, a one-of--a-kind test pressing. The picture is a black–and–white, full–face shot of Denny. The record is a tribute to Elvis by Paul Lichter. This same recording was used on the following picture discs also: **BEATLES; GEORGE HARRISON; JOHN LENNON; JOHN LENNON/ELVIS PRESLEY; PAUL McCARTNEY; RINGO STARR; WINGS.**

744   LASER BEAMS   Wizardo 382   (LP)

1. *Live And Let Die*	7. *Yesterday*
2. *Picasso's Last Words*	8. *Magneto And Titanium Man*
3. *Richard Cory*	9. *Go Now*
4. *Bluebird*	10. *Band On The Run*
5. *I've Just Seen A Face*	11. *Hi Hi Hi*
6. *Blackbird*	12. *Soilie*

Cuts 1–12: Recorded at the L.A. Forum, June 23, 1976.

745   LEEDS, ENGLAND   King Kong 647; King Kong 1050   (LP)

1. *Soilie*	6. *My Little Woman*
2. *Big Barn Red*	7. *C Moon*
3. *When The Night*	8. *Live And Let Die*
4. *Wildlife*	9. *Maybe I'm Amazed*

LIVE FROM LIVERPOOL

NOVEMBER 25, 1979

Let It Be/Yesterday (45)   Ll10 A/B (Entry 747)

5. *Keep That Woman (Seaside
   Woman)*
10. *My Love*
11. *Go Now*
12. *The Mess*

Cuts 1--12: Recorded in Leeds, England, May 19, 1973.

746 LEEDS '73 Unknown (LP)

1. *Live And Let Die*
2. *Hi Hi Hi*
3. *Soilie*
4. *When The Night*
5. *Wildlife*

6. *C Moon*
7. *My Love*
8. *The Mess*
9. *Little Woman Love*

Cuts 1--9: Recorded in Leeds, England, May 19, 1973.

747 *LET IT BE/YESTERDAY* LL 10 A/B (45)
NOTES: Recorded live in Liverpool, November 25, 1979. There is a little
bit of *Maggie Mae* before *Yesterday*. Came with a black--and--white picture
sleeve showing Paul and Denny at the mike. This is a small--holed 45 rpm.

748 LIGHT AS A FEATHER ZAP 7875 (LP)

1. *Venus And Mars Rock Show*
2. *Jet*
3. *Let Me Roll It*
4. *Spirits Of Ancient Egypt*

5. *Medicine Jar*
6. *Maybe I'm Amazed*
7. *Call Me Back Again*
8. *Lady Madonna*
9. *Long And Winding Road*

Cuts 1--9: Recorded live in concert at the Capitol Centre in Largo, Maryland,
May 15, 1976.

749 LIQUID PAPER TWM 1805 (LP)

1. *Venus And Mars*
2. *Rock Show*
3. *Jet*
4. *Let Me Roll It*
5. *Spirits of Ancient Egypt*

6. *Medicine Jar*
7. *Maybe I'm Amazed*
8. *Call Me Back Again*
9. *Lady Madonna*
10. *Long And Winding Road*

Cuts 1--10: Recorded live at the L.A. Forum, June 23, 1976.
NOTES: This is sides one and two of **WINGS FROM THE WINGS** (Idle Mind
1117--1119).

750 LIVE BRR 002 (LP)

1. *Rock Show*
2. *Jet*
3. *Let Me Roll It*
4. *Spirits of Ancient Egypt*
5. *Medicine Jar*
6. *Maybe I'm Amazed*

7. *Call Me Back Again*
8. *Lady Madonna*
9. *Long And Winding Road*
10. *Live And Let Die*
11. *Picasso's Last Words*
12. *Richard Cory*
13. *Bluebird*

Cuts 1--13: Recorded live at Maple Leaf Gardens, Toronto, Canada on May 9,
1976.
NOTES: Issued on multi--color vinyl.

751 LIVE AND LET DIE/I LIE AROUND Apple 1863 (LP)
NOTES: This is a black--and--white picture sleeve only. No sleeve was issued with
the original record. Same picture appears on both sides and shows Paul at
mike singing and playing bass.

Liverpool Live (LP)   Ayatollah ARC-011-50 (Entry 757)

752 **LIVE AT L.A. JUNE 23, 1976** 3006 (3 LPs)
NOTES: Re--release of **WINGS FROM THE WINGS** (Idle Mind 1117–1119).
Issued on colored vinyl.

753 **LIVE IN BELGIUM** CBM 1016 (LP)
NOTES: Same as **BELGIUM 1972**, but different song order.

754 **LIVE IN COPENHAGEN** TMOQ 0002 (2 LPs)

1. *Venus And Mars Rock Show*
2. *Jet*
3. *Let Me Roll It*
4. *Spirits Of Ancient Egypt*
5. *Maybe I'm Amazed*
6. *Call Me Back Again*

7. *Lady Madonna*
8. *Long And Winding Road*
9. *Live And Let Die*
10. *Picasso's Last Words*
11. *Richard Cory*
12. *Bluebird*

13. *Yesterday*
14. *You Gave Me The Answer*
15. *Magneto And Titanium Man*
16. *My Love*
17. *Let 'Em In*
18. *Silly Love Songs*

19. *Beware My Love*
20. *Letting Go*
21. *Band On The Run*
22. *Hi Hi Hi*
23. *Soilie*

Cuts 1–23: Recorded live at the Falkoner Theatre in Copenhagen March 21, 1976.

755 **LIVE IN HANOVER GERMANY 1972** Wizardo 500 (LP)
NOTES: Same as **1882**.
SEE ALSO: **McCARTNEY LIVE IN HANOVER GERMANY 1972**.

756 **LIVE IN SCOTLAND** Wizardo 302 (LP)

1. *Wildlife*
2. *Seaside Woman*
3. *C Moon*
4. *Little Woman Love*
5. *Live And Let Die*
6. *Maybe I'm Amazed*

7. *My Love*
8. *Go Now*
9. *Say You Don't Mean It*
10. *The Mess*
11. *Hi Hi Hi*
12. *Long Tall Sally*

Cuts 1–12: Recorded in Edinburgh, Scotland, May 23, 1973.
NOTES: Same number as **IN SCOTLAND**, but different titles listed.

757 **LIVERPOOL LIVE** Ayatollah Records ARC--011--50 (LP)

1. *Got To Get You Into My Life*
2. *Getting Closer*
3. *Every Night*
4. *I've Had Enough*
5. *No Words*
6. *Old Siam, Sir*

7. *The Fool On The Hill*
8. *Spin It On*
9. *Arrow Through Me*
10. *Wonderful Christmas Time*
11. *Hot As Sun*
12. *Twenty Flight Rock*
13. *Mull Of Kintyre*

Cuts 1--13: Recorded at the Liverpool Royal Court Theatre, November 25, 1979.
NOTES: Black--and--white laminated cover.

758 *LONG TALL SALLY/HOUND DOG* Heavy 101 (45)
NOTES: *Long Tall Sally* was recorded by Paul and Wings March 18, 1973,
while *Hound Dog* was recorded by John and Elephant's Memory August 30,
1972. Issued with a black--and--white picture sleeve.

759 *LOVE IS STRANGE*   Original Rock 45--1012   (45)
NOTES: This 45 has McCartney's version of *Love Is Strange* on one side and the original version by Mickey & Sylvia on the other side.

760 **MAPLE LEAF GARDENS TORONTO**   TMOQ 0002; ZAP 7887   (LP)
NOTES: Same as **LIVE** (BRR 002).

761 *MAYBE I'M AMAZED/HI HI HI*   RAM 104   (45)
NOTES: These are the original recordings with comments by Alan Parsons who engineered them. They were taken from the DJ album **AUDIO GUIDE TO THE ALAN PARSONS PROJECT** (Arista SP 68), released in 1979.

762 **McCARTNEY & WINGS/FORT WORTH & SEATTLE LIVE**   King Kong 4599   (LP)
NOTES: Same as **FORT WORTH & SEATTLE.**

763 **McCARTNEY COLD CUTS**   K0--405   (LP)
NOTES: Exact cuts unknown, but presumably originals.

764 **McCARTNEY HITS AGAIN**   Capitol STAX 33452   (LP)
NOTES: Exact cuts unknown. Made to look like a legitimate Capitol greatest hits album.

765 **McCARTNEY LIVE IN HANOVER GERMANY 1972**   Wizardo 500   (LP)
NOTES: Same as **1882.**
SEE ALSO: **LIVE IN HANOVER GERMANY 1972.**

766 **McCARTNEY: LONDON TOWN**   RAM 101   (LP)
NOTES: This is a 30--minute interview with Paul about the **LONDON TOWN** album. It was broadcast on the BBC May 14, 1978.

767 **McCARTNEY, PAUL**   92444 C/D   (EP)
NOTES: Special test pressing picture disc. There are 35 different McCartney picture discs available. Paul does not sing on the record. Instead it is a tribute to Elvis done by Paul Lichter. This same recording was also used for the following picture discs: **BEATLES; GEORGE HARRISON; JOHN LENNON; JOHN LENNON/ELVIS PRESLEY; RINGO STARR; WINGS.**

768 *McCARTNEY SHOW*   RAM 105   (45)

1. *Promo*   3. *Uncle Albert*
2. *Interview With Paul*
NOTES: From the "Weekly Top--30 Show" of October 20, 1979, hosted by Mark Elliott.

769 *MY DARK HOUR/GOD BLESS CALIFORNIA*   RAM 106   (45)
NOTES: Both songs are originals. *My Dark Hour* was recorded in London in 1969 with Steve Miller on guitar and lead vocals and Paul on bass, drums and vocals. *God Bless California* is from the album **PASS ON THIS SIDE** by Thornton, Fradkin and Unger. Paul and Linda add some vocals and Wings' member Denny Seiwell is on drums.

770 **MY LOVE**   Berkeley 2028   (LP)
NOTES: Same as **JAMES PAUL McCARTNEY** (Berkeley 45). Issued with a deluxe black--and--white cover.

771   **NASHVILLE DIARY**   PRO 1234A/B   (EP)

    1. *My Love*   3. *Hi Hi Hi*
    2. *One Hand Clapping*   4. *Soily*
    Cuts 1–4: Studio outtakes from Nashville, 1975.
    NOTES: Came with a brown–tone picture sleeve.

772   **NATURE SCAPES**   Highway Hi Fi HHCER 116   (LP)

    1. *Lucille*   7. *The Mess*
    2. *Give Ireland Back To The Irish*   8. *Bip Bop*
    3. *Blue Moon Of Kentucky*   9. *Say Darling*
    4. *Introductions*   10. *Smile Away*
    5. *Help Me Darling*   11. *My Love*
    6. *Some People Never Know*
    Cuts 1–11: Recorded during the British tour in February in 1972, possibly Leeds
    or Hull University.

773   **9mm AUTOMATIC**   ZAP 7878   (LP)

    1. *Venus And Mars*   10. *Beware My Love*
    2. *Rock Show*   11. *Letting Go*
    3. *Jet*   12. *Band On The Run*
    4. *Let Me Roll It*   13. *Hi Hi Hi*
    5. *Maybe I'm Amazed*   14. *Liar–Cheater (Soily)*
    6. *I've Just Seen A Face*
    7. *Blackbird*
    8. *Yesterday*
    9. *Listen To What The Man Said*
    Cuts 1–9: Recorded live at Horden Pavillion in Sydney, Australia November 7,
    1975.
    Cuts 10–14: Recorded live at the Capitol Centre in Largo, Maryland on May 15,
    1976.

774   **OPEN END INTERVIEW**   CO 8447 A/B (Capitol)   (LP)
    NOTES: Same as **BAND ON THE RUN -- OPEN END INTERVIEW WITH
    WINGS TO PROMOTE LP.**

775   **ORIENTAL NIGHTFISH**   HAR 169   (2 LPs)

    1. *Eat At Home*   7. *Bip Bop*
    2. *Mumbo*   8. *Smile Away*
    3. *Why Do You Treat Me So Badly*   9. *Give Ireland Back To The Irish*
    4. *1882*   10. *The Mess*
    5. *I Will Only Smile*   11. *Mary Had A Little Lamb*
    6. *Oriental Nightfish*

    12. *Jet*   17. *Mine For Me*
    13. *Magneto And Titanium Man*   18. *Jet*
    14. *My Love*   19. *Zoo Gang*
    15. *Beware My Love*   20. *Country Dreamer*
    16. *Soilie*   21. *I Lie Around*
                            22. *Mary Had A Little Lamb*
                            23. *Uncle Albert*
    Cuts 1–5: Unknown, but probably from the 1972 tour.
    Cut 6: Paul and Linda demo from 1973.
    Cuts 7–11: From the Hanover, Germany concert of August 16, 1972.
    Cuts 12–16: From the San Diego concert, June 16, 1976.
    Cut 17: From "Midnight Special" (1975) with Paul and Linda harmonizing with

Rod Stewart on this song written by Paul for Rod.
Cut 18: Original. The DJ edited version of the song.
Cuts 19–21: Originals.
Cuts 22–23: From the "James Paul McCartney" TV special of April 16, 1973.
NOTES: Deluxe, laminated cover. Issued on color vinyl.

776 **ORIENTAL NIGHTFISH PART 2** Unknown (LP)
NOTES: Exact cuts unknown, but does contain some cuts from Germany, 1972.
Issued on colored vinyl.

777 **PAUL McCARTNEY AND WINGS IN CONCERT IN COPENHAGEN** TMOQ 1401 (LP)
NOTES: Same as **COPENHAGEN** (TMOQ 8205/6).

778 **PAUL McCARTNEY AND WINGS LIVE** Unknown (LP)

1. *Big Barn Red*
2. *My Little Love*
3. *My Love*
4. *The Mess*
5. *Maybe I'm Amazed*
6. *Long Tall Sally*
7. *Another Day*
8. *Hi Hi Hi*
9. *Oh Woman Oh Why*
10. *Gotta Sing–Gotta Dance*
11. *Live And Let Die*
12. Medley:
    Bluebird
    Michelle
    Heart Of The Country
13. *Yesterday*

Cuts 1–13: From the TV special "James Paul McCartney" April 16, 1973.

779 **PAUL McCARTNEY AND WINGS MEET BILL GRAHAM 1976** Wizardo 503 (LP)

1. *My Love*
2. *Letting Go*
3. *Silly Love Songs*
4. *Time To Hide*
5. *You Gave Me The Answer*
6. *Let 'Em In*
7. *Listen To What The Man Said*
8. *Beware My Love*
9. *Hi Hi Hi*

Cuts 1–9: Recorded at the Cow Palace in San Francisco on June 14, 1976.
SEE ALSO: **WINGS OVER FRISCO.**

780 *PLASTIC MACS COMING UP* RAM 111 (45)
NOTES: From the promo film for the studio version of *Coming Up* in which
Paul plays all the musicians. This version is slightly longer than the released
version. This is a one–sided disc, made to look like a test pressing.

781 **RIDE A KILLER BIRD** TWM 1806 (LP)

1. *Live And Let Die*
2. *Picasso's Last Words*
3. *Bluebird*
4. *I've Just Seen A Face*
5. *Blackbird*
6. *Yesterday*
7. *You Gave Me The Answer*
8. *Magneto And Titanium Man*
9. *Go Now*
10. *My Love*

Cuts 1–10: Recorded live at the L.A. Forum June 23, 1976.
NOTES: This album is sides three and four of **WINGS FROM THE WINGS** (Idle
Mind 1117–1119).

782 **ROCK SHOW** MARC (LP)

1. *Venus And Mars*
2. *Rock Show*
3. *Jet*
4. *Let Me Roll It*
5. *Maybe I'm Amazed*
9. *Listen To What The Man Said*
10. *Call Me Back Again*
11. *Letting Go*
12. *Band On The Run*
13. *Hi Hi Hi*

6. *I've Just Seen A Face*　　　　14. *Radio Announcement*
7. *Blackbird*　　　　　　　　　15. *Bluebird*
8. *Yesterday*

Cuts 1--15: Recorded at the Myer Music Bowl in Melbourne, Australia on November 13, 1975. The show was broadcast on Japanese radio station JOZR.
NOTES: Japanese bootleg with deluxe cover.
SEE ALSO: **ROCK SHOW '75.**

783　**ROCK SHOW '75**　MARC　(LP)
　　　NOTES: Same as **ROCK SHOW** (MARC).

784　**SAN DIEGO 1976**　BR 10004　(2 LPs)
　　　NOTES: Exact cuts unknown, but all from the San Diego concert, June 16, 1976.

785　**SCOTLAND**　King Kong 646　(LP)
　　　NOTES: Exact cuts unknown, but probably recorded in Edinburgh on May 23, 1973.

786　**SCOTLAND '73**　Instant Analysis　(LP)
　　　NOTES: Same as IN SCOTLAND (Wizardo 302), except *Hi Hi Hi* appears before *Long Tall Sally.*

787　**SCOTLAND 1973**　Instant Analysis　(LP)
　　　NOTES: Same as **SCOTLAND '73.**

788　**SUNSHINE SUPERMEN/THE MELVIN BRAGG INTERVIEW**　Cx296A/Cx296B
　　　(LP)

1. *How Do You Do*　　　　　　9. *Paul McCartney Interview By*
2. *Blackbird*　　　　　　　　　　*Melvin Bragg*
3. *The Unicorn*
4. *Lalena*
5. *Heather*
6. *Mr. Wind*
7. *The Walrus And The Carpenter*
8. *Land Of Gisch*

Cuts 1--8: Paul and Donovan.
Cut 9: This interview was done in October, 1977 during the recording of *Mull Of Kintyre.*
NOTES: Issued on purple vinyl.

789　**TELEVISION OUT--TAKES**　Tobe--Milo 4Q 3--4　(LP)
　　　NOTES: See this listing under George Harrison for complete details.

790　**TORONTO**　Unknown　(LP)

1. *Venus And Mars Rock Show*　　8. *Lady Madonna*
2. *Jet*　　　　　　　　　　　　9. *Long And Winding Road*
3. *Let Me Roll It*　　　　　　　10. *Live And Let Die*
4. *Spirits Of Ancient Egypt*　　　11. *Picasso's Last Words*
5. *Medicine Jar*　　　　　　　12. *Richard Cory*
6. *Maybe I'm Amazed*　　　　　13. *Bluebird*
7. *Call Me Back Again*

Cuts 1--13: Recorded live at Maple Leaf Gardens in Toronto on May 9, 1976.

Venus And Mars Rock Show (45)   Capitol 4175 (Entry 795)

791   *TWENTY FLIGHT ROCK*   Original Rock 45--1013   (45)
        NOTES: Side one is McCartney live at the Liverpool Royal Court Theatre on
        November 25, 1979. The other side is the original version of this song by
        Eddie Cochran.

792   *TWENTY FLIGHT ROCK/WONDERFUL CHRISTMASTIME*   RAM 107   (45)
        NOTES: Both songs were recorded live in concert at the Liverpool Royal Court
        Theatre on November 25, 1979.

793   **20/20 EYESIGHT**   RAM 113   (LP)
        NOTES: Paul on the TV show "20/20" being interviewed by Geraldo Rivera on
        November 1, 1979. Bits of many songs are heard throughout the interview,
        including: *Arrow Through Me, Yesterday, Maybe I'm Amazed, Getting
        Closer, Bip Bop, All My Loving, Ticket To Ride, Revolution, Come
        Together* and *Goodnight Tonight.*

794   **VENUS AND MARS**   CBM 402   (LP)
        NOTES: Exact cuts unknown, but recorded live in Manchester, England on
        September 12, 1975.

795   **VENUS AND MARS ROCK SHOW**   Capitol 4175   (45 sleeve)
        NOTES: This is a black--and--white picture sleeve. No sleeve was issued
        originally with this record. Both sides of the sleeve are the same and show
        all five Wings' members.

796   *WALKING IN THE PARK WITH ELOISE/BRIDGE ON THE RIVER SUITE*
        S45--X--48905 F2/S45--X--48906 F2   (45)
        NOTES: This is a seven--inch picture disc. The picture is the same as that used
        for the picture sleeve that accompanied this record. Both sides say *Walking
        In The Park With Eloise*, but one side is, in fact, *Bridge On The River Suite.*
        The picture is the same on both sides of the record. The record is listed as
        being by the Country Hams. The Country Hams are Paul McCartney,
        Geoff Britton, Chet Atkins and Floyd Cramer. It was recorded in Nashville
        in June, 1974.

797   **WINGS**   92444 C/D   (EP)
        NOTES: This is a special test pressing picture record. Four different picture
        discs were available. The record is actually an Elvis tribute by Paul Lichter.
        This same recording was also used on the following picture records:
        **BEATLES; GEORGE HARRISON; DENNY LAINE; JOHN LENNON;
        JOHN LENNON/ELVIS PRESLEY; PAUL McCARTNEY; RINGO STARR.**

798   **WINGS ACROSS THE WATER**   IMP 1115   (LP)
        NOTES: Exact cuts unknown, but recorded live at the L.A. Forum on June 21,
        1976.

799   **WINGS AT HULL UNIVERSITY**   Wizardo 370   (LP)
        NOTES: Same as **BELGIUM** (Wizardo 370).

800   **WINGS AT THE FORUM**   Unknown   (3 LPs)
        NOTES: Exact cuts unknown, but recorded at the L.A. Forum on June 21,
        1976. Since this is a three--record set, it is probably the entire concert.

801   **WINGS FROM THE WINGS**   Idle Mind Productions 1117–1119   (3 LPs)

        1. *Venus And Mars*   7. *Maybe I'm Amazed*
        2. *Rock Show*   8. *Call Me Back Again*
        3. *Jet*   9. *Lady Madonna*
        4. *Let Me Roll It*   10. *Long And Winding Road*

222

Wings On The Radio (LP)   **Berkeley 61007 (Entry 807)**

5. *Spirits Of Ancient Egypt*
6. *Medicine Jar*

11. *Live And Let Die*
12. *Picasso's Last Words*
13. *Richard Cory*
14. *Bluebird*
15. *I've Just Seen A Face*
16. *Blackbird*
17. *Yesterday*

18. *You Gave Me The Answer*
19. *Magneto And Titanium Man*
20. *Go Now*
21. *My Love*

22. *Listen To What The Man Said*
23. *Let 'Em In*
24. *Time To Hide*
25. *Silly Love Songs*
26. *Beware My Love*

27. *Letting Go*
28. *Band On The Run*
29. *Hi Hi Hi*
30. *Soilie*

Cuts 1–30: Recorded live at the L.A. Forum on June 23, 1976.
NOTES: Each disc was a different color. For the bicentennial year, one was red, one white, and one blue. Sides one and two were also released as **LIQUID PAPER**; sides three and four as **RIDE A KILLER BIRD**; and sides five and six as **FLASH BOMBS**.

802 **WINGS GREAT DANE -- LIVE IN COPENHAGEN** PAV 1; TMOQ 8205/6 (LP)
NOTES: Same as **COPENHAGEN**.
SEE ALSO: **GREAT DANE**.

803 *WINGS GREATEST HITS* RAM 115 (45)
NOTES: This one--sided disc contains a 60--second radio commercial for **WINGS GREATEST HITS** album.

804 **WINGS IN BELGIUM** CBM 1126 (LP)
NOTES: Same as **BELGIUM** (Wizardo 370).

805 *WINGS – I'VE HAD ENOUGH* RAM 114 (45)
NOTES: This is a one--sided disc containing a 60--second radio spot for the Wings' single *I've Had Enough.*

806 **WINGS L.A. 1976** TKRWM 2805 (2 LPs)
NOTES: Same as **L.A. FORUM**.

807 **WINGS ON THE RADIO** Berkeley 61007; Highway Hi Fi HHCER 106 (LP)

1. *Country Dreamer*
2. *The Mess*
3. *Mary Had A Little Lamb*
4. *Little Woman Love*
5. *Another Day*

6. *C Moon*
7. *Hi Hi Hi*
8. *My Love*
9. *Live And Let Die*
10. *I Lie Around*

Cuts 1–10: Original recordings with bits of radio shows between them.

808 **WINGS OVER AMERICA** CBM A108 (2 LPs)
NOTES: Exact cuts and concert unknown, but from the 1976 U.S. tour.

809 **WINGS OVER AMERICA LANDING GEAR DOWN** ZAP 7876 (LP)

1. *Live And Let Die*
2. *Picasso's Last Words*
3. *Richard Cory*
4. *Bluebird*

8. *You Gave Me The Answer*
9. *My Love*
10. *Listen To What The Man Said*
11. *Let 'Em In*

5. *I've Just Seen A Face*   12. *Silly Love Songs*
6. *Blackbird*
7. *Yesterday*
Cuts 1–12: Recorded live at the Capitol Centre in Largo, Maryland on May 15, 1976.

810   **WINGS OVER ATLANTA**   Melvin MM03   (LP)

1. *Venus And Mars Rock Show*   6. *Yesterday*
2. *Jet*   7. *Silly Love Songs*
3. *Let Me Roll It*   8. *Beware My Love*
4. *Long And Winding Road*   9. *Soilie*
5. *Live And Let Die*
Cuts 1–9: Recorded at the Omni in Atlanta, Georgia, on May 19, 1976.
NOTES: Deluxe cover. Only 500 pressed.

811   **WINGS OVER FRISCO**   Wizardo 503   (LP)
NOTES: Same as **PAUL McCARTNEY & WINGS MEET BILL GRAHAM 1976.**

812   **WINGS OVER THE WORLD**   WOW 1616   (2 LPs)
NOTES: From the TV special "Wings Over The World." The albums consist mainly of interviews and songs from Paul and Wings' 1976 tour of the U.S. There are also bits from England and Australia. Some of the songs included are: *Band On The Run; Jet; Bip Bop; Lucille; Maybe I'm Amazed; Live And Let Die; Letting Go; You Gave Me The Answer; Yesterday; Long And Winding Road; Magneto And Titanium Man; Silly Love Songs; Beware My Love; Let 'Em In; Venus And Mars; Rock Show; Hi Hi Hi; Ringo On Stage With Paul; Soily.*

813   **WINGS OVER WEMBLEY**   Melvin MM–13   (2 LPs)

1. *Got To Get You Into My Life*   7. *Cook Of The House*
2. *Getting Closer*   8. *Old Siam Sir*
3. *Ev'ry Night*   9. *Maybe I'm Amazed*
4. *Again And Again*   10. *The Fool On The Hill*
5. *I've Had Enough*   11. *Let It Be*
6. *No Words*   12. *Hot As Sun*

13. *Spin It On*   18. *Coming Up*
14. *Twenty Flight Rock*   19. *Goodnight Tonight*
15. *Go Now*   20. *Yesterday*
16. *Arrow Through Me*   21. *Mull Of Kintyre*
17. *Wonderful Christmastime*   22. *Band On The Run*
Cuts 1–22: Recorded live at Wembley Stadium, London, on December 7, 1979.

814   **WINGS: PAUL McCARTNEY, LINDA McCARTNEY, DENNY LAINE**
      Wizardo 505   (3 LPs)

1. *Paul Apologizing For Not Coming*   6. *Interview – Paul*
   To Japan   7. *Letting Go*
2. *Bluebird*   8. *Bip Bop*
3. *Soily*   9. *Magneto And Titanium Man*
4. *Wildlife*   10. *When The Night*
5. *Band On The Run*

11. *Interview*   17. *Interview*
12. *Hi Hi Hi*   18. *I've Just Seen A Face*
13. *Beware My Love*   19. *Chicago*

14. *Interview -- Paul*
15. Medley:
    Little Woman Love
    C Moon
    Little Woman Love
16. *Let Me Roll It*

20. *Yesterday*
21. *Helen Wheels*
22. *Big Barn Red*
23. *Silly Love Songs*

24. *Interview -- Paul*
25. *Venus And Mars*
26. *Rock Show*
27. *Jet*
28. *Interview -- Paul*
29. *Live And Let Die*
30. *Go Now*

31. *Interview -- Paul & Linda*
32. *Maybe I'm Amazed*
33. *Yesterday*
34. *Call Me Back Again*
35. *Medicine Show*

NOTES: Cuts are taken from many different sources. Among those listed on the album are Boston (May 22, 1976), Chicago (June 1--2, 1976), San Diego (June 16, 1976), San Francisco (June 13--14, 1976), England 1973 and far east tour 1975. Also cut 5 and cut 21 are listed as outtakes from 1973.

815   **WINGS WILD LIFE**   Unknown   (LP)

1. *Mumbo*
2. *Bip Bop*
3. *Love Is Strange*
4. *Wild Life*

5. *Some People Never Know*
6. *I Am Your Singer*
7. *Tomorrow*
8. *Dear Friend*

NOTES: Same as original album.

816   **YESTERDAY AND TOMORROW**   RAM 112   (LP)

NOTES: Paul and Linda and the NBC--TV show "Tomorrow" with host Tom Snyder. The show was taped December 5, 1979, just before Wings went on stage at the London Rainbow Theatre. Denny Laine and Laurence Juber are also interviewed. There are bits of the following songs on this record: *Silly Love Songs; Spin It On; Wonderful Christmastime; With A Little Luck; Yesterday (live).*

817   **ZOO GANG**   IMP 1117   (LP)

1. *Spirits Of Ancient Egypt*
2. *Lady Madonna*
3. *Long And Winding Road*
4. *Picasso's Last Words*
5. *You Gave Me The Answer*
6. *Magneto And Titanium Man*
7. *Go Now*

8. *My Love*
9. *Let 'Em In*
10. *Silly Love Songs*
11. *Beware My Love*
12. *Soily*
13. *Zoo Gang*

Cuts 1--12: Recorded live in San Francisco and Los Angeles during the 1976 concert tour.
Cut 13: Original recording.
NOTES: Japanese bootleg.

Ringo Starr

818 *A MAN LIKE ME/A MOUSE LIKE ME*   Ring 710   (45)
NOTES: Both cuts are originals. *A Mouse Like Me* is from the cartoon "Scouse The Mouse."

819   **DOWN AND OUT**   Melvin MS10   (LP)

1. *Down And Out*
2. *Six O'Clock*
3. *Heart On My Sleeve*
4. *Hard Times*
5. *Band Of Steel*
6. *A Man Like Me*
7. *Living In A Pet Shop*
8. *Scouse's Dream*
9. *Running Free*
10. *Boat Ride*
11. *Scouse The Mouse*
12. *I Know A Place*
13. *S.O.S.*
14. *A Mouse Like Me*

Cuts 1--2, 5: Original recordings. Cut 2 is the long version of the song. Cut 5 is done by Guthrie Thomas. Ringo wrote the song, plays drums and sings on the recording. It was originally recorded for Thomas' 1976 album **LIES AND ALIBIES.**
Cuts 3--4, 6: From Ringo's TV special of April 26, 1978.
Cuts 7–12: From the British TV "Scouse The Mouse" cartoon special. Only Ringo's parts are included here.
NOTES: Laminated cover. Picture label with two different pictures of Ringo. Front cover of the album shows Ringo lying on the floor with five topless beauties standing over him.

820   *FIDDLE ABOUT/TOMMY'S HOLIDAY CAMP*   Ring 706   (45)
NOTES: Both cuts are original recordings from the **TOMMY** LP (Ode 99001) from 1972. Ringo sang his part on the album, but never appeared on stage with the show.

821   *I'VE GOT A WOMAN*   Unknown   (45)
NOTES: This bootleg was supposedly released in 1964. No information could be found about it however.

822   *THE KIDS ARE ALRIGHT*   PRODUCTION 198 CR 3926   (45)
NOTES: This one–sided disc contains radio spots for the Who's movie "The Kids Are Alright" (New World Pictures, Inc.). There are two 30--second spots, but both are the same. The originals have CR 3926 stamped in the run–off wax, the boots do not.

823   *MEN'S ROOM, L.A./HUNTING SCENE*   Ring 709   (45)
NOTES: Both of these cuts are originals. *Men's Room, L.A.* is from Kinky Friedman's album **LASSO FROM EL PASO** (Epic 34304). Ringo appears as the voice of Jesus. *Hunting Scene* is taken from the soundtrack of the film "The Magic Christian."

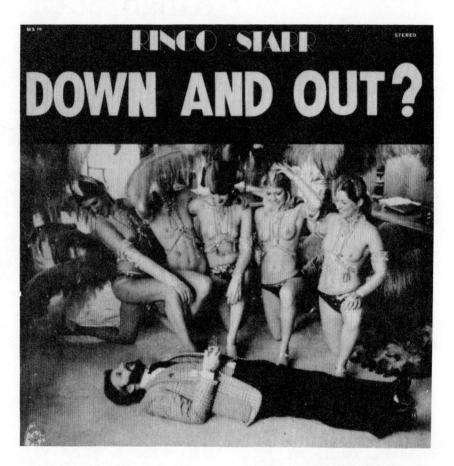

Down And Out (LP)   Melvin MS10 (Entry 819)

824 *NO NO SONG/SUIT COMMERCIAL*   Ring 708   (45)

NOTES: The *No No Song* is from Ringo's appearance on the "Smothers Brothers" TV show on April 28, 1975. The flip side is a Japanese commercial for leisure suits done by Ringo.

825 **RINGO INTERVIEW**   Ring 704   (LP)

NOTES: Complete 60-minute interview of Ringo by Dave Herman done September 4, 1977.

826 **RINGO INTERVIEW BY MIKE DOUGLAS**   Ring 703   (LP)

NOTES: Just before his 1978 TV special, Ringo appeared on the "Mike Douglas Show" to plug it. This is his appearance on that show.

827 **RINGO TV SPECIAL**   Ring 702   (LP)

NOTES: The entire soundtrack to the TV special "Ringo" as shown on NBC–TV, April 26, 1978. Besides Ringo, the show also starred Art Carney, Angie Dickinson, Mike Douglas, Carrie Fisher, Vincent Price, John Ritter and George Harrison. The following songs, in part or total, are on the album:

1. *I Am The Greatest*
2. *Act Naturally*
3. *It Don't Come Easy*
4. *Yellow Submarine*
5. *You're Sixteen*
6. *Octopusses Garden*
7. *With A Little Help From My Friends*
8. *Cry* (Johnny Ray)
9. *Only The Lonely* (Roy Orbison)
10. *Whole Lotta Shakin' Goin' On –* (Jerry Lee Lewis)
11. *Johnny B. Goode* (Chuck Berry)
12. *Hound Dog* (Elvis Presley)
13. *Peggy Sue* (Buddy Holly)
14. *Heart On My Sleeve*
15. *Hard Times*
16. *A Man Like Me*

828 **RINGO vs THE WORLD VOL. I**   Original Rock 1014   (LP)

1. *Hey Baby*
2. *Hey Baby*
3. *No No Song*
4. *No No Song*
5. *Only You*
6. *Only You*
7. *You're Sixteen*
8. *You're Sixteen*
9. *Drowning In The Sea Of Love*
10. *Drowning In The Sea Of Love*
11. *Love Is A Many Splendored Thing*
12. *Love Is A Many Splendored Thing*

Cuts 1, 3, 5, 7, 9, 11: Originals by Ringo.
Cut 2: Original by Bruce Channel.
Cut 4: Original by Hoyt Axton.
Cut 6: Original by the Platters.
Cut 8: Original by Johnny Burnette.
Cut 10: Original by Joe Simon.
Cut 12: Original by the Four Aces.

829 **RINGO vs THE WORLD VOL. II**   Original Rock 1015   (LP)

1. *Can She Do It Like She Dances*
2. *Can She Do It Like She Dances*
3. *Beaucoups Of Blues*
4. *Beaucoups Of Blues*
5. *Easy For Me*
7. *Husbands And Wives*
8. *Husbands And Wives*
9. *Occapella*
10. *Occapella*
11. *You Always Hurt The One You*

6. *Easy For Me* *Love*
12. *You Always Hurt The One You Love*

Cuts 1, 3, 5, 7, 9, 11: Originals by Ringo.
Cut 2: Original by Gold Rush.
Cut 4: Original by Buzz Rabin.
Cut 6: Original by Nilsson.
Cut 8: Original by Roger Miller.
Cut 10: Original by Lee Dorsey.
Cut 12: Original by the Mills Brothers.

830   SCOUSE THE MOUSE   Cx368A/Cx368B   **(LP)**

1. *Living In A Pet Shop*
2. *Sing A Song Fro Tragopan*
3. *Scouse's Dream*
4. *Snow Up Your Nose For Christmas*
5. *Running Free*
6. *America, A Mouse's Dream*
7. *Scousey*
8. *Boat Ride*
9. *Scouse The Mouse*
10. *Passenger*
11. *I Know A Place*
12. *Caterwaul (Instrumental)*
13. *S.O.S.*
14. *Ask Lovey*
15. *A Mouse Like Me*

Cuts 1, 3, 5, 8--9, 11, 13, 15: Ringo's parts in this film.
Cuts 2, 4, 6--7, 10, 12, 14: Ringo not on these cuts.
NOTES: Issued on purple vinyl.

831   SING ONE FOR MY KIDS   Ring 705   **(EP)**

1. *Introduction Of The Band*
2. *Money*
3. *Twist And Shout* (just a bit)
4. *Jumpin' Jack Flash*
5. *Introduction Of Ringo*

NOTES: All cuts are from a jam session at the superdance at the Los Vegas
Convention Center which appeared on the "Jerry Lewis Telethon" on
September 3, 1979. In the band, along with Ringo were Todd Rundgren,
Doug Kershaw, Bill Wyman, Dave Mason, Kiki Dee and Joni Harris. Comes
with a special hard picture sleeve.

832   STARR, RINGO   92444 C/D   **(EP)**
NOTES: This is a special one--of--a--kind test pressing picture disc. Nine
different Ringo discs are available. Ringo does not sing on the record.
Instead, it is an Elvis tribute by Paul Lichter. This same recording was also
used on the following picture discs: **BEATLES; GEORGE HARRISON;
DENNY LAINE; JOHN LENNON; JOHN LENNON/ELVIS PRESLEY;
PAUL McCARTNEY; WINGS.**

833   *STARR SHOW*   Ring 707   (45)

1. *Promo*
2. *Interview With Ringo*
3. *Photograph*

NOTES: From the "Weekly Top--30 Show" which aired October 27, 1979, with
host Mark Elliott.

834   *YOU'RE 16/BAND OF STEEL*   Ring 701   (45)
NOTES: *You're 16* is a duet between Ringo and Carrie Fisher and is from
Ringo's TV special of April 26, 1978. *Band Of Steel* is by Guthrie
Thomas. Ringo wrote it, plays drums and sings on the recording. It's
from the 1976 album **LIES AND ALIBIES.**

The Beatles
(group & solo)

835 ABBEY ROAD   Apple 383   (LP)

1. *Come Together*
2. *Something*
3. *Maxwell's Silver Hammer*
4. *Oh! Darling*
5. *Octopuss's Garden*
6. *I Want You (She's So Heavy)*
7. *Here Comes The Sun*
8. *Because*
9. *You Never Give Me Your Money*
10. *Sun King*
11. *Mean Mr. Mustard*
12. *Polythene Pam*
13. *She Came In Through The Bathroom Window*
14. *Golden Slumbers*
15. *Carry That Weight*
16. *The End*
17. *Her Majesty*

ORIGINAL vs COUNTERFEIT: The cover picture on the counterfeit is some—what fuzzy, off--color and on many copies is tilted slightly off center.

836   *AIN'T SHE SWEET/NOBODY'S CHILD*   Atco 6308 (45)
ORIGINAL vs COUNTERFEIT: The label color is somewhat faded and the printing is not always clear. There are no markings on the inner wax, or, if there are, they are not clear.

837   *AIN'T SHE SWEET/NOBODY'S CHILD*   Atco 6308   (45)
ORIGINAL vs COUNTERFEIT: This is a copy of the DJ single. The label is white, but the record has been pressed on colored vinyl.

838   *AIN'T SHE SWEET/NOBODY'S CHILD*   Atco 6308   (PS)
ORIGINAL vs COUNTERFEIT: This is a counterfeit of just the picture sleeve that was issued with the original single. The lettering on the originals was more turquoise than the blue used on the counterfeits. The counterfcits show no wear, which you would expect even on originals that were treated well. Some dealers are known to have wiped alcohol on the counterfeits to give them an "aged" look.

839   *ALL YOU NEED IS LOVE/BABY YOU'RE A RICH MAN*   Capitol 5964   (PS)
ORIGINAL vs COUNTERFEIT: This is a picture sleeve only. The copy is a good one, but the lettering is slightly fuzzy and the folding is different.

840   **AMERICAN TOUR WITH ED RUDY**   Radio Pulasebeat News Documentary No. 2
(LP)
ORIGINAL vs COUNTERFEIT: The counterfeit has no spine writing. There are no markings in the inner wax of the record.

841   **THE BEATLES AND FRANK IFIELD ON STAGE**   Vee Jay 1085   (LP)

1. *Please Please Me*
2. *Anytime* (F.I.)
7. *I Remember You* (F.I.)
8. *Ask Me Why*

3. *Lovesick Blues* (F.I.)
4. *I'm Smiling Now* (F.I.)
5. *Nobody's Darling*
6. *From Me To You*

9. *Thank You Girl*
10. *The Wayward Wind* (F.I.)
11. *Unchained Melody* (F.I.)
12. *I Listen To Me Heart* (F.I.)

ORIGINAL vs COUNTERFEIT: This is a copy of the cover showing the Beatle painting, the same one used for the *LOVE ME DO/P.S. I LOVE YOU* picture sleeve. The counterfeits have no writing on the spine. The edges of the lettering on the front and back of the cover are somewhat fuzzy. The blue color of the cover is uneven on the copy. The inner wax markings on the record are not there or they are hard to read.

NOTES: This album also was released with another cover picture and a slightly different title. For information on that version see **JOLLY WHAT – THE BEATLES AND FRANK IFIELD ON STAGE.**

842　**THE BEATLES CHRISTMAS ALBUM**　Apple 100　(LP)

1. *1963*
2. *1964*
3. *1965*
4. *1966*

5. *1967*
6. *1968*
7. *1969*

ORIGINAL vs COUNTERFEIT: The originals were released to members of the Beatle fan club on December 18, 1970. The counterfeit picture cover is slightly off focus. The inner wax markings on the record are not very clear.

843　**BEATLES VS. THE FOUR SEASONS**　Vee Jay 30　(2 LPs)

1. *I Saw Her Standing There*
2. *Misery*
3. *Anna*
4. *Chains*
5. *Boys*
6. *Ask Me Why*

7. *Please Please Me*
8. *Baby It's You*
9. *Do You Want To Know A Secret*
10. *A Taste Of Honey*
11. *There's A Place*
12. *Twist And Shout*

13. *Sherry*
14. *I've Cried Before*
15. *Marlena*
16. *Soon (I'll Be Home Again)*
17. *Ain't That A Shame*
18. *Walk Like A Man*

19. *Connie--O*
20. *Big Girls Don't Cry*
21. *Starmaker*
22. *Candy Girl*
23. *Silver Wings*
24. *Peanuts*

ORIGINAL vs COUNTERFEIT: The counterfeits were first released in 1977. They had no writing on the spine as the originals did. The originals say "FREE BONUS 8" X 15" FULL COLOR BEATLE PICTURE SUITABLE FOR FRAMING." This is left off the counterfeits.

844　**THE BEATLES WITH TONY SHERIDAN AND GUESTS**　MGM 4215　(LP)

1. *My Bonnie*
2. *Cry For A Shadow*
3. *Johnson Rag* (Titans)
4. *Swanee River* (Tony Sheridan)
5. *Flying Beat* (Titans)
6. *The Darktown Strutters Ball* (Titans)

7. *The Saints*
8. *Rye Beat* (Titans)
9. *You Are My Sunshine* (Tony Sheridan)
10. *Summertime Beat* (Titans)
11. *Why*
12. *Happy New Year Beat* (Titans)

ORIGINAL vs COUNTERFEIT: Counterfeits are similar, but there is no spine writing and the album number is left off the jacket.

845　**BEST OF THE BEATLES**　Savage BM 71　(LP)

1. *Last Night*
2. *Why Did You Leave Me Baby*
3. *Shimmy Like My Sister Kate*
4. *I Need Your Lovin'*
5. *Nobody But You*
6. *I Can't Do Without You Now*
7. *Casting My Spell*
8. *Wait And See*
9. *Some Other Guy*
10. *I'm Blue*
11. *She's Alright*
12. *Keys To My Heart*

ORIGINAL vs COUNTERFEIT: Original was pressed on a very heavy record, others are on a lighter vinyl. Picture on cover is fuzzy on counterfeits.

846　*CAN'T BUY ME LOVE/YOU CAN'T DO THAT*　Capitol 5150　(PS)
ORIGINAL vs COUNTERFEIT: The picture sleeve was counterfeited twice. The first time was on a rough textured paper with a glossy finish with colors similar to the original. The picture was slightly off center and the lettering was not as clear as the original. The second counterfeit was not good at all. The lettering showed definite fuzziness and the Capitol number was left off the sleeve.

847　*CHRISTMAS SLEEVE*　Originals released with Tollie 9001　(LP)
ORIGINAL vs COUNTERFEIT: The originals were printed on thin paper, while the counterfeits were on heavy paper and the color was slightly distorted.

848　*DECADE -- 10TH ANNIVERSARY RADIO SPOTS*　MBRF 55551　(45)
ORIGINAL vs COUNTERFEIT: Contains a 30--second and a 60--second radio spot for the Beatles' 10th anniversary with Capitol. The counterfeits have no markings in the inner wax.

849　*DO YOU WANT TO KNOW A SECRET/THANK YOU GIRL*　Oldies 45 149　(45)
ORIGINAL vs COUNTERFEIT: There are no inner wax markings on the counter-- feits, or, if there are, they are hard to read.

850　*DO YOU WANT TO KNOW A SECRET/THANK YOU GIRL*　Vee Jay 587　(PS)
ORIGINAL vs COUNTERFEIT: On the original picture sleeve the words "THE BEATLES" are in white, "Do You Want To Know A Secret" is in yellow and the paper used is very thin. On the counterfeits, all printing is in white.

851　**ED RUDY WITH NEW U.S. TOUR VOLUME 3**　Radio Pulsebeat News 1001/1002 (LP)
ORIGINAL vs COUNTERFEIT: Counterfeit has no writings on the spine of the jacket. Inner wax markings are missing or not clear.

852　*EIGHT DAYS A WEEK/I DON'T WANT TO SPOIL THE PARTY*　Capitol 5371 (PS)
ORIGINAL vs COUNTERFEIT: There is some doubt that this sleeve was ever counterfeited. Some say it may have been counterfeited on thin paper with the picture less clear than the original.

853　**THE FAMILY WAY**　London 82007　(LP)
ORIGINAL vs COUNTERFEIT: McCartney did the soundtrack for this film. The counterfeits are somewhat fuzzy in appearance. The coloring on the jacket is not the same as on the originals.

854　*FROM ME TO YOU/THANK YOU GIRL*　Vee Jay 522　(45)
ORIGINAL vs COUNTERFEIT: The counterfeit has a silver VJ, a grey label with silver printing and a white swirl around the label. The originals had no swirl of any kind.

**John Lennon Sings The Great
Rock & Roll Hits (LP)**

Adam VIII A8018 (Entry 859)

855 *GIRL/YOU'RE GONNA LOSE THAT GIRL* Capitol 4506 (45)

ORIGINAL vs COUNTERFEIT: The originals were released only as a DJ single with the number P–4506. These were not counterfeited. No stock copies were released by Capitol, but the labels had been printed. Apparently someone got these labels and pressed the records themselves and released them in the original picture sleeves, also printed by Capitol. The recording was also booted and more information can be found in that section of this book.

856 **HEAR THE BEATLES TELL IT ALL** Vee Jay PRO–202 (LP)

ORIGINAL vs COUNTERFEIT: Original was issued to radio stations only. Counterfeits have no spine writing and the printing, especially the pictures on the back of the cover, are fuzzy.

857 **HERE'S TO THE VETERANS** FP 72196–1 (LP)

1. *Paul Introduction*
2. *I'll Cry Instead*
3. *Announcer*
4. *Paul Introduction*
5. *Eleanor Rigby*
6. *Announcer*
7. *Paul Introduction*
8. *Ob–La--Di Ob–La–Da*
9. *Paul Introduction*
10. *Hey Jude*
11. *Announcer*
12. *The Phil Harris Show Vintage Radio*

Cuts 1–12: Program No. 1406 put out by the Veterans' Administration.

ORIGINAL vs COUNTERFEIT: Originally released only to radio stations. Counterfeits are pressed on a much thinner vinyl and have a much glossier label than the originals.

858 **INTRODUCING THE BEATLES** Vee Jay 1062 (LP)

1. *I Saw Her Standing There*
2. *Misery*
3. *Anna*
4. *Chains*
5. *Boys*
6. *Love Me Do* (or *Ask Me Why*)
7. *P.S. I Love You* (or *Please Please Me*)
8. *Baby It's You*
9. *Do You Want To Know A Secret*
10. *A Taste Of Honey*
11. *There's A Place*
12. *Twist And Shout*

ORIGINAL vs COUNTERFEIT: This has been counterfeited several times, each producing its own variations. Some of the variations include the following. Originals have "Introducing The Beatles" above the record hole and "The Beatles" below the hole. Counterfeits have the wording divided on either side of the hole. Labels are often sloppy with double printing, burn marks, broken letters and may be off center. The inner wax markings on the counterfeits are barely visible. Many of the counterfeits have no spine writing. The front cover picture on the originals is sharp enough to read the time on John or Ringo's watch, while the counterfeits are fuzzy and the times cannot be read. A new counterfeit appeared in late 1979 which had the front picture framed by a brown border.

859 **JOHN LENNON SINGS THE GREAT ROCK & ROLL HITS** Adam VIII A8018 (LP)

1. *Be–Bop–A–Lula*
2. *Ain't That A Shame*
3. *Stand By Me*
9. *Bony Moronie*
10. *Peggy Sue*
11. *Bring It On Home To Me*

4. *Sweet Little Sixteen*
5. *Rip It Up*
6. *Angel Baby*
7. *Do You Want To Dance*
8. *You Can't Catch Me*

12. *Slippin' And Slidin'*
13. *Be My Baby*
14. *Ya Ya*
15. *Just Because*

ORIGINAL vs COUNTERFEIT: The counterfeit does have spine writing like the original, but it says "JOHN LENNON SINGS THE GREATEST ROCK & ROLL HITS." It should be GREAT, not GREATEST. The inner sleeve of the originals had ads for other Adam VIII albums or they had a heavy brown sleeve. The counterfeits have just a plain white sleeve.

860   JOLLY WHAT – THE BEATLES & FRANK IFIELD ON STAGE   Vee Jay 1085   (LP)

1. *Please Please Me*
2. *Anytime* (F.I.)
3. *Lovesick Blues* (F.I.)
4. *I'm Smiling Now* (F.I.)
5. *Nobody's Darling* (F.I.)
5. *From Me To You*

7. *I Remember You* (F.I.)
8. *Ask Me Why*
9. *Thank You Girl*
10. *The Wayward Wind* (F.I.)
11. *Unchained Melody* (F.I.)
12. *I Listen To My Heart* (F.I.)

ORIGINAL vs COUNTERFEIT: The counterfeits have no spine writing. There is some fuzziness along the edges of the lettering on both the front and back of the cover. Originals are blue and orange, while the counterfeits show black and orangish--red on the front cover. There are no markings in the inner wax of the record, or, if there are, they are hard to read.

NOTES: This is a counterfeit of the cover showing a man with a long moustache. There was also another cover originally released with a painting of the Beatles on it. That has also been counterfeited and can be found listed elsewhere under its title of **THE BEATLES AND FRANK IFIELD ON STAGE.**

861   *LADY MADONNA/THE INNER LIGHT*   Capitol 2138   (45)
ORIGINAL vs COUNTERFEIT: Both the record and the sleeve were counter--feited in 1979. The copy is pretty good, but there are some things that will help you separate them. On the label, the Capitol logo (top of the Capitol building) is somewhat fuzzy and not as detailed as the original. Also the word "Capitol" at the bottom of the label is not clear. The background color on the sleeve is more of a purple than was used on the original and the color bleeds over into the picture in spots.

862   LET IT BE   Apple 34001   (LP)

1. *Two Of Us*
2. *I Dig A Pony*
3. *Across The Universe*
4. *I Me Mine*
5. *Dig It*
6. *Let It Be*
7. *Maggie Mae*

8. *I've Got A Feeling*
9. *One After 909*
10. *The Long And Winding Road*
11. *For You Blue*
12. *Get Back*

ORIGINAL vs COUNTERFEIT: The pictures used on the cover are fuzzy on the counterfeits. On the originals "Phil & Ronnie" was scratched into the inner wax. The counterfeits do not have this, or, if they do, it is not clear.

863   *LOVE ME DO/P.S. I LOVE YOU*   Oldies 45 151   (45)
ORIGINAL vs COUNTERFEIT: The inner wax markings are missing from the counterfeit. If they are there, they are hard to read.

864 *LOVE ME DO/P.S. I LOVE YOU* Tollie 9008 (45)
ORIGINAL vs COUNTERFEIT: The counterfeited version has a yellow label with black lettering. The printing is very thin. The inner wax markings are barely visible.

865 *MY BONNIE/THE SAINTS* Decca 31382 (45)
ORIGINAL vs COUNTERFEIT: Has been counterfeited in both DJ and stock copy style. The printing on both is not as clear as on the original. The inner wax markings on both are not clear. The black label of the stock copy is more of a grey on the counterfeit.

866 *MY BONNIE/THE SAINTS* MGM 12312 (45)
ORIGINAL vs COUNTERFEIT: The counterfeit has *My Bonnie* on both sides. One side has the German introduction and the other has the English introduction.

867 *NOWHERE MAN/WHAT GOES ON* Capitol 5587 (45)
ORIGINAL vs COUNTERFEIT: Both record and sleeve were counterfeited in 1979. The copies are good, but the printing of the Capitol logo on the left side of the label is not as clear as the originals and the "Reg. U.S. PAT. OFF." is very hard to read. The white, written Capitol at the bottom of the label is also hard to read. The edges of the lettering on the sleeve are ragged and there is some bleeding of the picture colors into the white area above.

868 *PAPERBACK WRITER/RAIN* Capitol 5651 (45)
ORIGINAL vs COUNTERFEIT: Both the record and the sleeve were counter-- feited in 1979. The copy is very good, but the Capitol logo on the left side of the label is not clear and the words "REG. U.S. PAT. OFF." are very hard to make out. Also, the white, written Capitol at the bottom of the label is hard to read. The lettering on the sleeve is not as clear as the original's and the pictures are also less clear.

869 *PENNY LANE/STRAWBERRY FIELDS FOREVER* Capitol 5810 (45)
ORIGINAL vs COUNTERFEIT: This is a copy of the DJ version of *Penny Lane* with the trumpet ending. The label shows burn marks and the printing is crooked.

870 *PENNY LANE/STRAWBERRY FIELDS FOREVER* Capitol 5810 (PS)
ORIGINAL vs COUNTERFEIT: The picture sleeve is counterfeited on a red tinted paper, while the original was on plain white paper. The pictures on the counterfeit are not nearly as clear as those on the originals.

871 *PLEASE PLEASE ME/FROM ME TO YOU* Oldies 45 150 (45)
ORIGINAL vs COUNTERFEIT: The inner wax markings on the counterfeits are absent, or, if they exist, they are hard to read.

872 *PLEASE PLEASE ME/FROM ME TO YOU* Vee Jay 581 (PS)
ORIGINAL vs COUNTERFEIT: On the counterfeits, "THE BEATLES" is in green and all other lettering is black. The picture is not as clear as the originals.

873 **SGT. PEPPER'S LONELY HEARTS CLUB BAND** Capitol 2653 (LP)

1. *Sgt. Pepper's Lonely Hearts Club Band*
2. *Lucy In The Sky With Diamonds*
3. *Getting Better*
7. *Within You Without You*
8. *When I'm Sixty–Four*
9. *Lovely Rita*
10. *Good Morning, Good Morning*

4. *Fixing A Hole*
5. *She's Leaving Home*
6. *Being For the Benefit Of Mr. Kite*

11. *Sgt. Pepper's Lonely Hearts*
    Club Band Reprise
12. *A Day In The Life*

ORIGINAL vs COUNTERFEIT: The album was counterfeited in 1976. The cover on the counterfeit does not fold open.

874 **SAVAGE YOUNG BEATLES** Savage BM 69 (LP)

1. *Cry For A Shadow*
2. *Let's Dance*
3. *If You Love Me Baby*
4. *What I Say*

5. *Sweet Georgia Brown*
6. *Ruby Baby*
7. *Ya–Ya*
8. *Why*

ORIGINAL vs COUNTERFEIT: The originals were released in mid--1964 and again in 1966. There was no spine writing, even on the originals. The counterfeit cover says "Stereo," but there was no stereo edition of this album. The counterfeit record is pressed on a thin vinyl, not the thick, heavy vinyl that was used on the original.

875 **SEASIDE WOMAN** Epic ASF 361 (12--inch DJ)
ORIGINAL vs COUNTERFEIT: This special 12--inch disc with the same song on both sides was released to radio stations to help promote the Suzy & The Red Stripes single. The counterfeits look much the same as the originals. They are on a white label with black printing and the printing is clear. However, the originals were issued in a plain white jacket on which was embossed in gold "FOR PROMOTION ONLY Ownership Reserved By CBS Sale Is Unlawful." The counterfeits came in a plain white sleeve with no markings.

876 *SHE LOVES YOU/I'LL GET YOU* Swan 4152 (45)
ORIGINAL vs COUNTERFEIT: The label color and lettering color varies on the counterfeits, but none are exactly the same as the original's. The original has "Mastered at Philadelphia" or "Virtue Studio" stamped in the runoff wax. This is not present on the counterfeits.

877 *SHE LOVES YOU/I'LL GET YOU* Swan 4152 (PS)
ORIGINAL vs COUNTERFEIT: The picture on the counterfeit sleeve is not nearly as clear as that on the original. Also, the counterfeit sleeve has slightly perforated edges which cause it to split open easily.

878 *SLOW DOWN/MATCHBOX* Capitol 5327 (PS)
ORIGINAL vs COUNTERFEIT: The original picture sleeve was in color, while this one is in black and white. It is, however, the same picture. Some dealers have tried to pass this off as a rare DJ sleeve, but it is just a counterfeit.

879 **SONGS AND PICTURES OF THE FABULOUS BEATLES** Vee Jay 1092 (LP)

1. *I Saw Her Standing There*
2. *Misery*
3. *Anna*
4. *Chains*
5. *Boys*
6. *Ask Me Why*

7. *Please Please Me*
8. *Baby It's You*
9. *Do You Want To Know A Secret*
10. *A Taste Of Honey*
11. *There's A Place*
12. *Twist And Shout*

ORIGINAL vs COUNTERFEIT: The title of the original album is **SONGS, PICTURES AND STORIES OF THE FABULOUS BEATLES.** The "STORIES" has been dropped from the title of the counterfeit. Also, the cover on the original opened to reveal a short history of each Beatle. The cover of the counterfeit does not open at all.

238

880   *SWEET GEORGIA BROWN/TAKE OUT SOME INSURANCE ON ME BABY*
       Atco 6302   (45)
       ORIGINAL vs COUNTERFEIT: The label color (especially the yellow) is
       slightly faded on the counterfeits. The originals had an "AT" stamped in
       the inner wax of the record. This is missing on the counterfeits.

881   TICKET TO RIDE/YES IT IS   Capitol 5407   (45)
       ORIGINAL vs COUNTERFEIT: Both record and sleeve were counterfeited in
       1979. The copy is good, but the Capitol logo on the left side of the label
       is not as clear as the original and it is very hard to read the "REG. U.S.
       PAT. OFF." under that logo. The white, written Capitol at the bottom of
       the label is also hard to read. The sleeve color is slightly off the original
       color and there is some fuzziness to the edge of the lettering.

882   *TWIST AND SHOUT/THERE'S A PLACE*   Oldies 45 152   (45)
       ORIGINAL vs COUNTERFEIT: The counterfeits have no inner wax markings, or,
       if they do, are very hard to read.

883   *TWIST AND SHOUT/THERE'S A PLACE*   Tollie 9001   (45)
       ORIGINAL vs COUNTERFEIT: The counterfeit has a yellow label with black
       printing. The label is shiny, unlike the original.

884   UNFINISHED MUSIC NO. 1 – TWO VIRGINS   Apple 5001   (LP)
       ORIGINAL vs COUNTERFEIT: The originals had a dark tan textured outer
       cover, while the counterfeits have a smooth tan cover. The inside cover of
       the originals are off--white, while the counterfeit is a glossy white. John
       and Yoko's nude pictures are not as clear on the counterfeits. The originals
       had a sticker to keep the outer cover closed. This is missing from the
       counterfeits.

885   UNFINISHED MUSIC NO. 2: LIFE WITH THE LIONS   Zapple 3357   (LP)

       1. *Cambridge 1969*   2. *No Bed For Beatle John*
                                        3. *Baby's Heartbeat*
                                        4. *Two Minutes Silence*
                                        5. *Radio Play*
       ORIGINAL vs COUNTERFEIT: In the upper right hand corner of the back
       cover of the original album is the word "ZAPPLE." This has been left off
       the counterfeit copies.

886   *WE CAN WORK IT OUT/DAY TRIPPER*   Capitol 5555   (45)
       ORIGINAL vs COUNTERFEIT: Both sleeve and record were counterfeited in
       1979. The counterfeits are good, but the Capitol logo on the left side of
       the record is not clear and the words "REG. U.S. PAT. OFF." are barely
       discernible. Some of the letters on the sleeve are a little ragged.

887   WEDDING ALBUM   Apple 3361   (LP)

       1. *John And Yoko*   2. *Amsterdam*
       ORIGINAL vs COUNTERFEIT: The counterfeit did not come in a box, nor
       did it contain any of the material that came with the original album.

888   THE WORLD'S BEST   EMI–Odeon 27--408--4   (LP)

       1. *Good Day Sunshine*   9. *Things We Said Today*
       2. *All My Loving* (with hi–hat)   10. *Michelle*
       3. *Eight Days A Week*   11. *Dr. Robert*
       4. *No Reply*   12. *Yellow Submarine*

<table>
<tr><td>5. Rock And Roll Music</td><td>13. If I Fell</td></tr>
<tr><td>6. A Hard Day's Night</td><td>14. And Your Bird Can Sing</td></tr>
<tr><td>7. I Should Have Known Better</td><td>15. Girl</td></tr>
<tr><td>8. All My Loving</td><td>16. Eleanor Rigby</td></tr>
</table>

5. *Rock And Roll Music*　　13. *If I Fell*
6. *A Hard Day's Night*　　14. *And Your Bird Can Sing*
7. *I Should Have Known Better*　　15. *Girl*
8. *All My Loving*　　16. *Eleanor Rigby*

ORIGINAL vs COUNTERFEIT: The original was released in Germany. When it went out of print, this counterfeit was issued here in the U.S.

889　*YELLOW SUBMARINE/ELEANOR RIGBY*　Capitol 5715　(45)
ORIGINAL vs COUNTERFEIT: Both record and sleeve were counterfeited in 1979. The copy is good, but the Capitol logo on the left side of the label is not as clear as on the original and the words "REG. U.S. PAT. OFF." are just barely readable. Some of the lettering on the sleeve is rough around the edges.

890　*YESTERDAY/ACT NATURALLY*　Capitol 5498　(45)
ORIGINAL vs COUNTERFEIT: Both record and sleeve were counterfeited in 1979. The copy is good, but the Capitol logo on the left side of the label is not as clear as on the original and the words "REG. U.S. PAT. OFF." are very hard to read. Sleeve lettering is uneven and fuzzy around the edges.

891　**YESTERDAY AND TODAY**　Capitol 2553　(Cover Art)
ORIGINAL vs COUNTERFEIT: The famous "butcher" picture has been counterfeited. The counterfeits show a slight haze around the lettering. Also, the Beatles' turtleneck sweaters are grey, instead of black. Some persons have pasted this picture over the real album in an effort to trick an unsuspecting buyer.

Personal Name Index

McCartney, Linda, continued
297, 511, 513, 569, 714,
730, 769, 775, 814, 816
McCartney, Paul 001, 005,
044, 051, 059, 068, 069,
070, 094, 095, 096, 097,
098, 099, 100, 101, 102,
103, 104, 105, 106, 107,
109, 110, 113, 138, 144,
155, 168, 169. 171, 189,
191, 245, 297, 301, 337,
367, 386, 393, 397, 461,
481, 494, 511, 513, 514,
545, 548, 556, 569, 632,
658, 666, 670, 671, 707,
708, 714, 715, 717, 720,
721, 730, 731, 732, 738,
739, 740, 743, 747, 751,
755, 758, 759, 762, 763,
764, 765, 766, 767, 769,
770, 775, 777, 778, 779,
780, 788, 791, 793, 796,
797, 811, 812, 814, 816,
832, 853, 857
McCulloch, Jimmy 730
McGowan, Cathy 502
McQuickly, Dirk 011
Melvin, Hank 502
Mickey & Sylvia 759
Midler, Bette 251
Miller, Roger 829
Miller, Steve 769
Mills Brothers 829
Miracles 135
Mitchell, Mitch 656, 662,
664, 687, 688
Monkees 142
Moore, Dudley 037, 149,
151, 195, 391
Mott The Hoople 549
Move 549
Murdock, Charlie 605
Murray The K 024, 034,
150, 256, 320, 414, 495,
562, 564
Mushroom Tabernacle Choir
549
Nasty, Ron 011
Neufield, Joanne 101
Newton–John, Olivia 251
Nicol, Jimmy 071, 115,
178, 305
Nilsson 829
Nurk Twins 113, 272, 337,
367, 393, 397, 562, 564
O'Boogie, Dr. Winston see
also Boogie, Dr. Winston O.
O'Boogie, Dr. Winston 661

O'Hara, Stig 011
Olympics 678
Ono, Yoko 103, 109, 158,
168, 171, 238, 239, 240,
242, 243, 276, 471, 545,
656, 662, 664, 687, 688,
884, 887
Orbison, Roy 827
The Originals, Rosie &
679
Otto, Dave 577
Owens, Buck 134
Palmer, Robert 059
Parnes, Larry 094
Parsons, Alan 006, 295,
761
Pease, Gayleen 005
Perkins, Carl 131
Peter & Gordon 068, 069,
070, 473
Phrank, Phast 122
Platters 031, 828
Pope, Joe 510, 511
Presley, Elvis 031, 044,
094, 135, 206, 251, 632,
670, 671, 743, 767, 797,
827, 832
Preston, Billy 059, 614,
620, 627, 639, 640, 642,
644, 645, 651
Price, Jim 628
Price, Lloyd 677
Price, Vincent 827
Proby, P.J. 466
Procol Harum 549
Purtan, Dick 577
Rabin, Buzz 829
Radle, Carl 628
Ray, Johnny 094, 827
The Redstripes, Suzy &
875
Reed, Lou 176
Remus, Uncle 118
Residents 115
Richard, Cliff 502
Richard, Keith 656, 662,
664, 687, 688
Richard, Little 031, 130,
251, 678
Righteous Brothers 031
Riley, Ron 577, 602
The Rippers, Bernice &
510
Ritter, John 827
Rivera, Geraldo 730, 793
Robbins, Fred 277, 278,
279, 280, 281, 282
Roberts, Art 577, 602

Robinson, Red 108
Rodriguez, Chi Chi 119
Roe, Tommy 133
Rolling Stones 030, 039,
050, 092, 093, 199, 200,
408, 471, 481, 494, 654,
656, 662, 664, 668, 687,
688, 689
Ronettes 679
Ronstadt, Linda 251
Rosie & The Originals 679
Rudy, Ed 015, 016, 202,
203, 204, 420, 421, 840,
841
Rundgren, Todd 831
Rush, Merrilee 281, 283
Russell, Leon 613, 614,
615, 620, 631, 633, 643
Rutles 011, 472, 549
Sable, Jimmy 277
Scott, Tom 640, 651
Seiwell, Denny 769
Seville, Jimmy 099
Shankar, Ravi 297, 621
Shannon, Del 031
Shapiro, Helen 097
Shaw, Rick 605
Shaw, Sandie 502
Sheridan, Tony 007, 094,
844
Sherwood, Lee 605
Shipper, Mark 301
Shirelles 132
Silkie 466
Simon And Garfunkel 251,
549
Simon, Joe 828
Simon, Paul 011, 511, 512,
569, 648
Sinatra, Frank 251
Sinclair, John 168, 654,
659, 682, 684, 685, 701
"Small" Stan 009
Smith, Norman 095
Smothers Brothers 511,
574, 648, 824
Snyder, Tom 661, 816
Sommerville, Brian 098
Sorbi, Jack 605
Sounds, Inc. 067
Spector, Phil 004, 072,
323, 386, 441,
Sperling, Klaus 099
Spirit 549
Splinter 621
Springfield, Dusty 502
Springsteen, Bruce 549

Song & Album Title Index

201, 333
Tokyo, Budokan Hall (7--2--66) 080,
    083, 089, 090, 091, 111, 216, 217,
    244, 252, 327, 351, 375, 376, 432,
    433, 476, 507, 555, 557, 559, 560,
    585, 598
Baby You're A Rich Man
    Original   012, 057, 136, 250, 307,
    593, 839
    Picture Sleeve   839
    "Yellow Submarine" Soundtrack
    164, 610
Back In The Jungle see *Rockin' In The
Jungle*
Back In The U.S.S.R.
    Original   013, 098, 137, 594
Back Off Boogaloo (R)
    Original   106, 464, 465
Back Of My Car (Correct title: *Back Seat
Of My Car)* (P)
    Original   013, 105, 137, 594
Back To Commonwealth
    "Let It Be" Sessions (1--69)   020,
    081, 253, 254, 275, 289, 394, 537,
    538, 540, 542, 545, 571, 572, 583
Bad Boy
    Original   095, 130, 425
    Larry Williams   130
Ballad see *Ballad Of John And Yoko*
Ballad Of John And Yoko
    Original   012, 031, 046, 103, 136,
    250, 307, 593
Ballad Of Sir Frankie Crisp (G)
    Original   617
Baltke
    Eric Clapton   626
Band Of Steel (R)
    Original (With Guthrie Thomas)
    819, 834
Band On The Run (P)
    Australia 1975   736
    Bernice & The Rippers (1975)   510
    Copenhagen (3--21--76)   733, 754
    Los Angeles Forum (6--21--76)   742,
    806
    Los Angeles Forum (6--23--76)   726,
    744, 752, 801
    Largo, Maryland, Capitol Centre
    (5--15--76)   773
    Melbourne, Australia (11--13--75)
    727, 728, 782, 783
    Original   708, 774
    Outtake   814
    Unknown (1976 Tour)   729, 762,
    812
    Wembley Stadium, London (12--7--79)
    813
Bangla Desh (G)

Bangla Desh Concert (8--1--71)   106,
    613, 614, 615, 620, 631, 633, 641,
    643,
    Original   012, 136, 145, 250, 464,
    465, 466, 593
Bathroom Window see *She Came In
Through The Bathroom Window*
Batman/Warmup (P)
    Melbourne, Australia (11--13--75)
    727, 728
Beatle Music Montage
    Various   278, 283
THE BEATLES AND MURRAY THE K
    024
Beatles Christmas Message
    BBC--TV (1963)   115
The Beatles Christmas Record 1963
    Original   143, 156, 157, 160, 172,
    173, 174, 552
Beatles Friends
    Billy Preston & Robert Palmer   059
BEATLES INTERVIEWS 1966
    210
**BEATLES RARITIES AND TRUE
COLLECTOR'S ITEMS**
    393
Beaucoups Of Blues (R)
    Original   104, 465, 829
    Buzz Rabin   829
BEFORE PHIL SPECTOR
    323, 441
Be--Bop--A--Lula (J)
    Adam VIII Original   677, 690, 691,
    692, 859
    "Let It Be" Sessions (1--69)   021,
    153, 253, 254, 289, 537, 541, 543,
    546
    Star Club   508
    Gene Vincent   677
Because
    Original   047, 835
Being For The Benefit Of Mr. Kite
    Original   013, 047, 137, 594, 873
Be My Baby (J)
    Adam VIII Version   654, 655, 679,
    690, 691, 692, 859
    Ronettes   679
Be My Friend see *Big Barn Red*
Besame Mucho
    Decca Audition Session (1--1--62)
    140, 141, 187, 189, 190, 191
    "Let It Be" Sessions (1--69)
    084, 113, 151, 161, 232, 235, 237,
    260, 261, 262, 263, 329, 412, 422,
    424, 454, 473, 498, 529, 530, 571,
    586, 591
    Star Club   508

443, 444, 515, 517, 518, 603
Devil In His Heart
Donays 132, 514
Dialogue
"Let It Be" Sessions (1–69) 532,
533
Dialogue From The Beatles
"Let It Be" Sessions (1–69) 192,
324
Dialogue From Magical Mystery Tour
Original 500
Diddy Wah Diddy
Capt. Beefheart 017, 139, 426, 549,
664
Did We Meet Somewhere Before (P)
From the film "Rock And Roll
High School" 720
Dig It
"Let It Be" Sessions (1–69) 004,
035, 036, 037, 072, 085, 086, 113,
143, 151, 161, 173, 176, 196, 211,
226, 227, 228, 230, 231, 232, 233,
234, 236, 312, 313, 314, 323, 325,
326, 327, 329, 380, 411, 412, 419,
424, 438, 441, 473, 493, 498, 529,
530, 579, 588
Original 046, 862
Ding Dong (G)
Demo 513
Dizzy Miss Lizzy
BBC Radio (1964) 150
Forest Hills (8–29–64) 218, 129, 220
Original 001, 013, 094, 130, 137,
244, 260, 261, 262, 263, 556, 594
Outtake (1962) 555
Sam Houston Coliseum (8--19--65)
067, 076, 144, 339
Shea Stadium (8–15--65) 022, 031,
154, 319, 320, 346, 381, 477, 482,
483, 487
Shea Stadium (8–16--65) 073, 181,
201, 333
Toronto – Varsity Stadium (9–13--
69) 103
Unknown 034, 035, 036, 217, 221,
290, 300, 396, 454, 476, 579
Larry Williams 130
Dr. Robert
Original 013, 137, 195, 594, 888
Domino see *I Me Mine*
Don't Be Cruel
Elvis Presley 031
Don't Bother Me
"A Hard Day's Night" Soundtrack
007, 008, 177, 258
Don't Keep Me Waiting see *Long And
Winding Road*
Don't Leave Me Waiting Here see *Long
And Winding Road*

Don't Let Me Down
"Let It Be" Sessions (1–69) 004,
020, 026, 072, 086, 149, 153, 158,
159, 161, 176, 211, 226, 227, 228,
229, 230, 231, 232, 233, 234, 236,
238, 239, 240, 241, 242, 243, 253,
254, 262, 275, 289, 306, 310, 311,
312, 314, 315, 316, 321, 322, 323,
325, 326, 327, 329, 380, 391, 392,
419, 424, 438, 441, 455, 493, 498,
537, 538, 540, 541, 542, 587, 596,
597, 681
Original 046, 463
Press Conference (Fall '68) 001,
002, 155, 217, 300, 396, 556
Don't Lie To Me
Rolling Stones 408, 481
Don't Pass Me By
Original 102
Don't Worry Kyoko (J)
Picture Sleeve 657
Do The Oz (J)
Original 145, 495, 497, 684
Doubleback Alley
Rutles 011
Down And Out (R)
Original 145, 819
Down In The Flood
Bob Dylan 200
Down To The Wire
Buffalo Springfield 688
Do You Want To Dance (J)
Adam VIII Original 677, 690, 691,
692, 859
Bobby Freeman 677
Do You Want To Know A Secret
Original 012, 046, 097, 136, 250,
317, 439, 440, 493, 518, 843, 849,
858, 879
Picture sleeve 850
Studio outtakes (Possibly original)
030, 050, 093, 184, 303, 304, 317,
369, 422, 442, 444, 453, 510, 516,
518, 603
Unknown 084, 586
Drive My Car
Original 013, 137, 594
Drivin' South
Jimi Hendrix 663, 715
Dropout
Bonzo Dog Band 387
Drowning In The Sea Of Love (R)
Original 828
Joe Simon 828
Duke Of Earl
Gene Chandler 031
Early In The Morning – Hi Ho Silver
"Let It Be" Sessions (1–69) 573,

458, 460
Happy Birthday Mike Love
   Rishikesh, India (3–15–68) 019,
     297, 511
Happy Christmas 1968
   Original 156, 157, 160, 172, 173,
     174, 552, 600
Happy Christmas 1969
   Original 156, 157, 160, 172, 173,
     174, 337, 365, 552, 600
Happy New Year Beat
   Titans 844
Happy Wanderer see MEDLEY Section
Happy X–Mas (War Is Over) (J)
   Original 464, 465, 466, 514
A Hard Day's Night
   BBC Radio (July & August 1964)
     217, 396
   Hollywood Bowl Concert (8–23–
     64) 017, 029, 032, 033, 074,
     079, 139, 244, 285, 341, 342, 344,
     347, 360, 377, 378, 426, 476, 484,
     488, 507, 555, 601
   Live (Unknown) 082, 383, 411
   Original 012, 046, 098, 136, 250,
     593, 888
   Outtake 009, 469
   Paris Concert (6–20–65) 352, 353,
     354, 446, 447, 448, 449, 506
   Radio Commercials for Film 115,
     513
   Sam Houston Coliseum Concert
     (8–19–66) 067, 339
   Shea Stadium Concert (8–15–65)
     084, 087, 319, 320, 346, 381,
     482, 483, 487, 586, 589
   Shea Stadium Concert (8–16–65)
     073, 181, 201, 333
   Film Soundtrack 007, 008, 165,
     177, 258
   Studio Version (Unreleased) 225
   "Top Of The Pops" BBC Radio (7–
     8–64) 272, 300, 337, 365,
     367, 397, 398, 417, 418, 422, 561,
     562, 564, 599
   Vancouver Concert (8–22–64) 040,
     147, 403, 580, 581, 582
   "Whiskey Flat" 010, 049, 062, 296,
     348, 355, 356, 357, 361, 368
A HARD DAY'S NIGHT
007
**A HARD DAY'S NIGHT + SKINNIE
MINNIE**
008
Hard Knights see *A Hard Day's Night*
A Hard Rain's Gonna Fall
   Bangla Desh Concert/Bob Dylan
     (8–1–71) 613, 615, 631, 633,
     641, 643

Hard Times (R)
   Ringo TV Special (4–26–78) 819, 827
Hare Krsna Mantra
   "Let It Be" Sessions (1–69) 573,
     574, 596
   Hare Krsna Temple Original 103
Hari's On Tour (G)
   Fort Worth, Texas (11–22–74) 624,
     625, 629
   Long Beach, California (12–10–74)
     639, 642, 650
   Unknown ('74 Tour) 644, 645
Harris Show Vintage Radio, Phil
   Original 857
HARRISON, GEORGE
   Picture Disc 632
Have Some Fun Tonight see *Long Tall
Sally*
Have You Heard The Word (J)
   John & Bee Gees (6–70) 001, 002,
     037, 087, 110, 149, 151, 155, 195,
     217, 260, 261, 262, 263, 264, 300,
     383, 396, 411, 529, 530, 556, 571,
     589
Hear Me Lord (G)
   Original 617
Hear My Train A–Comin'
   Jimi Hendrix 696
HEAR THE BEATLES TELL ALL see
   INTERVIEWS in **Topical Index**
Heartbreak Hotel
   Elvis Presley 094
Heart Of The Country (P)
   "James Paul McCartney" TV Special
     (4–16–73) 168, 169
   Original 013, 137, 594
   see also MEDLEY Section
Heart On My Sleeve (R)
   Ringo TV Special (4–26–78) 819,
     827
The Heart That You Broke (P)
   Nashville (1975) 514
Heather (P)
   Paul & Donovan 423, 512, 569, 788
Helen Wheels (P)
   Original 708, 774
   Outtake 814
Hello Goodbye
   Original 012, 101, 102, 136, 250,
     593
Hello Little Girl
   Decca Auditions (1–1–62) 187, 188,
     189, 190, 191, 266, 267, 268, 269,
     572
Hello Mabel
   Bonzo Dog Band 387
Help
   "Blackpool Night Out" TV Special
     (8–1–65) 509

Rutles 011
HOLLYWOOD BOWL
524
Homeward Bound (G)
Taping for "Saturday Night Live"
with Paul Simon (11--18--76)
511, 648
Honey Don't
BBC Radio (1963) 034, 035, 036,
115, 150, 454, 579
Original 012, 131, 136, 250, 518,
593
Outtake 183, 317, 515, 603
Carl Perkins 131
Unknown 221, 443, 444, 517, 518
Honey Hush see *Hi Ho Silver*
Honeymoon Song see *Bound By Love*
Honky Tonk Woman
Rolling Stones 199, 656, 698
Hooray For Capt. Spaulding
Groucho Marx 549
Hop On The Bus
"Magical Mystery Tour" Soundtrack
499
Hot As Sun (P)
Royal Court Theatre, Liverpool (11--
25--79) 757
Wembley Stadium, London (12--7--
79) 813
Hound Dog (J)
Jimi Hendrix 663, 696
Elvis Presley 031, 827
"One--To--One Concert" (8--30--72)
658, 665, 666, 667, 673, 686
House Of The Rising Sun
"Let It Be" Sessions (1--69) 020,
042, 081, 253, 254, 275, 289, 394,
537, 538, 540, 542, 545, 583
House That Jack Built
Aretha Franklin 279, 283
How Do You Do
Paul & Donovan 423, 788
How Do You Do It
Recorded 11--26--62 188, 290, 291,
292, 469, 473, 572
How Do You Sleep (J)
Original 105
How Many Times
Rolling Stones 039, 224
Hunting Scene (R)
From "The Magic Christian" Sound--
track 823
Hurt
Elvis Presley/Timi Yuro 251
Husbands And Wives (R)
Roger Miller 829
Original 829
I Am Missing You

Ravi Shankar 621, 647
I Am The Greatest (R)
Original 095
Ringo TV Special (4--26--78) 827
I Am The Walrus
Demo 019, 107, 297
"Magical Mystery Tour" Soundtrack
167, 393
Original 013, 057, 102, 137, 594
I Am Your Singer (P)
Hanover, Germany (8--16--72) 721,
755, 765
Original 815
I Call Your Name
Original 063, 064, 249
I Can't Be Satisfied
Rolling Stones 200
I Can't Do Without You
Pete Best 452, 845
I'd Have You Anytime (G)
Dylan--Harrison Outtake 060, 569,
649
Original 617
I Dig A Pony
"Let It Be" Sessions (1--69) 004,
072, 086, 087, 149, 161, 176, 211,
226, 227, 228, 229, 230, 231, 232,
233, 234, 235, 236, 237, 238, 239,
240, 241, 242, 243, 306, 310, 311,
312, 313, 314, 315, 316, 322, 323,
326, 326, 327, 329, 380, 383, 391,
392, 412, 419, 424, 438, 441, 455,
498, 588, 589, 591
Original 013, 106, 137, 322, 594 862
I Dig Love (G)
Original 617
I Don't Care Anymore (G)
Original 145
I Don't Know Why (G)
George with Delaney & Bonnie &
Friends in Copenhagen (12--69)
628
I Don't Want To See You Again
Peter & Gordon 068, 069, 070, 473
I Don't Want To Spoil The Party
Original 013, 137, 594 852
Picture Sleeve 852
I Feel Fine
"Blackpool Night Out" TV Show (8--
1--65) 509
Circus Krone, Munich, Germany (6--
24--66) 208, 359, 364, 366, 372,
413, 429, 430, 565
Cleveland, Ohio (8--14--66) 138, 590
Forest Hills 218, 219, 220
Original 012, 047, 057, 063, 064,
099, 136, 249, 250, 593
Paris (6--20--65) 043, 045, 352, 373,

446, 447, 448, 449, 491, 506
Sam Houston Coliseum (8–19–66)
   067, 339
San Francisco (8–29–66)   340
Shea Stadium (8–15–65)   022, 154,
   319, 320, 346, 381, 477, 482, 483,
   487
Shea Stadium (8–16–65)   073, 181,
   201, 333
"Ed Sullivan Show" (9–12–65)
   039, 073, 181, 201, 224, 333, 450
Tokyo (7–1–66)   375, 559, 598
Tokyo (7–2–66)   080, 083, 085, 089,
   090, 091, 111, 216, 217, 244, 252,
   327, 351, 376, 432, 433, 476, 507,
   555, 557, 560, 585
If I Fell
   "A Hard Day's Night" Soundtrack
      007, 008, 037, 061, 152, 165, 255,
      458, 460, 527, 528, 531, 532, 534
   Hollywood Bowl (8–23–64)   029,
      032, 033, 079, 244, 285, 318, 341,
      342, 344, 360, 372, 377, 378, 413,
      476, 484, 488, 507, 555, 566
   Original   012, 046, 047, 136, 250,
      593, 681, 888
   Outtake   019
   Studio   225
   Unknown   082, 104
   Vancouver (8–22–64)   040, 147,
      580, 581, 582
   "Whiskey Flat"   010, 049, 062, 296,
      348, 355, 356, 357, 361, 368
If I Needed Someone
   Circus Krone, Munich, Germany (6–
      24–66)   566, 567
   Original   047
   San Francisco (8–29–66)   340
   Tokyo (7–1–66)   375, 559, 598
   Tokyo (7–2–66)   080, 083, 089,
      090, 091, 111, 216, 217, 221, 244,
      252, 351, 360, 376, 432, 433, 476,
      507, 555, 557, 560, 585, 601
If Not For You (G)
   Original   637
   Bob Dylan   637
I Forgot To Remember
   BBC (11–62)   094, 185, 249, 260,
      261, 262, 263, 436, 437
   BBC Radio (1962)   473, 612
If You Can't Get Her
   Pete Best   393, 399, 452
If You Don't Help Me Darling (P)   see
   Henry's Blues
If You Love Me Baby
   Original   874
If You Wanna Be Me
   Cat Stevens   549

If You Want It You Can Dig It   see   *Dig It*
I Got A Feeling   see   *I've Got A Feeling*
I Got A Woman
   BBC Radio (11–62)   025, 185, 186,
      196, 222, 294, 308, 436, 437, 606,
      607
   Outtake (1963)   468, 495, 497
   Lennon Outtake (WABC Radio)   150
   Unknown   290, 436, 437
I Got Stung
   Elvis Presley/Johnny Hallyday   251
I Just Don't Understand
   BBC Radio (11–62)   025, 110, 185,
      186, 196, 222, 294, 308, 436, 437,
      606, 607
I Just Want To Make Love To You
   Rolling Stones   030, 050, 093
I Know A Place (R)
   "Scouse The Mouse" Soundtrack
      819, 830
I Lie Around (P)
   Original   732, 734, 775, 807
   Picture Sleeve   751
I LIE AROUND
   751
I Listen To My Heart
   Frank Ifield   841, 860
I'll Be Back
   Original   012, 047, 136, 250, 593
I'll Be Mine   see   *I Me Mine*
I'll Be On My Way
   BBC Radio (Fall '62)   115, 256, 257,
      393, 399, 473, 495
I'll Cry Instead
   Original   098
   Original with Paul's Intro.   857
I'll Follow The Sun
   Original   012, 058, 099, 136, 250,
      593
I'll Get You
   Original   098, 439, 440, 490, 876,
   Picture sleeve   877
I Love You Girl   see   *For You Blue*
I Love You Too
   Fourmost   297
Imagine (J)
   "Mike Douglas Show" (Week of 2–
      14–72)   658, 672, 693
   "Jerry Lewis Telethon" (9–6–72)
      659, 660
   One–To–One Concert (8–30–72)
      654, 655, 668, 682, 684, 685, 686
   Original   012, 051, 105, 136, 250,
      593
   Outtake   513
   "Salute To Sir Lew Grade" TV Special
      (6–13–75)   511, 569, 686
   "Weekly Top–30" (11–3–79)   676
I'm A Loser

261

Original   104, 463, 464, 465
"Top Of The Pops" BBC–TV Show
   (2–12–70)   158, 159, 322, 499,
   500
Instrumentals (Unknown titles)
   Cream   688
   Bob Dylan   638
   Jimi Hendrix   696
   "Let It Be" Sessions (1–69)   176,
   327
   Unknown   469
Instrumental No. 42
   "Let It Be" Sessions (1–69)   086,
   176, 327, 419, 588
In The Bottom
   Rolling Stones   039, 224
Introducing The Beatles
   Unknown   301
I Remember You
   Frank Ifield   133, 841, 860
   Star Club   133, 508
I Sat Belonely (J)
   John Reading Poem   513
I Saw Her Standing There
   Christmas Show at Liverpool
      Empire (12–22–63)   058, 612
   John Lennon with Elton John
      (11–26–74)   652, 653
   Melbourne, Australia (6–16–64)
      034, 150, 362, 371, 401, 402, 403,
      434, 476
   Original   012, 046, 047, 095, 136,
      250, 317, 593, 843, 858, 879
   Outtake   183, 515, 518, 603
   Star Club   508
   "Ed Sullivan Show" (2–16–64)
      001, 002, 175, 462, 556
   Swedish TV Show "Drop In" (11–3–
      63)   284, 370, 509, 520, 535,
      536, 604
   Unknown   082, 218, 220, 429, 430,
      443, 444, 517, 518
   Unknown (Possibly The Who)   514
   Washington, D.C. (2–11–64)   078,
      213, 214, 223, 362, 379, 401, 434,
      568
I Shot The Sheriff
   Eric Clapton   626
I Should Have Known Better
   "A Hard Day's Night" Soundtrack
      007, 008, 019, 037, 061, 152, 165,
      255, 458, 460, 527, 528, 531, 532,
      534
   Original   012, 046, 047, 136, 250,
      302, 593, 888
   Studio (False Start)   225
   Studio (With Harmonica)   225
   Studio (Without Harmonica)   225

Isn't It A Pity (G)
   Original   051, 104
I Started A Joke
   Bee Gees   280, 283
It Ain't Easy   see   *It Don't Come Easy*
It Ain't Me Babe
   Bob Dylan   200
It Don't Come Easy (R)
   Bangla Desh Concert (8–1–71)   104,
      614, 620
   Original   047, 464, 465
   Ringo TV Special (4–26–78)   827
I Threw It All Away
   "Let It Be" Sessions (1–69)   543
It's All Too Much
   "Yellow Submarine" Soundtrack
      164, 610
It's For You
   Cilla Black   473
   Cilla Black with Lennon Intro.   068,
      069, 070
It's Getting Better
   Original   047
It's Hard To Wait   see   *It's So Hard*
It's Only Love
   Outtake   297
It's So Hard (J)
   "Mike Douglas Show" Week of 2–14–
      72   668, 672, 693
   "One–To–One Concert" (8–30–72)
      658, 665, 667, 673
It Takes A Lot To Laugh
   Bob Dylan, Bangla Desh Concert
      (8–1–71)   613, 615, 631, 633,
      641, 643
It Won't Be Long
   Original   012, 046, 047, 098, 136,
      250, 400, 593
I've Cried Before
   Four Seasons   843
I've Got A Feeling
   "Let It Be" Sessions (1–69)   004,
      020, 026, 072, 086, 149, 153, 161,
      176, 211, 226, 227, 228, 229, 230,
      231, 232, 233, 234, 236, 238, 239,
      240, 241, 242, 243, 253, 254, 275,
      289, 306, 310, 311, 312, 313, 314,
      315, 316, 321, 322, 323, 327, 329,
      391, 392, 419, 424, 438, 441, 455,
      463, 537, 538, 540, 541, 542, 543,
      588
   Original   013, 047, 137, 594, 862
I've Got A Woman (R)
   Unknown   821
I've Had Enough (P)
   Radio Spot   805
   Royal Court Theatre, Liverpool (11–
      25–79)   757

Wembley Stadium, London (12–7–79)
813
I've Just Seen A Face (P)
Australia (11–75) 727, 728, 736
Copenhagen (3–21–76) 733, 735,
802
Fort Worth, Texas (5–3–76) 724
Largo, Maryland (5–15–76) 809
Los Angeles, California (6–23–76)
744, 752, 781, 801
Melbourne, Australia (11–13–75)
782, 783
Original (Beatles) 013, 137, 594
Sydney, Australia (11–7–75) 773
Unknown 814
I Wanna Be Your Man
"A Hard Day's Night" Soundtrack
007, 008, 165, 255
"Around The Beatles" TV Show
(5–6–64) 023, 168, 169, 207, 499,
500
BBC Radio (1964) 217, 396
"Big Night Out" TV Show (2–29–
64) 384, 519
"From Us To You" BBC Radio Show
(12–26–63) 300, 370, 458, 460,
536, 589, 604
Hollywood Bowl (8–23–64) 029
Houston (8–19–65) 339
Original 095
Paris (6–20–65) 352, 353, 354, 446,
447, 448, 449, 506
San Francisco (8–29–66) 340
Tokyo (7–1–66) 375, 559, 598
Tokyo (7–2–66) 080, 083, 089, 090,
091, 111, 216, 217, 244, 252, 351,
376, 432, 433, 476, 507, 555, 557,
560, 601
Unknown 071, 178, 305
Unknown ('64 Tour) 048
Washington, D.C. (2–11–64) 078,
193, 194, 213, 214, 223, 362, 379,
401, 434, 568
"Whiskey Flat" 010, 049, 062, 296,
348, 355, 356, 357, 361, 368
I Want A Beatle For Christmas
Becky Lee Beck 512
I Want To Be Loved
Rolling Stones 494
I Want To Hold Your Hand
Christmas Show, Liverpool Empire
(12–22–63) 058, 612
Hollywood Bowl (8–23–64) 032,
033, 079, 087, 244, 285, 318, 341,
342, 344, 360, 372, 377, 378, 413,
476, 484, 488, 507, 555, 566, 589
Original 012, 046, 047, 063, 064,
098, 136, 199, 250, 400, 439, 440

"Scene At 6:30" TV Show (8–19–63)
061, 255, 458, 460
"Ed Sullivan Show" (2–16–64) 001,
002, 205, 370, 462, 556
"Sunday Night At The London
Palladium" (10–13–63) 003, 075,
219, 334, 384, 519
"Sunday Night At The London
Palladium" (1–12–64) 384, 519
Unknown 043, 045, 082, 085, 383,
411.
Vancouver (8–22–64) 147, 582
Washington, D.C. (2–11–64) 078,
193, 194, 213, 214, 223, 379, 401,
434, 491, 535, 536, 566, 567, 568,
604
"Whiskey Flat" 010, 049, 062, 296,
348, 355, 356, 357, 361, 368
see also   MEDLEY Section
I Want You
Unknown 321
I Want You (She's So Heavy)
Original 835
I Wish I Was In London
Bob Dylan 638
I Would Only Smile (P)
Hanover, Germany (8–16–72) 721,
755, 765
Unknown (Possibly '72 Tour) 775
Jailhouse Rock
Elvis Presley 031
Jam see *Hari's On Tour*
Jam
"Let It Be" Sessions (1–69) 228
Jazz Piano Theme see *Whole Lotta
Shakin'*
Jerk With A Badge
Minneapolis Policeman talking (8–21–
65) 592
Jessie's Dream
"Magical Mystery Tour" Soundtrack
393
Jet (P)
Atlanta, Georgia (5–19–76) 810
Australia (11–75) 727, 728, 736
Copenhagen (3–21–76) 718, 719,
733, 735, 754, 777, 802
Fort Worth, Texas (5–3–76) 724
Largo, Maryland (5–15–76) 748
Los Angeles, California (6–21–76)
742, 806
Los Angeles, California (6–23–76)
749, 752, 801
Melbourne, Australia (11–13–75)
782, 783
Original 708, 740, 774
Original DJ Edit 775
San Diego (6–16–76) 775

263

726, 752, 801
Melbourne, Australia (11--13--75)
  782, 782
San Francisco, California (6--14--75)
  779, 811
Sydney, Australia (11--7--75)   773

Little Beatle Boy
Angels   513

Little Drummer Boy
Jimi Hendrix   715

Little Drummer Boy/Silent Night/Auld
Lang Syne
Jimi Hendrix   549

Little Miss Lover
Jimi Hendrix   663

Little Queenie
Chuck Berry   114
Star Club   114, 508
Rolling Stones   494

Little Woman Love (P)
Edinburgh, Scotland (5--23--73)
  737, 756, 786, 787
"James Paul McCartney" TV Special
  (4--16--73)   169, 731, 732, 739,
  770, 778
Leeds, England (5--19--73)   745, 746
Original   106, 734, 807

Live And Let Die (P)
Atlanta, Georgia (5--19--76)   810
Bernice & The Rippers (Boston, 1975)
  510
Copenhagen (3--21--76)   718, 719,
  733, 735, 754, 777, 802
Edinburgh, Scotland (5--23--73)
  737, 756, 786, 787
Fort Worth, Texas (5--3--76)   724
Largo, Maryland (5--15--76)   809
Leeds, England (5--19--73)   745, 746
Los Angeles, California (6--21--76)
  742, 806
Los Angeles, California (6--23--76)
  744, 752, 781, 801
"James Paul McCartney" TV Special
  (4--16--72)   168, 169, 731, 732,
  738, 739, 770, 778
Original   807
Picture Sleeve   751
Toronto, Canada (5--9--76)   750, 760,
  790
Unknown   812, 814

LIVE AT SHEA
320

LIVE IN COPENHAGEN
802

Living In A Pet Shop (R)
"Scouse The Mouse" Soundtrack
  514, 819, 830

Living In Hope

Rutles   011

LONDON TOWN
766

Lonesome Tears In My Eyes
BBC Radio (11--62)   025, 134, 185,
  186, 196, 222, 294, 308, 436, 437,
  572, 606, 607
Johnny Burnette Trio   134

Long And Winding Road
Atlanta, Georgia (5--19--76) (P)   810
Australia (11--75) (P)   727, 728
Copenhagen (3--21--76) (P)   718,
  719, 733, 735, 754, 777, 802
Fort Worth, Texas (5--3--76) (P)   724
"Let It Be" Sessions (1--69)   004,
  021, 072, 086, 113, 149, 152, 158,
  159, 161, 200, 211, 226, 227, 228,
  229, 230, 231, 232, 233, 234, 236,
  260, 261, 262, 263, 289, 306, 310,
  312, 313, 314, 315, 316, 323, 325,
  326, 329, 419, 438, 441, 463, 473,
  493, 498, 527, 531, 534, 538, 546,
  588
Largo, Maryland (5--15--76) (P)   748
Los Angeles, California (6--23--76) (P)
  749, 752, 801
Original   012, 046, 047, 104, 136,
  206, 250, 593, 862
Original with Dialogue by Mark Elliott
  386
Toronto, Canada (5--9--76) (P)   750,
  760, 790
Unknown   812
Unknown ('76 Tour – San Francisco
  or L.A.) (P)   817

Long May You Run
Crosby, Stills, Nash & Young   549

Long Tall Sally
"Around The Beatles" TV Show (5--
  6--64)   022, 023, 154, 155, 168,
  169, 207, 477, 499, 500
Delaney & Bonnie & Friends (12--69)
  (G)   628
Edinburgh, Scotland (5--23--73) (P)
  737, 756, 786, 787
Hollywood Bowl (8--23--64)   017,
  029, 032, 033, 074, 079, 087, 139,
  244, 284, 285, 318, 341, 342, 344,
  345, 346, 360, 372, 377, 378, 413,
  426, 476, 484, 488, 507, 520, 555,
  565, 589, 601
"James Paul McCartney" TV Special
  (4--16--73) (P)   168, 169, 731,
  732, 738, 739, 758, 770, 778
Little Richard   130
Melbourne, Australia (6--16--64)
  150, 468

Magical Mystery Tour
  "Magical Mystery Tour" Soundtrack
    167, 393
  Original   013, 031, 102, 137, 594
MAGICAL MYSTERY TOUR
  167
MAGICAL MYSTERY TOUR AND APPLE
  102
Magneto And Titanium Man (P)
  Copenhagen (3--21--76)   718, 719,
    733, 735, 754, 777, 802
  Fort Worth, Texas (5-3-76)   724
  Los Angeles, California (6--23--76)
    744, 752, 781, 801
  San Diego, California (6--16--76)
    775
  Unknown   812, 814
  Unknown ('76 Tour -- San Francisco
    or Los Angeles)   817
THE MAKING OF SGT. PEPPER
  101
A Man Like Me (R)
  Original   818
  Ringo TV Special   819, 827
Marlena
  Four Seasons   843
Mary Had A Little Lamb (P)
  Hanover, Germany (8--16--72)   775
  "James Paul McCartney" TV Special
    (4--16--73)   168, 775
  Original   106, 734, 807
  see also   MEDLEY Section
Mary Jane   see   *What's Yer New Mary Jane*
Matchbox
  Original   063, 064, 131, 249
  Carl Perkins   131
  Picture sleeve   878
  Star Club   508
Maxwell's Silver Hammer
  ABBEY ROAD Outtake   115, 423, 469,
  "Let It Be" Sessions   037, 084, 149,
    151, 161, 232, 235, 237, 262, 329,
    391, 392, 412, 422, 424, 454, 473,
    498, 529, 530, 586, 591
  Original   013, 047, 137, 594, 835
  Original with comments by Alan
    Parsons   295
Maya Love (G)
  Long Beach, California (12--10--74)
    639, 642, 650
  Seattle, Washington (11--4--74)   635
  Unknown ('74 Tour)   623, 627, 645
  Vancouver (11--2--74)   640, 646, 651
Maybe Baby (J)   see   MEDLEY Section
Maybe I'm Amazed (P)
  Australia (11--75)   727, 728, 736
  Copenhagen (3--21--76)   718, 719,
    733, 735, 754, 777, 802
  Edinburgh, Scotland (5--23--73)   737,
    756, 786, 787

Fort Worth, Texas (5--3--76)   724
"James Paul McCartney" TV Special
  (4--16--73)   168, 169, 731, 732,
  738, 739, 770, 778
Largo, Maryland (5--15--76)   748
Leeds, England (5--19--73)   745
Los Angeles, California (6--21--76)
  742, 806
Los Angeles, California (6--23--76)
  749, 752, 801
Melbourne, Australia (11--13--75)
  782, 783
Original   012, 051, 102, 104, 136,
  250, 593
Original with comments by Alan
  Parsons   761
Sydney, Australia (11--7--75)   773
Toronto, Canada (5--9--76)   750,
  760, 790
Unknown   812, 814
Wembley Stadium, London (12--7--
  79)   813
McCARTNEY, PAUL
  Picture Disc   767
Mean Mr. Mustard
  "Let It Be" Sessions with Extra Verse
    596, 597
  Original   013, 137, 594, 835
  Outtake   393, 399, 556
Medicine Jar (P)
  Fort Worth, Texas (5--3--76)   724
  Largo, Maryland (5--15--76)   748
  Los Angeles, California (6--21--76)
    742, 806
  Los Angeles, California (6--23--76)
    749, 752, 801
  Toronto, Canada (5--9--76)   750,
    760, 790
  Unknown   814
MEDLEY: *Baby Please Don't Go/Rock
  Island Line/Maybe Baby/Peggy Sue* (J)
  Unknown   658
MEDLEY: *Besame Mucho/Cottonfields/
  When You Walk/Whole Lotta Shakin'
  Goin On/Suzy Parker*
  110
MEDLEY: *Blackbird/Bluebird/Michelle/
  Heart Of The Country/Yesterday* (P)
  "James Paul McCartney" TV Special
    (4--16--73)   169, 731, 738, 739,
    770, 778
MEDLEY: *Bluebird/Mommas Little Girl/
  Michelle/Heart Of The Country* (P)
  "James Paul McCartney" TV Special
    Outtake   569
MEDLEY: *Little Woman Love/C Moon/
  Little Woman Love* (P)
  "James Paul McCartney" TV Special
    (4--16--73)   738, 770, 814
MEDLEY: *Love Me Do/Please Please Me/*

268

270

Original   680, 885
Nobody But You
    Pete Best   452, 845
Nobody's Child
    Original   836, 837, 838
    Picture sleeve   838
Nobody's Darling
    Frank Ifield   841, 860
No Expectations
    Rolling Stones   689
No No Song (R)
    Hoyt Axton   828
    Original   828
    "Smothers Brothers Show" (4--28--75)
    511, 648, 824
No Pakistanis
    "Let It Be" Sessions (1–69)   020,
    084, 153, 253, 254, 275, 289, 422,
    454, 537, 538, 540, 541, 542, 549,
    586
No Particular Place To Go
    Chuck Berry   094
No Reply
    Original   013, 137, 594, 888
Norwegian Wood
    "Let It Be" Sessions (1–69)   021,
    153, 253, 254, 289, 537, 538, 541,
    543, 546
    Original   013, 031, 094, 100, 137,
    594
Not Guilty
    Outtake (1968)   297
Nothing From Nothing
    Billy Preston on George Harrison
    Tour (Long Beach, 12–10–74)
    639, 642, 650
    Unknown: Billy Preston On '74
    Harrison Tour   627, 644, 645
    Billy Preston On Harrison Tour
    (Vancouver, 11–2–74)   640, 646,
    651
Nothing Is Easy
    Jethro Tull   143, 173, 196
Nothing's Gonna Change My Life see
Across The Universe
Now Hear This Song Of Mine (P)
    From **RAM** Promo disc   701, 703,
    705, 706, 732
Nowhere Man
    Circus Krone, Munich, Germany (6--
    24--66)   208, 359, 364, 366, 372,
    413, 429, 430, 491, 565, 566, 567
    Original   012, 031, 100, 136, 250,
    593, 867
    Picture Sleeve   867
    San Francisco, California (8--29--66)
    340
    Tokyo (7–1–66)   375, 559, 598
    Tokyo (7–2–66)   080, 083, 084, 085,

090, 216, 217, 244, 327, 351, 360,
376, 422, 432, 433, 454, 476, 507,
549, 557, 560, 585, 586, 601
    Unknown   043, 045
    "Yellow Submarine" Soundtrack
    164, 610
No Words (P)
    Royal Court Theatre, Liverpool (11–
    25–79)   757
    Wembley Stadium, London (12-7–
    79)   813
Number One
    Rutles   011
Ob–La–Di Ob–La–Da
    Original   012, 094, 136, 250, 593
    Original with Paul's Intro.   857
    Outtake   681
Occapella (R)
    Lee Dorsey   829
    Original   829
Octopus's Garden (Spellings will vary
  slightly for different versions)
    ABBEY ROAD Outtake   423, 469
    "Let It Be" Sessions   149, 161, 260,
    261, 262, 263, 329, 424, 498
    Original   047, 835
    Ringo TV Special (4--26--78)   827
Oh Carol see *Carol*
Oh Darling
    ABBEY ROAD Outtake   423, 469,
    512, 569
    "Let It Be" Sessions   161, 329, 391,
    392, 424, 498
    Original   018, 047, 835
Oh Darling (P) see *Say Darling*
Oh Lord (G)
    Delaney & Bonnie & Friends, Copen-
    hagen (12–69)   628
Oh My Love (J)
    Beatles Outtake   107
    Recorded at Weybridge (7–75)   652,
    653
Oh Sisters see *Sisters Oh Sisters*
Oh Woman Oh Why (P)
    "James Paul McCartney" TV Special
    (4--16--73)   169, 731, 732, 738,
    739, 770, 778
Oh Yeah see *I've Got A Feeling*
Oh Yoko (J)
    Original   013, 137, 594
Old Brown Shoe
    Original   047, 307
Old Hillbilly Way see *Tennessee*
Old Siam Sir (P)
    Royal Court Theatre, Liverpool (11–
    25–79)   757
    Wembley Stadium, London (12-7–79)
    813

"Yellow Submarine" Soundtrack
164, 610
Shades Of Orange
Rolling Stones (with possible Beatle
involvement) 060, 408, 481, 494
Shake A Hand
Elvis Presley/Little Richard 251
Shake And Roll see *Shake Rattle And
Roll*
Shake It (J)
"Mike Douglas Show" (Week of 2--
14--72) 672, 693
Shake, Rattle And Roll
"Let It Be" Sessions (1--69) 037,
113, 134, 151, 161, 232, 235, 237,
329, 412, 424, 450, 473, 498, 529,
530, 572, 591
Joe Turner 134
Shakin' In The Sixties
"Let It Be" Sessions (1--69) 021, 042,
081, 253, 254, 289, 394, 537, 538,
543, 545, 546, 583
She Belongs To Me
Bob Dylan 638
She Bop
Unknown (Not Beatles) 031
*She Came In Through The Bathroom
Window*
"Let It Be" Sessions (1--69) 021,
153, 253, 254, 289, 537, 538, 541,
543, 546, 596, 597
Original 013, 047, 137, 594, 835
She Loves You
"A Hard Day's Night" Soundtrack
007, 008, 165
"Around The Beatles" TV Show (5--6--
64) 154, 155
Christmas Show, Liverpool Empire
(12--22--63) 058, 612
Copenhagen (6--4--64) 071, 178, 305
Hollywood Bowl (8--23--64) 029,
032, 033, 074, 079, 221, 244, 284,
285, 318, 341, 342, 343, 345, 347,
360, 377, 378, 476, 484, 488, 507,
520, 555, 562, 566, 567, 601
"Magical Mystery Tour" Soundtrack
(Instrumental) 393
Manchester, England (11--20--63) 003,
075, 334, 470
Melbourne, Australia (6--16--64) 150,
362, 371, 401, 402, 403, 434, 468
Original 012, 046, 047, 098, 136,
199, 250, 317, 439, 490, 876
Outtakes 184, 443, 444, 515, 517,
518,
Picture Sleeve 877
Royal Command Variety Show (11--
4--63) 054, 055, 056

"Ed Sullivan Show" (2--9--64) 205,
462
"Ed Sullivan Show" (2--16--64) 001,
002, 022, 477, 556
Swedish TV Show "Drop In" (11--3--
63) 284, 370, 509, 520, 535,
536, 604
Unknown 071, 082, 178, 305, 383,
425, 429, 430
Vancouver (8--22--64) 147, 377, 378,
403, 582
Washington, D.C. (2--11--64) 194,
213, 214, 223, 362, 401, 434, 568
"Whiskey Flat" 010, 049, 062, 296,
348, 355, 356, 357, 361, 368
see also MEDLEY Section
Sherry
Four Seasons 843
She Said She Said
"Let It Be" Sessions (1--69) 596,
597
Original 013, 137, 594
She's Alright
Pete Best 452, 845
She's A Rainbow
Rolling Stones 494
She's A Woman
Circus Krone, Munich, Germany (6--
24--66) 566, 567
Houston (8--19--66) 067, 339
Minneapolis (8--21--65) 592
Original 057, 063, 064, 099, 249
Paris (6--20--65) 043, 045, 176, 304,
327, 352, 353, 354, 446, 447, 448,
449, 491, 506
San Francisco (8--29--66) 340
Tokyo (7--1--66) 375, 559, 598
Tokyo (7--2--66) 080, 083, 089, 090,
091, 111, 216, 217, 244, 252, 351,
376, 432, 433, 476, 507, 555, 557,
560, 585, 601
She's Leaving Home
Original 873
She's Your Lover Now
Bob Dylan 638
Sheik Of Araby
Decca Auditions (1--1--62) 187, 188,
189, 190, 191, 478, 479, 480
Sheila
Tommy Roe 133
Star Club 133
Shimmy Like My Sister Kate
Pete Best 452, 845
Shimmy Shake
Star Club 508
Shirley's Wild Accordian
"Magical Mystery Tour" Soundtrack
393

167
Original 012, 031, 099, 136, 199, 250, 593, 890
Picture sleeve 890
Royal Court Theatre, Liverpool (11--25--79) (P) 747
San Francisco (8--29--66) 340
Seattle (6--10--76) (P) 730
"Ed Sullivan Show" (9--12--65) 039, 073, 181, 201, 224, 333, 391, 392, 450
Sydney, Australia (11--7--75) (P) 773
Tokyo (7--1--66) 375, 559, 598
Tokyo (7--2--66) 080, 083, 085, 089, 090, 091, 111, 216, 217, 252, 327, 351, 360, 376, 432, 433, 476, 555, 557, 560, 585, 601
Unknown 043, 045
Unknown (P) 812, 814
Unknown ('76 Tour -- Fort Worth or Seattle) (P) 729, 762
"Weekly Top--30" (7--21--79) 088
Wembley Stadium, London (12--7--79) (P) 813
Yesterday And Today (LP)
Cover Picture 891
Yoko Sings see *Midsummer New York*
You Ain't Going Nowhere
Not Beatles 200
You Always Hurt The One You Love (R)
Mills Brothers 829
Original 829
You And Me Babe (R)
Original 102
You Are My Sunshine
Tony Sheridan 844
see also MEDLEY Section
You Can Dig It see *Dig It*
You Can Make It If You Try
Rolling Stones 030, 050, 093
You Can't Always Get What You Want
Rolling Stones 689
You Can't Catch Me (J)
Adam VIII Original 679, 690, 691, 692, 859
Chuck Berry 679
You Can't Do That
Hollywood Bowl (8--23--64) 017, 029, 032, 033, 035, 036, 074, 079, 085, 139, 221, 244, 285, 318, 341, 342, 343, 345, 347, 360, 372, 411, 413, 426, 476, 484, 507, 555, 562, 565, 566, 567, 579, 601
Melbourne, Australia (6--16--64) 150, 362, 371, 401, 402, 403, 434
Original 012, 136, 250, 303, 304, 369, 593, 846
Original for KFWB Radio 415
Paris (6--20--65) 303, 304, 369

Picture Sleeve 846
Unknown 030, 050, 084, 093
Unknown (Live '64) 586
Unknown (Live '65) 422
Vancouver (8--22--64) 040, 147, 377, 378, 403, 580, 581, 582
"Whiskey Flat" 010, 049, 062, 296, 348, 355, 356, 357, 361, 368
You Don't Know Me
Elvis Presley/Bette Midler 251
You Don't Know Where Your Interest Lies
Simon & Garfunkel 549
You Gave Me A Mountain
Elvis Presley/Frankie Laine 251
You Gave Me The Answer (P)
Copenhagen (3--21--76) 718, 719, 733, 735, 754, 777, 802
Fort Worth, Texas (5--3--76) 724
Largo, Maryland (5--15--76) 809
Los Angeles, California (6--23--76) 752, 781, 801
San Francisco (6--14--76) 779, 811
Unknown 812
Unknown ('76 Tour -- Los Angeles or San Francisco) 817
You Just Want Meat
Jackson Browne 549
You Know My Name (Look Up My Number)
Original 057, 158, 322, 367, 397, 398, 417, 418, 466, 599
You Need Feet
Rutles 011, 472
You Never Give Me Your Money
ABBEY ROAD Outtakes 423, 469
Original 013, 047, 103, 137, 594, 835
Youngblood
BBC Radio (1962) 572, 612
The Young Ones
Bonzo Dog Band 387
You Really Got A Hold On Me
"Let It Be" Sessions (1--69) 085, 149, 161, 260, 261, 262, 263, 329, 424, 529, 530, 586
Miracles 135
Original 096, 135, 249
Outtakes 184, 317, 422, 442, 444, 515, 516, 518, 603
"Saturday Club" BBC Radio (5--25--63) 043, 045, 061, 255, 256, 257, 458, 460, 491
Swedish TV Show "Drop In" (11--3--63) 001, 002, 037, 151, 155, 284, 370, 520, 529, 530, 535, 536, 556, 604
Unknown 037, 151, 217, 300, 396, 429, 430
You're Gonna Lose That Girl

285

Label Index

label number	entry number
BERKELEY continued	
2008	499
2009	450
2027	032
2028	770
2033	464
61007	807
no. unknown	260, 285
BEST SELLER RECORDS	
ES–LP–50	206
BR	
10004	784
BRB	
100	452
BRK	
1001	633
BRR	
002	750
BS	
1000	094
1001	095
1002	096
1003	097
1004	098
1005	099
1006	100
1007	101
1008	102
1009	103
1010	104
1011	105
1012	106
BV	
1966	138, 590
CAPITOL	
444	492
2138	861
PRO 2549	400
2553	891
2653	873
PRO 2720	069
PRO 2720/2721	068
4175	795
4506	245, 855
5150	546
5327	878
5371	852
5407	881
5498	890
5555	886
5587	867
5651	868
5715	889
5810	451, 869, 870
5964	839
SPRO–6210	714

label number	entry number
CO 8447	708, 774
9431	561
SPRO–9462	057
STAX 33452	764
CARNABY	
SAD 1/2	643
no. unknown	026, 633
CATSO	
no. unknown	026
CBM (CONTRABAND MUSIC)	
2	173
2 C1/C2	607
X3	045
no. 15	310
77	448
A101	520
A102	521
A103	522
A104	523
A105	524
A106	525
A107	526
A108	808
A109	722
A110	368
B201	275
B202	183
B203	149
B204	607
B205	155
B206	552
B207	527
B208	496
B209	239
B210	575
B211	163
B212	162
B213	459
B215	501
B218	020
B219	021
401	738
402	794
403	628
404	691
1000	215
1001	348
1002	359
1003	335
1005	391
1016	711, 753
1018	528, 531
1022	495
1044	618
1100	193
1101	506
1103	335

label number	entry number	label number	entry number
CBM continued		CONTRABAND MUSIC (see CBM)	
1126	804	COTILLION	
1168	619	104/105	674
1882	739	CRASH	
1900	560	1016	051
2315	487	CUSTOM	
2999	337, 358, 365	RB–2637/	415
3316	025, 196	RB–2638	
3426	656	DARK HORSE	
3519	240, 242	8313	622
3552	355, 356	no. unknown	621
3571	364	DECCA	
3585	397, 417, 418, 553,	31382	416, 865
	554, 599	DECCAGONE	
3587	638	1100	266, 267
3620	261	1101	478, 479
3624	262	1102	404, 405
3626	391, 396	1103	330, 331
3640	516	1104	409, 410
3640/3641	184	1105	179, 180
3641	517	1106	140, 141
3665	703	1108	055, 056
3670	450	DEMO DISC	
3687	384, 519	L–1389	548
3688	353, 446	DE WEINTRAUB	
3711	693	426	216
3795	193, 379, 536, 604	DITTOLINO DISCS	
3795 C1/3571B	078, 535	0001	025, 222
3813	499	no. unknown	230, 287, 318
3906	154	EAGLE	
3907	002, 556	1832	251
3922	151, 529	EMI–ODEON	
3923	152	27 408–4	888
4020	161	EPIC	
4022C/3665A	168	361	875
4162	371, 377	ESR	
4178	033	no. unknown	018
4178/Instant	369	EVA–TONE	
Analysis 1038		10207521 A&B	510
4181	546	12877 A&B	511
4182	542	1123772 A&B	512
4184	644	128781	513
4228	220	117801	514
4242	659	EXCLUSIVE BEATLES INTERVIEW	
4438	275	66x53A/66x53B	210
4450	628	610x11	209
5020	466	FAIRWAY	
5030	061, 255, 458	526	024
5040	665, 667, 673	FIGA	
7879	634	no. unknown	341
no. unknown	143, 164, 165, 167,	FL	
	175, 315, 321, 460,	1178	249
	465, 530, 633, 682	FP	
CIRCUIT		72196–1	857
4438	189, 190	FRENIA	
4450	053	no. unknown	617
CLUB			
no. 3	390		

label number	entry number
KO continued	
402	463
404	464
405	466, 763
408	025
KUM BACK	
no. 1	312
KUSTOM RECORDS	
002	262, 427, 488
003	307
KYA	
69A/69B	669
LA SOOT RECORDS	
346	202
LEE ALAN PRESENTS	
no. unknown	027
LEMON	
123	226
143	032
510A	357
LIVE RECORDS	
101	319
LL	
10 A/B	747
LONDON	
82007	853
LYN	
996	502
MAK	
S 1/2	211
5 S 1/2	313
MARC	
75112	366
76057	598
no. unknown	232, 498, 782, 783
MBRF	
55551	182, 848
MELVIN	
MM001	110
MM02	570
MM03	810
MM05	205
MM06	572
MM08	115
MM09	658
MS10	819
MM13	813
MMEP 001	592
MERCURY	
MK 2--121	577
MGM	
4215	844
12312	866
MICHAEL & ALLISON	
HH 1/2	412
no. unknown	230

label number	entry number
MILO (see also TOBE--MILO)	
5Q 1/2	076
10Q 3/4	067, 077
MOTD	
1269	681
MUSHROOM	
4	335, 662, 697
12	376
13	412
no. unknown	288
N	
2027	039
NAPOLEON	
11044	017, 139, 426
NEWSOUND	
909	537
NW	
8 AR 8--69	423
ODD--FOUR--A/ODD--FIVE--B	
no. unknown	058
OLDIES 45	
149	198, 849
150	871
151	863
152	882
ORFEH	
276	302
ORIGINAL ROCK	
1000	114
1001	129
1002	130
1003	131
1004	132
1005	133
1006	134
1007	135
1008	637
1009	677
1010	678
1011	679
1012	759
1013	791
1014	828
1015	829
PARLOPHONE	
31506	063, 064
PAV	
1	802
PBR	
7005/6	109
PHOENIX	
44784	253
PHONYGRAF	
1114	650
1115	207
no. unknown	688

label number	entry number	label number	entry number
PIG'S EYE		007	664
no. 1	080, 432	ROLLING THUNDER RECORDS	
PINE TREE RECORDS		695	649
S2131/2132	233	RP	
2531/2532	489	no. 23	240
PR		RR	
100	389	360	213
PRO		725	462
909	153	726	463
1234	771	1001	463
PRODUCTION		1002	462
198 CR3926	822	RS	
PYE		2597	481
106	268	RTS	
206	480	A/B	890
306	332	RUT	
406	406	546	011
QUAYE/TRIDENT		547	472
3419	675	RUTHLESS RHYMES	
RADIO PULSEBEAT NEWS		LMW–281F	225
NO. 2	840	no. unknown	482, 569, 653
1001/1002	851	RYDE	
RAM		5226	716
101	766	SAVAGE	
102	730	69	874
103	707	71	845
104	761	SEAN MARK	
105	768	HAR 170	686
106	769	SFF/SOK	
107	792	21	292
108	720	SHALOM	
109	740	3316C/3316D	607
110	717	3688	352, 354
111	780	3795/8430	284
112	816	3906/3907	155
113	793	4178A/3688A	304
114	805	4228/3687	219
115	803	4598	724
RECORD PROMOTIONS		8410	275
ATRBH TVP	594	8420	628
9--16		SHARE	
REIGN		6699	631
001	473	SHEA	
RING		S–2531	248
701	834	SILVER GREATEST RECORDS	
702	827	LB1	326, 380
703	826	SINGER ORIGINAL DOUBLE DISC	
704	825	(SODD)	
705	831	005	640, 646
706	820	SLIPPED DISC	
707	833	979	697, 715
708	824	SMILIN' EARS	
709	823	2--7700	092, 494
710	818	7701	188
RIVERBREEZE DISCS		7702	574
no. unknown	038	7704	089, 091
RL			

label number	entry number	label number	entry number
009	476	24	039
SPEED RECORDS		79	296
3001	408	104	174
STONED		111	231
3	663	115	286, 349
SUNSHINE MUSIC		118	237
501--4	250	S–201	361
SUTRA		D–207	445
6667	440	S–208	029
SWAN		D–211	580
4152	490, 876, 877	501	319
4182	301	513	606
4197	291	517	693
no. unknown	309	519	442
SXTT		543	396, 504
979	263	0002	754, 760
THE AMAZING KORNYPHONE RECORD		1016	712
LABEL (TAKRL, TKBWM, TWM)		1018	152
Λ/B/C/D Bozo 1	549	1383	688
1373	645	1401	777
1374	207	1702	464
1803	668	1704	296, 335
1805	749	1800	319
1806	781	1801	231
1807	726	1834	693
1900	080, 432	1852	462
1922	387	1882	738
1969	036	1892	237, 504
1985	081, 583	1893	237
1986	082, 584	5101	319
1987	083, 585	7508	444
1988	084, 586	8205/6	718, 733, 802
1989	085, 587	70417/70418	361
1995	086, 588	70418	296, 348
1998	087, 589	71007	062, 296, 348
2805	742, 806	71012	319
2807	719	71015	174
2950	254	71024	231
TOBE--MILO (see also MILO)		71026	462
4Q 1/2	060	71032	606
4Q 3/4	648, 695, 789	71046	693
4Q 5/6	713	71048	442
4Q 7/10	090	71049	443
4Q 11/12	107	71065	336
4Q 13/14	680	71068	237, 412, 591
5Q 1/2	338	71076	396, 504
5Q 3	005	72012	580
10Q 1/2	144	73001	462
TOLLIE		73002	463
EP1–8091	551	73018	738
9001	576, 847, 883	73030	043
9008	864	73032	464
TORONTO RECORDS		no. unknown	148, 212, 246, 265,
23	243		272, 287, 382
TRADEMARK OF QUALITY (TMOQ)		TV	
19	348	8467	136

label number	entry number
ZAKATECAS	
ST 57 633XV	042
ZAPPLE	
999	337, 365
3357	885
ZE ANONYM PLATTENSPIELER (ZAP)	
1900	433
7853	422
7857	156, 475
7861	567
7864	035, 579
7866	419
7869	383
7870	372, 413, 565
7872	034
7873	468
7875	748
7876	809
7878	773
7879	626
7887	760
ZTSC	
97436/7	461

Topical Index

8. *Hallelujah I Love Her So*
9. *Hippy Hippy Shake*
10. *I Remember You*
11. *I Saw Her Standing There*
12. *Kansas City*
13. *Lend Me Your Comb*
14. *Little Queenie*
15. *Long Tall Sally*
16. *Matchbox*
17. *Mr. Moonlight*
18. *Red Sails In The Sunset*
19. *Reminiscing*
20. *Roll Over Beethoven*
21. *Shimmy Shake*
22. *Sweet Little Sixteen*
23. *Talkin' 'Bout You*
24. *To Know Her Is To Love Her*
25. *Twist And Shout*
26. *Your Feets Too Big*
114, 115, 129, 133, 135, 508

CONCERT: TOP TEN CLUB, LONDON
8–63
1. *Long Tall Sally*
260, 261, 262, 263

CONCERT: ROYAL COMMAND VARIETY
SHOW, PRINCE OF WALES THEATRE
11–4–63
Recorded by the BBC and broadcast 11–
10–63.
1. *From Me To You*
2. *She Loves You*
3. *Till There Was You*
4. *Twist And Shout*
054, 055, 056, 247

CONCERT: ARDWICK APOLLO,
MANCHESTER, ENGLAND
11–20–63
Filmed by Pathe British News and shown
in movie houses. Released 12–22–63, the
film ran about 8½ minutes.
1. *She Loves You*
2. *Twist And Shout*
003, 075, 334, 470

CONCERT: CHRISTMAS SHOW AT
LIVERPOOL EMPIRE 12–22–63
1. *All My Loving*
2. *Boys*
3. *From Me To You*
4. *I Saw Her Standing There*
5. *I Wanna Be Your Man*
6. *I Want To Hold Your Hand*
7. *Money*
8. *Roll Over Beethoven*
9. *She Loves You*

10. *This Boy*
11. *Till There Was You*
12. *Twist And Shout*
058, 612

CONCERT: WASHINGTON, D.C.
COLOSSEUM 2–11–64
Part of this concert was filmed and
shown on CBS–TV. The songs recorded
were *Till There Was You* and *I Want
To Hold Your Hand*.
1. *All My Loving*
2. *From Me To You*
3. *I Saw Her Standing There*
4. *I Wanna Be Your Man*
5. *I Want To Hold Your Hand*
6. *Please Please Me*
7. *Roll Over Beethoven*
8. *She Loves You*
9. *This Boy*
10. *Till There Was You*
078, 082, 193, 194, 213, 214, 223, 362,
379, 401, 434, 491, 535, 536, 566, 567,
568, 584, 604

CONCERT: KB HALL, COPENHAGEN,
DENMARK 6–4–64
Jimmy Nicol replaced Ringo on drums
at this concert.
1. *All My Loving*
2. *Can't Buy Me Love*
3. *I Saw Her Standing There*
4. *I Want To Hold Your Hand*
5. *Roll Over Beethoven*
6. *She Loves You*
7. *This Boy*
8. *Till There Was You*
9. *Twist And Shout*
071, 115, 178, 305

CONCERT: FESTIVAL HALL, MEL–
BOURNE, AUSTRALIA 6–16–64
Ringo returned from his illness for this
concert. Some records contain an
announcement of this.
1. *All My Loving*
2. *Can't Buy Me Love*
3. *I Saw Her Standing There*
4. *Long Tall Sally*
5. *Roll Over Beethoven*
6. *She Loves You*
7. *This Boy*
8. *Till There Was You*
9. *You Can't Do That*
034, 150, 362, 371, 401, 402, 403, 434,
468, 476, 523

CONCERT: EMPIRE STADIUM, VAN--
COUVER, BRITISH COLUMBIA,
CANADA 8--22--64
1. *A Hard Day's Night*
2. *All My Loving*
3. *Boys*
4. *Can't Buy Me Love*
5. *If I Fell*
6. *I Want To Hold Your Hand*
7. *Long Tall Sally*
8. *Roll Over Beethoven*
9. *She Loves You*
10. *Things We Said Today*
11. *Twist And Shout*
12. *You Can't Do That*
040, 147, 377, 378, 403, 523, 580, 581,
582

CONCERT: HOLLYWOOD BOWL, LOS
ANGELES, CALIFORNIA 8--23--64
This concert was recorded by Capitol
for possible release. Several cuts (2, 3,
7–10) were later released on the album
**THE BEATLES AT THE HOLLYWOOD
BOWL.**
1. *A Hard Day's Night*
2. *All My Loving*
3. *Boys*
4. *Can't Buy Me Love*
5. *If I Fell*
6. *I Want To Hold Your Hand*
7. *Long Tall Sally*
8. *Roll Over Beethoven*
9. *She Loves You*
10. *Things We Said Today*
11. *Twist And Shout*
12. *You Can't Do That*
017, 029, 032, 033, 035, 036, 074, 079,
082, 085, 087, 115, 139, 221, 244, 284,
285, 286, 287, 288, 318, 336, 341, 342,
343, 344, 345, 347, 349, 350, 360, 372,
377, 378, 411, 413, 422, 426, 427, 428,
454, 476, 484, 485, 486, 488, 489, 507,
520, 555, 562, 565, 566, 567, 579, 584,
587, 589, 601

CONCERT: FOREST HILLS TENNIS
STADIUM, NEW YORK 8--29--64
Concert was taped and later broadcast
over station WBOX. Most of the bootlegs
are from that broadcast and not the actual
concert.
1. *A Hard Day's Night*
2. *All My Loving*
3. *Boys*
4. *Can't Buy Me Love*
5. *If I Fell*
6. *I Want To Hold Your Hand*

7. *Long Tall Sally*
8. *Roll Over Beethoven*
9. *She Loves You*
10. *Things We Said Today*
11. *Twist And Shout*
12. *You Can't Do That*
218, 219, 220, 525

CONCERT: WHISKEY FLAT
The correct history of this concert(s)
may be lost forever. Different albums
will list the source as Hollywood Bowl
(8--23--64), Atlantic City (8--30--64) or
Philadelphia (9--2--64). The exact source
may be only one of these concerts, or a
combination of all three.
1. *A Hard Day's Night*
2. *All My Loving*
3. *Boys*
4. *Can't Buy Me Love*
5. *If I Fell*
6. *I Want To Hold Your Hand*
7. *Long Tall Sally*
8. *Roll Over Beethoven*
9. *She Loves You*
10. *Things We Said Today*
11. *Twist And Shout*
12. *You Can't Do That*
010, 049, 062, 296, 348, 355, 356,
357, 361, 368

CONCERT: PARIS SPORTS PALACE
6--20--65
Parts of this concert were recorded and
later broadcast on French TV (ORTF).
1. *A Hard Day's Night*
2. *Baby's In Black*
3. *Can't Buy Me Love*
4. *Everybody's Trying To Be My
Baby*
5. *I Feel Fine*
6. *I'm A Loser*
7. *I Wanna Be Your Man*
8. *Long Tall Sally*
9. *Rock And Roll Music*
10. *She's A Woman*
11. *Ticket To Ride*
12. *Twist And Shout*
043, 045, 176, 303, 304, 327, 352, 353,
354, 369, 373, 446, 447, 448, 449, 491,
506, 522

CONCERT: SHEA STADIUM 8--15--65
This concert was filmed for TV broadcast
and was first shown in England on May 1,
1966. Not all the songs actually performed
made the final film.
1. *Act Naturally*

2. *A Hard Day's Night*
3. *Baby's In Black*
4. *Can't Buy Me Love*
5. *Dizzy Miss Lizzie*
6. *Help*
7. *I Feel Fine*
8. *I'm Down*
9. *Ticket To Ride*
10. *Twist And Shout*

022, 031, 082, 084, 087, 154, 319, 320, 345, 346, 381, 477, 482, 483, 487, 584, 586, 589, 681

CONCERT: SHEA STADIUM 8--16--65
1. *A Hard Day's Night*
2. *Baby's In Black*
3. *Can't Buy Me Love*
4. *Dizzy Miss Lizzie*
5. *Everybody's Trying To Be My Baby*
6. *Help*
7. *I Feel Fine*
8. *I'm Down*
9. *I Wanna Be Your Man*
10. *She's A Woman*
11. *Ticket To Ride*
12. *Twist And Shout*

073, 181, 201, 333

CONCERT: SAM HOUSTON COLISEUM, HOUSTON, TEXAS 8-19-65
Both the afternoon and evening shows were recorded and appear on bootlegs.
1. *A Hard Day's Night*
2. *Baby's In Black*
3. *Can't Buy Me Love*
4. *Dizzy Miss Lizzie*
5. *Everybody's Trying To Be My Baby*
6. *Help*
7. *I Feel Fine*
8. *I'm Down*
9. *I Wanna Be Your Man*
10. *She's A Woman*
11. *Ticket To Ride*
12. *Twist And Shout*

067, 076, 077, 144, 338, 339

CONCERT: METROPOLITAN STADIUM, MINNEAPOLIS, MINNESOTA 8-21-65
Thus far only cuts 5, 10, and 12 have appeared on any bootlegs.
1. *A Hard Day's Night*
2. *Baby's In Black*
3. *Can't Buy Me Love*
4. *Dizzy Miss Lizzie*
5. *Everybody's Trying To Be My Baby*

6. *Help*
7. *I Feel Fine*
8. *I Wanna Be Your Man*
9. *I'm Down*
10. *She's A Woman*
11. *Ticket To Ride*
12. *Twist And Shout*

592

CONCERT: CIRCUS KRONE, MUNICH, GERMANY 6-24--66
There were two shows, one of which was recorded for German TV.
1. *Baby's In Black*
2. *Day Tripper*
3. *I Feel Fine*
4. *If I Needed Someone*
5. *I'm Down*
6. *I Wanna Be Your Man*
7. *Nowhere Man*
8. *Paperback Writer*
9. *She's A Woman*
10. *Rock And Roll Music*
11. *Yesterday*

208, 359, 364, 366, 372, 413, 429, 430, 491, 565, 566, 567

CONCERT: BUDOKAN HALL, TOKYO, JAPAN 7-2-66
There were two Japanese concerts, one on July 1 and this one on the 2nd. The songs were the same for both concerts and apparently only three bootlegs exist for the July 1 concert (375, 559, 598) so they are all listed together here.
1. *Baby's In Black*
2. *Day Tripper*
3. *I Feel Fine*
4. *If I Needed Someone*
5. *I'm Down*
6. *I Wanna Be Your Man*
7. *Nowhere Man*
8. *Paperback Writer*
9. *Rock And Roll Music*
10. *She's A Woman*
11. *Yesterday*

035, 036, 080, 083, 084, 085, 087, 089, 090, 091, 111, 144, 150, 176, 216, 217, 221, 244, 252, 327, 351, 360, 375, 376, 411, 422, 431, 432, 433, 454, 476, 507, 549, 555, 557, 559, 560, 579, 585, 586, 587, 589, 598, 601

CONCERT: MUNICIPAL STADIUM, CLEVELAND, OHIO 8-14--66
Thus far only one song from this concert, *I Feel Fine,* has appeared on any bootlegs.
1. *Baby's In Black*
2. *Day Tripper*

3. *I Feel Fine*
4. *If I Needed Someone*
5. *I'm Down*
6. *I Wanna Be Your Man*
7. *Nowhere Man*
8. *Paperback Writer*
9. *Rock And Roll Music*
10. *She's A Woman*
11. *Yesterday*
138, 590

CONCERT: CANDLESTICK PARK, SAN
FRANCISCO, CALIFORNIA
8--29--66
The group's last U.S. concert as the
Beatles.
1. *Baby's In Black*
2. *Day Tripper*
3. *I Feel Fine*
4. *If I Needed Someone*
5. *I'm Down*
6. *I Wanna Be Your Man*
7. *Nowhere Man*
8. *Paperback Writer*
9. *Rock And Roll Music*
10. *She's A Woman*
11. *Yesterday*
340

CONCERT: VARSITY STADIUM,
TORONTO, CANADA. ROCK AND
PEACE FESTIVAL 9-13--69 (J)
John, Yoko and the Plastic Ono Band
featuring Eric Clapton, Klaus Voorman
and Alan White.
1. *Blue Suede Shoes*
2. *Money*
3. *Dizzy Miss Lizzy*
4. *Cold Turkey*
5. *Give Peace A Chance*
6. *Don't Worry Kyoko*
7. *John John (Let's Hope For
Peace)*
103,131

CONCERT: FALKONER THEATRE,
COPENHAGEN, DENMARK
December 10--12, 1969 (G)
Recorded during a Delaney & Bonnie &
Friends tour. The "Friends" included
George Harrison on guitar. Also in the
group were Eric Clapton, Dave Mason,
Carl Radle, John Gordon, Tex Johnson,
Bobby Whitlock, Jim Price, Bobby Keys
and Rita Coolidge.
1. *Coming Home*
2. *I Don't Want To Discuss It*
3. *Medley:*
Long Tall Sally

Jenny Jenny
The Girl Can't Help It
Tutti Frutti
4. *Only You Know And I Know*
5. *Poor Elijah – Tribute To
Johnson*
6. *That's What My Man Is For*
7. *Things Get Better*
8. *Where There's A Will There's
A Way*
628

CONCERT: BANGLA DESH, MADISON
SQUARE GARDEN, NEW YORK
8-1--71 (G)
Appearing with George were Eric Clapton,
Bob Dylan, Ringo Starr, Billy Preston,
Leon Russell and a host of other rock
stars including the members of Bad--
finger. There was an afternoon show
and an evening show, the later filmed
for theatrical release.
1. *Awaiting On You All*
2. *Bangla Desh*
3. *Bangla Dhun*
4. *Beware Of Darkness*
5. *Blowin' In The Wind*
6. *Dadra Tal*
7. *A Hard Rain's Gonna Fall*
8. *Here Comes The Sun*
9. *It Don't Come Easy*
10. *It Takes A Lot To Laugh*
11. *Jumpin' Jack Flash*
12. *Just Like A Woman*
13. *Mr. Tambourine Man*
14. *My Sweet Lord*
15. *Sitar And Sarod Duet*
16. *Something*
17. *Teentall*
18. *That's The Way God Planned It*
19. *Wah Wah*
20. *While My Guitar Gently Weeps*
21. *Youngblood*
613, 614, 615, 616, 620, 631, 633, 638,
641, 643

CONCERT: JOHN SINCLAIR BENEFIT,
ANN ARBOR, MICHIGAN 12--18--71
(J)
John and Yoko with no less than Jerry
Rubin on bongos.
1. *Attica State*
2. *John Sinclair*
3. *Luck Of The Irish*
4. *Sisters Oh Sisters*
168, 654, 655, 659, 660, 682, 683, 684,
685, 701, 702, 703, 704, 705, 706

CONCERT: YORK UNIVERSITY,

301

ENGLAND 2–10–72 (P)
Wings first, unannounced tour. They
played as the support band for Brinsley
Schwarz and used that band's equipment.
1. *Bip Bop*
2. *Blue Moon Of Kentucky*
3. *Give Ireland Back To The Irish*
4. *Help Me Darling*
5. *Henry's Blues*
6. *Long Tall Sally*
7. *Lucille*
8. *The Mess*
9. *My Love*
10. *Say Darling*
11. *Seaside Woman*
12. *Smile Away*
13. *Some People Never Know*
14. *Wild Life*
712

CONCERT: HANOVER, GERMANY
8–16–72 (P)
1. *Best Friends*
2. *Bip Bop*
3. *Blue Moon Of Kentucky*
4. *1882*
5. *Give Ireland Back To The Irish*
6. *Henry's Blues*
7. *Hi Hi Hi*
8. *I'm Your Singer*
9. *I Would Only Smile*
10. *Long Tall Sally*
11. *Mary Had A Little Lamb*
12. *Maybe I'm Amazed*
13. *The Mess*
14. *My Love*
15. *Say You Don't Mind*
16. *Seaside Woman*
17. *Smile Away*
18. *Soilie*
19. *Wild Life*
The following songs may also have been
performed:
1. *Green Acorn*
2. *Lucille*
3. *Say Darling*
4. *Some People Never Know*
5. *Take Me For A Ride Momma*
721, 755, 765, 775

CONCERT: CINE ROMA, ANTWERP,
BELGIUM 8–22–72 (P)
1. *Best Friends*
2. *Bip Bop*
3. *Blue Moon Of Kentucky*
4. *1882*
5. *Give Ireland Back To The Irish*
6. *Henry's Blues*

7. *Hi Hi Hi*
8. *I'm Your Singer*
9. *I Would Only Smile*
10. *Long Tall Sally*
11. *Mary Had A Little Lamb*
12. *Maybe I'm Amazed*
13. *The Mess*
14. *My Love*
15. *Say You Don't Mind*
16. *Seaside Woman*
17. *Smile Away*
18. *Soilie*
19. *Wild Life*
The following songs may also have been
performed:
1. *Green Acorn*
2. *Lucille*
3. *Say Darling*
4. *Some People Never Know*
5. *Take Me For A Ride Momma*
709, 710, 711, 753, 799, 804

CONCERT: ONE TO ONE, MADISON
SQUARE GARDEN, NEW YORK
8–30–72 (J)
These two shows, afternoon and evening,
were performed for the benefit of the
Willowbrook School for Children. Be--
sides John and Yoko, Roberta Flack, Sha
Na Na and Stevie Wonder also performed.
1. *Born In A Prison*
2. *Cold Turkey*
3. *Come Together*
4. *Give Peace A Chance*
5. *Hound Dog*
6. *Imagine*
7. *Instant Karma*
8. *Midsummer New York City*
9. *Mother*
10. *Sisters Oh Sisters*
11. *We're All Water*
12. *Woman Is The Nigger Of The
World*
Some sources also list the following twc
songs as having been performed:
1. *It's So Hard*
2. *Move On Fast*
654, 655, 658, 665, 666, 667, 668, 673,
682, 683, 684, 685, 686

CONCERT: LEEDS UNIVERSITY
5–19–73 (P)
1. *Big Barn Red*
2. *C Moon*
3. *Go Now*
4. *Little Woman Love*
5. *Live And Let Die*
6. *Long Tall Sally*

7. *Maybe I'm Amazed*
8. *The Mess*
9. *My Love*
10. *Say You Don't Mind*
11. *Seaside Woman*
12. *Soilie*
13. *When The Night*
14. *Wildlife*
745, 746

CONCERT: ODEON, EDINBURGH,
   SCOTLAND 5–23–73 (P)
There were two shows performed here.
1. *Big Barn Red*
2. *C Moon*
3. *Go Now*
4. *Little Woman Love*
5. *Live And Let Die*
6. *Long Tall Sally*
7. *Maybe I'm Amazed*
8. *The Mess*
9. *My Love*
10. *Say You Don't Mind*
11. *Seaside Woman*
12. *Soilie*
13. *When The Night*
14. *Wildlife*
737, 756, 785, 786, 787

CONCERT: PACIFIC COLISEUM,
   VANCOUVER, BRITISH COLUMBIA,
   CANADA 11–2–74 (G)
This was the first performance of the
1974 U.S. tour. Numbers 9 and 10 were
done by Billy Preston and 14 by Tom
Scott. Ravi Shankar also performed a
spot during the concert.
1. *All Right As A Lumberjack*
2. *Dark Horse*
3. *For You Blue*
4. *Give Me Love*
5. *Hari's On Tour*
6. *In My Life*
7. *Maya Love*
8. *My Sweet Lord*
9. *Nothing From Nothing*
10. *Outta Space*
11. *Something*
12. *Soundstage '74*
13. *Sue Me Sue You Blues*
14. *Tomcat*
15. *What Is Life*
16. *While My Guitar Gently Weeps*
635, 640, 646, 651

CONCERT: SEATTLE CENTER
   COLISEUM, SEATTLE, WASHING–
   TON 11–4–74 (G)
For complete song listing, see Vancouver

11–2–74. All songs are the same.
635

CONCERT: FORT WORTH, TEXAS
   11–22–74 (G)
For complete song listing see Vancouver
11–2–74. All songs are the same.
624, 625, 629, 630

CONCERT: MADISON SQUARE
   GARDEN, NEW YORK 11–26–74 (J)
John made an unannounced visit to the
stage during an Elton John performance.
They sang three songs together. *I Saw
Her Standing There* was released as the
flip to Elton's *Philadelphia Freedom*
(MCA 40364) in early 1975.
1. *Whatever Gets You Through The Night*
2. *Lucy In The Sky With Diamonds*
3. *I Saw Her Standing There*
652, 653, 686

CONCERT: CHICAGO STADIUM,
   CHICAGO, ILLINOIS 11–30–74 (G)
For complete song listing see Vancouver
11–2–74. All songs are the same.
618, 619

CONCERT: LONG BEACH ARENA,
   LONG BEACH, CALIFORNIA
   12–10–74 (G)
For complete song listing see Vancouver
11–2–74. All songs are the same.
627, 639, 642, 650

CONCERT: FREE TRADE HALL,
   MANCHESTER, ENGLAND
   9–12–75 (P)
1. *Band On The Run*
2. *Bluebird*
3. *Call Me Back Again*
4. *C Moon*
5. *Go Now*
6. *Hi Hi Hi*
7. *Jet*
8. *Lady Madonna*
9. *Let Me Roll It*
10. *Letting Go*
11. *Listen To What The Man Said*
12. *Live And Let Die*
13. *Long And Winding Road*
14. *Magneto And Titanium Man*
15. *Maybe I'm Amazed*
16. *Medicine Jar*
17. *My Love*
18. *Picasso's Last Words*
19. *Richard Cory*
20. *Rock Show*
21. *Soilie*

303

22. *Spirits Of Ancient Egypt*
23. *Venus And Mars*
24. *Yesterday*
25. *You Gave Me The Answer*
794

CONCERT: AUSTRALIA 11--75 (P)
Site of this particular concert is unknown,
but it is more than likely either Melbourne
or Sydney.
1. *Band On The Run*
2. *Blackbird*
3. *Bluebird*
4. *Call Me Back Again*
5. *C Moon*
6. *Go Now*
7. *Hi Hi Hi*
8. *I've Just Seen A Face*
9. *Jet*
10. *Lady Madonna*
11. *Let Me Roll It*
12. *Letting Go*
13. *Listen To What The Man Said*
14. *Live And Let Die*
15. *Long And Winding Road*
16. *Maybe I'm Amazed*
17. *Medicine Jar*
18. *Magneto And Titanium Man*
19. *My Love*
20. *Picasso's Last Words*
21. *Richard Cory*
22. *Rock Show*
23. *Soilie*
24. *Spirits Of Ancient Egypt*
25. *Venus And Mars*
26. *Yesterday*
27. *You Gave Me The Answer*
727, 728, 736, 814

CONCERT: HORDEN PAVILLION,
SYDNEY, AUSTRALIA 11--7--75 (P)
For complete song listing see Australia
11--75. All songs performed are the same.
773

CONCERT: MYER MUSIC BOWL, MEL--
BOURNE, AUSTRALIA 11-13--75 (P)
For complete listing see Australia 11--75.
All songs performed are the same.
782, 783

CONCERT: FALKONER THEATRE,
COPENHAGEN, DENMARK
3--21--76 (P)
1. *Band On The Run*
2. *Beware My Love*
3. *Blackbird*
4. *Bluebird*

5. *Call Me Back Again*
6. *Hi Hi Hi*
7. *I've Just Seen A Face*
8. *Jet*
9. *Lady Madonna*
10. *Let 'Em In*
11. *Let Me Roll It*
12. *Letting Go*
13. *Listen To What The Man Said*
14. *Live And Let Die*
15. *Long And Winding Road*
16. *Magneto And Titanium Man*
17. *Maybe I'm Amazed*
18. *Medicine Jar*
19. *My Love*
20. *Picasso's Last Words*
21. *Richard Cory*
22. *Rock Show*
23. *Silly Love Songs*
24. *Soilie*
25. *Spirits Of Ancient Egypt*
26. *Time To Hide*
27. *Venus And Mars*
28. *Yesterday*
29. *You Gave Me The Answer*
718, 719, 733, 735, 754, 777, 802

CONCERT: TARRANT COUNTY CON--
VENTION HALL, FORT WORTH,
TEXAS 5--3--76 (P)
First stop on 1976 U.S. tour.
1. *Band On The Run*
2. *Beware My Love*
3. *Blackbird*
4. *Bluebird*
5. *Call Me Back Again*
6. *Go Now*
7. *Hi Hi Hi*
8. *I've Just Seen A Face*
9. *Jet*
10. *Lady Madonna*
11. *Let 'Em In*
12. *Let Me Roll It*
13. *Letting Go*
14. *Listen To What The Man Said*
15. *Live And Let Die*
16. *Long And Winding Road*
17. *Magneto And Titanium Man*
18. *Maybe I'm Amazed*
19. *Medicine Jar*
20. *My Love*
21. *Picasso's Last Words*
22. *Richard Cory*
23. *Rock Show*
24. *Silly Love Songs*
25. *Soilie*
26. *Spirits Of Ancient Egypt*
27. *Time To Hide*

28. *Venus And Mars*
29. *Yesterday*
30. *You Gave Me The Answer*
723, 724, 729, 762

CONCERT: MAPLE LEAF GARDENS,
TORONTO, CANADA 5–9--76 (P)
For complete song listing see Fort Worth,
Texas, 5--3--76. All songs the same.
750, 760, 790

CONCERT: MARYLAND CAPITOL
CENTRE, LARGO, MARYLAND
5–15–76 (P)
For complete song listing see Fort Worth,
Texas, 5--3--76. All songs the same.
748, 773, 809.

CONCERT: OMNI, ATLANTA, GEORGIA
5--19–76 (P)
For complete song listing see Fort Worth,
Texas, 5--3--76. All songs are the same.
810

CONCERT: BOSTON GARDENS,
BOSTON, MASSACHUSETTS
5--22–76 (P)
For complete song listing see Fort Worth,
Texas, 5--3--76. All songs the same.
814

CONCERT: CHICAGO STADIUM,
CHICAGO, ILLINOIS 6–1 & 2–76 (P)
For complete song listing see Fort Worth,
Texas, 5--3--76. All songs are the same. A
small portion of the song *Chicago* was
also performed here. There were two
concerts on separate days and it is not
certain from which the cuts were taken.
814

CONCERT: KINGDOME, SEATTLE,
WASHINGTON 6–10–76 (P)
For complete song listing see Fort Worth,
Texas 5--3--76. All songs are the same.
A portion of this concert was filmed
and parts were shown on the ABC–TV
show "Goodnight America." Paul and
Linda were also interviewed by Geraldo
Rivera on that show.
729, 730, 741, 762

CONCERT: COW PALACE, SAN FRAN–
CISCO, CALIFORNIA 6–14–76 (P)
For complete song listing see Fort Worth,
Texas, 5--3--76. All songs are the same.
There was also a concert here on 6–13,
but all bootlegs are marked as having
come from the concert on the 14th.

779, 811, 814, 817

CONCERT: SPORTS ARENA, SAN
DIEGO, CALIFORNIA 6–16–76 (P)
For complete song listing see Fort Worth,
Texas, 5--3--76. All songs are the same.
775, 784, 814

CONCERT: LOS ANGELES FORUM, LOS
ANGELES, CALIFORNIA 6–21–76/
6--23–76 (P)
For complete song listing see Fort Worth,
Texas, 5--3--76. All songs are the same.
There was also a third concert here on
6--22, but all bootlegs appear to be only
from the 21st or 23rd dates. During the
concert of the 23rd, Ringo appeared on
stage and gave Paul a bouquet of flowers.
He did not sing or play the drums,
however.
6--21 concert: 742, 798, 800, 806
6--23 concert: 726, 744, 749, 752, 781,
801, 817

CONCERT: ROYAL COURT THEATRE,
LIVERPOOL, ENGLAND 11--25–79
(P)
1. *Again And Again*
2. *Arrow Through Me*
3. *Band On The Run*
4. *Coming Up*
5. *Cook Of The House*
6. *Ev'ry Night*
7. *Fool On The Hill*
8. *Getting Closer*
9. *Go Now*
10. *Goodnight Tonight*
11. *Got To Get You Into My Life*
12. *Hot As Sun*
13. *I've Had Enough*
14. *Let It Be*
15. *Maybe I'm Amazed*
16. *Mull Of Kintyre*
17. *No Words*
18. *Old Siam*
19. *Spin It On*
20. *Twenty Flight Rock*
21. *Wonderful Christmastime*
22. *Yesterday*
747, 757, 791, 792

CONCERT: BRIGHTON, ENGLAND
12--2–79 (P)
For complete song listing see Royal
Court Theatre, Liverpool, 11--25–79.
All songs are the same. Only one song
(*Wonderful Christmastime*) from this
concert has thus far appeared on any

(6--23--76) 812
'76 Tour 729, 762
"Tomorrow Show" (12–5–79) 816
"20/20 Show" (11–1–79) 793
"Weekley Top–30" (10–20–79) 768
"Weekley Top–30" (6–7–80) 717
Miscellaneous 715, 814

INTERVIEWS: RINGO STARR
"Mike Douglas Show" 826
Dave Herman (9–4–77) 825
Ringo On Stage With Paul In Los Angeles
(6–23--76) 812
Ringo with George and Jackie Stewart
514
"Weekly Top–30" (10--27–79) 833
Miscellaneous 457, 513

INTERVIEWS: NON--BEATLES
Tony Barrow on Butcher Cover
499, 500
Richard DiLello 510
Brian Jones (Rolling Stones) 494
Liverpool Accent 280, 283
Peter McCabe 510
Robert Palmer on playing with Paul,
George & Ringo at Eric Clapton's
wedding 059
Joe Pope 510, 511
Billy Preston on meeting Beatles 059
Rolling Stones 494
Jurgen Volmer 510
Allan Williams 395

"LET IT BE" SESSIONS, TWICKENHAM
STUDIOS, LONDON, ENGLAND
EARLY 1969
There were many songs recorded during
these sessions, many were just short bits
of songs. Many have never been released,
even on bootlegs. Different sources do
not seem to agree on the exact cuts in--
cluded on these tapes. There appear to
be about 106 songs that were performed.
These are all listed below. Those with an
asterisk (*) behind them have not as yet
appeared on any bootlegs.
1. Across The Universe
2. All Along The Watchtower*
3. All Shook Up*
4. All Things Must Pass
5. Ba Ba Black Sheep
6. Baby I Don't Care*
7. Back To Commonwealth
8. Bad Boy*
9. Be Bop A Lula
10. Besame Mucho
11. Blowing In The Wind

12. Blue Suede Shoes*
13. Carol*
14. Come On Everybody*
15. Da Doo Run Run*
16. Devil In Her Heart*
17. Dig A Pony
18. Dig It
19. Dizzy Miss Lizzy*
20. Don't Be Cruel*
21. Don't Let Me Down
22. A Fool Like Me
23. For You Blue
24. Get Back
25. Good Golly Miss Molly
26. Good Rockin' Tonight
27. High Heel Sneakers
28. Hi Ho Silver (Yackety Yack)
29. Hippy Hippy Shake*
30. Hitchhike*
31. Hot As Sun*
32. House Of The Rising Sun
33. I Me Mine
34. I Shall Be Released*
35. I Threw It All Away
36. It's Only Make Believe*
37. It's So Easy*
38. I've Got A Feeling
39. Johnny B. Goode*
40. Kansas City
41. Lawdy Miss Clawdy
42. Lend Me Your Comb*
43. Let It Be
44. Little Queenie*
45. Long And Winding Road
46. Lotta Lovin*
47. Love Me Do*
48. Lucille*
49. Maggie Mae
50. Maxwell's Silver Hammer
51. Maybelline*
52. Memphis*
53. Michael Row The Boat Ashore*
54. Midnight Special*
55. Miss Ann
56. Momma You've Been On My Mind
57. Money*
58. Norwegian Wood
59. Nowhere Man*
60. Octopuss's Garden
61. Oh Darling
62. Oh My Soul*
63. One After 909
64. Penina
65. Piano Boogie
66. Piano Theme
67. Piece Of My Heart*
68. Please Please Me*
69. Right String, Wrong Yo Yo*

307

"Let It Be" Sessions continued . . .
70. Rock And Roll Music*
71. Rock Island Line*
72. Roll Over Beethoven*
73. Save The Last Dance For Me
74. Send Me Some Lovin'*
75. Shake, Rattle And Roll
76. Shakin' In The 60's
77. She Came In Through The
    Bathroom Window
78. She Said, She Said*
79. Short Fat Fanny*
80. Singing The Blues*
81. Some Other Guy
82. Somethin' Else*
83. Stairway To Paradise*
84. Stand By Me
85. Sure To Fall*
86. Suzy Parker
87. Sweet Little 16*
88. Tea For Two*
89. Teddy Boy
90. Tennessee
91. Think It Over*
92. Third Man Theme
93. Thirty Days*
94. Three Cool Cats
95. True Love*
96. Turn Around*
97. Twenty Flight Rock*
98. Two Of Us
99. When Irish Eyes Are Smiling*
100. When You Walk
101. White Power/Promenade
102. Whole Lotta Loving*
103. Why Don't We Do It In The Road
104. You Can't Do That*
105. You Really Got A Hold On Me
106. You Win Again

Although some of these titles may not
appear in the song title index of this
book, they may in fact be found on some
bootlegs. They are usually so short that
the bootleggers do not take the time to
list them on the jacket or label.
004, 019, 020, 021, 026, 035, 036, 037,
042, 072, 081, 083, 084, 085, 086, 087,
107, 110, 113, 130, 134, 135, 143, 149,
151, 152, 153, 158, 159, 161, 163, 173,
176, 192, 196, 200, 211, 226, 227, 228,
229, 230, 231, 232, 233, 234, 235, 236,
237, 238, 239, 240, 241, 242, 243, 253,
254, 260, 261, 262, 263, 275, 289, 306,
310, 311, 312, 313, 314, 315, 316, 321,
322, 323, 324, 325, 326, 327, 328, 329,
380, 383, 385, 391, 392, 394, 411, 412,
419, 422, 424, 438, 441, 450, 454, 455,
463, 473, 493, 498, 527, 528, 529, 530,

531, 532, 533, 534, 537, 538, 539, 540,
541, 542, 543, 544, 545, 546, 571, 572,
573, 574, 579, 583, 586, 587, 588, 589,
591, 596, 597, 649, 681

ORIGINAL RECORDINGS
The following bootlegs contain original
recordings by the Beatles as a group or
as solo artists, as well as originals by
other artists. On some albums songs are
described as outtakes, when they may in
fact be originals; these are all correctly
identified here. The original fan club
Christmas records are not indexed here
(see CHRISTMAS RECORDS).
001, 005, 006, 007, 008, 011, 012, 013,
014, 018, 019, 031, 035, 036, 046, 047,
051, 057, 058, 063, 064, 068, 069, 070,
083, 088, 094, 095, 096, 097, 098, 099,
100, 101, 102, 103, 104, 105, 106, 114,
129, 130, 131, 132, 133, 134, 135, 136,
137, 142, 145, 146, 158, 184, 195, 196,
198, 199, 206, 207, 221, 228, 244, 245,
249, 250, 251, 260, 261, 262, 263, 277,
283, 291, 295, 297, 301, 302, 306, 307,
309, 317, 322, 337, 358, 359, 365, 367,
369, 383, 386, 388, 397, 398, 400, 415,
416, 417, 418, 425, 429, 440, 442, 443,
444, 451, 452, 454, 463, 464, 465, 466,
467, 472, 473, 476, 490, 492, 495, 497,
503, 507, 511, 512, 513, 514, 515, 516,
517, 518, 522, 549, 551, 553, 554, 555,
556, 564, 579, 585, 593, 594, 595, 599,
603, 607, 617, 621, 636, 637, 647, 659,
676, 677, 678, 679, 680, 681, 684, 686,
708, 717, 732, 734, 740, 759, 761, 763,
764, 768, 769, 774, 780, 791, 807, 815,
817, 819, 820, 823, 838, 829, 832, 833,
834, 835, 891

OUTTAKES see ALTERNATE TAKES

PICTURE DISCS – SEVEN–INCH
044, 503, 632, 670, 671, 743, 767, 796,
797, 832

PICTURE DISCS – TWELVE–INCH
064, 189, 191, 351, 541, 545

PICTURE SLEEVES: COUNTERFEIT
These are copies of picture sleeves that
were issued with regularly released
records.
716. 838, 839, 846, 847, 850, 852, 861,
867, 868, 870, 872, 877, 878, 881, 886,
889, 890

PICTURE SLEEVES: NEW

308

Listed here are seven–inch 45s and EPs
that were issued strictly as bootlegs and
came with picture sleeves. Some sleeves
are in color, some in black and white.
009. 054, 055. 056, 060, 066, 076, 090,
107, 140, 141, 170, 179, 180, 209, 210,
266, 267, 268, 269, 277, 278, 279, 280,
281, 282, 292, 299, 330, 331, 332, 338,
343, 344, 366, 389, 390, 400, 404, 405,
406, 409, 410, 414, 478, 479, 480, 502,
548, 551, 561, 573, 592, 597, 648, 657,
666, 680, 695, 713, 747, 758, 771, 789,
831

PICTURE SLEEVES: FOR REGULARLY ISSUED RECORDS THAT DID NOT COME WITH SLEEVES

These are bootleg sleeves that were made
for records that originally were issued
without sleeves. In most cases these were
put out by fan clubs in very limited
quantities, usually about 50.
171, 273, 547, 550, 576, 622, 751, 795

RADIO: BBC "LIGHT & POPULAR" AND "STRAMASH" 1962

1. *Crying, Waiting, Hoping*
2. *Devil In Her Heart*
3. *Hippy Hippy Shake*
4. *I Forgot To Remember*
5. *Kansas City*
6. *Memphis*
7. *A Shot Of Rhythm And Blues*
8. *Sure To Fall*
9. *Sweet Little Sixteen*
10. *Too Much Monkey Business*
11. *Youngblood*
115, 572, 612

RADIO: BBC FALL 1962

1. *I'll Be On My Way*
115, 256, 257, 393, 399, 473, 495

RADIO: BBC 11–62

1. *Ain't Nothin' Shakin'*
2. *A Shot Of Rhythm And Blues*
3. *Bound By Love (Honeymoon Song)*
4. *Crying, Waiting, Hoping*
5. *Everyone Wants Someone*
6. *Glad All Over*
7. *I Forgot To Remember (?)*
8. *I Got A Woman*
9. *I Just Don't Understand*
10. *I'm Gonna Sit Right Down And Cry Over You*
11. *Lonesome Tears In My Eyes*
12. *Please Don't Ever Change*

13. *Slow Down*
14. *Sure To Fall*
15. *To Know Her Is To Love Her*
025, 034, 035, 036, 037, 042, 110, 129,
131, 134, 150, 151, 183, 184, 185, 186,
188, 196, 221, 222, 260, 261, 262, 263,
294, 308, 317, 436, 437, 443, 444, 453,
454, 473, 517, 518, 529, 530, 571, 572,
579, 606, 607

RADIO: RADIO LUXEMBOURG 1–18–63

1. *Carol*
2. *Lend Me Your Comb*
114, 115, 131, 150, 170, 294, 436, 437,
450, 453, 468, 473

RADIO: BBC MARCH 1963

1. *Hippy Hippy Shake*
2. *Lucille*
3. *Roll Over Beethoven*
087, 110, 130, 133, 150, 183, 184, 256,
257, 259, 260, 261, 263, 317, 383, 411,
436, 437, 442, 443, 444, 468, 473, 499,
500, 516, 517, 518, 571, 572, 589

RADIO: BBC 1963

1. *Honey Don't* (John on lead vocals)
034, 035, 036, 115, 150, 454, 579

RADIO: BBC "SATURDAY CLUB" 5–25–63

The songs for this broadcast were re-–
corded at a concert in Sheffield City
Hall.
1. *Happy Birthday*
2. *Johnny B. Goode*
3. *Memphis*
4. *You Really Got A Hold On Me*
034, 043, 045, 061, 087, 150, 255, 256,
257, 383, 411, 458, 460, 468, 491, 589

RADIO: BBC "POP GOES THE BEATLES"

"Pop Goes The Beatles" was a series of
15 weekly radio shows featuring the
Beatles. The shows were 30 minutes in
length. They began 6–4–63 and ran
through 9–-10–63.
1. *Pop Goes The Beatles*
061, 256, 257, 453

RADIO: BBC "FROM US TO YOU" 12–-26–63

1. *All My Loving*
2. *From Us To You*
3. *I Wanna Be Your Man*
4. *Roll Over Beethoven*
019, 087, 255, 300, 370, 383, 458, 460,

499, 500, 535, 536, 589, 604

RADIO: BBC "TOP OF THE POPS"
7--8--64
1. *A Hard Day's Night* (with long
   fade)
2. *Interview By Brian Matthews*
3. *Long Tall Sally*
4. *Things We Said Today*
272, 300, 337, 358, 365, 367, 397, 398,
417, 418, 422, 467, 553, 554, 561, 562,
564, 599

RADIO: BBC 1964
1. *Roll Over Beethoven*
2. *Shout*
043, 045, 061

RADIO: TOP OF THE POPS 12--2--65
1. *Day Tripper*
2. *We Can Work It Out*
429, 430

RADIO: LONDON RADIO ONE'S "TOP
GEAR" 10--67
John Lennon with Jimi Hendrix.
1. *Day Tripper*
652, 653, 659, 660, 663, 696

RADIO: "HIT HEARD ROUND THE
WORLD" 9--30--68
1. *Early Beatles Appearances*
2. *Fool On The Hill*
3. *Love Me Do*
4. *Strawberry Fields Forever*
277, 283

RADIO: "HIT HEARD ROUND THE
WORLD" 10--14--68
1. *Beatle Music Montage*
2. *Interview With John Lennon*
3. *Think* (Aretha Franklin)
278, 283

RADIO: "HIT HEARD ROUND THE
WORLD" 11--6--68
1. *Hey Jude And Beatle Talk*
2. *House That Jack Built* (Aretha
   Franklin)
3. *Those Were The Days* (Mary
   Hopkin)
279, 283

RADIO: "HIT HEARD ROUND THE
WORLD" 11--18--68
1. *Apple Label*
2. *I Started A Joke* (Bee Gees)
3. *Liverpool Accent*

4. *Sour Milk Sea* (Jackie
   Lomax)
5. *Thingumybob* (Black Dyke Mills
   Band)
280, 283

RADIO: "HIT HEARD ROUND THE
WORLD" 11--21--68
1. *Angel Of The Morning* (Merrilee
   Rush)
2. *Sour Milk Sea* (Jackie Lomax)
3. *Times Were* (Cats)
281, 283

RADIO: "HIT HEARD ROUND THE
WORLD" 2--3--69
1. *Hey Bulldog*
2. *Yellow Submarine* (LP & music)
282, 283

RADIO: WEEKLY TOP--30 7--21--79
1. *Yesterday*
2. *Interview*
088

RADIO: WEEKLY TOP--30 10--20--79
1. *Uncle Albert*
2. *Interview*
768

RADIO: WEEKLY TOP--30 10--27--79
1. *Photograph*
2. *Interview*
833

RADIO: WEEKLY TOP--30 11--3--79
1. *Imagine*
2. *Interview*
676

RADIO: WEEKLY TOP--30 11--10--79
1. *My Sweet Lord*
2. *Interview*
636

RADIO: WEEKLY TOP--30 4--19--80
1. *Jet*
2. *Interview*
740

RADIO: WEEKLY TOP--30 5--17--80
1. *Long And Winding Road*
2. *My Sweet Lord*
386

RADIO: WEEKLY TOP--30 6--7--80
1. *Coming Up*
2. *Interview*

717

SOUNDTRACK: "A HARD DAY'S NIGHT"
Recorded at EMI Abbey Road Studios from 3-2-64 through 4-27-64.
1. *A Hard Day's Night*
2. *All My Loving*
3. *And I Love Her*
4. *Can't Buy Me Love*
5. *Don't Bother Me*
6. *If I Fell*
7. *I'll Cry Instead*
8. *I'm Happy Just To Dance With You*
9. *I Should Have Known Better*
10. *I Wanna Be Your Man*
11. *She Loves You*
12. *Tell Me Why*
13. *This Boy*
007, 008, 019, 037, 061, 152, 165, 177, 255, 258, 458, 460, 527, 528, 531, 532, 534

SOUNDTRACK: "HELP"
Recorded February through May of 1965
1. *Another Girl*
2. *Help*
3. *I Need You*
4. *The Night Before*
5. *She's A Woman*
6. *Ticket To Ride*
7. *You're Gonna Lose That Girl*
8. *You've Got To Hide Your Love Away*
035, 036, 166, 270, 271, 454, 572, 579

SOUNDTRACK: "MAGICAL MYSTERY TOUR"
Recorded September and October 1967. Song 2 is by the Bonzo Dog Band, and 7 and 10 are by Shirley Collins.
1. *Blue Jay Way*
2. *Death Cab For Cutie*
3. *Flying*
4. *Fool On The Hill*
5. *Hello Goodbye*
6. *I Am The Walrus*
7. *Jessie's Dream*
8. *Magical Mystery Tour*
9. *Medley:*
   Tu Tu Tutsy Goodbye
   Happy Wanderer
   When Irish Eyes Are Smiling
   Never On Sunday
10. *Shirley's Wild Accordian*
11. *Yesterday*
12. *Your Mother Should Know*
115, 167, 393, 499, 500, 512

SOUNDTRACK: "YELLOW SUBMARINE"
Recorded late 1967 into early 1968.
1. *A Day In The Life*
2. *All Together Now*
3. *All You Need Is Love*
4. *Baby You're A Rich Man*
5. *Eleanor Rigby*
6. *It's All Too Much*
7. *It's Only A Northern Song*
8. *Lucy In The Sky With Diamonds*
9. *Nowhere Man*
10. *Penny Lane*
11. *Sgt. Pepper*
12. *When I'm Sixty-Four*
13. *With A Little Help From My Friends*
14. *Within You Without You*
15. *Yellow Submarine*
115, 164, 511, 609, 610

SOUNDTRACK: "SCOUSE THE MOUSE" (R)
Ringo does the voice of Scouse the Mouse in this animated film for British TV. He appears only on the following cuts: 3, 5, 6, 7, 9, 10, 11, 15.
1. *America, A Mouse's Dream*
2. *Ask Lovey*
3. *Boat Ride*
4. *Caterwaul*
5. *I Know A Place*
6. *Living In A Pet Shop*
7. *A Mouse Like Me*
8. *Passenger*
9. *Running Free*
10. *Scouse's Dream*
11. *Scouse The Mouse*
12. *Scousey*
13. *Sing A Song For Tragopan*
14. *Snow Up Your Nose For Christmas*
15. *S.O.S.*
514, 819, 830

SOUNDTRACK: "ROCK AND ROLL HIGH SCHOOL" (P)
Neither McCartney nor Wings are seen in the film, but the song appears twice. The song was not released on the soundtrack of the film and has never been released commercially in any form by Paul.
1. *Did We Meet Somewhere Before*
720

TV: "PEOPLE AND PLACES"
Recorded at the Cavern Club (10-13-62) by Granada TV. The show aired 11-7-62. There is some difference of opinion by the experts on these dates.
1. *Some Other Guy*

311

043, 045, 095, 150, 188, 256, 257, 468, 473, 491, 499, 500, 571

TV: "SCENE AT 6:30" 8–19–63
Shown on Granada TV.
1. *I Want To Hold Your Hand*
2. *This Boy*
3. *Twist And Shout*
061, 255, 458, 460

TV: "SUNDAY NIGHT AT THE LONDON
    PALLADIUM" 10–13–63
This was the Beatles first major TV
appearance. It was broadcast live by AT
1. *All My Loving*
2. *I Want To Hold Your Hand*
3. *Money*
4. *This Boy*
5. *Twist And Shout*
003, 075, 219, 334, 384, 519, 525

TV: SWEDISH TV SHOW "DROP IN"
Recorded 10–30–63; aired 11–3–63.
1. *From Me To You*
2. *I Saw Her Standing There*
3. *Long Tall Sally*
4. *Money*
5. *She Loves You*
6. *Twist And Shout*
7. *You Really Got A Hold On Me*
001, 002, 037, 151, 155, 260, 261, 263, 284, 370, 509, 520, 529, 530, 535, 536, 556, 604

TV: "SUNDAY NIGHT AT THE LONDON
    PALLADIUM" 1–12–64
1. *I Want To Hold Your Hand*
2. *Please Mr. Postman*
384, 519

TV: "ED SULLIVAN SHOW"
Recorded in New York on 2–7–64, the
show aired 2–9–64.
1. *All My Loving*
2. *She Loves You*
3. *This Boy*
4. *Till There Was You*
001, 002, 175, 205, 370, 462, 491, 495, 497, 555, 556

TV: "ED SULLIVAN SHOW" 2–16–64
Broadcast from the Deauville Hotel in
Miami Beach, Florida. There were 3,400
fans in attendance.
001, 002, 003, 022, 175, 205, 370, 462, 477, 555, 556

TV: "BIG NIGHT OUT"

Recorded at Teddington Studios on
2–23–64 and shown 2–29–64.
1. *All My Loving*
2. *I Wanna Be Your Man*
3. *Please Mr. Postman*
4. *Till There Was You*
084, 384, 519, 586

TV: "AROUND THE BEATLES"
Recorded for Rediffusion TV on April
27 and 28, 1964. The show aired
5–6–64 in England. Portions of the
show were later shown on ABC–TV
in the U.S.
1. *Can't Buy Me Love*
2. *I Wanna Be Your Man*
3. *Long Tall Sally*
4. *Medley:*
   Love Me Do
   Please Please Me
   From Me To You
   She Loves You
   I Want To Hold Your Hand
5. *Roll Over Beethoven*
6. *Shout*
7. *Twist And Shout*
022, 023, 048, 069, 084, 113, 129, 150, 154, 155, 168, 169, 207, 214, 247, 256, 257, 272, 397, 398, 417, 418, 422, 467, 468, 473, 477, 491, 499, 500, 553, 554, 568, 571, 586, 599

TV: "SHINDIG" 1–20–65
Songs were recorded at Granville Theatre
in London 10–9–64. *House Of The Rising
Sun* was not used on the show and has
not appeared on any bootlegs.
1. *Boys*
2. *House Of The Rising Sun*
3. *I'm A Loser*
4. *Kansas City*
078, 150, 169, 193, 208, 359, 364, 379, 393, 399

TV: "BLACKPOOL NIGHT OUT"
Songs were recorded 7–17–65, while the
show aired 8–1–65.
1. *Act Naturally*
2. *Help*
3. *I Do Like To Be By The Seaside*
4. *I Feel Fine*
5. *I'm Down*
6. *Ticket To Ride*
7. *Yesterday*
509

TV: "ED SULLIVAN SHOW"
Taped 8–14–65 before a live audience.

312

The show aired 9–12–65.
1. *Act Naturally*
2. *Help*
3. *I Feel Fine*
4. *I'm Down*
5. *Ticket To Ride*
6. *Yesterday*
039, 073, 181, 201, 224, 333, 391, 392, 450

TV: "TOP OF THE POPS" 12–2–65
1. *Day Tripper*
2. *We Can Work It Out*
429, 430

TV: "TOP OF THE POPS" 6–16–66
Broadcast over BBC on the above date. The same tape was later shown on "Thank Your Lucky Stars" (6–25–66) and on the "Ed Sullivan Show" in August.
1. *Paperback Writer*
2. *Rain*
003, 037, 075, 152, 334, 470, 527, 528, 531, 532, 533, 534

TV: "OUR WORLD" 6–25–67
The Beatles are shown at EMI during a recording session.
1. *All You Need Is Love*
115, 391, 392

TV: "THE CILLA BLACK SHOW"
2–6–68 (R)
Ringo dueting with Cilla.
1. *Act Naturally*
383, 411, 499, 500

TV: "FROST ON SUNDAY"
David Frost show recorded 9–4–68 and aired 9–8–68. An audience of about 300 persons joins the Beatles in singing their song.
1. *Hey Jude*
078, 193, 208, 272, 300, 337, 358, 359, 364, 365, 379, 391, 392, 562, 564

TV: "TOP OF THE POPS" 9–19–68
1. *Revolution*
078, 188, 193, 208, 272, 290, 292, 337, 358, 359, 364, 365, 379, 562, 564

TV: "ROCK AND ROLL CIRCUS" (J)
On December 11, 1968) (some sources say 69), John and Yoko performed at the filming of the Rolling Stones TV show "Rock And Roll Circus." The show never was shown on TV, but John and Yoko's song has shown up in bootleg form.

1. *Yer Blues*
654, 655, 656, 662, 664, 668, 687, 688, 689, 697, 698, 699, 700

TV: "TOP OF THE POPS" 2–12–70 (J)
John and Yoko's back–up band for this performance included Klaus Voorman (bass), Alan White (drums), and Mal Evans (watch).
1. *Instant Karma*
158, 159, 322, 499, 500

TV: "ED SULLIVAN SHOW" 5–17–70 (R)
1. *Sentimental Journey*
495, 497

TV: "MIKE DOUGLAS SHOW" (J)
John and Yoko serve as guest hosts during the week of 2–14/18–72. During the week they perform 12 songs with Elephant's Memory Band backing them. Two songs, *Johnny B. Goode* and *Memphis* are performed with Chuck Berry.
1. *Attica State*
2. *Imagine*
3. *It's So Hard*
4. *Johnny B. Goode*
5. *John Sinclair*
6. *The Luck Of The Irish*
7. *Memphis*
8. *Sakura*
9. *Shake It*
10. *Sisters Oh Sisters*
11. *We're All Water*
12. *Woman Is The Nigger Of The World*
658, 668, 672, 693, 694

TV: "DICK CAVETT SHOW"
5–11–72 (J)
1. *Woman Is The Nigger Of The World*
672, 693

TV: "JERRY LEWIS MUSCULAR DYSTROPHY TELETHON"
9–6–72 (J)
The second song has not appeared on any bootlegs.
1. *Imagine*
2. *Now Or Never*
659, 660

TV: BOREHAM WOODS STUDIOS, LONDON 3–18–73 (P)
Four songs were recorded live which

would later be included in the show "James Paul McCartney" which aired in the U.S. on 4-16-73.
1. *Big Barn Red*
2. *Long Tall Sally*
3. *Maybe I'm Amazed*
4. *The Mess*
168, 169, 569, 731, 732, 738, 739, 758, 770, 775, 778

TV: "JAMES PAUL McCARTNEY" TV SPECIAL 4-16-73 (P)
See also listing for Boreham Woods (3-18-73) for four additional songs that appeared in this show.
1. *Another Day*
2. *C Moon*
3. *Gotta Sing, Gotta Dance*
4. *Hi Hi Hi*
5. *Little Woman Love*
6. *Live And Let Die*
7. *Mary Had A Little Lamb*
8. *Medley:*
   Blackbird
   Bluebird
   Michelle
   Heart Of The Country
9. *My Love*
10. *Oh Woman Oh Why*
11. *Uncle Albert/Admiral Halsey*
12. *Yesterday*
168, 169, 569, 731, 732, 738, 739, 758, 770, 775, 778

TV: "OLD GREY WHISTLE TEST" 4-18-75 (J)
1. *Slippin' And Slidin'*
2. *Stand By Me*
652, 653

TV: "TOMORROW SHOW" 4-28-75 (J)
John and his lawyer, Leon Wildes, with Tom Snyder on NBC-TV's "Tomorrow Show."
661

TV: "SMOTHERS BROTHERS SHOW" 4-28-75 (R)
Song 3 was performed by John Stewart. He was backed by Ringo and the entire cast of the show, including Dick and Tom Smothers, Don Novello, Pat Paulson, Lily Tomlin and Steve Martin. This hasn't appeared on any bootlegs to date.
1. *No No Song*
2. *Snookeroo*
3. *Survival (Can You Hear Me)*
511, 648, 824

TV: "SALUTE TO SIR LEW GRADE" 6-13-75 (J)
1. *Imagine*
2. *Slippin' And Slidin'*
511, 569, 574, 686, 695

TV: "RUTLAND WEEKEND TELEVISION CHRISTMAS SHOW" 12-25-75 (G)
1. *The Pirate Song*
297

TV: SIMPLE LIFE COMMERCIAL (R)
Ringo on Japanese TV plugging leisure suits.
513, 569, 824

TV: "MIDNIGHT SPECIAL" 1975 (P)
Paul and Linda harmonizing with Rod Stewart on a song that Paul had written for Rod.
1. *Mine For Me*
511. 775

TV: ED SULLIVAN MEMORIAL TV SHOW
1. *And The House Came Down When . . .*
144, 574, 648

TV: "SATURDAY NIGHT LIVE" (G)
Seven songs were recorded on 11-16-76, but only two were shown in the final show which aired 11-18-76. Numbers 2, 4-6 are George with Paul Simon. Only 4 and 5 were aired.
1. *Bridge Over Troubled Water*
2. *Bye Bye Love*
3. *Don't Let Me Wait Too Long*
4. *Here Comes The Sun*
5. *Homeward Bound*
6. *Rock Island Line*
7. *Yesterday*
511, 512, 569, 648

TV: "MIKE DOUGLAS SHOW" 4-78 (R)
No songs; Ringo was interviewed about his upcoming TV special.
826

TV: RINGO SPECIAL 4-26-78 (R)
1. *Act Naturally*
2. *Cry* (Johnny Ray)
3. *Hard Times*
4. *Heart On My Sleeve*
5. *Hound Dog* (Elvis)
6. *I Am The Greatest*
7. *It Don't Come Easy*
8. *Johnny B. Goode* (C. Berry)

314

9. *A Man Like Me*
10. *Octopusses Garden*
11. *Only The Lonely* (Roy Orbison)
12. *Peggy Sue* (Buddy Holly)
13. *Whole Lotta Shakin' Goin' On* (Jerry Lee Lewis)
14. *With A Little Help From My Friends*
15. *Yellow Submarine*
16. *You're Sixteen* (Duet with Carrie Fisher)

819, 827, 834

TV: "JERRY LEWIS MUSCULAR DYSTROPHY TELETHON" 9--3–79 (R)
1. *Jumpin' Jack Flash*
2. *Money*
3. *Ringo Talking*
4. *Twist And Shout*
Ringo plays drums only in this super--band made--up of Ringo, Todd Rundgren, Bill Wyman, Doug Kershaw, Dave Mason, Kiki Dee and Joni Harris. Just a small bit of *Twist And Shout* can be heard before Jerry cuts them off.

831

TV: ABC–TV "20/20" 11--1–79 (P)
Paul and Linda interviewed by Geraldo Rivera. Only small bits of songs are included.

793

TV: "TOMORROW SHOW" 12--5--79 (P)
Paul, Linda and Wings members are interviewed by Tom Snyder. Only small bits of their music can be heard.

816

UNRELEASED SINGLES see ALTERNATE TAKES

I Want To Hold Your Hand
& Other Favorites (LP)

Sutton 329 (Entry 1019)

Novelty Records

1000 ALLEN, STEVE & THE GENTLE PLAYERS
Here Comes Sgt. Pepper/Flowers Of Love   Dunhill 4097   1967

This record by comedian, musician and author Steve Allen was produced by jazz
great Bob Thiele.

1001 ALLEN, TINA
John, Paul, George And Ringo   Granite 537   1976

Before being picked up by Granite, this record appeared on the Tara label. The DJ
copies were recorded at 33 1/3 rpm on one side and 45 rpm on the other.

1002-- AMERICAN BEATLES
1005 *She's Mine/Theme Of The American Beatles*   BYP 1001   1964
       It's My Last Night In Town/You're Getting To Me   BYP 101   1964
       Don't Be Unkind/You Did It To Me   Roulette 4550   1964
       School Days/Hey Hey Girl   Roulette 4559   1964

The American Beatles were led by song--writer/producer Bob Yorey. See also
AMERICAN BEETLES.

1006 AMERICAN BEETLES
It's My Last Night In Town/You're Getting To Me   BYP 102   1964

Also released on BYP 101 as by the American Beatles.

1007-- ANGELS
1008 *Little Beatle Boy/Java*   Smash 1885   1964
       HALO TO YOU (LP)   Smash 27048   1964

The Angels were Peggy Santiglia, Phyllis Allbut and her sister Barbara Allbut. In
1964, when they recorded this Beatles' novelty, they were in the declining
days of their popularity. That popularity had peaked in the summer of 1963
when *My Boyfriend's Back* (Smash 1834) was number one in the country.
The group is still together today but the members have changed. *Little
Beatle Boy* was written and produced by the team of Bob Feldman, Jerry
Goldstein and Richard Gottehrer. This team was also responsible for Angie
& The Chicklettes' *Treat Him Tender Maureen*. They also recorded and had
several hits in the 60's under the names Strangeloves and Sheep. *Little
Beatle Boy* also appears on the album **HALO TO YOU**. See number 513
in bootleg section.

1009 ANGIE & THE CHICKLETTES
Treat Him Tender Maureen/Tommy   Apt 25080   1965

This novelty was released in 1965 when Ringo married Maureen Cox. The song was produced by Bob Feldman, Jerry Goldstein and Richard Gottehrer who also wrote and produced *Little Beatle Boy* for the Angels.

1010 ANNIE & THE ORPHANS
My Girl's Been Bitten By The Beatle Bug/   Capitol 5144   1964
A Place Called Happiness

This one was originally released with a picture sleeve.

1011 BABY BUGS
Bingo/Bongo's Bongo Bingo Party   Vee Jay 594   1964

Originally released with a picture sleeve which showed four Beatle–like figures. The sleeve also announced, "It's a take off on you know who."

1012 BADBEATS
One And One Is Two/Tip Of My Tongue   Beatbad 1000   1979

The Badbeats have done new versions of two early Lennon/McCartney songs that were never released by the Beatles. It's being listed as a novelty because of the picture sleeve that came with the record. It shows the Badbeats in an early Beatle–like pose. It's also black and white, like the early Beatle sleeves. The label is a copy of the Capitol orange/yellow swirl label.

1013 BAGELS
I Wanna Hold Your Hair/Yeah, Yeah, Yeah, Yeah   Warner Bros. 5420   1964

1014 BAKER, PENNY & THE PILLOWS
Bring Back The Beatles/Gonna Win Him   Witch 123   1964

Originals came with a picture sleeve.

1015 BALDWIN, CLIVE
Now It's Paul McCartney, Stevie Wonder, Alice   Mercury 73680   1975
Cooper, Elton John/The Disco Rag

Written by I. Levine and L. Russell Brown who have been responsible for many pop hits over the years.

1016 BAND OF THE IRISH GUARDS
Marching With The Beatles   Tower 5046   1965

The Beatles' music done by bagpipes.

1017-- BARCLAY JAMES HARVEST
1018   *Titles*   Polydor 15118   1975
     TIME HONOURED GHOSTS (LP)   Polydor 6517   1975

The group Barclay James Harvest is made up of Stewart "Wooley" Wolstenholme, John Lees, Les Holroyd and Mel Pritchard. The lyrics to *Titles* consist of the titles to many Bealtes' songs. Those songs include: *The Long And Winding Road, Here Comes The Sun, All You Need Is Love, Lady Madonna, Let It Be, Something, Yesterday, Across The Universe, One After 909, I've Got A Feeling, For You Blue, I Feel Fine*. The LP **TIME HONOURED GHOSTS** also contains the song *Titles*.

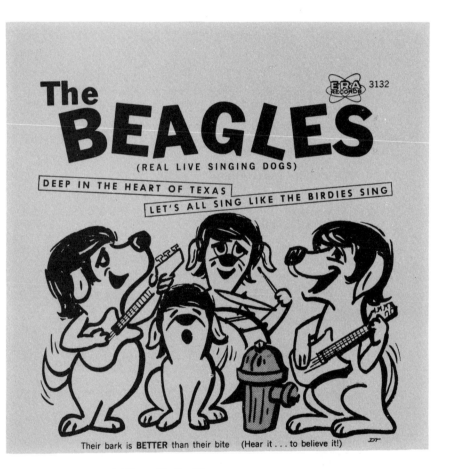

**Deep In The Heart Of Texas/Let's All
Sing Like The Birdies Sing (45)**

ERA 3132 (Entry 1020)

1019　THE BEAGLE & THE FOUR LIVERPOOL WHIGS
　　　　I WANT TO HOLD YOUR HAND & OTHER　　　Sutton 329　　　1964
　　　　FAVORITES (LP)
　　　　　Rap–A–Way　　　　　　　　　*My Sheila*
　　　　　Painless Thoughts　　　　　　*He's My Blue Guy*
　　　　　Tear A Love　　　　　　　　　*Give A Love*
　　　　　I Want To Hold Your Hand　　*The Cheat*
　　　　　Should We Love　　　　　　　*Pillow Thoughts*

　　　　The cover of this album shows four guys in Beatles' wigs and a beagle. The album
　　　　itself is incredibly bad. It has bad harmony, bad timing and is just a poor
　　　　recording.

1020　BEAGLES
　　　　Deep In The Heart Of Texas/Let's All Sing Like　　Era 3132　　　1964
　　　　The Birdies Sing

　　　　The Beagles were a group of singing dogs. The record came with a picture sleeve
　　　　showing a drawing of four dogs, all wearing Beatle wigs and playing various
　　　　instruments.

1021　BEAGLES
　　　　Can't Buy Me Love/White On White　　　　Hit 113　　　1964

　　　　The artist on *White On White* is listed as Fred York.

1022　BEARCUTS
　　　　BEATLEMANIA (LP)　　　　　　　　　Somerset 20800　　1964
　　　　　I Want To Hold Your Hand　　　*She Loves You*
　　　　　Twist And Shout　　　　　　　*Liverpool Stomp*
　　　　　Your Barber Is A Beatle Too　*Love Me Do*
　　　　　Please Please Me　　　　　　　*Bearcut Haircut*
　　　　　Monkey On Down To London Town　*From Me To You*

　　　　The Beatles' songs *I Want To Hold Your Hand, Twist And Shout, Please Please
　　　　Me, She Loves You, Love Me Do* and *From Me To You* are all vocals. The
　　　　remaining cuts are instrumentals.

1023
　　　　BEAT--A--MANIA (LP)　　　　　　　　　Spectrum 172　　1964
　　　　　She Loves You　　　　　　　*Please Please Me*
　　　　　In A Little While　　　　　*Baby You Can Do No Wrong*
　　　　　Tell Me Now　　　　　　　　*I Don't Need You*
　　　　　Night Without End　　　　　*What Shall I Do*
　　　　　Won't You Come Home Tonight　*Don't Tell Me You Don't Know*

　　　　No group is listed on this LP, so it has been listed here by title only.

1024　BEATLE BUDDIES
　　　　THE BEATLE BUDDIES (LP)　　　　　　　Diplomat 2313　　1964

　　　　The Beatle Buddies are an all--girl group.

1025　BEATLE--BUGS
　　　　Where Did Ringo Go　　　　　　　　　　Castle 101　　　1964

1026

BEATLERAMA VOL. 1 (LP) Guest Star 2307 1964
Diplomat 2307 1964
No group is listed on this album, so it is listed here by title only. The same album
was released on two different labels, but with the same release number.
See MANCHESTERS.

1027– BEATLE–ETTES
1028 *Yes You Can Hold My Hand* Assult 1893 1964
Only Seventeen/Now We're Together Jubilee 5472 1965

Yes You Can Hold My Hand was originally issued on red vinyl. *Only Seventeen*
is not a direct take–off on *I Saw Her Standing There*, but it does contain
references like "saw her standing there" and "let you hold my hand."

1029

THE BEATLES CRACKER SUITE (EP) 1965
It's For You *From Me To You*
Help *Ticket To Ride*
She Loves You *All My Loving*

One of the first records released setting Beatle tunes to a classical style. Released
in the U.K. only.

1030 BEATLES
The Girl I Love/For Yon Tunas Only Quest 101 1965

This is NOT the Beatles. These novelty artists went out of their way to make it
look like the real Beatles had something to do with this record. The song
was co–written by J. Lemmon and the publisher is listed as Maclen Pub.
The song is listed as "A Miracle Production (If it sells . . . it's a miracle!)."
The artist on *For Yon Tunas Only* is given as Jerry Blabber (a take–off on
popular Philadelphia DJ Jerry Blavet).

1031

BEATLES BLAST AT STADIUM DESCRIBED BY Audio Journal 1 1966
ERUPTING FANS (LP)

This LP was recorded during the Beatles' August 15, 1965 concert at Shea
Stadium. It's mostly noise, but the thoughts of some of the fans who
witnessed the concert are preserved forever on the disc.

1032 BEATLES COSTELLO
WASHING THE DEFECTIVES (EP) Pious JP 310 1978

This one's a take–off on both the Beatles and Elvis Costello. The man behind this
EP is Joe Pope, who runs the Beatle fan club, Strawberry Fields Forever.
The EP contains four songs: *Soldier Of Love, I Feel Fine, Theme From A*
Summer Place and *Out Of Limits. Soldier Of Love*, a song done by the
Beatles and appearing on several of their bootleg albums, is the only vocal
on the EP. The record comes with a picture sleeve which gives a brief
history of the group. The Beatles Costello are Eric "Slowhand" Rosenfeld,
Andy Paley, Jim Freeman, Chuck Chaplin, Jim Skinner and Joe Pope.

1033 BEATLES REVIVAL BAND
The Beatles Revival Song

This one was released in West Germany. Record label and year of release are
unknown.

1034 BEAT MERCHANTS
So Fine   Tower 127   1965

So Fine was released as the flip side of Freddie & The Dreamers top–5 hit *You Were Made For Me*. Nobody apparently thought much about the song until the mid--70's when someone decided that the Beat Merchants might actually be the early Beatles. After that statement was made, the record began selling for high prices. It doesn't really sound all that much like the Beatles but it is included here for its novelty value.

1035 BEATS
THE MERSEYSIDE SOUND (LP)   Design 170   1964
I Want To Hold You Hand   *I Saw Her Standing There*
This Is What I Mean   *Seems To Me*
Tell Me I'm The One   *Got To Get Another Girl*
Joshua   *Your Kind Of Love*
Maybe I Will   *There I Go*

This same album was released on the Rondo label as by the Liverpool Beats. See their entry.

1036 BECKY LEE BECK
I Want A Beatle For Christmas/Puppy Dog   Challenge 9372   1964

Also see number 512 in bootleg section.

1037 BEDBUGS
Yeah Yeah/Lucy Lucy   Liberty 55679   1964

The man behind the Bedbugs was none other than Ross Bagdasarian who, in the 50's, had been the mastermind behind the popular Chipmunks. Bagdasarian used the stage name David Seville. The Chipmunks also recorded some Beatle novelties. See their entry for a complete listing.

1038 BEDBUGS

The Bedbugs are a Beatles novelty group who starred on a segment of the popular TV series "F Troop." The Bedbugs were four guys from Boston with collarless suits and long hair. They played acoustic guitars on the show, but an electric sound came out of them. They played only instrumentals on the show, mainly *Camptown Races*. Corporal Agarn decided to leave the Army to manage the group. To get Agarn back, the other characters form their own group . . . the Termites, another Beatle novelty name. The Termites were Captain Parmenter, Wrangler Jane, Sgt. O'Rourke, Dobbs and Vanderbuilt. They too wore Beatle wigs while singing *Lemon Tree* and *Mr. Tambourine Man*. At the end of the show we learn that the Bedbugs have gone to Liverpool, England and become big hits. They even performed for the Queen. The Bedbugs were played by members of the Factory, a group led by Lowell George, who later became famous with the group Little Feat.

1039 BEE, TOMMY
Beatle Dance   September 103   1964

1040 BEEHIVES
I Want To Hold Your Hand/She Loves You   King 5881   1964

1041 BEETLES
Ain't That Love/Welcome To My Heart   Blue Cat 115   1965

322

1042 BELL, JESSICA
    Ode To Four   Fire--Sign 74501   1977

    Jessica Bell also wrote this Beatle novelty.

1043 BENNY & THE BEDBUGS
    The Beatle Beat/Roll Over Beethoven   DCP 1008   1964

    Originals came with a picture sleeve. *The Beatle Beat* was written by Don Costa.
    DCP was his label and the letters stand for Don Costa Productions. Several
    other novelties also appear on this label.

1044 BERRY, CHUCK
    Liverpool Beat   Chess 1488   1964

    This was part of Chuck's album **ST. LOUIS TO LIVERPOOL.**

1045 BERWICK, BRAD
    I'm Better Than The Beatles/Walkin' On Easy Street   Clinton 1012   1964

    Berwick's back--up band were the Bugs. The record came with a picture sleeve
    complete with notes on Berwick by Jane Mansfield. Berwick was also an
    actor and appeared with Robert Young on the TV series "Window On Main
    Street."

1046-- BEST, PETE
1051 *I'm Gonna Knock On Your Door/Why Did I*   Decca 11929 (UK) 1964
     Fall In Love With You
    (I'll Try) Anyway/I Wanna Be There   Beatles 800   1964
    I Can't Do Without You Now/Keys To My Heart   Mr. Maestro 711   1964
    Casting My Spell/I'm Blue   Mr. Maestro 712   1964
    Boys/Kansas City   Cameo 391   1964
    BEST OF THE BEATLES (LP)   Savage 71   1964

    Pete Best was the drummer for the Beatles from about August of 1960 until 1962
    when he was replaced by Ringo Starr. He played drums on the songs
    recorded by the Beatles in Germany with Tony Sheridan. His *Boys/Kansas*
    City was a direct copy of the Beatles Capitol Starline single (6066). This
    one came with a picture sleeve. The album, **BEST OF THE BEATLES,**
    contained the following songs:

Last Night	*Casting My Spell*
Why Did You Leave Me Baby	*Wait And See*
Shimmy Like My Sister Kate	*Some Other Guy*
I Need Your Lovin'	*I'm Blue*
Nobody But You	*She's Alright*
I Can't Do Without You Now	*Keys To My Heart*

1052 BIG BEN BANJO BAND
    HAPPY BANJOS PLAY THE BEATLES (LP)   Capitol 2642   1967

    The leader of the Big Ben Banjo Band was Norrie Paramor. All the songs on the
    album were medleys of Beatle tunes.

1. *All My Loving*	1. *Paperback Writer*
She's A Woman	*Eight Days A Week*
You Can't Do That	*I'll Get You*

2.	*World Without Love*	2.	*Michelle*
	Any Time At All		*This Boy*
	And I Love Her		*Yesterday*
3.	*Ticket To Ride*	3.	*Norwegian Wood*
	I'm Happy Just To Dance With You		*Rain*
	Things We Said Today		*Nowhere Man*
4.	*I Should Have Known Better*	4.	*Don't Bother Me*
	I'm A Loser		*No Reply*
	It Won't Be Long		*Little Child*
5.	*A Hard Day's Night*	5.	*Tell Me Why*
	I Feel Fine		*The Word*
	Can't Buy Me Love		*I'll Be Back*

1053 BLOWFISH
BLOWFISH IN THE NEW WAVE (EP) Varulven Blo–1 1977

Blowfish is Paul Lovell. The EP contains the following cuts:

George Harrison Outtake (1970)	*Hit Me Wid De X–Lax*
Glue England Music City	*Rock And Roll Cook*
40 Seconds Of The Ramones	*Chord Book Blues*
Live At The Rat	*Pew England Music City*

Both *George Harrison Outtake (1970)* and *Rock And Roll Cook* are about the *My Sweet Lord/He's So Fine* law suit. *Live At The Rat* mentions the Beatles.

1054 BLUE BEAT
THE BEATLE BEAT (LP) A.A. 133 1964

1055 BOCKY & THE VISIONS
The Spirit Of '64/Mo–Jo–Hanna Philips 40224 1964

1056 BOLL WEEVILS
Please Please Me/My Bonnie Hit 107 1964

1057 BON BONS
What's Wrong With Ringo/Come On Baby Coral 62402 1964

After the Bon Bons unsuccessful attempt at a hit with this Beatle Novelty, they changed their name to the Shangri–Las and had a string of hits including the number 1 *Leader Of The Pack*. The members of the group were Mary Weiss, Marge Ganser and her sister Mary Ann Ganser.

1058 BONNIE & THE BUTTERFLYS
I Saw Him Standing There/Dust Storm Smash 1878 1964

This is the female version of the Beatles' *I Saw Her Standing There*.

1059 BOOKER T. AND THE MG'S

See RANDLE, DEL.

1060 BOOTLES
I'll Let You Hold My Hand/Never Till Now GNP Crescendo 311 1964

1061 BO–WEEVILS
The Beatles Will Getcha United States 1934 1964

Do The Beetle (LP)   **Crown 399 (Entry 1065)**

1062   BRAMLETT, DELANEY
        Are You A Beatle Or A Rolling Stone   Columbia 45950   1973

        This novelty was written and produced by Delaney Bramlett and Doug Gilmore.
        Doug was formerly with Mott The Hoople.

1063   B.R.A.T.T.S.
        Secret Weapon (The British Are Coming)/   Tollie 9024   1964
        Jealous Kind Of Woman

        B.R.A.T.T.S. stands for Brotherhood for the Re–establishment of American Top
        Ten Supremacy. This particular record did absolutely nothing to further
        that cause.

1064   BRET & TERRY
        Beatle Fever/The Beatle Hop   Prestige 313   1964

        The Beatle Hop was co–written by Frank Slay who also produced both sides of
        this record. Slay produced many hits for Swan Records during their
        heyday of the late–50's and early 60's.

1065   BROCK, B. & THE SULTANS
        DO THE BEETLE (LP)   Crown 399   1964
        I Want To Hold Your Hand   *Feed The Beetle*
        The Saints   *Fast Beetle*
        Beetle Walk   *Mexican Beetle*
        30 Lb. Beetle   *Little Brown Beetle*
        My Bonnie   *Do The Beetle*

        The mono and stereo versions of this album have different release numbers – 399
        is the stereo number, the mono LP's have the number 5399.

1066   BROOKS, BONNIE
        Bring Back My Beatles (To Me)/A Letter From   United Artists 708 1964
        My Love

        This one is sung to the tune of *My Bonnie*.

1067   BROTHERS FOUR
        Ratman & Bobbin In The Clipper Caper/   Columbia 43547   1969
        Muleskinner

        This entire record is spoken with the theme from Batman serving as the background
        music. The story is that someone called the Mad Barber is out to shave the
        heads of all the rock stars. The Rolling Stones and Sonny & Cher have
        already gotten it and now he's after the Beatles. But Ratman and Bobbin
        capture him before the Beatles are shorn. The Mad Barber, by the way, turns
        out to be Lawrence Welk, or at least someone who sounds like him.

1068   BRYAN, DORA
        All I Want For Christmas Is A Beatle/If I Were A Fairy Fontana 427   1963

        This was released in England in late 1963 and made the charts there in December.
        It remained on the charts for six weeks and reached the number 22 position.
        This was probably the first of the Beatle novelties.

1069   BUCHANAN & GREENFIELD
        The Invasion/What A Lovely Party   Novel 711   1964

        This novelty record is of the break–in type made famous by Bill Buchanan and

The Beatle Beat (LP)   **Coronet 212 (Entry 1073)**

Dickie Goodman in their hit, *The Flying Saucer*. Dickie Goodman also went on to use many Beatle songs in his solo efforts. Bill made only this one Beatle novelty with partner Howie Greenfield (who co--wrote many of Neil Sedaka's early hits with Sedaka). Buchanan and Greenfield wrote *The Invasion*. No Beatle songs were actually used in this one, but we do hear "yeah, yeah, yeah" sung several times throughout the song.

1070 BUDDIES
　　The Beatle/Pulse Beat　　　　　　　　　　Swan 4170　　　1964

1071 BUG COLLECTORS
　　Beatle Bug/Thief In The Night　　　　　　Catch 103　　　1964

1072 BUGGS
　　Buggs vs. The Beatles/She Loves Me　　　Soma 1413　　　1964

This is definitely not the same group as number 1073.

1073 BUGGS
　　THE BEATLE BEAT (LP)　　　　　　　　Coronet 212　　1964
　　　　I Want To Hold Your Hand　　　　　　*She Loves You*
　　　　Mersey Mercy　　　　　　　　　　　*Liverpool Drag*
　　　　Soho Mash　　　　　　　　　　　　*Swingin' Thames*
　　　　East End　　　　　　　　　　　　　*Big Ben Hop*
　　　　London Town Swing　　　　　　　　*Teddy Boy Stomp*

Not the same group as number 1072. These guys went far out of the way to make the titles of all their instrumentals sound very British.

1074 BUG MEN
　　Beatle You Bug Me/Bloomin' Bird　　　　Dot 16592　　　1964

1075– BUGS
1076　*She Loves You/Dawn (Go Away)*　　　　Hit 106　　　　1964
　　　Twist And Shout/Stay　　　　　　　　Hit 111　　　　1964

The flips of both of these records were sung by the Chellows and were current hits by the Four Seasons. The Hit label specialized in selling hit songs by their own artists for a cheaper price than the major labels could sell them. If you didn't mind sound--alikes, the records were usually O.K.

1077 BUGS
　　Slide/Pretty Girl　　　　　　　　　　　Astor 002　　　1964

1078 BUGS

See MOSQUITOES.

1079 BULLDOGS
　　John, Paul, George & Ringo/What Do I See　　Mercury 72262　　1964

1080 BUMBLERS
　　?　　　　　　　　　　　　　　　　　　　?　　　　　　1964

In 1964, the English music paper *New Musical Express* reported that a group made--up of Frank Sinatra, Sammy Davis, Jr., Bing Crosby and Dean Martin would record a parody of the Beatles using the name Bumblers. If such a record was ever made, it would probably be on the Reprise label, since all of the above recorded for that label.

1081	BUTLER, DAWS		
	Bingo, Ringo/Clementine	Merri 6011	1964

> This one came with a picture sleeve. Daws Butler was the voice of Huckleberry Hound and this record was done using that voice. See HUCKLEBERRY HOUND.

1082–	CAFE CREME		
1084	*Unlimited Citations*		1978
	Discomania Pt. 1/Pt. 2	RSO 899	1978
	DISCOMANIA (LP)	RSO 3035	1978

> *Unlimited Citations* was the first of these three to be released. It was released in Spain in 1978 and reached number 4 on the charts in that country. The record and group were picked up in the U.S.A. by RSO Records and a single and album were quickly released. The records used the titles of Beatles' songs to make up the lyrics. The Beatles' songs used in *Discomania Pt. 1/Pt. 2* include: *Hey Jude, Day Tripper, Get Back, Back In The U.S.S.R., I Want To Hold Your Hand, Yellow Submarine, Ob–La–Di, Ob–La–Da, Lucy In The Sky With Diamonds, Michelle, All My Loving, With A Little Help From My Friends, Penny Lane, Eleanor Rigby, Twistin' In The Sixties* (not a Beatle song) / *Hey Jude, Twist And Shout, Good Day Sunshine, Let It Be, Sgt. Pepper's Lonely Hearts Club Band, Eight Days A Week, Strawberry Fields Forever, Day Tripper, Eleanor Rigby, I Saw Her Standing There, Come Together, From Me To You, Something, Hello Goodbye.* The LP contains the above, plus *Unlimited Citations (Rock),* including: *Eight Days A Week, Please Please Me, Tell Me Why, Blackbird, I Wanna Be Your Man, Ticket To Ride, A Hard Day's Night, Got To Get You Into My Life, I Should Have Known Better, Honey Pie, All You Need Is Love, All My Loving, I'm A Loser, She Loves You, Love Me Do, Can't Buy Me Love, She's A Woman, Revolution, Taxman, The Night Before, Drive My Car, I Feel Fine, You Won't See Me, When I'm Sixty--Four.* The other Beatle novelty on the album is *Unlimited Citations (Slow),* including: *Long And Winding Road, You're Gonna Lose That Girl, Girl, Here, There And Everywhere, Julia, Don't Let Me Down, She's Leaving Home, For No One, Because, Sexy Sadie, Don't Let Me Down, Something, Rocky Raccoon, You Never Give Me Your Money, Golden Slumbers, We Can Work It Out, If I Fell, Fool On The Hill, I Am The Walrus, Cry Baby Cry, Oh! Darling, Girl, Here, There And Everywhere, A Day In The Life.* The three remaining songs on the album, *Tell Me Please Little Girl, It Was Yesterday* and *Twistin' In The Sixties* are not Beatle novelties.

1085--	CANADIAN BEATLES		
1086	*Think I'm Gonna Cry/I'll Show You The Way*	Tide 2003	1964
	Love Walk Away/I'm Comin' Home	Tide 2006	1964

1087	CANDOLI, PETE		
	Beatle Bug Jump/You Made Me Love You	Nan 3004	1964

1088--	CAREFREES		
1089	*We Love You Beatles/Hot Blooded Lover*	London International 10614	1964
	FROM ENGLAND! THE CAREFREES (LP)	London 3379	1964

> This single came with a picture sleeve and on two different label colors, red and gold. *We Love You Beatles* made the *Billboard* charts in April 1964 and remained on the charts for five weeks, while attaining number 39, making it the most successful of all the Beatle novelties released in this country.

> The album contained *We Love You Beatles, All My Loving* and other popular British songs of the era. The group consisted of Lyn Cornell, Betty Prescott,

Barbara Kay, Johnny Evans, John Stevens and Don Riddell. Lyn and Betty had been in The Vernon Girls, a group which also had a Beatle novelty. See their listing for full details.

1090	CARL & HAIRCUTS		
	Ringo Pt. 1/Pt. 2	Day Dell 1002	1964
1091	CATERPILLARS		
	The Caterpillar Song/Hello Happy Happy Goodbye	Port 70033	1964
1092	CHARLES RIVER BOYS		
	BEATLE COUNTRY (LP)	Elektra 74006	1967
1093	CHIFFONS		
	My Sweet Lord/Main Nerve	Laurie 3630	1975

The Chiffons are Barbara Lee, Patricia Bennett and Sylvia Peterson. In 1963, with lead singer Judy Craig, the Chiffons hit it big with *He's So Fine*. Later in the 70's, George was sued for having copied that song when he wrote *My Sweet Lord*. The Chiffons then put out their own version of *My Sweet Lord*, mixing in the lyrics of *He's So Fine*. This was undoubtedly an attempt to show how much the two songs sounded alike.

1094--	CHIPMUNKS		
1096	**THE CHIPMUNKS SING THE BEATLES HITS** (LP)	Liberty 3388	1964
	THE CHIPMUNKS SING THE BEATLES HITS (EP)	Liberty 7388	1964
	All My Loving/Do You Want To Know A Secret	Liberty 55134	1964

The Chipmunks – Theodore, Simon and Alvin – were the brainchild of Ross Bagdasarian, who was better known by his stage name, David Seville. As Seville, he had a number one hit in 1958 with *Witch Doctor*. When he started doing the Chipmunks, he hit number one again with *The Chipmunk Song*. The LP in this series was popular enough to be re–released as Sunset 7388. The album contains the following songs:

All My Loving	*A Hard Day's Night*
Do You Want To Know A Secret	*P.S. I Love You*
She Loves You	*I Saw Her Standing There*
From Me To You	*Can't Buy Me Love*
Love Me Do	*Please Please Me*
Twist And Shout	*I Want To Hold Your Hand*

1097	CHUG AND DOUG		
	Ringo Comes To Town/My Girl	Charger 101	1964
1098	CLIFTON, BILL		
	Beatle Crazy/Little Girl Dressed In Blue	London 9638	1964
1099	COLLINS KIDS		
	Beetle Bug Bop	Columbia 21470	
1100	COLLINS, TOMMY		
	All The Monkeys Ain't In The Zoo/Don't Let Me Stand In His Footsteps	Capitol 5345	1965
1101	COMSTOCK, BOBBY & THE COUNTS		
	The Beatle Bounce/Since You Been Gone	Lawn 229	1964

Comstock scored a big hit in 1963 with *Let's Stomp*, but his career went rapidly downhill from there. The counts were: Gus Eframson, Dale Sherwood,

A DAY
IN THE LIFE
OF GREEN ACRES

Asinine
Records
6120 Barrows Drive
Los Angeles, California
90048

DAMASKAS: Vocals, Piano, Violin Abuse
ARTIE BARNES: Vocals, Electronic Keyboards
ART BARNES: Bass, Electric & Accoustic Guitars
                Maracas, Seat Cushion & Engineering

Recorded in Lumania

A Day In The Life Of Green Acres/
    Makin' Love In A Subaru (45)   Asinine 1 (Entry 1110)

Chuck Ciaschi and Freddy Ciaschi. Comstock co–wrote *The Beatle Bounce.*

1102   COOK & MOORE
L.S. Bumblebee/Bee Side   Decca 12551   1967

This one was released in Britain in January of 1967. *L.S. Bumblebee* has often been credited as being a Beatles' song and has even been included in many Beatle bootleg albums. But the song was actually done by British comedians Peter Cook and Dudley Moore.

1103   COOPER, GARNELL & THE KINFOLKS

See RANDLE, DEL.

1104   CORNISH, GENE & THE UNBEETABLES
I Wanna Be A Beatle/Oh Misery   Dawn 551   1964

Cornish later was to become a member of the Young Rascals, one of the most popular American groups of the 60's. Gene arranged and co–wrote *I Wanna Be A Beatle.*

1105   CROSS, JIMMY
I Want My Baby Back/Play The Other Side   Tollie 9039   1965

I Want My Baby Back was written and produced by Perry Botkin and Gil Garfield. Botkin is well known as a song writer, producer and artist. His most recent and well known song is *Nadia's Theme.* Gil Garfield was an original member of the Cheers, whose biggest hit was *Black Denim Trousers* in 1955. Bert Convy was also a member of that group.
The song tells the story of a couple on their way home from a Beatle concert. They are in an accident and the girl dies. The boy is willing to do anything to get her back, including robbing the coffin. It has to be one of the worst "death–rock" songs of all time.

1106–   CURTIS, SONNY
1109   *A Beatle I Want To Be/So Used To Loving You*   Dimension 1024   1964
         BEATLE HITS FLAMENCO STYLE (LP)   Imperial 12276   1964
         Do You Remember Roll Over Beethoven   Elektra 46568   1979
         SONNY CURTIS (LP)   Elektra 6E–227   1979

Curtis was at one time a member of the Crickets, Buddy Holly's group. His most recent claim to fame came when he wrote the theme for the TV series "The Mary Tyler Moore Show." *Do You Remember Roll Over Beethoven* was a minor country/western hit early in 1980. The song mentions the Beatles, Lennon and McCartney by name, and tells how the group helped us all get through the sixties. The song also appears on the LP **SONNY CURTIS.**

1110   DAMASKAS, BARNES & BARNES
A Day In The Life Of Green Acres/Makin' Love   Asinine 1   1979
In A Subaru

This group consists of Damaskas, Artie Barnes and Art Barnes. The song is basically the theme from the TV series "Green Acres" sung to the tune of the Beatles' *A Day In The Life.* At the end of the record, the group apologizes to the Beatles for what they had done to their song.

1111   DAVIS, LINK
Beatle Bug/I Keep Wanting You More   Kook 1026   1964

332

1112 DAVIS, RONNY
      Let's Beetle In The Rocket   Sheridan 573   1964

1113 DBM
      Beatlemania/Kiss Me   AVI 12--182   1978

      DBM stand for Disco Beatlemania. This 12--inch disco single uses Beatle song
      titles to make up its lyrics. Song titles used include: *I Saw Her Standing
      There, Twist And Shout, Eleanor Rigby, Get Back, Day Tripper, Sgt.
      Pepper's Lonely Hearts Club Band, Ob–La–Di Ob–La–Da*, and *I Want To
      Hold Your Hand*. In addition, you hear instrumental sections from *A Hard
      Day's Night, From Me To You* and *Day Tripper*. At several places in the
      song we also hear "the Beatles go disco" and "George, John, Paul and
      Ringo."

1114 DEAN, BOB
      Ringo   Summit 2   1964

1115 DEFENDERS
      Beatles We Want Our Girls Back   Realm 001   1964

1116 DEL RICOS
      Beatle Crawl/Beatle Hootenanny   "620" 1008   1964

1117-- DETOURS
1118 *Bring Back My Beatles To Me/Money*   McSherry 1285   1964
      Bring Back My Beatles/Money   McSherry 1285   1964

      This record was apparently released with two, slightly different titles.

1119 DICKY & THE WATERGATE BUGS
      We Can Work It Out/Help   Steady Records 053 1973

      An obvious take--off on our ex--president.

1120 DILLON, ZIG
      Beetle Bug/Bird Song Boogie   "R" 512   1964

1121 DONELL, DELMAR
      The Beatle Bit My Dog   Lave He 1008   1964

1122 DOODLES
      I Want To Hold Your Hand   Hit 104   1964

1123 DORSEY BIG BAND JACK
      Ringo's Dog/March Of The Gonks   Parkway 938   1964

1124 DOUD, EARLE/ALEN ROBIN
      LYNDON JOHNSON'S LONELY HEARTS CLUB   Acto 230   1968
      BAND (LP)

      The jacket picture for this album was based on the Beatles' **SGT. PEPPER** cover.
      The album made the charts in January of 1968, and remained there for five
      weeks, making the number 176 position.

1125 DOUGLAS, SCOTT
      The Beatles Barber/The Wall Paper Song   Apogee 105   1964

1126-- DOVAL, JIM & THE GOUCHOS
1127   *Stranded In The Pool/Right Now*   Diplomacy X5   1964
             Beatle Rule/Pink Elephants   Diplomacy X6   1964

The "pool" in *Stranded In The Pool* is Liverpool. It is also a take–off on the 1956 hit *Stranded In The Jungle.*

1128   EGGHEADS
       Why Don't They Stop Fooling Around   1964

It was the Eggheads themselves that were the Beatle novelty here. They went totally opposite the Beatles and shaved their heads bare.

1129

       EINE KLEINE BEATLEMUSIK (EP)   HMV 7EG8887   1964
         She Loves You   *Please Please Me*
         A Hard Day's Night   *I Want To Hold Your Hand*
         All My Loving   *I'll Get You*

An EP made up of Beatles' songs set in a classical tone. This was one of the first attempts to do this. The EP was devised by Fritz Spiegel and was arranged by Harry Wild.

1130-- EXTERMINATORS
1131   *The Beetle Bomb/Stomp 'Em Out*   Chancellor 1145   1964
             Beatle Stomp/Stomp 'Em Out   1964

1132   FAIR, CARLO
       Beetle Bounce   Express 801   1964

1133   FANS
       I Want A Beatle For Christmas/How Far Should   Dot 16688   1964
          My Heart Go

1134   FEMALE BEATLES
       I Want You/Don't Want To Cry   20th Century 531   1964

1135   FERRA, TINA
       R (Is For Ringo)/Modern Youth   Limelight 3022   1964

1136   FERRIER, GARRY
       Ringo–Deer/Just My Luck   Academy 112   1964

Ferrier also wrote this novelty.

1137   FINNEGAN, LARRY
       A Tribute To Ringo Starr (The Other Ringo)/When   Ric 146   1964
         My Love Passes By

Finnegan had a 1962 hit with *Dear One.* At the time he recorded that song he was a student at Notre Dame University. Larry's brother John wrote *A Tribute To Ringo Starr* and Larry produced it. The tune for the song was taken from Lorne Greene's number one hit *Ringo*, a song which had nothing to do with the real Ringo.

1138   FINSTER, WERBLEY
       So Long, Paul/Here Comes Werbley   RCA 74–0290   1969

The label says Werbley Finster, but there's little doubt that this is really Jose

It's A Beatle World (LP)   Swan 514 (Entry 1139)

Feliciano. His name appears as writer or co–writer of both songs and there's no mistaking his voice or guitar style. This one was done as the peak of the "Paul is dead" rumors.

1139 FISHER, AL & LOU MARKS

IT'S A BEATLE WORLD (LP)   Swan 514   1964

Instant Beatle   *Ringo, Ringo Little Star*
On The Plane   *Mr. President & Mr. Minister*
At The Concert (We Love Rock & Roll)   *Sunday At 8:00*
The Fifth "Coo Coo"   *Are You Putting Me On*
Paul, George, John & Ringo (All The   *Scotland From The Yard*
*   Way To The Bank)*   *The Real Fisher And Marks*
Bella 'N Boris
Does She Love Me

A comedy album with almost all the cuts pertaining to the Beatles in one way or another. There's even a little bit of singing.

1140 FITZGERALD, ELLA
Ringo Beat/I'm Falling In Love   Verve 10340   1964

Even the reigning "Queen of jazz" did a Beatle novelty, such was the popularity that the group generated.

1141 FONDETTES
The Beatles Are In Town   Arhoolie 507   1964

1142 FOOTMAN, JOHN
A Broken Heart/Same   Beatle 554–14   1975

It's the label that's the novelty here. Notice the name.

1143– FOSTER, BRUCE
1144 *Platinum Heroes/I Remember*   Millenium 602   1977
      AFTER THE SHOW (LP)   Millenium 8000   1977

Foster wrote and co–produced *Platinum Heroes,* his tribute to the Beatles. DJ copies of the single came with a picture sleeve. The record made the charts in July of 1977. It made number 63 during its five–week stay on the charts. The song also appears on his album.

1145 FOSTER, JERRY
I Ain't No Beatle   Spar 30014   1964

1146 FOTO–FI FOUR
Stand Up And Holler/Ismael   Foto–Fi 107   1964

This is a rather remarkable novelty which may have only been issued to radio stations. The record came in a cardboard sleeve which read "The Beatles arrive in America! Have fun running the film with this specially scored recording. A Foto–Fi Film Presentation." A film of the Beatles arriving in the U.S. accompanied the record. The back of the sleeve says that more films are on the way and gave an address to write for more information. *Stand Up And Holler* was written by Harry Nilsson. Nilsson himself would later do a Beatle novelty and would become a personal friend of the Beatles.

1147 FOUR PREPS
A Letter To The Beatles/College Cannonball   Capitol 5143   1964

The Four Preps were Marvin Inabnett, Bruce Bellard, Glen Larson and Ed Cobb. The group had many hits including *26 Miles* and *Big Man*. By 1964 they had started to fade and this Beatles' novelty provided them with their last charted hit. It reached number 85 in three weeks on the charts in March of 1964.

1148 FOUR SHILLINGS
Do You Want Me To   Limelight 3017   1964

1149 FOUR SISTERS
I Want Ringo For Christmas   Hermatage 822   1964

1150 FRENCHY & THE CHESSMEN
Beetle Bebop/E Tacos   Temple 2081   1964

1151 GLORIEUX, FRANCOIS
PLAYS THE BEATLES (LP)   Vanguard 79417   1978
Yesterday (Chopin)   *Yellow Submarine* (Beethoven)
Help/Let It Be (Schumann)   *Girl/Ob–La–Di Ob–La–Da*
Can't Buy Me Love (Gershwin/   (Brahms)
Prokofiev)   *Norwegian Wood* (Milhaud)
Ob–La–Di Ob–La–Da (Mozart)   *The Fool On The Hill*
Hey Jude (Bach)   (Rachmaninoff)
Michelle (Ravel)   *In My Life* (Debussy)
          Eleanor Rigby (Bartok)

Francois Glorieux, at the piano, plays the above Beatles songs in the style of the composer listed after each. The cover, in caricature form, shows the Beatles' **ABBEY ROAD** sleeve with Glorieux between Paul and George and facing the wrong way.

1152 GORDON, ALAN
Beatles/I Ain't Gonna Cry Tonight   RCA 10641   1976

Gordon wrote *Beatles* which he recorded with the Extragordonary Band.

1153 GRASSHOPPERS
Mod Socks   Warner Bros. 5607   1965

1154 GREEN, KEITH
Sgt. Pepper's Epitaph/Country Store   Era/Happy Tiger   1970
          108

1155 GUARNIR, JOHNNY
To Kill A Beatle   Magnifique 18   1964

1156 HAIRCUTS
She Loves You/Love Me Do   Parkway 899   1964

Originals came with a picture sleeve.

1157 HALLOWAY, LARRY
Beatle Teen Beat/Going Up   Parkway 903   1964

Halloway wrote *Beatle Teen Beat*.

1158 HAMILTON, DAVE & HIS PEPPERS
 Beatle Walk/The Argentina   Fortune 861   1964

 Beatle Walk was written by Hamilton.

1159 HAMPTON, JOHNNY
 Beatle Dance/I Can't Get Along With You   Rose 002   1964

1160 HARDLY WORTHIT PLAYERS
 THE HARDLY WORTHIT REPORT (LP)   Parkway 7053   1967

 From the people who gave us *Wild Thing* by Senator Bobby comes this comedy
 album featuring the cut *Beatles/Pope Visits New York City*. The story line
 of the cut is that The Pope's (Paul VI) plane lands where the Beatles' were to
 have landed and vice versa. As a result there are a lot of people on hand when
 the Pope arrives and very few to greet the Beatles. The conclusion? "The
 Pope is more popular than the Beatles." The Hardly Worthit Players are
 Bill Minkin as Slander Van Oki, Chet Hardly as Murray The K, Dennis
 Wholey as David Worthit, Carol Morley as Nancy Dickering, and Steve Baron
 as Ed Nuisance.

1161 HARRIS, ROLF
 Ringo For President/Click Go The Shears   Epic 9721   1964

 Australian Rolf Harris was no stranger to the charts when he recorded this novelty.
 He had gone top–five in 1963 with *Tie Me Kangaroo Down Sport*. Although
 Click Go The Shears may sound like it's about cutting the Beatles' hair, it
 actually is about sheep and has nothing to do with the Beatles.

1162-- HOLMES, RUPERT
1163 *I Don't Want To Hold Your Hand/The Man*   Epic 50096   1975
       Behind The Woman
       RUPERT HOLMES (LP)   Epic 33443   1975

 Holmes wrote *I Don't Want To Hold Your Hand*. This one was not a hit for him,
 but four years later he topped the charts with *Escape (The Pinia Colada
 Song)*. This novelty also can be found on the album **RUPERT HOLMES**.

1164 HOMER & JETHRO
 I Want To Hold Your Hand/She Loves You   RCA 8345   1964

 Henry "Homer" Haynes and Kenneth "Jethro" Burns had been poking fun at top
 artists for years with their parody songs, and the Beatles could not escape
 their wit.

1165 HONEY BEES

 See MOSQUITOES

1166 HUCKLEBERRY HOUND
 Bingo Ringo/Clementine   Merri 6011   1964

 Originals came with a picture sleeve. The voice of Huck was Daws Butler. See
 BUTLER, DAWS.

1167 HUGHLEY, GEORGE
 Do The Beatle/My Love Is True   Gaye 004   1964

1168 HUNTER, CHRISTINE
Santa Bring Me Ringo/Where Were You Daddy   Roulette 4589   1964

1169 INNER CITY MISSION
Get Back John   Kama Sutra 510   1970

1170 INSECTS
Let's Bug The Beatles/Dear Beatles   Applause 1002   1964

Dear Beatles is by the Little Lady Beatles.

1171 JACKIE & JILL
I Want A Beatle For Christmas/Jingle Bells   USA 791   1964

1172 JAPANESE BEATLES
The Beatles Song (Japanese Style)/Pt. 2   Golden Crest 584   1964

1173 JAY, HAROLD
Don't Wanna Be A Beatle   Johnny CO 101   1964

1174 JECKYL & HYDE
Frankenstein Meets The Beatles/Dracula Drag   DCP 1126   1965

Frankenstein Meets The Beatles was written by Dickie Goodman and Bill Ramal. Goodman has several other Beatles novelties to his credit. Check his entry in the break–in section.

1175 JOEY & THE CLASSICS
Ringo's Walk/Hamburger   Teen 514   1964

Joey & The Classics wrote *Ringo's Walk* which was released on the Hawaiian label, Teen.

1176 JOHN & PAUL
To Be Or Not To Be/Would You Tell Her   Swan 4207   1964

This is NOT the real John and Paul, nor is it the same duo who performed the next entry.

1177 JOHN & PAUL
People Say/I'm Walkin'   Tip 1021   1965

Even though this is obviously not the real John and Paul, both of these songs very often appear on Beatle bootleg albums. There are rumors that the former Beatle Pete Best may be the artist on this record and some believe that it might also have been the Nurk Twins, a name used by John and Paul at one time. The record was released in Britain in October of 1965.

1178 JOHNNY & THE HURRICANES
Saga Of The Beatles/Rene   Atila 211   1964

This popular instrumental group was made up of Johnny Paris, Paul Tesluk, Dave Yorko, Lionel Mattice and Tony Kaye. They first came to national prominence in 1959 with their hit *Red River Rock*.

1179 JONES BOYS
Beatlemania/Honky   Sabra 555   1964

Beatlemania is listed as featuring Bongo Pete.

1180 JUDY & THE DUETS
Christmas With The Beatles/The Blind Boy   Ware 6000   1964

See also bootleg section number 514.

1181 JUSTICE DEPARTMENT
Let John And Yoko Stay In The USA   New Design 1008   1972

Originals came with an insert showing the lyrics. This song, written by Artie
Resnick and Paul Nauman, was a plea to keep John from being deported.

1182 KARINE, ANNE
Jeg Ensker Meg En Bitte Liten Beatle   MA 74   1964

Originals of this foreign novelty came with a picture sleeve.

1183 KASEM, CASEY
Letter From Elaina/Theme For Elaina   Warner Bros. 5475 1964

A spoken word novelty from one of the country's leading DJ's. The background
music is *And I Love Her.* Today Casey hosts the show "American Top–40"
on which he plays *Billboard* magazine's top–40 records of the week. *Theme
for Elaina* is by the Burbank Strings.

1184 KELLUM, MURRAY
I Dreamed I Was A Beatle/Oh How Sweet It Could Be M.O.C. 658   1964

Kellum was an artist on his way out after his 1963 hit *Long Tall Texan.* His
novelty try went nowhere.

1185 KENNY, GERARD & THE NEW YORK BAND
Get Back Beatles/Same   International Committee To Reunite The   1976
                                              Beatles 001

This one was put out by Alan Amron to help raise money to reunite the Beatles.
Gerard Kenny wrote *Get Back Beatles.*

1186 KING, DAVE
The Beatle Walk   Teia 1004   1964

1187 KING, LENORE & TOMMY ANDERSON
The Beatles Is Back Yea Yea/Ye Old Lion And His Her Majesty 101   1965
Feudin' Cousins

1188 KNIGHT, TERRY
Saint Paul/Legend Of William & Mary   Capitol 2506   1969

Terry has been involved in music for many years. In 1966 he and his group, the
Pack, had a national hit with *I (Who Have Nothing).* When that group broke
up, the Pack became Grand Funk Railroad and Terry became their manager.
Saint Paul deals with the "Paul is dead" rumor.

1189 LADY BUGS
Liverpool/How Do You Do It   Chattahoochie 637 1964

1190 LADY BUGS
Sooner Or Later   Del Fi 4233   1964

1191 LADY BUGS
Fraternity U.S.A./Who Sent This Love Note Legrand 1033 1964

Although the above three groups all share the same name, they are not the same group.

1192 LAINE, DENNY
Japanese Tears Arista 0511 1980

Wings' member Denny Laine wrote this song about Paul's Japanese drug bust.

1193 LAMONT, PAULA
Beatles Meets A Lady Bug/Greatest Love Under Loadstone 1605 1964
The Sun

1194 LARRY & JOHNNY
Beatle Time Pt. 1/Pt. 2 Jola 1000 1964

Larry and Johnny are Larry Williams and Johnny "Guitar" Watson. Williams had made the charts with *Dizzy Miss Lizzy* and *Bonie Moronie* in the late fifties. These songs were later done by the Beatles and John Lennon respec-- tively. Williams died, the victim of suicide, early in 1980. Watson is also a popular soul artist.

1195 LEE, VERONICA & THE MONIQUES
Ringo Did It/Foreign Boy Centaur 106 1964

1196 LEHMAN, FRANKIE
A Long Day's Fight/Nikita's Lament VJM Russ 4424 1964

1197 LEMON TRIO, JOHN
Beatle Shuffle/Afro Bossa Nova Trudel 1002 1964

John Lemon is listed as the writer of *Beatle Shuffle*. Also in the Trio were James Scott on organ and Robert Brooks on drums.

1198 LENNON, FREDDIE
That's Life/Next Time You Feel Important Jerden 792 1965

Freddie, John's long lost father, suddenly showed up after the Beatles' success. His record was a total failure on the charts. It was released in December, 1965 in the U.K., but wasn't released in the U.S. until February, 1966.

1199 LENNON, JOHN & THE BLEECHERS
Ram You Hard Punch 1970

Released only in the U.K. Of course, this is not the real John Lennon.

1200 LIL' WALLY & THE VENTURAS
Welcome Beatles/My Happiness Drum Boy 108 1965

1201 LIPSTICK
Come Back Beatles/The Fab Four--Four Polydor 725 1976

This was released only in the U.K. Lipstick is really the popular Irish group Horslips. The members of the group are Barry Devlin, Jimmy Fean, Jim Lockhart, Eamon Carr and Charles O'Connor.

Beattle Mash (LP)   Palace 777 (Entry 1213)

Beatlemania In The U.S.A. (LP)   Wyncote 9001 (Entry 1215)

1202 LITTLE CHERYL
     Yeh Yeh We Love 'Em All/Nick And Joe   Cameo 307   1964

    Nick And Joe was done by Little Cheryl's Friends.

1203 LITTLE LADY BEATLES
     Dear Beatles/Let's Bug The Beatles   Applause 1002   1964

    Let's Bug The Beatles was done by the Insects. See their listing also.

1204 LIVERPOOL BEATS
    NEW MERSEYSIDE SOUND (LP)   Rondo 2026   1964

I Want To Hold Your Hand	*I Saw Her Standing There*
This Is What I Mean	*Seems To Me*
Tell Me I'm The One	*Got To Get Another Girl*
Joshua	*You Kind Of Love*
Maybe I Will	*There I Go*

    This same LP was also released on the Design label as by the Beats. See their listing also.

1205 LIVERPOOL EXPRESS
     You Are My Love   Atco 7058   1975

1206-- LIVERPOOL FIVE
1212
If You Gotta Go Go Now/Too Far Now	RCA 8660	1965
Sister Love/She's Mine	RCA 8816	1966
New Directions/What A Crazy World	RCA 8906	1966
Anyway That You Want Me/The Snake	RCA 8968	1966
Cloudy/She's (Got Plenty Of Love)	RCA 9158	1967
ARRIVE (LP)	RCA 3583	1966
OUT OF SIGHT (LP)	RCA 3682	1966

    Anyway You Want It was on the charts for one week late in 1966 and only reached the number 98 position.

1213 LIVERPOOL KIDS
    BEATTLE MASH (LP)   Palace 777   1964

She Loves You	*Three Me Baby*
Why Don't You Set Me Free	*I'm Lost Without You*
Let Me Tell You	*You Are The One*
Take A Chance	*Pea Jacket Hop*
Swinging Papa	*Japanese Beatles*
	Lookout For Charlie

    The LP jacket says Liverpool Kids, the record label lists the Schoolboys. See Schoolboys also.

1214 LIVERPOOL LADS
     Scowser City   All Lloyds   1964

1215-- LIVERPOOLS
1216 **BEATLEMANIA IN THE U.S.A.** (LP)   Wyncote 9001 1964
    THE HIT SOUNDS FROM ENGLAND (LP)   Wyncote 9061 1964

    The Liverpools' versions of various Beatle songs are included on these albums, as well as some original material.

344

| 1217–
1219 | LIVERPOOL SET
Miss You So/Must I Tell You
Oh Gee Girl
Change Your Mind | Columbia 43351
Columbia 43512
Columbia 43813 | 1965
1966
1966 |

| 1220 | LIVERS
Beatle Time/This Is The Night | Constellation 118 | 1964 |

The Livers were formerly known as the Chicagoans.

| 1221 | LORD, DICK
Like Ringo/The Name On The Wall | Atco 6331 | 1964 |

Dick Lord co--wrote *Like Ringo.*

| 1222 | LORDS
Cut My Hair/John Brown's Body | Columbia 23529 | 1964 |

This one was released in Germany.

| 1223–
1224 | LYNN, DONNA
My Boyfriend Got A Beatle Haircut/That Winter Weekend
JAVA JONES/MY BOYFRIEND GOT A BEATLE HAIRCUT (LP) | Capitol 5127

Capitol 2085 | 1964

1964 |

The LP contains the following songs:

Java Jones
Roll Over Beethoven
The Things That I Feel
I Only Want To Be With You
Navy Blue
I Had A Dream I Was A Beatle

My Boyfriend Got A Beatle Haircut
My Bonnie (My Beatles)
Our Day Will Come
Ronnie
That Winter Weekend
That's Me – I'm The Brother

My Boyfriend Got A Beatle Haircut reached the *Billboard* charts in March, 1964. It stayed on the charts for four weeks and reached number 83.

| 1225 | MAD ENGLISHMEN & THE FURYS
Beatlemania/Janice | Vee Six 1023 | 1964 |

| 1226 | MANCHESTERS
BEATLERAMA (LP) | Diplomat 2307 | 1964 |

I Want To Hold Your Hand
She Loves You
Wearying, Worrying Blues
I Waited
My Bonnie Lies Over The Ocean

Blue Waves
Shortening Bread
Little Miss Margie
The Beatles Move
Oh, What A Sorry Day

Also see listing for **BEATLERAMA VOL. 1.** This LP has the same release number, but the artist was not listed there.

| 1227 | MANCHESTERS
I Don't Come From England/Dragonfly | Vee Jay 700 | 1965 |

David Gates (later leader of Bread) wrote and arranged this one and it also sounds like his voice doing the singing.

1228 MARCH, PEGGY
John, Paul, George Und Ringo

This was released in West Germany. Peggy March had a big hit in this country in 1963 with *I Will Follow Him.*

1229 MARESCA, ERNIE
The Beatle Dance/Theme From Lilly Lilly   Rust 5076   1964

Maresca was mainly a song writer, having written many songs with Dion Dimucci. In 1962 he had his own hit with *Shout Shout (Knock Yourself Out).*

1230 MARTIN SIX, AL
Baby Beatle Walk/Prego   Bell 605   1964

1231 MARTIN, TRADE
Liverpool Baby/Joanne   Coed 594   1964

Martin had a hit in 1962 entitled *That Stranger Used To Be My Girl.*

1232-- MASKED MARAUDERS
1233 **MASKED MARAUDERS** (LP)   Diety 6387   1969
I Can't Get No Nookie   Diety 0870   1969

The album contains the following songs:
I Can't Get No Nookie	*Later*
Duke Of Earl	*More Or Less Hudson's Bay Again*
Cow Pie	*Season Of The Witch*
I Am The Japanese Sandman	*Saturday Night At the Cow*
The Book Of Love	*Palace*

Before this album was released, it was reviewed in *Rolling Stone* magazine. The review, by T.M. Christian, appeared in the October 18, 1969 edition. It talked of an album by a supergroup made up of John Lennon, Paul McCartney, Mick Jagger, Bob Dylan and an un--named drummer. The review was a joke, but it drew so much response that Warner Brothers released an album on its Diety label to match the review. The album and single were released late in 1969. The album, which includes an insert showing the original review, reached the charts early in 1970 and remained there for 12 weeks. It made it as high as number 114.

1234 MASON, BONNIE JO
Ringo I Love You/Beatle Blues   Annette 1000   1964

Bonnie Jo Mason turned out to be none other than Cher. The record was produced by Phil Spector and was released on his Annette label. See also bootleg number 512.

1235 MERRY ELVES: MILTON, SLEEPY & RINGO
Rock & Roll Around The Christmas Tree/I Love   Argus 250   1973
Christmas
This Chipmunk--like group sported a drummer named Ringo.

1236 MERSEYBEATS
ENGLAND'S BEST SELLERS (LP)   ARC International 834   1964

1237 MERSEY BEATS OF LIVERPOOL
MERSEY HITS (LP)   Arc   1964

1238	MERSEYBOYS		
	15 GREATEST SONGS OF THE BEATLES (LP)	Vee Jay 1101	1964

1239	MERSEY LADS		
	Whatcha Gonna Do Baby/Johnny No Love	MGM 13481	1966

1240	MERSEY MONSTERS		
	I Feel Mine/Buried Across The Mersey	Fright 'N 1011	1965

Parodies of the Beatles' *I Feel Fine* and Gerry & The Pacemakers' *Ferry Cross The Mersey.*

1241	MERSEY SOUNDS		
	Get On Your Honda And Ride/Honda Holiday	Montel 966	1966

1242	MINUTE MEN		
	Please Keep The Beatles In England	Argo 5469	1964

1243	MONTE, LOU		
	I Want To Hold Your Hand/My Paison's Across The Way	Reprise 0326	1964

The Beatles, Italian style.

1244	MORAN		
	The Beatles Thing/Lady Loves Me	Epic 10987	1973

This Canadian group did a song about the break--up of the Beatles.

1245	MORRIE, TINY		
	Beetle And The Spider	Hurricane 1937	

1246	MORROW BIG BAND, BUD		
	BEATLEMANIA (LP)	Columbia 26095	1964

1247	MOSQUITOES

The Mosquitoes appeared on an episode of TV's "Gilligan's Island." The *TV Guide* description says, "The mop--topped Mosquitoes arrive on the island seeking refuge." The Mosquitoes are: Bingo, Bango, Bongo, and Irving. The group is played by Les Brown, Jr. and the Wellingtons, the group that sang the show's theme song. They sing *He's A Loser* and other miscellane--ous music in the show. The castaways want the group to leave so they can get help and be rescued. First the men form a group of their own, hoping the Mosquitoes will like them and want them for an opening act. They call themselves the Bugs. But, they're so bad that the Mosquitoes want nothing to do with them. Then it's the girls' turn. They form the Honey Bees and sing *You Need Me.* But they turn out to be so good that the Mosquitoes are afraid that if they take them back they will soon be more popular than the Mosquitoes. So the group leaves the island during the night and doesn't tell anyone about the castaways.

In Mark Shipper's book, *Paperback Writer,* Bob Denver, the star of "Gilligan's Island," visits John and Yoko during their Toronto Bed--In. And on the Beatles' reunion LP, **GET BACK**, appears the song *Gilligan's Island.* So the show itself is, in a way, a Beatle novelty.

1248--	MOSS, GENE		
1249	*I Want To Bite Your Hand/Ghoul Days (School Days)*	RCA 8438	1964
	DRACULA'S GREATEST HITS (LP)	RCA 2977	1964

Moss co--wrote *I Want To Bite Your Hand*. This song also appears on his album.

1250 MOTIONS
Beatle Drums/Long Hair   Mercury 72297   1964

1251 MULLINS, ZEKE
Beatle Fan/Worried Man   Timber   1964

1252 MYSTERY TOUR
Ballad Of Paul/Ballad Of Paul (Follow The   MGM 14097   1969
Bouncing Ball)

1253 NAN & JAN
Beatle Bop/Believe It Or Not   Debby 069   1964

1254-- NATIONAL LAMPOON
1257   **RADIO DINNER** (LP)   Banana 38   1972
       GOOD--BYE TO POP (LP)   Epic   1975
       A HISTORY OF THE BEATLES (EP)   Epic AE7--1095   1975
       GREATEST HITS OF THE NATIONAL LAMPOON   Visa 7008   1979
       (LP)

A History Of The Beatles appears on the album **GOOD--BYE TO POP** and the special EP issued to radio stations. It is a typical Lampoon spoof. The albums **RADIO DINNER** and **GREATEST HITS OF THE NATIONAL LAMPOON** both contain *Magical Misery Tour,* which is a take--of on John Lennon. The writers of this one were Michael O'Donoghue and Christopher Cerf. Tony Hendra does John Lennon and Melissa Manchester does Yoko. Melissa also plays piano, Jim Payne plays drums and John "Cooker" LoPresti plays bass. **RADIO DINNER** also contains some clues to Paul's death, and, in fact, we can even hear Paul get shot for singing *Give Ireland Back To The Irish.* Also on that album is a spoof called *Concert In Bangla Desh.*

1258 NICOL, JIMMY & THE SHUBDUBS
Humpty Dumpty/Night Train   Mar--Mar 313   1965

Jimmy was the drummer for the Beatles for a short time in 1964 while Ringo was ill. Both sides of this one are instrumentals and are very heavy on drums.

1259-- NILSSON
1261   *You Can't Do That/Ten Little Indians*   RCA 9298   1967
       PANDEMONIUM SHADOW SHOW (LP)   RCA 3874   1967
       SCATALOGUE (LP)   Wizardo 322

Harry Nilsson's *You Can't Do That* used titles and lyrics from many Beatles' songs for its own lyrics. These include: *You Can't Do That, She's A Woman, I'm Down, Drive My Car, You're Gonna Lose That Girl, Good Day Sunshine, A Hard Day's Night, Rain, I Want To Hold Your Hand, Day Tripper, Paperback Writer, Do You Want To Know A Secret, Yesterday* and *Strawberry Fields Forever.* This song and the Beatles' *She's Leaving Home* also appear on the album **PANDEMONIUM SHADOW SHOW. SCATA-- LOGUE** is a bootleg album and contains a Beatle medley. Nilsson also co-- wrote *Stand Up And Holler*, another Beatle novelty done by the Foto--Fi Four. See their listing for full details.

1262 OGNIR & THE NITE PEOPLE
I Found A New Love   Samron 102   1964

In case you hadn't noticed, Ognir spelled backwards is Ringo.

1263
ORIGINAL LIVERPOOL BEAT (LP)   20th Century 3144 1964

There is no artist listed for this LP, so it is listed here by its title.

1264 OUTSIDERS
The Guy With The Long Liverpool Hair/The Outsiders Karate 505   1965

This group most likely had nothing to do with the Outsiders who went top–5 in
1966 with *Time Won't Let Me.*

1265 PARKER, GIGI & THE LONELIES
Beatles Please Come Back/In This Room   MGM 13225   1964

1266 PATTY CAKES
I Understand Them (A Love Song To The Beatles)/ Tuff 378   1964
Same (Instrumental)

1267 PAUL, LAFAWN
You Can Hold My Hand   Vandan 609   1964

1268 PAXTON, TOM
Crazy John/Things I Notice Now   Elektra 45667   1969

Paxton also wrote this song about John Lennon.

1269– PEEL, DAVID
1270 *Bring Back The Beatles/Imagine*   Orange 1001   1977
        BRING BACK THE BEATLES (LP)   Orange 004   1977

Peel and his group, The Lower East Side, had recorded for the Beatles' Apple
label and their album – **THE POPE SMOKES DOPE** – was a chart item. This
new album contains the following cuts:

The Beatles Pledge Of Allegiance	*The Ballad Of James Paul*
Bring Back The Beatles	*McCartney*
Coconut Grove	*With A Little Help From My*
Imagine	*Friends*
Turn Me On	*My Fat Budgie*
Lollipop Fish	*Keep John Lennon In America*
The Wonderful World Of Abbey Road	*(The John Lennon Interview)*
Apple Beatle Foursome	*B–E–A–T–L–E–S*

The words for *My Fat Budgie* were written by John Lennon as a poem which
appeared in *A Spaniard In The Works.* Peel Is backed by the Apple Band
which includes: Leslie Fradkin, Jeff Gilman, Andy Pierce, Tom Doyle,
Mike Murray, Fred Kramer, Scott Bailey, Sal Spicolla and Michael Angelo.

1271 PEOPLE
Come Back Beatles/Same Continued   Zebra 102   1978

1272 PEPPER, BILLY & THE PEPPERPOTS
MERSEYMANIA (LP)

349

1273 PERRYMAN, PAUL
    Just To Hold My Hand   Duke 158   1964

1274-- PETER, PAUL & MARY
1275   *I Dig Rock & Roll Music*   Warner Bros. 7067 1967
      ALBUM 1700 (LP)   Warner Bros. 1700 1967

      Peter Yarrow, Paul Stookey and Mary Travers made--up this popular group of the
      sixties. In *I Dig Rock & Roll Music,* which also appears on the album, they
      imitate several artists including the Beatles, Donovan, and the Mamas And
      Papas.

1276 PEYTON, DORI
    Ringo Boy/In The Spring Of The Year   Ohie 101   1964

1277 PHAETONS
    Beatle Walk/Frantic   Sahara 103   1964

      Jan & Dean are reported to have been involved in the making of this record.
      However, their names do not appear anywhere on the label. *Frantic* is done
      by the Premiers.

1278 PILLAR, DICK & THE ORCHESTRA
    Beatle Song/Johnny's Polka   Steljo 602   1964

1279 PRINCE, VIV
    Minuet For Ringo/Light Of The Charge Brigade   Columbia 7960   1964

      This was released in the U.K., but not the U.S. Prince was also with the Pretty
      Things, the Jeff Beck Group and was in the String Band with Denny Laine.

1280 PROF & THE PROFETTES
    Mud On My Tyre   1977

      It was reported in a Beatle fan magazine that the punk group Prof & The
      Profettes were going to record this novelty based on McCartney's *Mull Of
      Kintyre.* Whether or not it was ever recorded and released is unknown.

1281 RAE, DONNY & THE DEFIANTS
    Beatle Mania/Hold On   Arlen 521   1964

1282 RAINBO
    John You Went Too Far This Time/C'mon Teach   Roulette 7030   1969
    Me To Love

      Rainbo was soon to be famous actress Sissy Spacek. In this novelty she scolded
      John for appearing nude on the cover of the album **TWO VIRGINS**. In a
      1979 interview in *Rolling Stone*, Sissy said that she didn't even keep a copy
      of this record for herself.

1283 RAINBOWS
    My Ringo/He's Hooked On J's   Dot 16612   1964

1284 RAJAHS
    BEATLEMANIA: TRIBUTE TO THE BEATLES (EP) Sunday Mirror 002 1964

      This is an Australian release. Originals came with a cardboard picture jacket.

1285 RANDLE, DEL
      Introducing The Beatles To Monkey Land/The   Shakari 101/102   1964
      Monkey & The Beatles

      Del Randle wrote both sides of this record. The A–side was done with Garnell
      Cooper & The Kinfolks, while the B–side featured Booker T. & The MG's.

1286 REAL ORIGINAL BEATLES
      The Beatles Story/Same Pt. 2   Dot 16655   1964

1287 RELLA, CINDY
      Bring Me A Beatle For Christmas/Cla–wence   Drum Boy 112   1964

      Teddy Phillips wrote *Bring Me A Beatle For Christmas* and his orchestra is
      featured on the record.

1288– RESIDENTS
1289   **MEET THE RESIDENTS** (LP)   Ralph RR 0677   1979
       Beyond The Valley Of A Day In The Life

      There are two different album jackets for the **MEET THE RESIDENTS** album.
      The first shows the Beatles **MEET THE BEATLES** jacket with moustaches,
      beards, fangs, horns, etc. drawn on the picture. The second cover shows a
      pose similar to the pose on the *She Loves You* picture sleeve. John, Paul
      and George have the heads of crayfish and Ringo has the head of a starfish.
      The names on the jackets are Paul McCrawfish, John Crawfish, George
      Crawfish and Ringo Starfish.
      Beyond The Valley Of A Day In The Life appears on the bootleg album
      BEATLES vs. DON HO (Melvin MM08). See number 115 in the bootleg
      section.

1290 RHAMY, GARY
      Invasion Of The Bagels   1964

1291 RIFKIN, JOSHUA
      THE BAROQUE BEATLES BOOK (LP)   Elektra 7306   1965
      The Royal Beatleworks Musicke, MBE 1963   *"Last Night I Said," Cantata For*
      1. Overture: I Want To Hold Your Hand   *The Third Saturday After Shea*
      2. Rejouissance: I'll Cry Instead   *Stadium, MBE 58,000*
      3. La Paix: Things We Said Today   *1. Chorus: "Last Night I Said"*
      4. L'Amour S'en Cachant: You've Got   *Please Please Me*
      *   To Hide Your Love Away*   *2. Recitative: "In They Came*
      Epstein Variations, MBE 69A   *Joking" Aria: "When I Was*
      *   Hold Me Tight*   *Younger"*
      *   Murray The Klavierkitzler*   *Help*
                                                      3. Chorale: "You Know, If You
                                                          Break My Heart"
                                                          I'll Be Back
                                                      Harold Breines, Helpentenor. The
                                                      Canby Singers, Edward Tatnall
                                                      Canby, Director
                                                  Trio Sonata: Das Kaferlein MBE 004
                                                                              1/4
                                                      4. Grave–Allegro–Grave
                                                          Eight Days A Week
                                                      5. Quodlibette:
                                                          She Loves You
                                                          Thank You Girl
                                                          Hard Day's Night

351

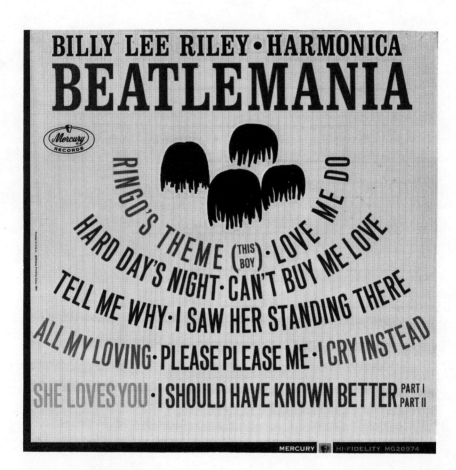

Beatlemania Harmonica (LP)   Mercury 20974 (Entry 1293)

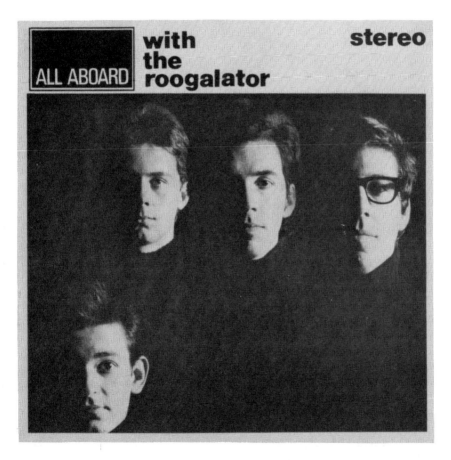

With The Roogalator (EP)   **Dynamite 45005 (Entry 1298)**

The full artist credit on this album reads Baroque Ensemble Of The Merseyside Kammermusickgesellschrft, Joshua Rifkin, conductor. The album made *Billboard* charts late in 1965. It remained on the charts for 17 weeks and reached number 83.

1292   RIGBY, ELEANOR
      Father McKenzie/Nudity   Amsterdam 85004   1970

Father McKenzie was co–written by Tom Scott and Bob Thiele and Scott also arranged and conducted the orchestra, while Thiele produced the record. Scott has been connected with the various Beatles on solo projects. Thiele also produced Steve Allen's Beatle novelty, *Here Comes Sgt. Pepper.*

1293   RILEY, BILLY LEE
      BEATLEMANIA HARMONICA (LP)   Mercury 20974   1964

Love Me Do	*Please Please Me*
I Cry Instead	*Tell My Why*
Hard Day's Night	*All My Loving*
Can't Buy Me Love	*I Should Have Known Better, Pt. 1*
She Loves You	*Ringo's Theme (This Boy)*
I Saw Her Standing There	*I Should Have Known Better, Pt. 2*

Riley, a popular rockabilly artist, had recorded *Red Hot* on Sun and had a 1972 hit with *I Got A Thing About You Baby.*

1294   RINGO, RON
      Ringo's Jerk/Queen Of The Jerk   Juggy 701   1964

1295   RINGOS
      Ain't No Big Thing/Blue Feeling   Hi 2071   1964

1296   ROACHES
      Beatlemania Blues/Angel Of Angels   Crossway 447   1964

1297   ROBERTS, BOBBY
      The Beatles For Christmas   1964

1298   ROOGALATOR
      WITH THE ROOGALATOR (EP)   Dynamite 45005   1976

The EP jacket for this record shows Roogalator in the exact same pose as the Beatles used on their album **WITH THE BEATLES**. The record was released in Holland. Roogalator is Danny Adler, Justin Heldreth, Nick Plytas and Julian Scott.

1299   RUFF, RAY & THE CHECKMATES
      Beatlemaniacs/Took A Liking To You   Lin 5034   1964

1300   RUSSELL, BOBBY & THE BEAGLES
      Roll Over Beethoven/Right Or Wrong   Spar 740   1964

1301   RYAN, PETER
      If We Try/I Can Hear Music   Ardvark 101   1973

1302   SANDERS, ARLEN
      Letter To Paul/Hopped Up Mustang   Faro 616   1964

The Beatles Greatest Hits (LP)   Canadian American 1017 (Entry 1304)

1303 SANDERS, GARY
      Ain't No Beatle/Ain't I Good To You   Warner Bros. 5676   1964

      Sanders was a popular DJ of this era. Sanders co–wrote this one with John Cale.
      It was produced by Cale and Leon Russell.

1304 SANTO & JOHNNY
      THE BEATLES GREATEST HITS (LP)   Canadian American 1017   1964
      A Hard Day's Night   *And I Love Her*
      Do You Want To Know A Secret   *All My Loving*
      She Loves You   *P.S. I Love You*
      I Want To Hold Your Hand   *Please Please Me*
      The Beatle Blues   *The Beatle Stomp*
      I Saw Her Standing There   *Can't Buy Me Love*

      Here, Santo and Johnny Farina do their instrumental versions of Beatle hits, plus
      a couple of Beatle novelties which they wrote. They are best remembered for
      their 1959 number 1 hit, *Sleep Walk*.

1305 SAXONS
      TRIBUTE TO THE BEATLES (EP)   Mordan 16084   1964

1306 SAXTONS
      The Beatle Dance/Sittin' On Top Of The World   Regina 305   1964

1307 SCHOOLBOYS
      BEATLEMANIA (LP)   Palace 778   1964

      This is the same LP as listed for the Liverpool Kids. See their entry for full details.

1308 SCRAMBLERS
      The Beatles Walk/The Beatles Blues   Del–Fi 4237   1964

1309 SELLERS, PETER
      A Hard Day's Night/Help   Capitol 5580   1966

      Done in a typical Sellers' comedy style.

1310 SEX BEATLES
      Will You Never/Fatal Fascination   1979

      A take–off of both the Beatles and the Sex Pistols. Released in the U.K.

1311 SHAGGY BOYS
      Stop The Clock   Red Bird 10–074   1966

1312 SHEARS, BILLY & THE ALL–AMERICANS
      Brother Paul/Message To Seymour   Silver Fox 121   1969

      Another novelty dealing with the "Paul is dead" rumor.

1313 SHEPPARD, NEIL
      You Can't Go Far Without A Guitar (Unless You're   Almont 314   1964
      Ringo Starr)/Betty Is The Girl

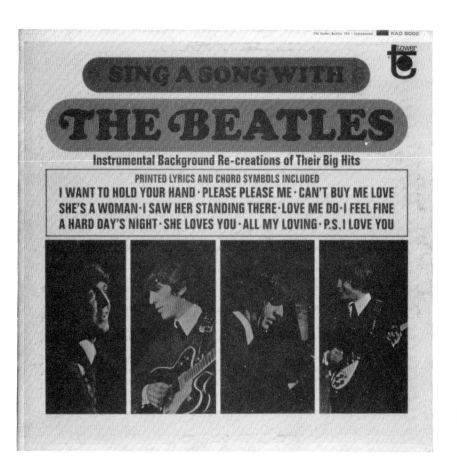

Sing Along With The Beatles (LP)   **Tower 5000 (Entry 1317)**

1314-- SHERMAN, ALLEN
1315   *I Hate The Beatles/Grow Mrs. Goldfarb*   Warner Bros. 5490 1964
    FOR SWINGIN' LIVERS ONLY (LP)   Warner Bros. 1569 1964

The album version of this novelty is titled *POP HATES THE BEATLES.* It is the same as the single even though the titles differ. It is done to the tune of *Pop Goes The Weasel* and is very well done. Sherman's parody and comedy records were well known before he recorded this Beatle novelty. His big hit had been *Hello Muddah, Hello Fadduh* in 1963.

1316 SILVER CONVENTION
    The Boys From Liverpool/A Song About The Boys   1978
    From Liverpool

This novelty by the popular disco group was released in West Germany.

1317

    SING ALONG WITH THE BEATLES -- INSTRUMENTAL   1965
    BACKGROUNDS (LP)   Tower 5000

A Hard Day's Night	*I Feel Fine*
I Saw Her Standing There	*P.S. I Love You*
Love Me Do	*Can't Buy Me Love*
She Loves You	*All My Lovin'*
Please Please Me	*I Want To Hold Your Hand*
She's A Woman	

The rumors run wild about this album, with some people claiming that the Beatles themselves are playing these instrumentals. True or not, the album commands a high price. The Beatles' pictures are on the jacket which also makes it a collector's item. The fold--open jacket has the lyrics to all the songs along with the chord symbols and guitar fingering charts.

1318 SONNY
    Beatle Squash   1964

Sonny Bono???

1319 SPADACHENE, SMITH
    Beatle Twist   Lynne 100   1964

1320 SPARROWS
    THAT MERSEY SOUND (LP)   Elkay 3009   1964

1321 STANDELLS
    Peppermint Beatle/The Shake   Liberty 55680   1964

1322 STARLETTES
    Ringo/All Dressed Up   Siana 717   1964

Written, arranged and produced by Anne Phillips of the Starlettes.

1323 STEEL, TRACY
    A Letter To Paul/Your Ring   Delaware 1705   1964

1324 STEIN, FRANKIE & HIS GHOULS
    MONSTER MELODIES (LP)   Power 341   1965

1. *Dr. Spook*	6. *Ghoulish Heart*
2. *In A Groovy Grave*	7. *Dressed To Kill*
3. *Frog Frug*	8. *All Choked Up*

4. *Melancholy Monsters*
5. *Haunted Mouse*

9. *Swingin' Head*
10. *Ain't Got No Body*

This album consists of saxaphone solos over Beatle and Kinks instrumentals.

1325 STERN, PAT & TINA
Sie Waren Die Helden Der 60er Jahre

A West German release. The title means "They Were The Heroes Of The 60's."

1326 STEWART, JUDY & HER BEATLE BUDDIES
Who Can I Believe/I'll Take You Back Again   Diplomat 0101   1964

1327 SWANS
The Boy With The Beatle Hair/Please Hurry Home   Cameo 302   1964

The Swans made the charts in March 1964. They remained on the charts for four week, hitting number 85.

1328 SWEETIES
Ich Wunsch Mir Sum Geburtstag Einin Beatle

A West German release. The title means "I Want A Beatle For My Birthday."

1329 TEEN BUGS
Yes You Can Hold My Hand/Teenitis   Blue River 208   1964

1330 TERMITES

See BEDBUGS.

1331 TERRI, DARLENE
Ringo Ringo/A Real Live Boy   Columbia 43042   1964

1332 THREE BLONDE MICE
Ringo Bells/The Twelve Days of Christmas   Atco 6342   1964

Ringo Bells is sung to the tune of *Jingle Bells*.

1333 TINY TIM
Bring Back The Beatles   1977

There has been talk of this record being recorded. Whether or not it was ever released is not known. Tiny Tim's real name is Herbert Khuarty. He appeared on the Beatles' *1968 CHRISTMAS RECORD* and sang *Nowhere Man*.

1334 TRIBUTES
Ringo Dingo/Here Comes Ringo   Donna 1391   1964

1335 TRIXIES
We Love You Beatles   Twinhit 5059   1964

1336 TURNBOW, JEANNE
Beattle Bug/Summertime   Ben–ron 1393   1964

1337 TWILITERS
My Beatle Hair Cut/Sweet Lips   Roulette 4546   1964

1338 TYSON, CLAY
The Marching Bedbugs   Winley 246   1964

1339 UPFRONTS
Do The Beatle/Most Of The Pretty Girls   Lummtone 114   1964

1340 U.S. BEATLEWIGS
She's Innocent (Oh Yeah)/Finger Poppin' Girl   Orbit 531   1964

1341 USHER, GARY
The Beetle/Jody   Capitol 5128   1964

Gary Usher and Roger Christian had produced the album, **THE BEATLES'
STORY** for Capitol Records. Usher and Christian wrote *The Beetle* and
Gary helped to produce it.

1342 VALENTINE, PENNY
I Want To Kiss Ringo Goodbye/Show Me The Way   Liberty 55774   1964
To Love You

Penny was a British newspaper columnist. She wrote for *Disc & Music Echo* and
Sounds.

1343 VARIOUS
BEATLES TRIBUTE ALBUM (LP)   SoN 119891

This bootleg album consists of the following Beatle novelties:

We Love You Beatles (Carefrees)
A Letter From Elaina (Casey Kasem)
Ringo For President (Young World
Singers)
Boy With The Beatle Hair (Swans)
The Beatles' Barber (Scott Douglas)
Beatlemania Blues (Roaches)
Christmas With The Beatles (Judy &
The Duets)
The Other Ringo (Larry Finnegan)

Little Beatle Boy (Angels)
Bring Back My Beatles (Detours)
Ringo Bells (Three Blond Mice)
A Letter To The Beatles (Four
Preps)
Treat Him Tender Maureen
(Angie & The Chicklettes)
*My Boyfriend Got A Beatle
Haircut* (Donna Lynn)
Interview With The Fab Four
(Harv Moore)

1344 VERNON GIRLS
We Love The Beatles/Her Lover Boy   Challenge 59234   1964

Lyn Cornell and Betty Prescott of this group were also members of the Carefrees,
who recorded their own Beatle novelty, *We Love You Beatles.* Lyn was
married to Andy White. White was the drummer that George Martin brought
in for the *Love Me Do/P.S. I Love You* sessions when he wasn't sure if
Ringo would fit in with the rest of the group.

1345 VICEROYS
Liverpool   U.S.A. 761   1964

1346 VITO & THE SALUTATIONS
Liverpool Bound/Can I Depend On You   Wells 1008   1964

Vito & The Salutations were Vito Balsamo, Shelly Buchansky, Randy Silverman,
Lenny Citrin and Frankie Fox. They had a 1963 hit with *Unchained
Melody* before recording this novelty.

1347 VULCANES
Liverpool/The Outrage   Capitol 5285   1964

1348 WAR
Beetles In A Bog/Cisco Kid   United Artists 163 1973

War is Howard Scott, B.B. Dickerson, Lonnie Jordan, Harold Brown, Papa Dee
Allen, Charles Miller and Lee Oskar.

1349 WEASELS
    THE LIVERPOOL BEAT (LP)   Wing 16282   1964

I Want To Hold Your Hand	*From Me To You*
She Loves You	*I Saw Her Standing There*
My Bonnie	*Way Down Upon The Swanee*
Green Sleeves	*River*
Danny Boy	*This Little Light Of Mine*
	Corrine, Corrina

1350 WEEKENDS
Ringo/I Want You   LeMans 001   1964

1351 WHIPPETS
Go Go With Ringo/I Want To Talk   Josie 921   1964

1352 WILDING, BOBBY
I Want To Be A Beatle/Since I've Been Wearing   DCP 1009   1964
My Hair Like A Beatle

1353 WOODS, LITTLE EDDIE
Bug Killer/Is It So Wrong   Comet 2165   1964

1354 WYNTER, PAT
Ringo, I Want To Know Your Secret   Take Five 631   1964

1355 YOUNG STRING CHORALE, LEON
John, Paul, George & Ringo/Westward Ho   Atco 6301   1964

1356 YOUNG WORLD SINGERS
Ringo For President/A Boy Like That   Decca 31660   1964

1357 ZACHARIAS & THE TREE PEOPLE
We're All Paul Bearers/Pt. II   Viking 1004   1969

Another novelty based on the "Paul is dead" rumor.

Break-In Novelties

The Beatle novelties that follow are of the break--in type. For those not familiar with this type of record, here is a brief description: This type of record, popularized in the late fifties by Buchanan and Goodman, used short clips from popular records as answers to questions asked by the artist. Beatle records have very often been used on this type of recording. Below are listed those break–ins that have used bits of Beatle records (group and solo). The record or records used are also listed. Flip sides have not been listed unless they too are Beatle novelties. The flip sides to many break--ins are simply instrumentals.

1358	**ALBEE & FRIENDS**		
	Hexorcist World Premiere	Nik Nik 74	1974
	You're Sixteen (Ringo Starr)		
1359	**APTER, BILL**		
	Hey Patty	Poly T 7968	1977
	Revolution (slow album version)		
	Give Peace A Chance (John Lennon)		

Also released on Unreleased Gold 799.

1360	**BRIDGER, BOBBY**		
	Interview Pt. 1/Pt. 2	Nugget 000	
1361--	**CHARLIE (REINHART)**		
1363	*Beatles/Best Ex–Beatle*	C&E 101	1979
	History Of The Beatles Pt. 1: Early Days/Hamburg Days	C&E 102/103	1980
	History Of The Beatles Pt. 2: Decca Audition/ Parlophone Session	C&E 104--104	1980

Beatles contains the following cuts: *Not A Second Time, Money, I'll Cry Instead, Anna, Dizzy Miss Lizzy, Dear Prudence, Sexy Sadie, I'm So Tired, A Hard Day's Night, Slow Down, Anytime At All, You Can't Do That, I'll Get You, Hello Goodbye, When I'm Sixty–Four, Long Tall Sally, Michelle, Eleanor Rigby, Lady Madonna, Martha My Dear, Kansas City, Got To Get You Into My Life, Here There And Everywhere, Fixing A Hole, She Came In Through The Bathroom Window, We Can Work It Out, Don't Bother Me, Piggies, Do You Want To Know A Secret, Everybody's Trying To Be My Baby, I Want To Tell You, Something, Devil In Her Heart, I'm Happy Just To Dance With You, Taxman, Long Long Long, What Goes On, Don't Pass Me By, The End, Act Naturally, With A Little Help From My Friends, Yellow Submarine* and *Good Night. Best Ex–Beatle* contains the following Pete Best records: *(I'll Try) Anything, Nobody But You, Last Night, Kansas City, I'm Blue, Just Wait And See, Shimmy Like My Sister Kate, Some Other Guy* and *Why Did You Leave Me Baby. Early Days* contains: *Six O'Clock, Oh My My, Mother, Bad Boy, Magneto And Titanium Man,*

Bip Bop, Ooh Baby (You Know That I Love You), All Things Must Pass, Sweet Little Sixteen, My Mummy's Dead, Not A Second Time, With A Little Luck, Paperback Writer, The Night Before, This Guitar, Bangla Desh, September In The Rain, Yes It Is, I Saw Her Standing There, It's So Hard, Roll Over Beethoven, Let 'Em In, Uncle Albert/Admiral Halsey, Well Well Well and *No Reply. Hamburg Days* contains *Mull Of Kintyre, Bye Bye Love, The Continuing Story Of Bungalow Bill, Norwegian Wood, Behind That Locked Door, Girl's School, How Do You Sleep, Beware Of Darkness, Man We Was Lonely, Bony Moronie, Sally G, Why Don't We Do It In The Road, Everybody's Trying To Be My Baby, Rock And Roll Music, Power To The People, A Hard Day's Night, It's Getting Better, Whatever Gets You Through The Night, I Want To Tell You, It's All Too Much, I Need You, The Mess, White Power/Promenade, Just Because, Nobody Loves You When You're Down And Out* and the following Pete Best records: *She's Alright, Keys To My Heart, Casting My Spell, I Can't Do Without You* and *I Need Your Lovin.' Decca Auditions* contains *Only People, When I'm Sixty–Four, Cold Turkey, Teddy Boy, Working Class Hero, Surprise Surprise, Listen To What The Man Said, Don't Let Me Wait Too Long, We Can Work It Out, Another Day, Out On The Streets, No No Song, Beaucoups Of Blues, Bless You, Hi Hi Hi, London Town, Penny Lane, The Continuing Story of Bungalow Bill, Maxwell's Silver Hammer, Deep Blue, Memphis, Love Of The Loved, Like Dreamers Do, Searchin', Sheik Of Araby, Sure To Fall, So Sad, The Answers In The End, I'm Down, I'm A Fool To Care, I Want You, Baby You're A Rich Man, Out Of The Blue, Maybe I'm Amazed, I'm Happy Just To Dance With You* and *Twist And Shout. Parlophone Sessions* contains: *No. 9 Dream, Cafe On The Left Bank, If I Needed Someone, Maybe I'm Amazed, Photographs, Hard Times, Down And Out, It's No Secret, Oo–Wee, All Together Now, Here There And Everywhere, Love Me Do, P.S. I Love You, Revolution No. 9, Let It Be, Back Off Boogaloo, Honey Don't, Please Please Me, This Song, Do You Want To Know A Secret, Boys, Band Of Gold (Ringo), When I Get Home, How Do You Do It* and *Isn't It A Pity.*

1364 CREEP
  Convention '76   NiXXXon 1976   1976
  Silly Love Songs (Wings)

CREEP stands for Committee to Rip off Each and Every Politician.

1365– GOODMAN, DICKIE
1369   *Presidential Interview (Flying Saucer '64)*   Audio Spectrum 75 1964
       A Hard Day's Night
       Batman And His Grandmother   Red Bird 10–058   1966
       Nowhere Man
       Watergrate   Rainy Wed. 202   1973
       My Love (Wings)
       Energy Crisis '74   Rainy Wed. 206   1974
         Helen Wheels (Wings); *Mind Games* (John Lennon); *You're Sixteen* (Ringo
         Starr)
       Mr. President   Rainy Wed. 207   1974
       Oh My My (Ringo Starr)

Four of Dickie Goodman's efforts made the charts. *Batman And His Grandmother* made it in May, 1966. It reached number 70 in its three weeks on the charts. In July, 1973, *Watergrate* started its seven week stay on the charts, during which time it reached number 42. In February, 1974, *Energy Crisis '74* started its eight week climb to number 33. Finally, in July of '74, *Mr. President* reached the charts. It hit number 73 during its four–week stay.

1370 GRAND CANYON
  Evil Boll–Weevil   Bang 713   1974
  Jet (Wings); *Baby, You're A Rich Man; Here, There And Everywhere*

  This one made the charts in November, 1974 and remained there five weeks, during which time it reached number 72.

1371 HARDSELL, HAROLD
  Speaking Of Streaking   Dunhill 4384 1974
  Oh My My (Ringo Starr)

  This was done using a Howard Cosell--like voice.

1372 HAGGENESS & WEST
  Doctor Gorrie's Laboratory   Clowd 7302   1973
  Live And Let Die (Wings)

  The artists are Fred Haggeness and Frank Wataschke.

1373 JERRY B. & THE SOUL AGENTS
  Double O Soul In Action   Double Check 4002 1976
  Yesterday

1374 J.P. AND THE REACTORS
  Three Mile Island Interlude Three Mile Island 3M--41379 1979
  Yesterday

  The artist here is J.P. Megonnell . . . the subject should be obvious.

1375 KALLUM, JOHNNY
  The Big Debate   Bang 730   1976
  Silly Love Songs (Wings); *Let 'Em In* (Wings)

1376 LEVINE, JEFF
  The Interview/(Wyatt Burp Meets) Silly The Kid//A Chip EP--2501 1978
  New Mr. President/San Clemente Report

  The Interview contains Paul McCartney's *Band On The Run.* Ringo's *Oh My My* can be heard on *Silly The Kid.* Anne Murray's version of the Beatles' *You Won't See Me* is on *San Clemente Report.* The EP is pressed on green vinyl.

1377 McNAUGHTON, BYRON
  Right From The Sharks Jaws   Jamie 1427   1975
  No No Song (Ringo Starr)

1378 MOORE, HARV
  Interview Of The Fab Four   American Artists 20 1964

  The songs used by Moore include: *I Want To Hold Your Hand, Honey Don't, I Should Have Known Better, I Feel Fine, No Reply, Mr. Moonlight, A Hard Day's Night, I'm A Loser, Long Tall Sally, Kansas City* and *She Loves You.*

1379 POPULAR DEMAND
  400 Mile Gas Line   Crunch 001   1979

  Help and *Get Back* are used in this break--in about the gas shortage.

1380 PROFESSOR BUG
    Beatlemania Pt. 1/Pt. 2   Beetle 1600   1964

    The Beatle songs used include: *Do You Want To Know A Secret, I'll Get You, It Won't Be Long, I Want To Hold Your Hand, Misery* and *She Loves You.*

1381
    Reunion   Club No. 3

    No artist is listed for this record. Beatle cuts used include: *Here Comes The Sun, She Came In Through The Bathroom Window, Something, Ticket To Ride, Get Back, You've Got To Hide Your Love Away, Everybody's Got Something To Hide Except For Me And My Monkey, Boys, Penny Lane, Back In The U.S.S.R., Yesterday, Fixing A Hole, Hello Goodbye, A Hard Day's Night, Paperback Writer, With A Little Help From My Friends, It Don't Come Easy, You Won't See Me, Drive My Car, Can't Buy Me Love, I Am The Walrus, We Can Work It Out, Till There Was You, Revolution, Ballad Of John And Yoko* and *She Loves You.*

1382 SCHWARTZ, PHIL & HAROLD WAGNER
    Interview Pt. 1/Pt. 2   Doctor–My–Eyes 20/20   1977
    No No Song (Ringo Starr)

1383 SOLOMON, ED
    The Beatle Flying Saucer   Diamond 160   1964

    Although it's called *The Beatle Flying Saucer*, there are only three Beatle songs used -- *I Saw Her Standing There, I Want To Hold Your Hand* and *She Loves You.*

1384 U AND I
    Report To The People   Black Patch 1   1976
    Let It Be; Come And Get It (Badfinger)

1385 WHITEHEAD, COL.
    Liverpool Landing   Counsel 050

Take-Offs & Rip-Offs, Put-Ons & Put-Downs

The remaining Beatle novelties have been separated from the rest for various reasons. Beatlemania, Klaatu and the Rutles were or are groups of people who have tried to imitate the Beatles, or, in the case of the Rutles, mock them. Costumes, songs, etc. are made to look and sound as much like the Beatles as possible. The Four Seasons and Herman's Hermits albums use drawings rather than songs to make them Beatle novelties.

1386– BEATLEMANIA
1387   BEATLEMANIA (LP)   Arista 8501   1978
       BEATLEMANIA (EP)   Eva–Tone 324771 1978

The two–record LP contains:

I Want To Hold Your Hand	*Eleanor Rigby*
She Loves You	*Nowhere Man*
Help	*Strawberry Fields Forever*
Can't Buy Me Love	*Penny Lane*
Day Tripper	*Magical Mystery Tour*
Yesterday	
Lady Madonna	*All You Need Is Love*
Fool On The Hill	*Revolution* ·
Got To Get You Into My Life	*Hey Jude*
Michelle	*I Am The Walrus*
Get Back	*The Long And Winding Road*
	Let It Be

The one–sided EP contains:
She Loves You
I Want To Hold Your Hand
A Hard Day's Night

The EP was issued to members of the Beatlemania Fan Club only. It was never commercially available. It was issued as a red flexi-disc.
This Broadway show was billed as "Not the Beatles. An incredible simulation." It was just that to many people. To others it was a rip–off of the Beatles. The Beatles themselves, or at least Apple, is suing the producers of Beatlemania. The pseudo–Beatles in the New York cast, and the ones appearing on these records are: Joe Pecorino, who plays rhythm guitar and serves as John; Mitch Weissman, bass player and Paul look––a––like; Leslie Fradkin who handles the part of George; and Justin McNiell on the drums as Ringo. They are backed up by off–stage musicians including Andrew Dorfman, Larry Davidson, Sally Rosoff, Mort Silver, Peter Van Dewater, Randy Clark, Reed Kailing, P.M. Howard and Bobby Taylor. Leslie Fradkin also appears on another Beatle novelty. He is part of the Apple Band that backs David Peel. The executive producers of Beatlemania are David Krebs and Steven Leber. The album was produced by Sandy Yagunda and Kenny Laguna. All songs were recorded live at the Winter Garden Theatre.

1388 FOUR SEASONS
   THE GENUINE LIFE IMITATION GAZETTE   Philips 600–290   1969
   (LP)

The LP jacket for this Four Seasons album is in the form of a six page imitation
newspaper. On one page is a cartoon showing the Beatles kneeling in front
of the Maharishi. They have their fingers crossed behind their backs. The
caption reads, "People worship crosses with fingers crossed." The back page,
serving as a sports page, has the "American Rock League Standings." These
baseball–like standings show the Four Seasons in first place and the Beatles
a distant second. The album also contains an eight–page advertising insert
printed on newsprint. On the back is an ad for A&P food stores showing
"Chocolate covered Beatles $1.08."

1389 HERMAN'S HERMITS
   BOTH SIDES OF HERMAN'S HERMITS (LP)   MGM 4386   1966

The cartoon–like drawing that serves as the back cover for this album shows
Herman's Hermits on stage performing. In the audience we see Paul, George
and Ringo. John is there too, but he has his back to us and we can't see his
face. Other dignitaries seated in the audience are: Fidel Castro, Nikita
Kruschev, Mao Tse Tung, Harry Truman, Lyndon Johnson, Ed Sullivan,
Anthony Armstrong Jones, Princess Margaret, Burt Lancaster, Elizabeth
Taylor and Barbra Streisand.

1390– KLAATU
1391   KLAATU (LP)   Capitol 11542   1976
   Sub–Rosa Subway/Calling Occupants   Capitol 4412   1977

In late August of 1976, when most of us were headed back to school, Capitol
Records released an album by a new group. The group called themselves
Klaatu, their album was titled **KLAATU** and all of the songs were published
•by Klaatoons. The album jacket contained no traces of the identity of the
members of the group. As is usually the case with the first record by an
unknown group, the album sat out the remainder of the year on radio station
and record store shelves. Then, early in 1977, a disc jockey named Charlie
Parker of station WDRC in Providence, R.I., played a cut from the album
over the air. The response was immediate -- hundreds of listeners phoned in
to ask if this was a new Beatle record that they were hearing. Is Klaatu the
Beatles? The great search was on. Record collectors, Beatle fans and DJ's
suddenly started playing the role of Columbo and began searching for clues
to the group's identity. The first people to be contacted were the officials
of Capitol Records, but they proved to be of little help. Capitol claimed
that they had never actually seen Klaatu. The tape had been brought to
them by Frank Davies of GRT Canada, who was acting as Klaatu's manager.
Capitol officials had bought the tape without ever seeing the group and
Davies had not told them anything about Klaatu. Next, Davies was asked
the big question, is Klaatu the Beatles? His answer amounted to a big
maybe. He wouldn't say it was and he wouldn't say it wasn't.
   After receiving no definite answer from these sources, the record sleuths turned to
looking for clues on the Klaatu album and on albums by ex–Beatle members.
Nearly 30 clues were quickly discovered. Some of the clues, as you might
imagine, were a lot more convincing than others. The clues are as follows:

1.   Klaatu was the name of a peace emissary sent to Earth in the 1951 film "The
     Day The Earth Stood Still." On the album jacket of Ringo's **GOODNIGHT
     VIENNA** Ringo appears dressed as Klaatu. With him is Gort, Klaatu's
     robot. This links at least one ex–Beatle with the name Klaatu.

2. In the movie mentioned above, Klaatu is asked where he is from. His answer is Venus and Mars, which is the title of an album by Paul and Wings.
3. Also in the film, Klaatu tells a young boy of a train with no obstacles. Could this have been the inspiration for the song *Sub--Rosa Subway,* one of the songs on the Klaatu album?
4. At the end of his concert in Boston in 1976, Paul shouted "See you when the Earth stands still." Could this have been another reference to the film?
5. McCartney wrote and recorded the song *Magneto And Titanium Man.* These two characters are from the Marvel Comics. Could the Marvel Comics have been the inspiration for the song *Dr. Marvello* on the Klaatu album?
6. McCartney had a poster of another Marvel character on stage with him during the '76 tour. The picture was of the Hulk and according to Marvel officials, the picture was from a story entitled "The Hulk--Klaatu Confrontation."
7. On McCartney's **VENUS AND MARS** LP, a Ken and Terry are thanked. Two of the people who work at the Toronto Sound Studio where much of the Klaatu album was recorded are named Ken Morris and Terry Brown. Just a coincidence?
8. In the booklet included with Paul's **RED ROSE SPEEDWAY** album, there are many pictures of rockets, spaceships and even a space station. More references to outer space.
9. Someone (nobody seems to know who) supposedly made a voiceprint of one of Klaatu's singers and claims that it matches McCartney's voiceprint.
10. On an ad for Ringo's **GOODNIGHT VIENNA** album which appeared in *Billboard* magazine, the following phrase appears: "Don't forget: Klaatu Barato Nikto." This is yet another reference to the film mentioned above.
11. On the inner jacket of Ringo's album **RINGO'S ROTOGRAVURE**, released shortly after the Klaatu album, this statement appears under a picture of Ringo: "I've been through the metaphaser." Could this mean that Ringo has been changed into Klaatu?
12. On the inner jacket of George's **33 1/3** LP there is a small picture of the sun which closely resembles the sun on the front of the Klaatu album.
13. On George's greatest hits album (U.S.) there is a strange drawing on the front of the jacket – could this be a rocket ship? Elsewhere on the jacket and sleeve are pictures of star clusters. More references to outer space.
14. In the booklet that came with John's **WALLS AND BRIDGES** album, John makes this quote: "On the 23rd August, 1974 at 9 o'clock I saw a U.F.O." Could this have been when Klaatu was formed? Four of the eight songs on the Klaatu album were copyrighted in 1974.
15. Klaatu is not a word in any Earth language. The closest anything comes to it is Klaatau, a small city in eastern Europe. The chief produce of the town is roses and Paul had an album called **RED ROSE SPEEDWAY.**
16. The songs on the Klaatu album are mainly about magic, mystery and touring. Every Beatle fan knows that the Beatles had an album entitled **MAGICAL MYSTERY TOUR.**
17. Frank Davies, Klaatu manager, worked for EMI from 1965 until 1967. The Beatles recorded at EMI during that period.
18. Is the title of the song *Sub--Rosa Subway* a clue to look at the roots on the front, bottom of the Klaatu album jacket?
19. With a little imagination, you can spell out the name Beatles in the roots mentioned in number 18.
20. The Beatles' albums were on Capitol. Klaatu's was also on Capitol.
21. In *Sub--Rosa Subway,* in the section where Klaatu is singing "to Brahmsian tunes" over and over again, there are several short bursts of something playing backwards. When this section is played in the right direction, they can be heard saying "it's us." It's us . . . the Beatles?
22. The Morse code message in *Sub--Rosa Subway* say they are calling a spaceship over London. More references to space, plus the Beatles' Apple Label was based in London.

23. In the song *Calling Occupants* is the line, "we are your friends." Are they our friends, the Beatles?
24. *California Jam* ends with "yeah, yeah, yeah," just as did the Beatles' own hit *She Loves You*.
25. In *Doctor Marvello* there is the line, "a sentimental journey was hazily recalled. Though it sounds absurd, we're completely cured and now we're fine." Is this a clue that the Beatles' differences have been patched and now they're back together again?
26. In the song *Sir Bodsworth Rugglesby III*, this line appears: "Officially presumed as dead. But the words he left behind still echo through my mind. I'm the only man who'll ever get to hell and back alive." Could Sir Rugglesby really be the Beatles? Presumed dead when they broke up, but their music wouldn't die so they got back together again.

There are also a few negative clues that have been uncovered. These include:

27. In the last song on the Klaatu album, *Little Neutrino,* is the line "it's only you, it can't be me for I myself refuse to be." Is this a declaration that Klaatu is not the Beatles because the Beatles refuse to get back together again?
28. In the March 26, 1977 issue of *Billboard* is an ad for the Klaatu album. The caption says simply, "Klaatu is Klaatu." Not the Beatles, not anyone else, just Klaatu.

Besides all these clues, it's easy for even the casual listener to hear the similarities between some of Klaatu's songs and those of the Beatles. They especially sound like the Beatle songs of the *Sgt. Pepper* era. But, after all the fuss over searching for clues and after Capitol undoubtedly sold many many more copies of the Klaatu album than they would have sold without all the Beatle publicity, the truth came out. Klaatu was not the Beatles! They were just a Toronto–based group of studio musicians. Klaatu is John Woloschuk (who is also known as Chip Dale and I.M. Carpenter), Cary Draper, David Long and Dino Tome.
Both the album and the single made the charts, but neither fared too well.

1392– RUTLES
1394

THE RUTLES (LP)	Warner Bros.	3151	1978
I Must Be In Love/Doubleback Alley	Warner Bros.	8560	1978
THE RUTLES (12–inch EP)	Warner Bros.	E723	1978

The songs included on the album are:

Hold My Hand	*Good Times Roll*
Number One	*Doubleback Alley*
With A Girl Like You	*Cheese And Onions*
I Must Be In Love	*Another Day*
Ouch	*Piggies In The Middle*
Living In Hope	*Let's Be Natural*
Love Life	
Nevertheless	

The 12–inch EP is pressed on yellow vinyl and includes these songs:

I Must Be In Love	*Another Day*
Doubleback Alley	*Let's Be Natural*
With A Girl Like You	

The Rutles' hour–and–a–half TV special, "All You Need Is Cash," was a spoof of the history of the Beatles and the album and all other records were from that special. The group deliberately tried to sound and act like the Beatles. The

Rutles are the brainchild of Neil Innes. He wrote all the songs on the album and also produced them. Neil played Ron Nasty, John's counterpart. The others were Eric Idle as Dirk McQuickly (Paul), Rikki Fataar as Stig O'Hara (George) and John Halsey as Barry Wom (Ringo). Besides looking and sounding like the Beatles, the album jacket and booklet contain take--offs on various Beatles' albums. We find albums like **MEET THE RUTLES, SGT. RUTTERS DARTS CLUB BAND, LET IT ROT, A HARD DAY'S RUT, OUCH** and **TRAGICAL HISTORY TOUR**. Even the songs on these albums are mocking Beatles' song titles. On **TRAGICAL HISTORY TOUR** are songs like *The Fool On The Pill, Lying, Blue Gay Way, Your Mother Should Go, I Am The Waitress, Hello Get Lost, W.C. Fields Forever, Denny Lane, Abie You're A Rich Man* and *All You Need Is Lunch.*

Francois Glorieux Plays The Beatles (LP)   Vanguard VSD 79417 (Entry 1151)

Personal Name Index

After consulting the main listing of people and groups listed alphabetically in the novelty section, this index may be used in two supplemental ways: (1) to find first *or additional* references to names of people and groups mentioned elsewhere within that section (i.e., other than as the main entry), and (2) to search for novelties under alternate versions of the main form of entry used in the novelty section. The former references appear in upper and lower case, the latter in capital LETTERS. References to the Beatles as a group are not given here, as nearly every entry mentions them in one way or another. However, references to the individual Beatles are recorded here. All references are to entry number.

Song & Album Title Index

This index contains references to all novelty album, EP, and song titles *except* for actual Beatles song titles. "Covered" versions or variations of Beatles songs done by other persons or groups in a novelty fashion are indexed separately. No flipsides are listed unless they, too, are novelties. All novelty album titles mentioned in the novelty section, however, are indexed here, whether their unusual quality is one of content, title, performer(s), or other Beatles association. Again, a variety of form of entry for titles has been used to facilitate location of titles; references are to entry numbers.

Cover Version Index

This index contains references to Beatles' group or solo song titles "covered" by people or groups listed in the novelty section. Novelty cover versions of songs written but not recorded by Lennon/McCartney are also included. To find album titles containing cover versions, consult the **Album & Song Title Index.** References are to the first entry number of the performer(s) who recorded the song.

A Hard Day's Night 1052, 1094, 1129, 1291, 1293, 1304, 1309, 1317
All My Loving 1029, 1052, 1088, 1094, 1129, 1293, 1304, 1317
All You Need Is Love 1386
And I Love Her 1052, 1304
Any Time At All 1052
Boys 1046
Can't Buy Me Love 1021, 1052, 1094, 1151, 1293, 1304, 1317, 1386
Day Tripper 1386
Don't Bother Me 1052
Do You Want To Know A Secret 1094, 1304
Eight Days A Week 1052, 1291
Eleanor Rigby 1151, 1386
Fool On The Hill 1151, 1386
From Me To You 1022, 1029, 1094, 1349
Get Back 1386
Girl 1151
Got To Get You Into My Life 1386
A Hard Day's Night 1052, 1094, 1129, 1291, 1295, 1304, 1309, 1317
Help 1029, 1119, 1151, 1291, 1309, 1386
Hey Jude 1386
Hold Me Tight 1291
I Am The Walrus 1386
I Feel Fine 1032, 1052, 1317
I'll Be Back 1052, 1291
I'll Cry Instead 1291, 1293
I'll Get You 1052, 1129
Imagine 1069
I'm A Loser 1052
I'm Happy Just To Dance With You 1052
In My Life 1151
I Saw Her Standing There 1035, 1094, 1293, 1304, 1317, 1349
I Should Have Known Better 1052, 1293
It's For You 1029
It Won't Be Long 1052
I Want To Hold Your Hand 1019, 1022, 1035,

1040, 1065, 1073, 1094, 1122, 1129, 1164, 1204, 1226, 1243, 1291, 1304, 1317, 1349, 1386
Kansas City 1046
Lady Madonna 1386
Let It Be 1151, 1386
Little Child 1052
The Long And Winding Road 1386
Love Me Do 1022, 1094, 1156, 1293, 1317
Magical Mystery Tour 1386
Michelle 1052, 1151, 1386
My Bonnie 1056, 1065, 1223, 1226, 1349
My Sweet Lord 1093
No Reply 1052
Norwegian Wood 1052, 1151
Nowhere Man 1052, 1386
Ob-La--Di, Ob--La Da 1151
One And One Is Two 1012
Paperback Writer 1052
Penny Lane 1386
Please Please Me 1022, 1023, 1056, 1094, 1129, 1291, 1293, 1304, 1317
P.S. I Love You 1094, 1304, 1317
Rain 1052
Revolution 1386
Ringo's Theme (This Boy) 1052, 1293
Roll Over Beethoven 1043, 1223, 1300
The Saints 1065
She Loves You 1022, 1023, 1029, 1040, 1073, 1075, 1094, 1129, 1156, 1164, 1213, 1226, 1291, 1293, 1304, 1317, 1349, 1386
She's A Woman 1052, 1317
Strawberry Fields Forever 1386
Tell Me Why 1052, 1293
Thank You Girl 1291
Things We Said Today 1052, 1291
This Boy 1052, 1293

381

Break-In Index

The **Break--In Index** contains references to all Beatles' group and solo songs used in break--in records listed in the novelty section. There are also several songs by Pete Best and others included in this index. If the same entry number appears twice after a particular song title, it means that a break--in of the song was used on two different records by the artist(s).

Titles-As-Lyrics Index

A number of Beatle novelty songs based their lyrical content on Beatles' song titles. This index contains references to the Beatles' songs used in novelties of this type. If the same entry number appears twice after a particular song title, it means that the song title was used in more than one song by the artist.

Across The Universe 1017
A Day In The Life 1082,
A Hard Day's Night 1082, 1082
All My Loving 1082, 1082
All You Need Is Love 1017, 1082
And I Love Her 1082
Back In The U.S.S.R. 1082
Because 1082
Birthday 1082
Blackbird 1082
Can't Buy Me Love 1082
Come Together 1082
Cry Baby Cry 1082
A Day In The Life 1082
Day Tripper 1082, 1113, 1259
Don't Let Me Down 1082
Do You Want To Know A Secret 1082, 1259
Drive My Car 1082, 1259
Eight Days A Week 1082, 1082
Eleanor Rigby 1082, 1113
Fool On The Hill 1082
For No One 1082
For You Blue 1017
From Me To You 1082
Get Back 1082, 1113
Girl 1082
Golden Slumbers 1082
Good Day Sunshine 1082, 1259
Got To Get You Into My Life 1082
A Hard Day's Night 1082, 1082
Hello Goodbye 1082
Help 1082
Here Comes The Sun 1017
Here, There And Everywhere 1082
Hey Jude 1082
Honey Pie 1082
I Am The Walrus 1082
I Feel Fine 1017, 1082
If I Fell 1082
I'm A Loser 1082

I'm Down 1259
I Saw Her Standing There 1082, 1113
I Should Have Known Better 1082
I've Got A Feeling 1017
I Wanna Be Your Man 1082
I Want To Hold Your Hand 1082, 1113, 1259
I Want You (She's So Heavy) 1082
Julia 1082
Lady Madonna 1017, 1082
Let It Be 1017, 1082
The Long And Winding Road 1017, 1082
Love Me Do 1082
Lucy In The Sky With Diamonds 1082
Michelle 1082
The Night Before 1082
Ob–La–Di, Ob–La–Da 1082, 1113
Oh Darling 1082
One After 909 1017
Paperback Writer 1082, 1259
Penny Lane 1082
Please Please Me 1082
Rain 1259
Revolution 1082
Rocky Raccoon 1082
Sgt. Pepper's Lonely Hearts Club Band 1082, 1113
Sexy Sadie 1082
She Loves You 1082
She's A Woman 1082, 1259
She's Leaving Home 1082
Something 1017, 1082, 1082
Strawberry Fields Forever 1082, 1259
Taxman 1082
Tell Me Why 1082
Ticket To Ride 1082
Twist And Shout 1082, 1113
We Can Work It Out 1082
When I'm Sixty-Four 1082
With A Little Help From My Friends 1082
Yellow Submarine 1082

Label Index

label number	entry number	label numbe	entry number	label number	entry number
A.A.		ATCO		391	1046
133	1054	230	1124	CANADIAN AMERICAN	
ACADEMY		6301	1355	1017	1304
112	1136	6331	1221	C & E	
ALL LLOYDS		6342	1332	101	1361
?	1214	7058	1205	102/103	1361
ALMONT		ATILA		104/105	1361
314	1313	211	1178	CAPITOL	
AMERICAN ARTISTS		AUDIO JOURNAL		2085	1223
20	1378	1	1031	2506	1188
AMSTERDAM		AUDIO SPECTRUM		2642	1052
85004	1292	75	1365	4412	1390
ANNETTE		AVI		5127	1223
1000	1234	12–182	1113	5128	1341
APOGEE		BANANA		5143	1147
105	1125	38	1254	5144	1010
APPLAUSE		BANG		5285	1347
1002	1170, 1203	713	1370	5345	1100
		730	1375	5580	1309
APT		BEATBAD		11542	1390
25080	1009	1000	1012	CASTLE	
ARC		BEATLE		101	1025
?	1237	554–14	1142	CATCH	
ARC INTERNATIONAL		BEATLES		103	1071
834	1236	800	1046	CENTAUR	
ARDVARK		BEETLE		106	1195
101	1301	1600	1380	CHALLENGE	
ARGO		BELL		9372	1036
5469	1242	605	1230	59234	1344
ARGUS		BEN--RON		CHANCELLOR	
250	1235	1393	1336	1145	1130
ARHOOLIE		BLACK PATCH		CHARGER	
507	1141	1	1384	101	1097
ARISTA		BLUE CAT		CHATTAHOOCHIE	
0511	1192	115	1041	637	1189
8501	1386	BLUE RIVER		CHESS	
ARLEN		208	1329	1488	1044
521	1281	BYP		CLINTON	
ASININE		101	1002	1012	1045
1	1110	102	1006	CHIP	
ASSULT		1001	1002	2501	1376
1893	1027	CAMEO		CLOWD	
ASTOR		302	1327	7302	1372
002	1077	307	1202		

389

label number	entry number	label number	entry number	label number	entry number
CLUB		DIMENSION		74501	1042
no. 3	1381	1024	1106	FONTANA	
COED		DIPLOMACY		427	1068
594	1231	X5	1126	FORTUNE	
COLUMBIA		X6	1126	861	1158
7960	1279	DIPLOMAT		FOTO–FI	
21470	1099	0101	1326	107	1146
23529	1222	2307	1026	FRIGHT 'N	
26095	1246	2307	1226	1011	1240
43042	1331	2313	1024	GAYE	
43351	1217	DOCTOR--MY--EYE		004	1167
43512	1217	20/20	1382	GNP–CRESCENDO	
43547	1067	DONNA		311	1060
43813	1217	1391	1334	GOLDEN CREST	
45950	1062	DOT		584	1172
COMET		16592	1074	GRANITE	
2165	1353	16612	1283	537	1001
CONSTELLATION		16655	1286	GUEST STAR	
118	1220	16688	1133	2307	1026
CORAL		DOUBLE CHECK		HER MAJESTY	
62402	1057	4002	1373	101	1187
CORONET		DRUM BOY		HERMATAGE	
212	1073	108	1200	822	1149
COUNSEL		112	1287	HI	
050	1385	DUKE		2071	1295
CROSSWAY		158	1273	HIT	
447	1296	DUNHILL		104	1122
CROWN		4097	1000	106	1075
399	1065	4384	1371	107	1056
CRUNCH		DYNAMITE		111	1075
001	1379	45005	1298	113	1021
DAWN		ELEKTRA		HMV	
551	1104	6E–227	1106	7EG68887	1129
DAY DELL		7306	1291	HURRICANE	
1002	1090	45667	1268	1937	1245
DCP		46568	1106	IMPERIAL	
1008	1043	74006	1092	12276	1106
1009	1352	ELKAY		INTERNATIONAL	
1126	1174	3009	1320	COMMITTEE TO RE–	
DEBBY		EPIC		UNITE THE BEATLES	
069	1253	AE7--1095	1254	001	1185
DECCA		9721	1161	JAMIE	
11929	1046	10983	1244	1427	1377
12551	1102	33443	1162	JERDEN	
31660	1356	50096	1162	792	1198
DELAWARE		?	1254	JOHNNY	
1705	1323	ERA		101	1173
DEL FI		3132	1020	JOLA	
4233	1190	ERA/HAPPY TIGER		1000	1194
4237	1308	108	1154	JOSIE	
DESIGN		EVA--TONE		921	1351
170	1035	324771	1386	JUBILEE	
DIAMOND		EXPRESS		5472	1027
160	1383	801	1132	JUGGY	
DIETY		FARO		701	1294
0870	1232	616	1302	KAMA SUTRA	
6387	1232	FIRE--SIGN		510	1169

label number	entry number	label number	entry number	label number	entry number
KARATE		13225	1265	341	1324
505	1264	13481	1239	PRESTIGE	
KING		14097	1252	313	1064
5881	1040	MILLENIUM		PUNCH	
KOOK		602	1143	?	1199
1026	1111	8000	1143	QUEST	
LAURIE		MR. MAESTRO		101	1030
3630	1093	711	1046	"R"	
LAVE HE		712	1046	512	1120
1008	1121	M.O.C.		RAINY WEDNESDAY	
LAWN		658	1184	202	1365
229	1101	MONTEL		206	1365
LEGRAND		966	1241	207	1365
1033	1191	MORDAN		RALPH	
LeMANS		16084	1305	RR0677	1288
001	1350	NAN		RCA	
LIBERTY		3004	1087	2977	1248
3388	1094	NEW DESIGN		3583	1206
7388	1094	1008	1181	3682	1206
55134	1094	NIK NIK		3874	1259
55679	1037	74	1358	8345	1164
55680	1321	NIXXXON		8438	1248
55774	1342	1976	1364	8660	1206
LIMELIGHT		NOVEL		8816	1206
3017	1148	711	1069	8906	1206
3022	1135	NUGGET		8968	1206
LIN		000	1360	9158	1206
5034	1299	OHIE		9298	1259
LOADSTONE		101	1276	10641	1152
1605	1193	ORANGE		74--0290	1138
LONDON		004	1269	REALM	
3379	1088	1001	1269	001	1115
9638	1098	ORBIT		RED BIRD	
10614	1088	531	1340	10--058	1365
LUMMTONE		PALACE		10--074	1311
114	1339	777	1213	REGINA	
LYNNE		778	1307	305	1306
100	1319	PARKWAY		REPRISE	
MA		899	1156	0326	1243
74	1182	903	1157	RIC	
MAGNIFIQUE		938	1123	146	1137
18	1155	7053	1160	RONDO	
MAR--MAR		PHILIPS		2026	1204
313	1258	40224	1055	ROSE	
McSHERRY		600--290	1388	002	1159
1285	1117	PIOUS		ROULETTE	
MERCURY		310	1032	4546	1337
20974	1293	POLYDOR		4550	1002
72262	1079	725	1201	4559	1002
72297	1250	6517	1017	4589	1168
73680	1015	15118	1017	7030	1282
MERRI		POLY T		RSO	
6011	1081, 1166	7968	1359	899	1082
		PORT		3035	1082
MGM		70033	1091	RUST	
4386	1389	POWER		5076	1229

Topical Index

ANSWER BEATLE SONGS (GROUP &
SOLO) & FEMALE VERSIONS OF
BEATLE SONGS
1027, 1058, 1060, 1162, 1267, 1273,
1329

BEATLES IN TITLE (THIS INCLUDES
BEETLES; JOHN, PAUL, GEORGE
AND RINGO; BEATLEMANIA;
FAB FOUR, ETC.)
1001, 1002, 1007, 1010, 1014, 1016,
1022, 1023, 1024, 1026, 1027, 1029,
1031, 1036, 1039, 1042, 1043, 1045,
1046, 1052, 1054, 1061, 1062, 1064,
1065, 1066, 1068, 1070, 1071, 1072,
1073, 1074, 1079, 1087, 1088, 1092,
1094, 1098, 1099, 1101, 1104, 1106,
1112, 1113, 1115, 1116, 1117, 1120,
1121, 1125, 1126, 1129, 1130, 1132,
1133, 1139, 1141, 1145, 1147, 1150,
1152, 1155, 1157, 1158, 1159, 1160,
1167, 1170, 1171, 1172, 1173, 1174,
1178, 1179, 1180, 1182, 1184, 1185,
1186, 1187, 1193, 1194, 1197, 1200,
1201, 1203, 1213, 1215, 1220, 1223,
1225, 1226, 1228, 1229, 1230, 1234,
1242, 1244, 1245, 1246, 1250, 1251,
1253, 1254, 1265, 1269, 1271, 1277,
1278, 1281, 1284, 1285, 1286, 1287,
1291, 1293, 1296, 1297, 1299, 1303,
1304, 1305, 1306, 1307, 1308, 1314,
1317, 1318, 1319, 1321, 1327, 1328,
1333, 1335, 1336, 1337, 1339, 1341,
1343, 1344, 1348, 1352, 1355, 1361,
1378, 1380, 1386

BEATLE SONGS MAKING UP LYRICS
TO OTHER SONGS
1017, 1082, 1113, 1259

CHRISTMAS NOVELTIES
1036, 1068, 1133, 1149, 1168, 1171,
1180, 1235, 1287, 1297, 1332, 1343

DANCES (INCLUDING THOSE ON LP'S)
1039, 1064, 1065, 1073, 1087, 1098,

1101, 1112, 1116, 1130, 1132, 1150,
1158, 1159, 1167, 1175, 1186, 1194,
1197, 1220, 1230, 1253, 1285, 1294,
1304, 1306, 1308, 1319, 1321, 1339,
1341

EX–BEATLES, FAMILY AND FRIENDS
1046, 1198, 1258, 1259

FEMALE VERSIONS OF BEATLE SONGS
see ANSWER BEATLE SONGS

HARRISON NOVELTIES
1053, 1093

LENNON NOVELTIES
1169, 1176, 1177, 1181, 1197, 1199,
1254, 1268, 1269, 1282

McCARTNEY NOVELTIES
1015, 1138, 1176, 1177, 1188, 1192,
1252, 1269, 1302, 1312, 1323, 1357

MENTION BEATLE SONGS IN TITLE
(IN FULL OR PART)
1000, 1110, 1124, 1154, 1196, 1240,
1288

MENTION LIVERPOOL/MERSEY IN
TITLE
1022, 1035, 1073, 1189, 1204, 1231,
1237, 1240, 1263, 1264, 1272, 1316,
1320, 1345, 1346, 1347, 1349, 1385

MOCK BEATLE SONGS (GROUP & SOLO)
OR BUILD NEW SONGS ON A
BEATLE SONG
1013, 1093, 1110, 1164, 1196, 1240,
1243, 1248, 1280, 1288, 1292

NOVELTY BECAUSE OF RECORD
SLEEVE
1012, 1124, 1288, 1298

NOVELTY IN NAME ONLY
1002, 1006, 1020, 1030, 1032, 1034,

1037, 1038, 1041, 1077, 1078, 1085,
1128, 1134, 1148, 1153, 1165, 1176,
1177, 1190, 1191, 1199, 1205, 1206,
1214, 1217, 1235, 1239, 1241, 1247,
1262, 1295, 1311, 1326, 1330, 1340

RECORD SLEEVE NOVELTIES see
NOVELTY BECAUSE OF
RECORD SLEEVE

SING OR PLAY BEATLE SONGS
(GROUP & SOLO), INCLUDING
SONGS NOT WRITTEN BY THE
BEATLES
1012, 1019, 1021. 1022, 1023, 1029,
1032, 1035, 1040, 1043, 1046, 1052,

1056, 1058, 1065, 1073, 1075, 1088,
1092, 1093, 1094, 1117, 1119, 1122,
1129, 1164, 1204, 1213, 1215, 1223,
1226, 1238, 1243, 1246, 1259, 1269,
1272, 1291, 1293, 1300, 1304, 1309,
1317, 1324, 1349

RINGO NOVELTIES
1009, 1011, 1025, 1057, 1081, 1090,
1097, 1114, 1123, 1135, 1136, 1137,
1139, 1140, 1149, 1161, 1166, 1168,
1175, 1195, 1221, 1234, 1235, 1262,
1276, 1279, 1283, 1294, 1295, 1313,
1322, 1331, 1332, 1334, 1342, 1343,
1350, 1351, 1354, 1356

APPENDIX I

EVERYTHING YOU ALWAYS WANTED TO KNOW ABOUT BOOTLEGS, BUT WERE TOO BUSY COLLECTING THEM TO ASK;
A Treatise on the Wages of Sinning for Sound
by
Tom Schultheiss

Charlie Reinhart's staggering discography of bootlegged, pirated and counterfeited Beatles' recordings will doubtless epitomize for some a totally wrong-headed misapplication of research energies because, for them, it will represent merely a consecration of the illicit, the illegal, the ephemeral, and the trivial. The recording industry will perhaps come to eventual but grudging terms with this book as, if nothing else, Volume One of its own *Index Recordorum Prohibitorum*. At the other extreme, there will be the vast number of avid fans and collectors who will delight in the appearance of this volume, either for the information it codifies or for the applications they will make of that information, or both.

It was clear to us in our acceptance of this book for publication that it would be praised or disparaged from a variety of perspectives, but also very clear that the fund of information which it organized and offered to future researchers, historians, and biographers more than justified its publication. While the subject it deals with is clearly illegal, only those unfriendly to the idea that the pursuit of knowledge is purely and legitimately self-justifying would severely disapprove of the publication of this book on that basis alone. It is not our aim, after all, to encourage or glorify bootlegs or bootlegging, but merely to detail the realities of recent recording history. Nor is it our place to resolve the legal and moral dilemmas involved, but simply to report on them.

The predicament for academic and public institutions which purchase this book will perhaps be further compounded by the question of whether, having added this discography to their library's collection (a decision based either on a professional assessment of its value or upon the urging of those served by the collection), they should not seek to acquire some of the rarities of recorded sound which are here cataloged. With that in mind, what follows is a brief discussion of what a "bootleg" recording is, the place it occupies in the realm of illegal recordings, and what it represents to those who view it from their own points of view.

It might be well to stress at this point, as was mentioned in the author's introduction, that *bootlegs, pirated* recordings, and *counterfeit* recordings are three different things, although they are forms of the same illegal activity: piracy. "Piracy," the misappropriation of another's property, is the general term applied to unauthorized duplication of any art form where ownership is claimed by and credited to the artist (part of any creator's rights to his or her work includes the sole right to license reproduction of that work by another party).

Record and tape piracy, the brand of misappropriation peculiar to the recording industry, is referred to in industry parlance as "disklegging" or the "unauthorized duplication of sound recordings." This unauthorized duplication can actually take *four* forms: pirated recordings, counterfeit recordings, bootleg recordings, and home recordings (made for personal use, the product of "personal piracy").

Pirated and counterfeit recordings are the end result of "dubbing," which is the process involved in the technically advanced mechanical, electrical or acoustical transfer of sounds from a copy of an authorized recording onto unauthorized blanks. ("Dubbing" is also sometimes used interchangeably with the term "disklegging," resulting in some uncertainty of usage; it should also not be confused with the "dubbing" of motion pictures.) Piracy and counterfeiting are motivated by the profits to be realized, large profits from current hits, smaller profits from the old, the rare, or the currently unavailable recording. Pirated and counterfeit recordings, products of the same process, are generally distinguished from one another on the basis of packaging: the "pirate" is usually repackaged with an album cover, inner sleeve, and label which bear little or no resemblance to the original; the counterfeit attempts to duplicate the packaging of the original so that it can be "passed off" as a genuine, authorized copy.

Bootleg recordings, also referred to as "underground recordings," are generally the product of "performance piracy," and represent the creation of unauthorized recordings not from preexisting ones, but from unauthorized taping of live performances or radio and TV broadcasts, or utilization of stolen tapes from unreleased studio sessions. Bootleg recordings are generally of poor quality, not having been recorded in a technically advanced fashion to begin with. Many so-called bootlegs, as this volume illustrates, are actually hybrids of genuine bootlegged material interspersed with pirated cuts from original recordings; the quality of even these cuts remains so poor, however, that their inclusion represents more of an effort to pad the bootleg recording than to compete with the original.

"Personal piracy" refers to several practices whereby individuals copy the contents of a recording for themselves (and/or a few friends) without the intention of duplicating copies on a large scale, but with the intention of avoiding purchase of the original recording itself.

The first two forms of record piracy, after a long struggle discussed below, are now subject to prosecution under provisions of the Federal copyright statute, while the latter two forms are not dealt with in the new Copyright Revision Act in specific terms, although their continued illegality remains otherwise quite clear.

ELIOT NESS AND ALL THAT

The *word* "bootleg" has been around for a long time. In mid-nineteenth century England and America, it was commonly used to refer to, of all things, the leg of a tall boot.* It was left to the enterprise and vision of Americans to see the potential that lay dormant within the word, and to reshape it from humble beginnings into something transcendent and truly meaningful. Hence, one can easily subsume the ingenious practice of "bootlegging" a bottle of whiskey or other article -- carrying it in one's *boot leg* (get it?), usually for the purposes of concealment -- as the origin for the now widely recognized and only legitimate and fitting meaning for the word: *illicit trading* in liquor or other commodities.

Application of the word to "other commodities" was not accomplished with ease, however. In the area of recordings, it was not until around 1929, when the entertainment publication *Variety*, in defiance of those trafficking in illegal spirits who wished to selfishly reserve use of the word unto themselves, dared to refer to the already huge market for "bootleg disk records." Some say that the St. Valentine's Day Massacre of "Bugs" Moran's Chicago-based bootlegging gang in early 1929 was actually a warning from a handful of over-zealous recording industry executives that exclusive use

---

*About as enlightened an origin for a word meaning as you'll ever find, reminiscent of Eve's penchant (in Mark Twain's "Extracts From Adam's Diary") for always naming things on the same pretext -- it *looks* like the thing being named: "There is the dodo, for instance. [She] says the moment one looks at it one sees at a glance that it 'looks like a dodo.' . . . Dodo! It looks no more like a dodo than I do." Imagine the flush of pride that must have gripped the first cobbler at his last who, when asked what he was doing, merely *looked* at his unfinished work and exclaimed (his mind whirling busily over the prospect of completing his newly fashioned but as yet unnamed leathery extension over the lower leg): "I'm working on the . . . er, um . . . *boot leg*!" Eureka!

of the word "bootleg" would no longer be tolerated, but I put little stock in the story . . .

. . . and neither should you, because I just made it up. The Recording Industry Association of America (R.I.A.A.) will perhaps forgive the fictitious transitional hyperbole if the connection between elements of organized crime and the large scale practice of record and tape piracy is here stressed. In mid-March, 1973, for example, a raid on a Tennessee-based record pirate's plant netted a local sheriff one of the FBI's "Ten Most Wanted" criminals. More recently, a counterfeiter wiretapped by Phoenix police was recorded discussing the volume of his production of pirated tapes (100,000 per week) with an organized crime figure in another state. "Bootlegging," then, to emphasize the difference, is not "counterfeiting," and is more a product of "unorganized crime" (some might prefer the designation "disorganized"). As for the R.I.A.A., given to more peaceful remedies to its problems, it simply coined the derivative term "disklegging" to 1951 to cover the industry's unauthorized duplication problems (a branch of which continues to be record bootlegging), thus avoiding altogether any harsh confrontations over use of the word "bootleg."

One can easily perceive the temptations for organized crime in the practice of record piracy simply by looking at the figures: legitimate annual recording industry sales moved from around $285 million in 1960 to some $1.2 billion by 1969 ($300 million in tape formats, $900 million in discs). Correspondingly, the annual figures for pirates and counterfeits show an increase from about $20 million loss to the industry in 1960, to $100 million lost in 1969, to $300 million lost in 1975, and $400 million in lost sales in 1980. In 1966, RCA Victor estimated that there were two million illicit copies of **The Sound of Music** in circulation. Beginning in 1969, sales of counterfeited tape formats reached $4 million *per week*, and it has been variously estimated since then that one of four, one of three, and even that *one of every two* prerecorded tapes sold in the U.S. is a counterfeit. And these are only domestic U.S. losses; large quantities of counterfeited tapes manufactured in the U.S. are shipped abroad for sale, bringing estimated annual industry losses to $1 billion worldwide.

By 1980, the Record Industry Association of America was devoting 70% of its annual budget to combatting record piracy: $1.25 million per year. Though the record industry's enormous losses represent the biggest chunk of the easy gains made by pirates, they are not the only losers when counterfeiters prosper. Pirates pay *no* royalties to artists and music publishers, they pay *no* fees to musicians, arrangers, engineers and technicians, they pay *no* expensive overhead costs growing out of inventory maintenance, distribution and records keeping, they pay *no* expensive production costs required for the recording and manufacture of high quality products, and they pay *no* taxes on most of the income they receive. They can select from the 10% of profitable hits released by the industry, and leave legitimate record companies to deal with the 90% of unprofitable releases which the hits were once able to support at a loss. The list of losers extends even farther than those directly connected with the recording industry, down to retailers who cannot compete with other retailers who traffic in pirated goods, and finally down to the public at large. The individual record buyer loses because he or she gets a poor quality counterfeit product, loses because variety diminishes when a hit-reliant industry is less and less able to support and invest in new or marginally unprofitable performers, groups and classical orchestras, and loses finally when more and more taxes must be paid to enable law enforcement agencies to cope with record pirates.

YANKEE INGENUITY

The *practice of making* a "bootleg" recording dates from the early 1900s, less than 30 years after the invention of the phonograph in 1877 (phonographs were fairly common in the U.S. by 1887). By the time the apparent "Father of Bootlegging," Lionel Mapleson, was in full stride, he had probably accumulated the worst sounding collection of live performances ever recorded on phonograph cylinders, thus setting the standard for most subsequent bootleg recordings. Mapleson, librarian at the Metropolitan Opera Company, recorded performances during the years 1901, 1902 and 1903 at the Metropolitan Opera House in New York, thus beginning the time-honored (if not otherwise honored) practices of not only "bootlegging" but also "performance piracy." (Bootleg recording, when thought of in terms of "performance piracy," was to have its Golden Era between 1920 and the mid-1950s, when the most accessible performances were those broadcast on the then premiere communications medium: radio.) The turn of the century period, quite apart from Mapleson's pioneering technological applications in the area of bootlegging, was also a period of burgeoning piracy of not only recorded sound, but of piano rolls!

These early infringements led record manufacturers to seek protection from Congress for their products under Article I, Section 8 of the Constitution of the United States, which empowered Congress to secure "for limited times to authors and inventors the exclusive right to their respective writings and discoveries . . . " (Congress first enacted a copyright law in 1790.) Record manufacturers were turned down because their products were not intelligible to the human eye, and were therefore not considered to be the "writings" stipulated by our Forefathers, nor were they considered to qualify for coverage by the subsequent protections of Title 17 of the U.S. Code dealing with "Copyrights." Fundamental opposition to extending copyright protection to sound recordings has always been advanced in the argument that records are not literary or artistic creations, but mere uses or applications of creative works in the form of physical objects.

Matters weren't helped when the Supreme Court decided, in a 1908 case, that composers had no existing legal right to control their own works on sound recordings because they could not submit "copies" of the works to the Library of Congress as specified in the U.S. Code, they could only submit "mechanical reproductions" not acceptable as "copies" of "writings." Material objects were subject to patenting, but not copyrighting.

The Copyright Act of 1909, a revision of Title 17, went on to establish that the only rights enjoyed by a composer (an "author") in his or her works were: the exclusive right to perform them, and; the exclusive right to record them *if written copies* of the contents of the recordings had been duly copyrighted. The recordings themselves remained *uncopyrightable*.

What had happened, in sum, was that Congress had refused legislatively to favorably interpret existing laws or enact new laws protecting recordings from piracy, and the Supreme Court had judicially affirmed that sound recordings enjoyed no protection under the Constitution or the statutes of the U.S. Code.

COURT ADJOURNED

Bootlegging and an irritating but tolerable level of record piracy and counterfeiting persisted throughout the first half of the century. From the viewpoint of record companies, most infringements were too small to justify becoming involved in expensive law suits, which could have been initiated on grounds other than copyright violation. There were a few significant cases, but record counterfeiting was a largely unaddressed issue in U.S. courts until the late 1940s and early 1950s. Legislative attempts to extend copyright coverage to sound recordings during this same period began in 1906, with a flurry of activity between 1925 and 1951 when at least 31 bills were introduced and reintroduced from one Congress to the next. Between 1909 and 1955, however, no court decision rendered in the U.S. held for the copyrightability of sound recordings, and no new legislation was enacted.

In the first half of the century, therefore, in the absence of copyright laws to guarantee protection for their recordings, recording

400

artists and record companies had two principal courses of legal redress, both of them involving the assertion of "property rights," and both of them available only under State "common law" (legal principles so old or widespread that they are commonly accepted norms): "common law copyright" and "unfair competition." Cases against record pirates had to be lodged case by case in State after State, with the judgments in such cases subject to limited jurisdictions and uncertain and varied outcomes – clearly an unending, expensive, and inefficient process.

"Common law copyright" in a sound recording asserts that, as an "original intellectual creation," recorded performances are protected under law against unauthorized use as long as they remain "unpublished" (the composer enjoys the right of first publication, in traditional terms, and the release of a sound recording was not viewed to constitute a "publication" in most court decisions). "Unfair competition" recognizes property rights in authorized sound recordings as business assets, protecting the investor against misappropriation by others who may seek to make unfair use of the money, time, skill and effort expended by the manufacturer of the recording.

Additional courses of action open to record companies seeking legal redress against infringers, apart from common law copyright and unfair competition, have included charges involving the right of privacy, misappropriation, interference with prospective economic advantage, disruption of contractual relations between artist and record company, interference with employer-employee relations, and protection of the special significance of sounds peculiar to a particular artist (much like the protection afforded trademarks), the uniqueness of which might be harmed by inferior unauthorized recordings which might tend to confuse the public about an artist's abilities (thereby devaluing the artist's talents and recordings in the minds of prospective record buyers). Interestingly, one important case, *Capitol Records, Inc. v. Greatest Records, Inc.*, involved recordings by The Beatles. Capitol Records sued Greatest Records to stop further production of an album containing songs by The Beatles taken from three of their albums. The New York State Supreme Court found for Capitol Records.*

---

*For those interested in case law, there follows a list of civil suits which figured importantly, in one way or another, in the development of legislative efforts leading to the decision to extend statutory copyright protection to sound recordings: *Victor Talking Machine Company v. Armstrong* (1904); *White-Smith Music Publishing Company v. Apollo Company* (1908); *Fonotipia Limited v. Bradley* (1909); *Aeolian Company v. Royal Music Roll Company* (1912); *International News Service v. The Associated Press* (1918); *Waring v. WDAS Broadcasting Station, Inc.* (1937); *RCA Manufacturing Company v. Whiteman* (1940); *Shapiro, Bernstein & Company v. Miracle*

SUE ME, SUE YOU BLUES

Music publishing and recording industry pressure to secure copyright protection for sound recordings grew in proportion to the increase in radio broadcasting. The final impetus for a dramatic change at mid-century was the widespread availability and application of magnetic tape technology in more compact, portable and inexpensive units, from professional mastering equipment down to battery-operated tape recorder/players. Pirating, which had cut its teeth beginning in the '30s by concentrating on filling the demand for out-of-print jazz classics, now ballooned in the U.S., branching into every area of possible profit. Pirates began to openly advertise their wares on a nationwide basis, even selling through legitimate retail outlets. Around 1951, record pirates, emboldened by not only lethargic industry opposition in the legal sphere but also by the complete lack of Federal copyright protection, switched from rarities and classics to pirating *current hits*. As a result, the early '50s were marked by a new cohesiveness within the recording industry, reflected in both a barrage of law suits against pirates and in the formation of the Recording Industry Association of America.

The beginnings of change in legal and legislative attitudes about the copyrightability of sound recordings also occurred at mid-century, a change apparent in a decision in the case called *Capitol Records, Inc. v. Mercury Records Corporation* (1955). The decision in this case established that recorded performances were *potentially copyrightable* in Constitutional terms, although they were not covered by the existing statute (the Act of 1909). Also, in the same year, the Legislative Appropriations Act of 1955 set aside funding for use by the Copyright Office which it could utilize to begin a study of complete copyright revision.

The early '60s saw the ever increasing replacement of phonograph records by less expensive prerecorded tapes, a situation which was growing more and more profitable for the recording industry and record pirates alike. By 1961, however, not only was there still no Federal statute prohibiting the unauthorized manufacture of

---

Record Company (1950); Supreme Records, Inc. v. Decca Records, Inc. (1950); Metropolitan Opera Association, Inc., et al. v. Wagner-Nichols Recorder Corp. (1950); Capitol Records, Inc. v. Mercury Records Corp. (1955); Gieseking v. Urania Records (1956); Sears, Roebuck & Company v. Stiffel Company (1964); Compco Corp. v. Day-Brite Lighting, Inc. (1964); Capitol Records, Inc. v. Greatest Records, Inc. (1964); Capitol Records v. Spies (1970); Columbia Broadcasting System v. Spies (1970); Capitol Records v. Erickson (1970); Tape Industries Association v. Younger (1971). Not all cases dealt specifically with sound recordings, but instead may have involved principles of law governing commercial practices which were later cited and applied by courts in deciding succeeding cases.

sound recordings, there were no State statutes against it either. The only anti-dubbing ordinance passed anywhere in the United States was apparently a 1948 provision by the City of Los Angeles which, in Section 42 of its Municipal Code, had made it "unlawful for any person to manufacture or reproduce for sale any phonograph records without the written consent of the owner of the reproduction rights thereto, . . . " (It's been estimated that at one point in the early 1970s, over 2,000 recording pirates were still in operation in Los Angeles.) In 1961, though, some progress was made when Congress received the "Report of the Register of Copyrights on the General Revision of the U.S. Copyright Law," work on which had begun in 1955. Also, in 1962, a Federal law was passed in the area of interstate commerce which made it a crime to transport, sell, offer or receive counterfeit records for sale. (Unfortunately, the law did not apply to pirated records upon which the pirate had put its own label!)

JOLLY ROGER MEETS THE F.B.I.

At last, State legislation began to spread following the enactment of the New York State record piracy statutes, which took effect on September 1, 1966. The New York legislation not only prohibited the manufacture, distribution and sale of counterfeit records, the law made it illegal to distribute or sell a recording without the name and address of the manufacturer on the jacket, or to indicate that a recording was stereophonic when it was not. In 1968, the California Legislature enacted Section 635h of its Penal Code, making record piracy a misdemeanor. Following the lead of New York and California, six more States passed anti-piracy laws in 1971: Arkansas, Tennessee, Arizona, Florida, Texas, and Pennsylvania.

On the national level, international governmental representatives met in Paris in March of 1971 at the "Convention for the Protection of Producers of Phonograms Against Unauthorized Duplication of Their Phonograms." The convention, jointly sponsored by UNESCO and the World Intellectual Property Organization, began work on a treaty subsequently signed in Geneva by 23 nations in October of 1971. The treaty was left open for signature by other nations, and the United States (a participant in drafting the provisions of the treaty, one of which required that signatories have national legislation to implement the agreement) was finally able to sign it in April of 1973, along with seven more nations.

The national legislation which the U.S. representative had to await was the Sound Recording Amendment to the Copyright Law of the United States (Public Law 92–140, Act of October 15, 1971) which extended copyright protection to sound recordings fixed

403

between February 15, 1972 and January 1, 1975. Thus, after more than 60 years of attempts to be protected under the 1909 Act, Congress finally could see the little "writings" fixed in sound recordings. The Amendment covered misappropriated recordings, both the unauthorized exact duplicates of commercial releases (counterfeits) and those issued in a different package (pirates). "Performance piracy" and "personal piracy," as noted above, were not specifically addressed by the Amendment, which was slightly modified and reenacted before expiration, effective December 31, 1974.

A complete revision of the copyright law, which incorporates terms of the Sound Recording Amendment, was signed into law on October 19, 1976, by President Ford as the Copyright Revision Act of 1976 (Public Law 94–553). The law provided for a transitional year (1977), and went into effect January 1, 1978. Recordings "fixed" prior to February 10, 1972 remain unprotected by the copyright statute, but violations remain actionable under State criminal and civil statutes. By 1980, all of the 50 States except Vermont had their own anti-piracy legislation. (Civil remedies are the least adequate; a pirate who loses a civil action is enjoined to stop producing a *particular* unauthorized recording, but another lawsuit is required if the pirate proceeds to "diskleg" a different recording. States with criminal statutes can prohibit *all* pirating by a disklegger as the result of one legal action.) The Copyright Revision Act of 1976 is acknowledged to have had considerable impact on the reduction of availability of unauthorized recordings in large discount houses and chain stores, although their availability in stores operated by individual retailers is apparently still widespread. (One chain store retailer, Sam Goody, Inc., was indicted in 1980 for involvement with counterfeited recordings.)

In contrast to the United States, the British Copyright Act of 1911 had explicitly set forth protection for sound recordings for not only Great Britain but the entire Commonwealth of Nations. Provisions of this protection were considerably expanded in the British Copyright Act of 1956. Other countries that had long ago at least mentioned sound recordings as qualifying for protection under their national copyright laws include the Republic of China (1944), the Dominican Republic (1947), Lebanon (1922), and Thailand (1931).

EVEN MONKEYS IN THE TREES DO IT

Most of the above has obviously dealt with the large scale "organized" crime of record piracy. This is not to say that all record pirates are members of "organized crime," as that term is commonly understood; elements of organized crime are involved in "disk-legging," other pirates are merely criminals. But what is the place of the garden variety "bootleg" in all this, the product of "unorganized" (or "disorganized") "performance piracy" with which this book is largely concerned?

The majority of bootlegs, contrary to the impression that may have been fostered by this volume, are not recordings of current "pop" or "rock" musicians, but are instead piracies of *classical and operatic performances*.* In fact, the first (and apparently the *only*) court case involving a bootleg recording dealt with the unauthorized duplication and sale of operatic performances broadcast over the radio: *Metropolitan Opera Association, Inc., et al. v. Wagner-Nichols Recorder Corporation* (1950). No additional cases of performance piracy seem to have reached U.S. courts from that time on, at least into the early 1970s, principally because most bootleggers are easily persuaded by the mere threat of prosecution to put a halt to circulation of a bootleg which a recording company may find particularly objectionable. Consequently, court dockets are not filled with bootlegging cases.

The reality is that record companies, for a variety of reasons, have hitherto largely turned a blind eye to most bootlegs. Strong opposition and official condemnation of bootlegs and performance piracy are given energetic lip service but, as evidenced by the low priority given them, there is obviously a more tolerant and charitable view of most bootlegs, culminating at worst in promises of lawsuits (assuming the bootlegger can be identified at all). The reasons for such an official position are clear: to do otherwise would only encourage bootlegging, as well as undermine respect for the law. Probably the most compelling underlying factor in this situation, however, is economic: the financial loss to record companies, who for the most part never intended to release the bootlegged performance in the first place, is virtually nil. Also, successful lawsuits against most bootleggers would probably be more trouble than they're worth, merely resulting in more expense to the company than the recovery would warrant. Failing compliance with company warnings of prosecution, legal actions against bootlegs would probably be taken only if the unauthorized recording were blatantly commercial and competitive with existing or proposed official releases, severely usurped property rights and potential financial interests, were of such a grossly inferior quality or content that it might in some way damage the reputation or public image of

---

*It is generally accepted that no really significant musical event of any kind held in the United States has eluded "performance piracy" in the past 20 years, even if recorded only by a single avid fan.

the artist or record company, or was offensive enough to the artist involved that he or she insisted that the company take action against it.

Certain other factors mitigate for the continued toleration enjoyed by the performance pirate, again unofficially. There is an awareness in the recording industry that bootleg recordings are the least harmful form of record piracy, that bootleg buyers are limited in numbers, generally concentrate on particular performers or types of performances, and acquire in a bootleg a performance which would not be considered for commercial release anyway. Avid fans with such focused and refined (or overpowering and compulsive, depending on your point of view) interests have usually already purchased every commercially released recording on the market, and will probably buy every new or repackaged release as well. Most bootlegs, as a result, pose little or no threat either competitively or financially. Then, too, many recording company executives are eager collectors of bootlegs, perhaps a source of empathy with other collectors.

There is even *some* grudging concession on the part of *some* parts of the recording industry that *some* bootlegs may actually offer *some* benefits to the public interest, preserving historically and musically valuable performances that would otherwise be lost. The archival value of the contents of such recordings to future biographers, or to social, musical and oral historians, is perhaps something that members of present generations are too familiar with to adequately recognize or assess. It is not hard to understand, though, why bootlegs of *current* live performances by especially valuable artists (in the commercial sense) receive very little sympathy from record manufacturers, despite small pressings (bootleg pressings seldom go beyond 2,000 copies) and complete lack of present intentions for commercial release. The *potential* for future release of the same material, as well as the *potential* for harmful influences on the public's perception of the artist's abilities growing out of poor quality bootlegs, govern the survivability of such bootlegs absolutely.

THE WORST OF BOTH WORLDS

Mitigating factors and charitable tolerance aside, bootleg recordings are, of course, embodiments of a theft, represent a violation of property rights (and now rights of copyright), are an infringement upon legitimate business interests, and their manufacture and sale continue to be actionable not only on a State "common law" and statutory level, but now on a Federal statutory level as well.

The judgment in the *Metropolitan Opera Association* case discussed above, which affirmed unfair competition based on misappropriation of another's work product, has been understood to be the grounds and precedent upon which all potential "performance piracy" litigation has its base. Such rights in property of commercial value are inviolate; it is also a performer's property right in his or her performance that it not be used as not intended.

Performances, as entities in and of themselves, cannot be copyrighted; that has been and continues to be the case. Previously, such performances and recordings of them were also not considered "writings" within the Constitutional definition, which is the reason that bootleg recordings could not be protected against under prior copyright law (any more than other recordings were protected). Before the recent revision period and subsequent Act of 1976, while performers and manufacturers could bring State-level unfair competition suits against bootleg recordings but could *not* bring suit for Federal copyright violation, *composers* could bring actions against unauthorized recordings in one of two ways. First, under the State-level common law property right in an unpublished work, *the right of first publication*. Second, under the longstanding copyright protection for transcribed works (published and copyrighted "writings," including lyrics and musical notation), *the exclusive mechanical recording right*.

An incredible conundrum thus developed between State and Federal law which placed these two composer rights at loggerheads. To take advantage of the State-level common law property right in an *unpublished* work, the composer could not copyright the work, a requirement of copyright being the work's *publication*. (State courts, in an effort to guarantee this common law right, were generally inclined to rule that release of a commercial recording *did not constitute a publication* of the lyrics or music.) If, on the other hand, a composer allowed release of a recording of an unpublished/ uncopyrighted composition, Federal copyright law *viewed this as a publication* without copyright protection for the lyrics and musical notation (even though it disallowed that the same recording so "published" constituted a "writing"), and the composition was thereby cast into the public domain from a Federal point of view.

BOOTLEGGERS BEWARE

In 1976, the dilemma was resolved through several provisions in the present copyright law, which not only guaranteed copyright protection to sound recordings for the first time, but guaranteed such statutory copyright protection *even to unpublished recordings*, provided "one complete copy or phonorecord" of such a recording was deposited with the Register of Copyrights. Thus, the previous requirement that a work be published -- released for sale to the public -- to qualify for copyright protection had been dropped, and even unpublished works (including unpublished sound recordings) could be copyrighted. In exchange, however, the Copyright Revision Act, as of January 1, 1978, preempts "any such right or equivalent right in any such work under common law or statutes of any State" in all classes of copyrightable material, although it specifies an exemption in the case of sound recordings, allowing that "any rights or remedies under common law or statutes of any State shall not be annulled or limited by this title until February 15, 2047."

The upshot of all this is that, within the interim exemption period, bootleg recordings are actionable on two levels of violation instead of one, although the prosecution preference would probably be on the Federal level. Live performances or unreleased studio sessions illegally duplicated on bootlegs can still be prosecuted by performers and manufacturers on a State level on the basis of misappropriation of another's work product (unfair competition) if a copyrighted commercial release has not appeared; or, unauthorized duplication can be prosecuted by composers whose work is unpublished and uncopyrighted on the basis of the property right of first publication. Conversely, live performances and unreleased studio sessions illegally duplicated on bootlegs are subject to prosecution on the Federal level under the new copyright act provided the copyright owner -- be it the composer, the performer, or the manufacturer -- has deposited a single copy (recording) of the same performance or session "fixed in a tangible medium of expression" as an *unpublished* work. Unpublished performances so deposited and copyrighted will lose the "equivalent right in any such work under the common law or statutes of any State," that is, the act of protecting a work with the Federal copyright law will divest it of its "common law" property right protections because these rights will be guaranteed statutorily – not an altogether inequitable exchange. Live performances not "fixed" in a tangible medium of expression, of course, continue to be uncopyrightable, as are commercially released sound recordings "fixed" before February 12, 1972.

INVITATION TO A BEHEADING

Resolution of the longstanding situation which had been perpetuated by the uncertain and variable outcomes of State-level civil and criminal actions against "diskleggers," touched on previously, is one of the principal corrective features of the Copyright Revision Act of 1976. The Act specifies explicit remedies for copyright infringement, but particularly stringent remedies are set forth for cases dealing with all forms of piracy against copyrighted sound recordings.

Courts in which a *civil* action is lodged for alleged violation of copyright can grant injunctions which can be served in any State of the Union to prevent further infringement; these can be enforced by any court having jurisdiction of the area where the offender operates. Courts can order impounding of all sound recordings, and the tapes and mastering plates used to reproduce them, while a resolution of the alleged violation is being sought.

The copyright owner in a civil action involving piracy of sound recordings is entitled to recover actual damages and any additional profits of the infringer unless, before a final judgment is made, the copyright owner elects to settle for statutory damages of from $250 to no more than $10,000 for all infringements covered by the action. If the action proceeds to a final judgment and the court finds willful infringement, the award of damages may be increased to no more than $50,000. The court may also levy payment of court costs and attorney fees on the infringer, and order destruction of all impounded recordings and "other articles" seized, at its discretion.

In cases involving *criminal* violations of copyright in sound recordings, the penalty for willful infringement "for purposes of commercial advantage or private financial gain" (which is otherwise not more than $10,000 or imprisonment for not more than one year, or both) is increased for the first offense to not more than $25,000 or imprisonment for not more than one year, or both. Subsequent offenses involving sound recordings call for a fine of not more than $50,000 or not more than two years imprisonment, or both. Here again, the court may order destruction of all offending recordings, "other articles," and also all other "devices for manufacturing, reproducing and assembling" unauthorized recordings.

... BUT I DON'T EVEN OWN A PORNOGRAPH

We come finally to the most common form of sound piracy, "personal piracy" or "home recording," so widespread and routine a pastime as to leave most practitioners of it largely unaware and undisturbed by the moral and ethical implications of what is, to the recording industry, simply another theft of its property. In 1970, an RCA recording executive estimated that "personal piracy" was in fact the largest single factor in the loss of potential record sales, exceeding even the amount lost to counterfeiters.

What, in the view of the recording industry, constitutes "personal piracy"? Answer: any private use of magnetic tape equipment which allows an individual to avoid the purchase of a commercially released record or tape. This includes taping from a radio broadcast, taping a recording from a friend's copy or a copy borrowed from a library collection, even making a tape of a recording which one *has purchased* to avoid wearing it out and having to buy a replacement copy. There is an awareness in industry circles, of course, that much of what is copied in this manner may involve recordings of which commercially released copies are no longer available or, for those that seek to preserve their original recordings by taping them, *will be* unavailable for replacement in the space of a few years.

These forms of "piracy" are unlikely ever to be the object of litigation; apparently no case has ever been heard on the subject of whether an individual may use privately owned taping equipment to duplicate a purchased or borrowed recording for personal enjoyment. The prosecution of single cases would be unending and the unfavorable public relations generated suicidal from a commercial standpoint; also, the industry recognizes that the lower quality of such copies certainly constitutes no competitive threat in the marketplace, except in terms of lost *potential* sales. There is simply no way to measure "home recording" activity or exact losses attributable to it, though both are accepted as being considerable. The closer that "personal piracy" gets to an organized or systematic practice designed to circumvent purchase, especially if it involves the use of professional duplicating equipment, the greater the risk to the pirate. Private, informal tape "clubs" of any significant size, whose members purchase recordings and then trade or sell taped copies amongst themselves, help underscore the legitimate industry concerns in this area, as do the activities of individuals whose regular custom it is to fraudulently return recordings to retailers as "defective" after having copied them.

Industry reaction even to these practices is unlikely to result in lawsuits. What has and possibly will result from an ever widening tendency in the public to use tape recording equipment in this way are, first, ever increasing prices for records and tapes and, second, ever mounting pressure to enact Federal regulative legislation for the licensing of home recording equipment. There already are countries with longstanding legislation making the private taping of recordings or broadcasts illegal (though such prohibitions would appear virtually unenforceable), and also countries where a surcharge is levied on privately purchased tape recorders in exchange for a "license" granting permission to practice "home recording" of this type. It is not an idle speculation, in view of this, to foresee a time when such licensing fees are collected from all purchasers of tape recording equipment in the U.S., either at the time of purchase, annually, or both. Collected monies would be dispersed to organizations representing composers, performers and record manufacturers, to reimburse them for revenue lost to energetic reel-to-reelers and cassetteers who haven't bought a record or tape since they learned the suspect pleasures of do-it-yourself recording.

ENOUGH IS ENOUGH

This overview of bootlegging and its place among other forms of record piracy should not be drawn to a close without the acknowledgment that it represents a distillation and synthesis of information contained in dozens of articles written about record piracy over the past twenty years, lest this writer be accused of piratical inclinations. Much of this material, published in law journals, would in any event have been difficult reading for many unfamiliar with legal practice and terminology, and it is hoped that this essay has made these efforts by others more accessible and understandable to the average reader. To the many writers whose works have been consulted and merged for this history and discussion, I fully admit my indebtedness and extend my acknowledgments.

I would have liked also to offer my appreciation for the assistance of the Recording Industry Association of America for information and statistics which they were invited to contribute to this survey. Unfortunately, after a phone call in which I explained my intentions to a person who declined to identify himself and insisted that to have my request considered I send a letter addressed only to "Anti-Piracy" at the R.I.A.A. (which I did), I received nothing in return. More's the pity since I paid for the call, unaware at the time that I could have dialed an R.I.A.A. toll-free number, 800–BAD–BEAT. But after all, in these inflationary times, what kind of office help can you expect to get for only $1.25 million?

APPENDIX II

THE BEATLES AT THE BEEB

When this book was first published in hardback edition (Pierian Press, 1981), very little research had been done on the Beatles' recordings for the BBC. Since then, two works have been published on this subject: *The Beatles At The Beeb*, by Kevin Howlett (BBC Publications, 1982); and "Yellow Matter Custard: Collecting Beatles Broadcast," an article by Richard M. Hochadel, appearing in the October 1982 issue of *Goldmine* magazine (#77). In addition, the three-hour radio show, "The Beatles At The Beeb," was broadcast to much of the world during the period from May 27 to May 30, 1983. That show contained at least parts of 40 commercially unreleased Beatle songs that had been broadcast on the BBC between 1962 and 1965. Many of these "newly discovered" tracks have now been bootlegged.

The object of this appendix is to show which BBC-recorded songs have been bootlegged and on which bootlegs they can be found. Recording date, broadcast date, and BBC show have been listed where possible. The hosts (they call them *presenters* in England) have also been listed. Finally, there is a listing of the bootlegs to check for this recording. All number listings are for bootlegs listed in this book. New bootlegs appearing after the original publication date are listed by title.

Only those songs that have been bootlegged are listed in this appendix. Songs that were broadcast, but not bootlegged, have been omitted. For instance, *Besame Mucho* was recorded and broadcast on "Here We Go," on June 15, 1962. But it hasn't been bootlegged, so there is no listing of it in this appendix. Similarly, *All My Loving* was performed on four different BBC shows, but only the version from the December 26, 1963, "From Us To You" show has been bootlegged. Therefore, only that show is listed here under the *All My Loving* heading. If you are interested in all the other sources, check the book and article mentioned above.

ALL MY LOVING
BROADCAST: December 26, 1963, "From Us To You," with Rolf Harris.
SEE: 217, 255, 300, 370, 396, 435, 458, 460, 536, 604, "From Us To You"

AND I LOVE HER
RECORDED: July 14, 1964, at Studio S2, Broadcasting House, London.
BROADCAST: July 16, 1964, on "Top Gear," with Brian Matthew.
NOTES: Some bootlegs have listed this as a "Top Of The Pops" show.
SEE: *The Beatles At the Beeb, Beatles BBC*

ANNA (GO TO HIM)
BROADCAST: "Pop Go The Beatles," August 27, 1963, with Rodney Burke.
SEE: 184, 443, 444, 515, 517, 518, 603

BEAUTIFUL DREAMER
RECORDED: January 22, 1963, at the Playhouse Theatre, London.
BROADCAST: January 26, 1963, "Saturday Club," with Brian Matthew.
SEE: *Beautiful Dreamer, Wonderful Picture of You*

BOYS
BROADCAST: "Pop Go The Beatles," September 17, 1963, with Rodney Burke.
SEE: 499, 500

CAN'T BUY ME LOVE
RECORDED: February 28, 1964, at Studio 1, Piccadilly Theatre.
BROADCAST: March 30, 1964, "From Us To You," with Alan Freeman.
SEE: *Airtime, The Beatles At The Beeb*

CAROL
RECORDED/BROADCAST:
#1: Recorded January 11, 1963, at EMI, London, before a live audience, and broadcast January 18, 1963, on Radio Luxembourg's "Friday Night Spectacular."
#2: Recorded July 2, 1963, at the BBC Maida Vale #5 Studio, and broadcast July 16, 1963, on "Pop Go The Beatles," with Rodney Burke.
SEE: #1: 114, 114, 150, 170, 436, 450, 468
#2: 170, 294, *The Beatles At The Beeb, Beatles BBC, Beatle Broadcasts, Carol/Lend Me Your Comb* (45)

CHAINS
RECORDED: September 3, 1963, at Aeolian Hall, London.
BROADCAST: "Pop Go The Beatles," September 17, 1963, with Rodney Burke.
NOTES: Usually listed on bootlegs as an outtake.
SEE: 443, 444, 453, 515, 517, 518, 603

CLARABELLA
RECORDED: July 2, 1963, at the BBC Maida Vale Studio #5.
BROADCAST: July 16, 1963, on "Pop Go The Beatles," with Rodney Burke.
NOTES: John Lennon introduces this song on some bootlegs.
SEE: 170, *The Beatles At The Beeb, Beatles BBC, The Beatle Broadcasts, Clarabella/Soldier of Love* (45)

CRYING, WAITING, HOPING
RECORDED: July 16, 1963, at the BBC Paris Studio, London.
BROADCAST: August 3, 1963, on "Pop Go The Beatles," with Rodney Burke.
SEE: 025, 042, 110, 129, 151, 186, 196, 222, 294, 308, 436, 437, 453, 529, 530, 606, 607, *The Beatles At The Beeb*

DAY TRIPPER
RECORDED: December 15, 1967, at the Playhouse Theatre, London.
BROADCAST: December 24, 1967, on "Top Gear."
NOTES: This is John Lennon with the Jimi Hendrix Experience.
SEE: 107, 652, 653, 659, 660, 663, 696

DEVIL IN HER HEART
RECORDED: July 16, 1963, at the BBC Paris Studio, London.
BROADCAST: August 20, 1963, "Pop Go The Beatles," with Rodney Burke.
SEE: 184, 443, 444, 515, 517, 518, 603, 612

DIZZY MISS LIZZIE
RECORDED: May 26, 1965, at BBC Studio 1, Piccadilly Theatre, London.
BROADCAST: June 7, 1965, on "The Beatles Invite You To Take A Ticket To Ride," with Denny Piercy.
NOTES: This is the last show for which the Beatles recorded special songs. Some bootlegs list this as an outtake.
SEE: 150, 221, 260, 261, 262, 263, 290, 396, 504, 505, 555, *Airtime, The Beatles At The Beeb, Recovered Tracks*

DO YOU WANT TO KNOW A SECRET
RECORDED/BROADCAST:
#1: Recorded May 24, 1963, at Aeolian Hall, London, and broadcast on "Pop Go The Beatles," on June 4, 1963, with Lee Peters.
#2: Recorded July 10, 1963, at Studio 2, Aeolian Hall, London, and broadcast July 30, 1963, on "Pop Go The Beatles," with Rodney Burke.
SEE: #1: 030, 050, 084, 092, 317, 422, 453, 515, 516, 518, 586, 603
#2: *The Beatles At The Beeb, The Beatle Broadcasts*

DON'T EVER CHANGE
RECORDED: August 1, 1963, at the Playhouse Theatre, Manchester.
BROADCAST: August 27, 1963, on "Pop Go The Beatles," with Rodney Burke.
SEE: 025, 110, 185, 196, 222, 294, 308, 436, 437, 606, 607, *The Beatles At The Beeb, Beatles BBC*

DREAM BABY
RECORDED: March 7, 1962, for "Teenager's Turn," with Ray Peters.
BROADCAST: March 8, 1962.
NOTES: This was the Beatles' first BBC broadcast.
SEE: *The Beatles At The Beeb, Wonderful Picture Of You*

EVERYBODY'S TRYING TO BE MY BABY
RECORDED/BROADCAST:
#1: Recorded November 17, 1964, at the Playhouse Theatre, Manchester, and broadcast November 26, 1964, on "Top Gear," with Brian Matthew.
#2: Recorded November 25, 1964, Studio 1, Aerolian Hall, London, and broadcast December 26, 1964, on "Saturday Club," with Brian Matthew.
SEE: #1: 115, *The Beatles At The Beeb, The Beatle Broadcasts*
#2: *Airtime*

FROM US TO YOU
RECORDED: February 28, 1964, at Studio 1, Piccadilly Theatre, London.
BROADCAST: Used as the theme song for all the "From Us To You" shows.
SEE: 019, 087, 095, 217, 225, 261, 370, 383, 396, 411, 499, 500, 535, 536, 589, 604, *The Beatles At The Beeb, Rough Notes*

GLAD ALL OVER
RECORDED: July 16, 1963, at the BBC Paris Studio, London.
BROADCAST: August 20, 1963, "Pop Go The Beatles," with Rodney Burke.
SEE: 025, 131, 185, 186, 196, 222, 294, 308, 436, 437, 572, 606, 607, *Beautiful Dreamer*

HAPPY BIRTHDAY
RECORDED: September 7, 1963, at the Playhouse Theatre, London.
BROADCAST: October 5, 1963, on the fifth anniversary "Saturday Club" show, with Brian Matthew.
NOTES: This is an 0:30 version of the traditional song with John providing this arrangement.
SEE: 043, 045, 061, 255, 256, 257, 458, 460, *The Beatles At The Beeb, Wonderful Picture Of You*

A HARD DAY'S NIGHT
   RECORDED/BROADCAST:
   #1: Recorded July 14, 1964, at Studio S2, Broadcasting House, London, and broadcast July 16, 1964, on "Top Gear," with Brian Matthew.
   #2: Recorded July 17, 1964, at the BBC Paris Studio, London, and broadcast August 3, 1964, on "From Us To You," with Don Wardell.
   NOTES: Version #1 is sometimes listed as being from a "Top Of The Pops" show.
   SEE: #1: 217, 300, 337, 365, 367, 396, 397, 398, 417, 418, 422, 561, 562, 564, 599, *The Beatles At The Beeb*
   #2: 009, 225, *Rarer Than Rare*

HIPPY HIPPY SHAKE
   RECORDED/BROADCAST:
   #1: Recorded May 24, 1963, at the BBC, Aeolian Hall, London, and broadcast on the June 4, 1963, "Pop Go The Beatles," with Lee Peters.
   #2: Recorded July 10, 1963, Studio 2, Aeolian Hall, London, and broadcast July 30, 1963, on "Pop Go The Beatles," with Rodney Burke.
   SEE: #1: 110, 133, 150, 183, 185, 258, 294, 317, 442, 444, 468, 473, 516, 518, 612
   #2: *The Beatles At The Beeb, The Beatle Broadcasts*

HONEY DON'T
   RECORDED/BROADCAST:
   #1: Recorded August 1, 1963, at the Playhouse Theatre, London, and broadcast on the September 3, 1963, "Pop Go The Beatles" show with Rodney Burke. This version features John Lennon, not Ringo, on lead vocals.
   #2: Recorded May 26, 1965, at Studio 1, Piccadilly Theatre, London, and broadcast June 7, 1965 on "The Beatles Invite You To Take A Ticket To Ride," with Denny Piercy.
   SEE: #1: 034, 035, 036, 115, 150, 454, 579
   #2: *The Beatles At The Beeb, Rough Notes*

THE HONEYMOON SONG
   RECORDED: July 16, 1963, at the BBC Paris Studio, London.
   BROADCAST: August 6, 1963, on "Pop Go The Beatles," with Rodney Burke.
   NOTES: Many bootlegs list this song under the title, "Bound By Love."
   SEE: 025, 042, 110, 185, 186, 188, 196, 222, 294, 308, 436, 437, 572, 606, 607, *Beautiful Dreamer*

I FEEL FINE
   RECORDED: November 17, 1964, at the Playhouse Theatre, London.
   BROADCAST: November 26, 1964, "Top Gear," with Brian Matthew.
   SEE: *The Beatles At The Beeb, The Beatle Broadcasts*

IF I FELL
   RECORDED: July 14, 1964, at Studio S2, Broadcasting House, London.
   BROADCAST: July 16, 1964, "Top Gear," with Brian Matthew.
   SEE: 225

I FORGOT TO REMEMBER TO FORGET
   RECORDED: May 1, 1964, at the BBC Paris Studio, London.
   BROADCAST: May 18, 1964, "From Us To You," with Alan Freeman.
   SEE: 094, 185, 260, 261, 262, 263, 436, 437, 473, 612, *Recovered Tracks*

I GOT A WOMAN
RECORDED/BROADCAST:
#1: Recorded July 16, 1963, at the BBC Paris Studio, London, and broadcast on August 13, 1963, on "Pop Go The Beatles," with Rodney Burke.
#2: Recorded March 31, 1964, at the Playhouse Theatre, Manchester, and broadcast April 4, 1964, on "Saturday Club," with Brian Matthew.
SEE: #1: 150, 186, 290, 294, 436, 468, 495, 496, 497, 607
#2: *The Beatles At The Beeb, The Beatle Broadcasts*

I GOT TO FIND MY BABY
RECORDED: June 1, 1963, at the BBC Paris Studio, London.
BROADCAST: June 11, 1963, "Pop Go The Beatles," with Lee Peters.
SEE: *The Beatles At The Beeb, Beautiful Dreamer*

I JUST DON'T UNDERSTAND
RECORDED: July 16, 1963, at the BBC Paris Studio, London.
BROADCAST: August 20, 1963, on "Pop Go The Beatles," with Rodney Burke.
SEE: 025, 110, 185, 186, 196, 222, 294, 308, 436, 437, 606, 607, *The Beatles At The Beeb*

I'LL BE ON MY WAY
RECORDED: April 4, 1963, at the BBC Paris Studio, London.
BROADCAST: June 24, 1963, on "Side By Side," with John Dunn.
SEE: 115, 256, 257, 393, 399, 473, 495, *The Beatles At The Beeb, Rough Notes*

I'LL FOLLOW THE SUN
RECORDED: November 17, 1964, at the Playhouse Theatre, Manchester.
BRAODCAST: November 26, 1964, on "Top Gear," with Brian Matthew.
SEE: *Beatles BBC, The Beatle Broadcasts*

I'LL GET YOU
RECORDED: August 1, 1963, at the Playhouse Theatre, Manchester.
BROADCAST: September 3, 1963, "Pop Go The Beatles," with Rodney Burke.
SEE: *Beautiful Dreamer*

I'M A LOSER
RECORDED: November 17, 1964, at the Playhouse Theatre, Manchester.
BROADCAST: November 26, 1964, on "Top Gear," with Brian Matthew.
SEE: *The Beatles At The Beeb, The Beatle Broadcasts*

I'M GONNA SIT RIGHT DOWN AND CRY (OVER YOU)
RECORDED: July 16, 1963, at the BBC Paris Studio, London.
BROADCAST: August 6, 1963, "Pop Go The Beatles," with Rodney Burke.
SEE: 025, 034, 042, 110, 150, 185, 186, 188, 196, 222, 294, 308, 436, 437, 453, 571, 606, 607, *Beautiful Dreamer*

I'M HAPPY JUST TO DANCE WITH YOU
RECORDED: July 17, 1964, at the BBC Paris Studio, London.
BROADCAST: August 3, 1964, "From Us To You," with Don Wardell.
NOTES: Two versions were recorded and bootlegged.
SEE: 225

(I'M) TALKING ABOUT YOU
BROADCAST: This song was broadcast live for the March 16, 1963,
"Saturday Club," with Brian Matthew, from Studio 3A, Broadcasting
House, Portland Place, London.
SEE: *Beautiful Dreamer*

I SAW HER STANDING THERE
RECORDED: September 3, 1963, at Studio 2, Aeolian Hall, London.
BROADCAST: September 24, 1963, "Pop Go The Beatles," with Rodney
Burke.
SEE: 317, 517, 603

I SHOULD HAVE KNOWN BETTER
RECORDED: July 17, 1964, at the BBC Paris Studio, London.
BROADCAST: August 3, 1963, "From Us To You," with Don Wardell.
NOTES: Two versions, one with and one without the harmonica, were
recorded. Both versions are on the bootlegs listed.
SEE: 225, *Rarer Than Rare*

I WANNA BE YOUR MAN
RECORDED: February 28, 1964, at Studio 1, Piccadilly Theatre, London.
BROADCAST: March 30, 1964, on "From Us To You," with Alan Freeman.
SEE: 255, 300, 396, 504, 505, 535, *The Beatles At The Beeb, Beatles BBC,
The Beatle Broadcasts*

JOHNNY B. GOODE
RECORDED: January 7, 1964, at the Playhouse Theatre, London.
BROADCAST: February 15, 1964, "Saturday Club," with Brian Matthew.
SEE: 034, 043, 045, 061, 087, 150, 255, 256, 257, 383, 458, 460, 491, 569, *The
Beatles At The Beeb, Beautiful Dreamer*

KANSAS CITY
RECORDED/BROADCAST:
#1: Recorded July 16, 1963, at the BBC Paris Studio, London, and
broadcast August 6, 1983, on "Pop Go The Beatles," with Rodney Burke.
#2: Recorded November 25, 1964, at Studio 1, Aeolian Hall, London,
and broadcast December 26, 1964, on "Saturday Club," with Brian
Matthew.
SEE: #1: 317, 468, 515, 516, 603
#2: *The Beatles At The Beeb*

KEEP YOUR HANDS OFF MY BABY
RECORDED: January 22, 1963, at Playhouse Theatre, London.
BROADCAST: January 26, 1963, "Saturday Club," with Brian Matthew.
SEE: *Beautiful Dreamer, Wonderful Picture Of You*

LEND ME YOUR COMB

RECORDED/BROADCAST:
#1: Recorded January 11, 1963, at EMI, London, and broadcast January
18, 1963, on Radio Luxembourg's "Friday Spectacular."
#2: Recorded July 2, 1963, at BBC Maida Vale Studio #5, and broadcast
July 16, 1963, on "Pop Go The Beatles," with Rodney Burke.
SEE: #1: 115, 131, 150, 294, 436, 450, 453, 468
#2: *The Beatles At The Beeb, Beatles BBC, The Beatle Broadcasts,
Clarabella* (EP), *Lend Me Your Comb/Carol* (45)

LONESOME TEARS IN MY EYES
    RECORDED: July 10, 1963, at Studio 2, Aeolian Hall, London.
    BROADCAST: July 23, 1963, "Pop Go The Beatles," with Rodney Burke.
    SEE: 025, 134, 185, 186, 196, 222, 294, 308, 436, 437, 572, 606, 607,
    "Airtime," *The Beatles At The Beeb, Beatles BBC*

LONG TALL SALLY
    RECORDED/BROADCAST:
    #1: Recorded July 16, 1963, at the BBC Paris Studio, London, and
    broadcast August 13, 1963, on "Pop Go The Beatles," with Rodney
    Burke.
    #2: Recorded March 31, 1964, at the Playhouse Theatre, Manchester,
    and broadcast April 4, 1964, on "Saturday Club," with Brian Matthew.
    #3: Recorded July 14, 1964, at Studio S2, Broadcasting House, London,
    and broadcast July 16, 1964, on "Top Gear," with Brian Matthew.
    #4: Recorded July 17, 1964, at the BBC Paris Studio, London, and
    broadcast August 3, 1964, on "From Us To You," with Don Wardell.
    NOTES: Version #3 is often listed as being from a "Top Of The Pops" show.
    SEE: #1: 317, 516, 518
    #2: *The Beatles At The Beeb, The Beatle Broadcasts*
    #3: 272, 300, 337, 358, 365, 367, 397, 398, 417, 418, 469, 561, 562, 564,
    599
    #4: 009, 225

LOVE ME DO
    RECORDED: July 10, 1963, at Studio 2, Aeolian Hall, London.
    BROADCAST: July 23, 1963, "Pop Go The Beatles," with Rodney Burke.
    SEE: 087, 317, 383, 516, 518, 589, 603

LUCILLE
    RECORDED: September 3, 1963, at Studio 2, Aeolian Hall, London.
    BROADCAST: September 17, 1963, "Pop Go The Beatles," with Rodney
    Burke.
    SEE: 130, 183, 256, 257, 260, 261, 262, 263, 425, 436, 443, 444, 468, 473, 499,
    500, 517, 518, 571, 572

MATCHBOX
    RECORDED: July 10, 1963, at Studio 2, Aeolian Hall, London.
    BROADCAST: July 30, 1963, "Pop Go The Beatles," with Rodney Burke.
    SEE: *The Beatles At The Beeb, The Beatle Broadcasts*

MEMPHIS
    RECORDED/BROADCAST:
    #1: Recorded June 24, 1963, at the Playhouse Theatre, London, and
    broadcast June 29, 1963, on "Saturday Club," with Brian Matthew.
    #2: Recorded July 10, 1963, at Studio 2, Aeolian Hall, London, and
    broadcast July 30, 1963, on "Pop Go The Beatles," with Rodney Burke.
    SEE: #1: *The Beatles At The Beeb, The Beatle Broadcasts, Wonderful Picture
    Of You*
    #2: 043, 045, 061, 150, 255, 256, 257, 458, 460, 468, 491

MISERY
    RECORDED: May 24, 1963, at Aeolian Hall, London.
    BROADCAST: June 4, 1963, "Pop Go The Beatles," with Lee Peters.
    SEE: 290, 317, 516, 518, *Recovered Tracks*

MONEY
RECORDED/BROADCAST:
#1: Recorded June 24, 1963, at the Playhouse Theatre, London, and broadcast June 29, 1963, on "Saturday Club," with Brian Matthew.
#2: Recorded August 1, 1963, at the Playhouse Theatre, Manchester, and broadcast September 3, 1963, on "Pop Go The Beatles," with Rodney Burke.
SEE: #1: 317, 516, 518
#2: 517, 518, 603

NOTHIN' SHAKIN' (BUT THE LEAVES ON THE TREES)

RECORDED: July 10, 1963, at Studio 2, Aeolian Hall, London.
BROADCAST: July 23, 1963, "Pop Go The Beatles," with Rodney Burke.
SEE: 025, 034, 042, 150, 185, 186, 188, 196, 222, 294, 308, 436, 437, 572, 606, 607, "Airtime," *The Beatles At The Beeb, The Beatle Broadcasts*

OH MY SOUL
RECORDED: August 1, 1963, at the Playhouse Theatre, Manchester.
BROADCAST: August 27, 1963, "Pop Go The Beatles," with Rodney Burke.
SEE: *Beautiful Dreamer, Wonderful Picture Of You*

A PICTURE OF YOU
BROADCAST: June 15, 1962, "Here We Go," with Ray Peters.
SEE: *Wonderful Picture Of You*

PLEASE MR. POSTMAN
RECORDED/BROADCAST:
#1: Recorded July 10, 1963, at Studio 2, Aeolian Hall, London, and broadcast July 30, 1963, on "Pop Go The Beatles," with Rodney Burke.
#2: Recorded February 28, 1964, at Studio 1, Piccadilly Theatre, London, and broadcast March 30, 1964, on "From Us To You," with Alan Freeman.
SEE: #1: *Airtime, The Beatles At The Beeb*
#2: *Rough Notes*
PLEASE PLEASE ME
RECORDED: July 16, 1963, at the BBC Paris Studio, London.
BROADCAST: August 13, 1963, on "Pop Go The Beatles," with Rodney Burke.
SEE: 030, 050, 093, 184, 317, 516, 518

POP GO THE BEATLES
RECORDED: May 24, 1963, at BBC Aeolian Hall, London.
BROADCAST: Theme song for all "Pop Go The Beatles" shows.
SEE: 061, 256, 257, 453, *The Beatles At The Beeb, The Beatle Broadcasts*

ROCK AND ROLL MUSIC
RECORDED: November 25, 1964, at Studio 1, Aeolian Hall, London.
BROADCAST: December 26, 1964, "Saturday Club," with Brian Matthew.
SEE: *Airtime, The Beatles At The Beeb*

ROLL OVER BEETHOVEN
RECORDED/BROADCAST:
#1: Recorded June 24, 1963, at the Playhouse Theatre, London, and broadcast June 29, 1963, on "Saturday Club," with Brian Matthew.
#2: Recorded February 28, 1964, at Studio 1, Piccadilly Theatre, London, and broadcast March 30, 1964, on "From Us To You," with Alan Freeman.
SEE: #1: 317, 516, 518, 603
#2: 255, 300, 396, 504, 505, 535, *The Beatles At The Beeb*

SHE LOVES YOU
RECORDED: July 16, 1963, at the BBC Paris Studio, London.
BROADCAST: August 20, 1964, on "Pop Go The Beatles," with Rodney Burke.
SEE: 083, 317, 383, 411, 517, 518, 589, 603

SHE'S A WOMAN
RECORDED: November 17, 1964, at the Playhouse Theatre, Manchester.
BROADCAST: November 26, 1964, on "Top Gear," with Brian Matthew.
SEE: *The Beatles At The Beeb, The Beatle Broadcasts*

A SHOT OF RHYTHM AND BLUES
RECORDED/BROADCAST:
#1: June 18, 1963, "Pop Go The Beatles," with Lee Peters.
#2: July 14, 1963, "Easy Beat," with Brian Matthew.
#3: Recorded August 1, 1963, at the Playhouse Theatre, Manchester, and broadcast August 27, 1963, on "Pop Go The Beatles," with Rodney Burke.
NOTES: Only the origina of version #3 are known for sure; all others are unknown.
SEE: (Unknown): 025, 042, 185, 186, 188, 196, 222, 294, 308, 436, 437, 453, 509, 571, 606, 607, 612
#3: *The Beatles At The Beeb, Beatles BBC*

SLOW DOWN
RECORDED: July 16, 1963, at the BBC Paris Studio, London.
BROADCAST: August 20, 1963, "Pop Go The Beatles," with Rodney Burke.
SEE: 025, 034, 150, 186, 196, 222, 294, 308, 606, 607

SO HOW COME (NO ONE LOVES ME)
RECORDED: July 10, 1963, at Studio #2, BBC Aeolian Hall, London.
BROADCAST: July 23, 1963, "Pop Go The Beatles," with Rodney Burke.
SEE: 025, 042, 185, 186, 188, 196, 222, 294, 308, 437, 606, 607, *Airtime, The Beatles At The Beeb*

SOLDIER OF LOVE
RECORDED: July 2, 1963, at BBC Maida Vale Studio #5.
BROADCAST: July 16, 1963, "Pop Go The Beatles," with Rodney Burke.
SEE: *The Beatles At The Beeb, Beatles BBC, Clarabella, Soldier Of Love/ Clarabella* (45)

SOME OTHER GUY
RECORDED: January 22, 1963, at the Playhouse Theatre, London.
BROADCAST: January 26, 1963, "Saturday Club," with Brian Matthew.
SEE: *The Beatles At The Beeb, Beautiful Dreamer, Wonderful Pictures Of You*

SURE TO FALL (IN LOVE WITH YOU)
RECORDED/BROADCAST:
#1: Recorded September 3, 1963, at Studio 2, Aeolian Hall, London, and broadcast September 24, 1963, on "Pop Go The Beatles," with Rodney Burke.
#2: Recorded March 31, 1963, at the Playhouse Theatre, Manchester, and broadcast April 4, 1963, on "Saturday Club," with Brian Matthew.
SEE: #1: 035, 036, 042, 131, 183, 187, 189, 190, 191, 221, 317, 409, 410, 436, 517, 606, 607
#2: *The Beatles At The Beeb, Beatles BBC, The Beatle Broadcasts*

SWEET LITTLE SIXTEEN
RECORDED: July 10, 1963, at Studio #2, BBC Aeolian Hall, London.
BROADCAST: July 23, 1963, "Pop Go The Beatles," with Rodney Burke.
SEE: 612, *Airtime, The Beatles At the Beeb, Beautiful Dreamer*

THAT'S ALL RIGHT MAMA
RECORDED: July 2, 1963, at BBC Maida Vale Studio #5.
BROADCAST: July 16, 1963, "Pop Go The Beatles," with Rodney Burke.
SEE: *The Beatles At The Beeb, Beautiful Dreamer*

THERE'S A PLACE
RECORDED: August 1, 1963, at the Playhouse Theatre, Manchester.
BROADCAST: September 3, 1963, on "Pop Go The Beatles," with Rodney Burke.
SEE: 515, 517, 603, *Beautiful Dreamer*

THINGS WE SAID TODAY
RECORDED/BROADCAST:
#1: Recorded July 14, 1964, at Studio S2, Broadcasting House, London, and broadcast July 16, 1964, on "Top Gear," with Brian Matthew.
#2: Recorded July 17, 1964, at BBC Paris Studio, London, . and broadcast August 3, 1964, on "From Us To You," with Don Wardell.
NOTES: Version #1 is usually listed as being from a "Top Of The Pops" show.
SEE: #1: 217, 272, 300, 337, 358, 365, 367, 396, 397, 398, 417, 418, 561, 562, 564, 599, *The Beatles At The Beeb*
#2: 225

THIS BOY
RECORDED/BROADCAST:
#1: Recorded December 17, 1963, at the Playhouse Theatre, London, and broadcast December 21, 1963, on "Saturday Club," with Brian Matthew.
#2: Recorded February 28, 1964, at Studio 1, Piccadilly Theatre, London, and broadcast March 30, 1964, on "From Us To You," with Alan Freeman.
SEE: #1: *The Beatles At The Beeb*
#2: *Rough Notes*

TICKET TO RIDE
RECORDED: May 26, 1965, at Studio 1, Piccadilly Theatre, London.
BROADCAST: June 7, 1965, "The Beatles Invite You To Take A Ticket To Ride," with Denny Piercy.
SEE: *Airtime, The Beatles At The Beeb*

TILL THERE WAS YOU
RECORDED/BROADCAST:
#1: Recorded June 24, 1963, at the Playhouse Theatre, London, and broadcast June 29, 1963, on "Saturday Club," with Brian Matthew.
#2: Recorded July 10, 1963, Studio 2, Aeolian Hall, London, and broadcast July 30, 1963, on "Pop Go The Beatles," with Rodney Burke.
#3: Recorded February 28, 1964, at Studio 1, Piccadilly Theatre, London, and broadcast March 30, 1963, on "From Us To You," with Alan Freeman.
SEE: #1: 317, 453, 516, 518, 603
#2: *The Beatle Broadcasts*
#3: *The Beatles At The Beeb*

TO KNOW HER IS TO LOVE HER
RECORDED: July 16, 1963, at the BBC Paris Studio, London.
BROADCAST: August 3, 1963, "Pop Go The Beatles," with Rodney Burke.
SEE: 025, 042, 186, 196, 222, 294, 308, 436, 437, 571, 606, 607, *The Beatles At The Beeb, The Beatle Broadcasts*

TOO MUCH MONKEY BUSINESS
RECORDED: June 1, 1963, at the BBC Paris Studio, London.
BROADCAST: June 11, 1963, "Pop Go The Beatles," with Lee Peters.
SEE: 115, 612, *The Beatles At The Beeb, Beatles BBC, Beautiful Dreamer, Wonderful Picture Of You*

WORDS OF LOVE
RECORDED: July 16, 1963, at the BBC Paris Studio, London.
BROADCAST: August 20, 1963, "Pop Go The Beatles," with Rodney Burke.
SEE: 183, 443, 444, 515, 517, 518, 603, *Beautiful Dreamer*

YOUNGBLOOD
RECORDED: June 1, 1963, at the BBC Paris Studio, London.
BROADCAST: June 11, 1963, "Pop Go The Beatles," with Lee Peters.
SEE: 572, 612, *Beautiful Dreamer, Wonderful Picture Of You*

YOU REALLY GOT A HOLD ON ME
RECORDED: May 24, 1963, at Aeolian Hall, London.
BROADCAST: June 4, 1963, "Pop Go The Beatles," with Lee Peters.
SEE: 043, 045, 061, 255, 256, 257, 458, 460, 491

THE DREAM IS OVER
John Lennon Tribute Records

Since 1964, the name *Beatles* and the phrase *novelty records* have been synonymous. But when John Lennon was killed on December 8, 1980, no flood of tribute records was unleashed on the market as had been the case when Elvis had died a few years earlier. After Presley's death, nearly 300 tributes were released. Thus far, the number of Lennon tributes has not reached 40. Why so few? Perhaps it is the fact that Lennon fans knew that John would not approve of someone making a quick dollar from his name.

What about those tributes that *were* released? They all had two things in common: they were done out of love for Lennon, and they were done in the very best of taste. Many of the tributes were released only to disc jockeys and are already quite rare. Some were issued with picture sleeves or posters, or both, that make them even more valuable. Some artists donated part or all of their earnings to John's charity, the Spirit Foundation.

1500   BAXTER, BAXTER & BAXTER
   John   Sun 1160   1980

> For 17 years the Baxter brothers, Rick, Mark, and Duncan, had been singing gospel music. Then, after John's death, they recorded *John,* which had been written by Stephen Kilgore, Virginia Fielder, and B. Castleman. It was produced for them by the owner of the Sun label, Shelby Singleton. Singleton also claims that this was the first Lennon tribute, since it was put on tape on December 9, the day after John's death. This is one of the few tributes that was commercially released. In fact, the flip side, *Take Me Back To The Country,* made the country charts. Mentioned in the lyrics of *John* are these Beatle songs: *A Hard Day's Night, Yesterday, I'll Follow The Sun, Ticket To Ride, Can't Buy Me Love,* and *Tell Me Why.* John's *Imagine* is also mentioned. The song's guitar part is based on the Beatles' *All My Loving.*

1501   BRADLEY, SID
   Elegy For The Walrus   VMS Promotions   1980

> According to an article in the December 27, 1980, issue of *Billboard,* this tribute was pressed in acetate copies only and mailed to major radio stations around the country. It may never have been released as a normal record. If this is the case, it would be extremely rare.

1502   CEE, JOEY
   Remember December   Niteflight   1981

> Cee, a Canadian, wrote and recorded this song for his own Niteflight record label. It was released on the first anniversary of John's death.

1503-
1504 CHARLENE with STEVIE WONDER
Used To Be   Motown 1650   1982
USED TO BE (LP)   Motown 6027   1982

Not a tribute in the strict sense of the word, but the death of John Lennon is mentioned in the line, "Someone took the Beatles' lead guitar." The song was written by Ron Miller and Ken Hirsch and produced by Miller. Charlene doesn't use her last name on the recording, but it is Duncan.

1505 CIRCLE OF FRIENDS
A Song For John   Vantage 1052   1983

This tribute was written by Bob Miele and, according to the label, is from the album *CHANGE OVER*, but it is not known if that album was ever released.

1506 DeCOTES, ALAN
Jazz On The Water   1982

Jazz On The Water is from the album *I LOOKED AND YOU WERE GONE* (True Luv Records-N-Tapes AD-1). This song, written by Joseph Borowski, was inspired by the seagulls that flew overhead during the vigil for John in Central Park. The jacket has a small photo of Lennon on the back and another on the back page of the 28-page booklet that comes with the album. DeCotes says the album is "dedicated to John Lennon, and I tried to keep the framework of the project on peace and love." The inner wax of side two has "Dedicated to John Lennon and Harry Chapin" scratched into it.

1507 DODSON, RICH
John Lennon Remembered   Marigold 705   1981

Dodson is a former member of the Stampeders. Although he is given credit on the A-side (*Lookin' Back*) of this single, no artist is listed for "John Lennon Remembered," and for good reason. The song is listed as being 10 minutes long, and it is, too. But it is 10 minutes of silence—not a sound is heard as the needle tracks through the groove.

1508 FAIRCLOTH, DAVID
The Dream Is Over   Nugget NST-8005   1980

Faircloth wrote *The Dream Is Over* and borrowed the title from the Lennon song *God*. The melody for the song, which is played on the piano throughout the recording, sounds very much like Lennon's *Imagine*. Faircloth's recording was produced by Robby Robertson.

1509 THE FANS
The Ballad Of John Lennon (They Finally Crucified You)/ Hey John   Egads 5047   1981

The Fans are: Steve Brosky, Pat Wallace, Peggy Salvatore, Paul Willistein, Pete Smoyer, and Scott Baliett. Steve and Paul wrote *The Ballad of John Lennon,* which features Brosky on lead vocals. *Hey John* was written by Pat and Paul and features Peggy on lead vocals. Willistein and Smoyer produced both songs.

1510   FARNSWORTH, BOB
John Would Agree   Hummingbird Productions   1980

Farnsworth, who wrote *John Would Agree,* is the president of a Nashville-based jingle company. The company is best known for their McDonald's jingles.

1511   FULL CIRCLE
I Did It For You   Mother GD2   1981

Full Circle is a play on words. The group consists mainly of Don Dannemann and his wife Eileen. In the sixties, Don was a member of the Cyrkle, a group named by John Lennon. The Cyrkle toured with the Beatles in 1966. *I Did It For You* was written by Eileen. Both the label and the sleeve state that the record is "in memory of John Lennon." The sleeve takes the form of a letter written to John by Full Circle. One thousand posters containing the song's lyrics and a picture of John were also printed and issued with the records.

1512   GILL, JOHN
The Legend Of Lennon   Sunlite 81001   1981

Gill also wrote and produced this tribute. The label states that the song is "in memory of John Lennon."

1513   GLASS ONION
Imagine: A Tribute To John   Onion UR 2317   1980

Glass Onion is led by Charles F. Rosenay III, who also heads Liverpool Productions, publishers of the Beatle fanzine *Good Day Sunshine.* Rosenay is the lead singer and is backed by Dean Falcone (bass), Steve Harris (keyboards), Mike Streeto (drums), and Myles Standish (additional instruments). The tune is Lennon's *Imagine,* with Rosenay adding the new lyrics. According to Rosenay, the lyrics were written on the night of December 8, 1980, immediately after he heard of John's death and were recorded the next day. Also see entry for Danny Lyons, artist on another tribute issued as the B-side of this record.

1514   HARDKNOX
Mr. Lennon (Can You Hear Me Now?)   1981

This was issued on the *HARDKNOX EP* (Rough Cut RC 1001) by the group. HardKnox is: Bob Barger, Wayne Gamache, Tom Marak, Tony Rondini, and Joe Walsh. Wayne Gamache wrote *Mr. Lennon.*

1515–
1517   HARRISON, GEORGE
All Those Years Ago   Dark Horse 49725   1981
All Those Years Ago (12″)   Dark Horse PRO-949   1981
SOMEWHERE IN ENGLAND (LP)   Dark Horse 3492   1981

The first Lennon tribute to be done by an ex-Beatle, and it was a mini-reunion of sorts. Both Ringo and Paul added to George's record. They were not all actually in the studio at the same time. George did the basic tracks, then Ringo got the tapes and added drums. Finally, Paul put the backing vocals onto the tape. This is one of the few Lennon tribute records to make the *Billboard* charts—peaking at #2. A video, featuring old Beatle clips, was made to help promote the song.

1518 HERNANDEZ, JUAN
Rest In Peace, John Lennon   JRH 8-24-46   1981

Hernandez wrote the song, which is one of the better tributes and one of the oddest. It is performed live. Hernandez introduces the song with a rather moving narrative on what the Beatles and Lennon meant to him and the rest of the world.

1519-
1521 JOHN, ELTON
Empty Garden (Hey Hey Johnny)   Geffen 50049   1982
Empty Garden (Hey Hey Johnny) (12″)   Geffen PRO-A-1018   1982
JUMP UP (LP)   Geffen GHS 2013   1982

John teamed once again with his old writing partner, Bernie Taupin, for this effort. Both the song and the video were very popular, with the single peaking at #13 on the *Billboard* chart. The 12″ single was issued to radio stations only.

1522 JOHN'S BIGGEST FAN
(We Need) Gun Control/Revolution 2   Dakota Records   1982

(We Need) Gun Control is done to the tune of *(Just Like) Starting Over* with new lyrics added by the artist. Only 300 copies of this tribute were pressed.

1523 KOSTER, IREN
We Won't Say Goodbye, John   TTR ZB 5814   1980

We Won't Say Goodbye, John was written by Koster on December 9, 1980, and recorded three days later. Although it was issued in several foreign countries, it was not released in the United States. According to the picture sleeve issued with the record, the proceeds from sales were to be donated to the Spirit Foundation. The artists appearing on the record donated their time and services in memory of John. At least two famous recording artists appear on the record—Peter Noone (of Herman's Hermits) and Bobby Hart (of Boyce and Hart), who both sing in the chorus. Others appearing are: Bruce Caton (drums), Steve Caton (guitar), Bill Armstrong (trumpet), Karen Childs (Rhodes and synthesizer), George Connor (guitar solo), Rick Kellis (piano and synthesizer), Steve Leshner (percussion), Michael Levin (guitar), and Bobby Lichtig (bass). Many of the musicians also sing in the chorus. They are joined by Midge Barnett, Eddy Estrada, Judy Hendershot, Mike Padilla, Tracey Silvers, Gary Skardina, Mary Ann Valli, and Lorna Wright.

1524 LAVIN, CHRISTINE
The Dakota   1981

From all available information, this song was not released on record, but instead was on a cassette tape. It was played over a New York City FM radio station on December 8, 1981.

1525 LYONS, DANNY
Have You Heard The News   Onion UR 2317   1980

Lyons, a disc jockey, put together this tribute, which consists of various Beatle/Lennon songs mixed with interviews and fan reactions to John's death. Lyons first aired the song on December 9, 1980. Among the songs used are: *A Day In The Life, I Want To Hold Your Hand, Yesterday, Please Please Me, Sgt. Pepper's Lonely Hearts Club Band, Come*

Together, I Found Out, The Ballad Of John And Yoko, Happy Xmas (War Is Over), Imagine, This Boy, and *(Just Like) Starting Over.* A second Lennon tribute was issued on the flip side of this record: See the entry for Glass Onion.

1526 McCARTNEY, PAUL
  Here Today   1982

Paul wrote and recorded his tribute to John for his album, *TUG OF WAR* (Columbia 37462). Paul is backed by a string quartet consisting of Jack Rothstein and Bernard Partridge on violins, Ian Jewel on viola, and Keith Harvey on cello. Because of Paul's closeness to John over the years, this is one of the more introspective of all the tributes. It has not been issued as a single.

1527 MEWBORN, BRANT
  A Love That Lasts Forever/Just Another Dreamer   Dreambeat DR 9   1982

Mewborn is a writer for *Rolling Stone.* His April 30, 1981, cover story on Ringo Starr inspired him to write and record his tribute. Mewborn wrote the music and put together the words from 21 Beatle songs, including: *Ticket To Ride, A Day In The Life, Happiness Is A Warm Gun, Imagine, We Can Work It Out, Don't Let Me Down, All You Need Is Love, Give Peace A Chance, Strawberry Fields Forever, I Am The Walrus, The Ballad Of John And Yoko, Baby You're A Rich Man, I'm So Tired, Lucy In the Sky With Diamonds, Revolution, A Hard Day's Night, Come Together, Mind Games, Across The Universe, Tomorrow Never Knows,* and *Yes It Is.* The song was produced by rock singer Cindy Bullens. The flipside, *Just Another Dreamer,* with words and music by Mewborn, is a tribute to Lennon and all dreamers. The disc was issued with a picture sleeve.

1528 NILSSON, HARRY
  With A Bullet   R-102982   1982

Lennon's friend Harry Nilsson recorded this song for the 1982 Beatlefest in New Jersey. It was pressed on red vinyl and came with a picture sleeve. Although it doesn't mention John directly, the proceeds of the record sales were earmarked for the National Coalition to Ban Handguns. Nilsson became quite an outspoken opponent of handguns following the shooting of Lennon.

1529 NOW SOUNDS ORCHESTRA
  A SALUTE TO JOHN LENNON AND THE BEATLES' GREATEST HITS
  (LP)   Tifton TS-96   1980

The album consists of the following tracks:
1. *(Just Like) Starting Over*
2. *My Sweet Lord*
3. *Yesterday*
4. *Nowhere Man*
5. *Michelle*
6. *Hey Jude*
7. *Whatever Gets You Thru The Night*
8. *All My Lovin'*
9. *All You Need Is Love*
10. *The Long And Winding Road*
The back cover of the album has four shots of John at various stages of his career. However, the picture of John as a boy is actually a picture of George.

1530   101 STRINGS
A TRIBUTE TO JOHN LENNON (LP)   Alshire 5380   1981

This album features a painting of John on its front cover and a photo on the back. The back also has a short history of John from his birth to his marriage to Yoko. The tracks included were:
1. *Hey Jude*
2. *Yesterday*
3. *Eleanor Rigby*
4. *She Loves You*
5. *Lucy In the Sky With Diamonds*
6. *A Hard Day's Night*
7. *I Want To Hold Your Hand*
8. *All You Need Is Love*
9. *Penny Lane*
10. *Michelle*

1531-
1532   QUEEN
Life Is Real (Song For Lennon)   Elektra 47452   1982
HOT SPACE (LP)   Elektra 60128   1982

Queen is Freddie Mercury, Brian May, John Deacon, and Roger Meadows-Taylor. Freddie Mercury wrote *Life Is Real.*

1533   RANKING JOE (JACKSON)
TRIBUTE TO JOHN LENNON (LP)   TADS 12181   1981

The album is entitled *TRIBUTE TO JOHN LENNON* and the first track on side one is also called *Tribute To John Lennon.* This is the only track on the album, however, that has anything to do with John. There are photos of John on both the front and back of the jacket. The song, done in the reggae "toasting" style, is a little hard to follow if you are not used to that type of music.

1534   ROXY MUSIC
Jealous Guy   Atco 7329   1981

Jealous Guy had been written by John Lennon and recorded for his album *IMAGINE.* The sleeve that accompanied the Roxy Music version says *Jealous Guy (A Tribute).* The song is also on the album *THE HIGH ROAD,* but with no mention of it being a tribute.

1535   SANDO
For The Walrus (Tribute To John Lennon)   All Star AS 111   1981

Sando, a Bob Dylan sound-alike, is Sando Parisi. He wrote this tribute in 1981 for the first anniversary of John's death. The label says that the single is from the album *FOR THE WALRUS,* but it is not known if that album was ever released.

1536   SIMON, PAUL
The Late Great Johnny Ace   1983

Simon and Garfunkel had done this song during their reunion concert in Central Park, but when the album of that concert was released, this track was not included. The only way to get it was on the video of the concert. Then in 1983, Paul Simon released the album *HEARTS AND BONES*

(Warner Brothers 23942) and included the song on that album. The lyrics, written by Simon, refer to blues singer Johnny Ace, the Beatles, Rolling Stones, and to the death of John Lennon.

1537 SQUIER, BILLY
Nobody Knows   1981

Nobody Knows was written by Squier and recorded for his 1981 album, *DON'T SAY NO* (Capitol 12146). The sleeve says that this song is "dedicated to the life of John Lennon."

1538 THOMPSON & LATHAM
Live With Love   Crescent 33036   1981

Live With Love was written and produced by Ross Hoffman, the owner of the Crescent label, and his wife Holly. It was recorded by Dawn Thompson and her daughter Daphne Latham. The single was issued with a picture sleeve. On that sleeve was the inscription "The sky is crying. The wind is crying too. Clouds were lying limp upon the hill, in a world suddenly stilled. Dec. 9, 1980. Dedicated to the living spirit of John Lennon."

1539 A TINT OF DARKNESS
To You Yoko: A Tribute To John   Roto 001   1981

Well, there was a reggae tribute, so why not a soul tribute? The melody borrows somewhat from *Let It Be,* and even the words are patterned after that Beatle song.

1540 VINTON, BOBBY
It Was Nice To Know You John   Tapestry TR005   1980

This one was written by Vinton and his son Robbie, with Vinton producing. Vinton had been one of the American artists that was wiped off the scene by the Beatles' invasion of 1964, but he apparently had no hard feelings, as he was one of the first artists to release a Lennon tribute.

1541 WELZ, JOEY
Voices In The Sky (A Tribute To John)   1981

This tribute is from Joey's album *I REMEMBER LOVE (AND ROCK AND ROLL)* (Music City 5008). Welz, keyboard player for Bill Haley and His Comets, joined with another rock legend, Link Wray, to write this tribute. On the album jacket, Welz talks of jamming with the Silver Beatles in Hamburg and also of turning them on to the music of Carl Perkins.

1542 ----
John Lennon Pt. 1 / Pt. 2   MA 1868   1981

This is actually a public service show issued to radio stations by TRAV for the Presbyterian Church in the United States. The program is entitled "What's It All About" and this represents show numbers 565 and 566. It was scheduled for broadcast in February, 1981. The shows feature interviews with Lennon and Beatle/Lennon songs, all pulled together by host Bill Huie. The songs (bits only) included are: *A Day In The Life, Help, I Am The Walrus, Strawberry Fields Forever, Lucy In The Sky With Diamonds, Revolution, Come Together, Imagine, Give Peace A Chance, The Ballad Of John And Yoko, Instant Karma, Whatever Gets You Thru The Night, (Just Like) Starting Over,* and *God.*